INDUSTRIAL MANAGEMENT
AND ECONOMIC REFORM IN CHINA,
1949–1984

INDUSTRIAL MANAGEMENT AND ECONOMIC REFORM IN CHINA, 1949-1984

PETER N. S. LEE

HONG KONG   OXFORD   NEW YORK
OXFORD UNIVERSITY PRESS
1987

Oxford University Press

Oxford   New York   Toronto
Petaling Jaya   Singapore   Hong Kong   Tokyo
Delhi   Bombay   Calcutta   Madras   Karachi
Nairobi   Dar es Salaam   Cape Town
Melbourne   Auckland

and associated companies in
Beirut   Berlin   Ibadan   Nicosia

First published 1987
Published in the United States
by Oxford University Press Inc., New York

Library of Congress Cataloging-in-Publication Data

Lee, Peter N. S., 1940–
Industrial management and economic reform in
China, 1949–1984.
Bibliography: p.
Includes index.
1. Industrial management—China. 2. China—Economic
policy—1949–   . I. Title.
HD70.C5L44   1987   338.951   87–13748
ISBN 0–19–584118–2

British Library Cataloguing in Publication Data

Lee, Peter N.S.
Industrial management and economic reform
in China, 1949–1984.
1. China—Economic policy—1949–1976
2. China—Economic policy—1976–
3. China—Politics and government—
1949–1976   4. China—Politics and
government—1976–
I. Title
330.951'05   HC427.9
ISBN 0–19–584118–2

Printed in Hong Kong by Kings Time Printing Press Ltd.
Published by Oxford University Press, Warwick House, Hong Kong

To Professor Tsou Tang

Preface

THIS book has two main concerns: the change in the policy output of industrial management at both the macro and the micro level in the People's Republic of China (PRC) since 1949; and the policy-making process in general, focusing on the area of industrial management in particular. These two concerns are intellectually connected, since one would find it difficult to appreciate the dynamics of policy change without investigating the policy-making process, and the policy-making process cannot be properly understood if the substance of policy has not been studied.

The present favourable research situation in China studies has two distinct advantages for the study of policy in the PRC. First, the publication 'explosion' in the post-Mao era has enabled China scholars to give a rich and detailed account of the process of the formation, implementation, outcomes, and feedback of major policies. It has become possible to examine the role of the key policy-makers of industrial management policy, such as Mao Zedong, Zhou Enlai, Chen Yun, Deng Xiaoping, Peng Zhen, Bo Yibo, Li Xiannian, Yu Quili, and so on, and the salient features of their interaction. There are now opportunities to reconstruct the sequence of the policy-making process, as well as the ideological and organizational context in which the key issues of industrial management have been raised.

The second advantage of the availability of new research materials and new academic contacts between foreign and Chinese specialists on China's industrial management is that they are able to re-examine some old empirical questions which have not been fully resolved (such as the rise of one-man management, the origin of the command economy, the dimensions of centralization versus decentralization, the charisma-inspired and mass-oriented style of enterprise management, the reform-oriented programmes in the radical periods, and so on). Furthermore an understanding of this historical background is essential for an appreciation of economic reform in the industrial sector in the post-Mao era.

This book breaks new ground in the analysis of policy in China by thoroughly examining the policy-making process in one area only, and by taking into account the existing body of Western literature on policy analysis and organization theory.

The book suggests that from 1949 to 1978 Chinese policy-makers tended to adopt a policy-making model resembling what is called 'conservative rationalism' or, in Charles E. Lindblom's terms, the 'synoptic model'. This model requires Chinese policy-makers to assume an exceedingly large and, in fact, an impossible role in the policy-making process. Within the context of this official expectation of omnipotence and omniscience, the sovereignty of the planner alternated with charismatic leadership from 1949, but did not provide an effective substitute. In the long term, the 'strategic model' (or 'incrementalism') would, as will be shown in this book, present as a more realistic alternative for policy-making. This strategic model took shape on a limited scale during the Great Leap Forward (1958–60), and has gained fresh momentum since 1978. The model entails a redefinition of the role of the State in economic and managerial spheres, the increasing importance of 'preference' rather than 'theory' as a guide for policy-making, the changing modes of State intervention (for example, towards indicative planning, the use of economic leverage, and so on), the development of the market mechanism, and the proliferation of policy-actors at various levels of the hierarchy.

With reference to meta-policy-making (that is, the factors affecting the change from one policy-making approach to another), the author proposes to focus on three independent variables: ideology, organization, and politics. They are metaphorically seen as 'windows', the opening of which is contingent upon specific historical circumstances. Thus it is entirely possible that an established doctrine or objective may search for political support and for the organizational means for its implementation; the available organizational means may look for an ideology and a political motive; and the political aim may seek an ideology and the organization to fulfil it. Since all three independent variables may not be activated at any one time, the policy-making process in China tends to be less than fully articulated ideologically, and to be partly co-ordinated at the political level, with or without the available organizational means for its implementation.

The author has considerable reservations about the ideological, organizational, and political approaches which have traditionally been employed in the China studies field. They are based upon the assumption of a fully articulated and coherent goal, the availability of organizational means, and a well-structured relationship in the political arena (see Chapter 10). While focusing on the theoretical limitations of the traditional modes of policy analysis in the Chinese case, the book also raises the question at the theoretical level of the validity of 'rationalism' and 'incrementalism', two major approaches to policy-making. The author suggests that the empirical findings concerning the policy-making process in the arena of industrial management in China are congruent with the 'garbage can model' which has gained currency in the fields of policy study and public administration in the West during the past two decades.

This study relies heavily upon documentary material for precise details of the development of policy-making in industrial management in China. However, the analytical framework of this book and major points of fact were confirmed and checked by means of exchanges with scholars both inside and outside China, and conversations with participants in the making of such policy. Furthermore, the author gained valuable insights from visits to enterprise units and in particular from interviews at the Beijing State-owned Number Two Cotton Textile Mills and the Guangzhou Nanhua Sewing Machine Works in 1972 and the Beijing Peoples' Printing Machine Works in 1979. Interview material filed at the former Union Research Institute in Hong Kong, covering the 1960s, complements the author's own interviews conducted in Hong Kong during the 1970s and 1980s. To all who assisted in these inquiries, the author is deeply grateful.

The author also wishes to express his appreciation for the support and assistance of a number of institutions and individuals during the preparation of this book. In the early stages of his research, the author received financial support from the Institute of Social Science and Humanities (now the Institute of Social Studies) at the Chinese University of Hong Kong, and from a Commonwealth Academic Staff Scholarship from the Commonwealth Scholarship Commission of the United Kingdom. The author is thankful to both the Contemporary China Institute and the Library of the School of Oriental and African Studies at the University of London, for facilities provided during his stay in 1980–1. His appreciation is also due to the Universities Service Centre, Hong Kong, for its fine collection and very helpful staff.

Some helpful comments were received from Professor Hung Yong Lee, Professor Lowell Dittmer, Dr Ronald Dore, Dr Martin Lockett, Mr Chang Xin, and Dr Richard A. Gambitter. The following persons also assisted the author at various stages of this book: Ms Lau Lai-chu, Ms Chao Kwok-mei, Ms Leung Fung-yee, Ms Yau Mei-mei, Mr Robin Hoggard, Ms Mary Lyons, Mr Tan Sui-yan, Mr Lam Tao-chu, Mr David Tsui, Ms Linda Ma, Ms Pollyanna So, Ms Elaine

Kurtenbach, Ms Marcie Wong, Mr Dennis Kalter, Ms Jean Xiong, Ms Dorris Wong, and Ms Elizabeth Lee.

The author thanks Chiu Hsia, his wife, not only for carrying out the Pinyin romanization for the entire book, but also for her moral support in his endeavour.

PETER N.S. LEE
Department of Government
and Public Administration
The Chinese University of Hong Kong
1987

Contents

Tables

Figures

1. The Theoretical Framework: The Policy-making Process in China

THE focus of this book is a group of State-run industrial enterprises in China. They constitute the main pillars of the Chinese Socialist economy and have represented approximately 90 per cent of the State revenue in the forms of taxation and profit remittance for three decades.[1] At both the macro and the micro level, the issues of industrial management highlight the core problems of modernization and economic growth. In addition, they reflect distributive justice and managerial and political participation in contemporary China. The evolution and development of China's industrial management have been marked by clashes between the human side and the technical side of modern organization,[2] the ideological conflicts between 'revolution and modernization',[3] and the dilemma of choice of policy between participation and inequality in the development process.[4]

This book is one of a small number of systematic studies which investigate the policy-making process of China on the basis of one selected policy area. In a historical perspective, this study covers the early origins of industrial management policy during the recovery period from 1949 to 1955, Mao's period from 1956 to 1976, and the transition period to the post-Mao era during the years 1977–84. Time periods in this case-history study overlap, because of the coexistence of more than one policy approach during certain periods. This study focuses on the formulation and implementation of major policy papers, on directives and regulations, on 'model experiences' and, in some cases, on implicit consensus and attitudes in the area of industrial management. Enterprise units are selected for empirical study in order to illustrate the important trend during certain historical periods.

In its transition to the post-Mao era, China has passed through two stages. The first stage (from 1977 to 1983) saw a restoration of old programmes and policy precedents which may be traced back to the 1950s and, to a lesser extent, to the 1960s. In the second stage (from 1984 onwards), many innovative reform ideas have been applied. Time is still too short for a full assessment of the results and consolidation of this new reform orientation. To put this continuing historical transformation of China in perspective it has been deemed necessary to bring the vast reservoir of policy precedents and past practice to light, thereby providing a foundation for projecting the existing trend into the future. The study of this historical trend is based upon a case study of policy-making approaches in the arena of industrial management from 1949 to 1984.

THE THESIS PROPOSED

This book proposes that the major deficiencies inherent within the policy-making process in China are derived from the exceedingly large and impossible role assigned to Chinese policy-makers by the official ideology, the organizational set-up, and the political system. Tensions arise as a result of the gap between the ideal and actual performance of policy-making. In adapting to these tensions Chinese policy-makers rely upon three specific policy-making approaches. Two of these, the 'administrative approach' and the 'preceptoral approach', alternated during the time of Mao Zedong. Both approaches have an idealistic belief in the infallibility of policy-makers and an exaggerated sense of the importance of theoretical knowledge, and therefore are not genuine alternatives. This explains why Mao Zedong's anti-bureaucratic efforts repeatedly ended with a high concentration of power, still more bureaucratization, and a multitude of unanticipated consequences.

The third approach, that is, the 'economic approach', first took shape paradoxically in the midst of the radical policy phases of the Great Leap Forward (1958–60) on a limited scale, and subsequently with greater salience in the post-Mao era. The ascendancy of the economic approach also marks the transformation from one theoretical dimension (the synoptic dimension) to another (the strategic dimension). Within this new dimension, 'preference' (or volition), rather than 'theory', assumes increasing importance in guiding policy-making. A further objective of this book is to assess whether this new development is likely to take hold in the post-Mao era.

This study of China's policy-making process is motivated by the following considerations. Firstly, a study of the policy-making process should enable analysts and observers to look more closely into the relationships of the independent variables (such as ideology, organization, and politics) to the patterns of policy output. Such an analysis is helpful in establishing the relevance of a number of factors which might have a bearing on policy formulation and execution in the Chinese context. Secondly, this study highlights the linkage of policy outcomes and feedback from them to yet another cycle of policy formulation. Chinese policy-makers often follow the complete policy cycle, from research and investigation, the drafting and formulation of position papers, trial implementation, and pilot programmes, to formal policy and its full-scale implementation. The policy output of the preceding period frequently becomes an input to policy formulation in the current process of policy-making.

Thirdly, the focus upon the policy-making process can inject some 'realism' into the study of public policy in China and highlight the irreducible area of irrationality, uncontrolled elements, and unintended consequences in the policy arena. This study presents a challenge to prevailing views of policy-making concerning the fully articulated policy premises and objectives, the total control over its implementation and consequences, and the well-structured relationship among policy-makers. Accordingly, this book raises the following questions. Why are there contradictions and inconsistencies in the process of policy formulation? Why is implementation often out of control? And why, in many cases, have the consequences been unanticipated? Why is the pattern of policy participation in some cases fluid? These questions become relevant, however, only if one assumes that the following premises are plausible: that the policy-makers have only limited intellectual faculties and real capacity; and that the decision-making situation is exceedingly complex and is constantly affected by environmental uncertainty.

THE POLICY-MAKING MODEL

The policy-making model in China refers to the set of relationships between independent and dependent variables pertaining to the policy-making process. The dependent variables are the changes in policy-making approaches and the tensions and conflicts allied with them. These dependent variables highlight issues concerning the role of policy-makers, the criteria of policy evaluation and choice, the process of decision-making, reasoning, the manner in which information and resources are used, the perception of unintended consequences, responses to feedback, the organizational form, and the fashion of implementation. The independent variables are taken as 'meta-policy-making' (that is, the policy governing policy-making), to use Yehezhel Dror's term.[5] They include ideology, organization, and politics which separately or jointly bring about a change from one policy-making approach to another.

For analytical purposes the term 'policy' here is defined as a direction and guide for actions taken by the Party and State organization. It includes a wide range of phenomena, from a coherent plan specifying objectives, strategy, schedule, and measures, to a very loose form of the adaptation of one actor to another in what Charles E. Lindblom calls 'mutual adjustment'.[6] 'Policy' could be both explicit (for example, written documents and public statements), and implicit regarding an orientation to specific actions (for example, 'spirit' or 'sentiments'). It might also be manifest in a collective form (as, for example, in a resolution of the Party), and in an individualistic fashion (for example, in unilateral action taken by a key actor). 'Policy' also refers to a concrete commitment to political and administrative action. It is, therefore, action-oriented in the sense that it represents an attempt to make a definite impact.

It is by no means easy to distinguish between policy and administration or between policy and implementation in either the Chinese or the Western context. Chinese policy-makers, however, do bear such distinctions in mind and usually use the terms 'measures' (*cuoshi*), 'arrangements' (*anpai*), 'methods' (*banfa*), or 'guarantees' (*baozheng*) to separate 'implementation and administration' from 'policy'. In some cases, model experiences are taken as an instrument of implementation in order to clarify the intent of a policy and suggest concrete ways to handle a particular problem. In addition, 'plan' (*jihua*), 'directive' (*zhishi*), 'order' (*mingling*), 'law' (*falü*), and 'regulation' (*guiding*) are also terms used in the process of implementation.[7]

Theoretically speaking, the policy-making system proper usually includes a diagnosis of the problem, the establishment of operational goals in some order of priority, the proposal of major alternatives, the assessment of the possible outcomes and the choice of those which might be the best or perhaps the correct ones. For an empirical study of the policy-making system, one has to extend both the forward and backward linkages of policy-making proper — for example, the phases in preparing and organizing policy formulation, and the adjustments made on the basis of feedback following implementation.

Leaning toward a cybernetic model of policy-making, Yehezhel Dror suggests that a policy-making system should include three stages: meta-policy-making, policy-making, and post-policy-making, and that these three stages are connected by various feedback routes.[8] Dror's analytical scheme is mainly normative but it is borrowed for the purpose of identifying the descriptive dimension of policy-making in the Chinese context (Fig. 1). In China, policy-makers are theoretically expected to proceed from meta-policy-making to policy-making proper (that is, from ideological premises to policy), and from policy-making proper to post-policy-making (that is, from policy papers of a general nature to specific laws and directives). However, such a sequence might not always be followed through in the actual process of policy formulation. It is likely that an ideological position would be formulated following the implementation of concrete measures, such as the Hundred Flowers campaign in 1957, and the Socialist Education Movement (1963–6). In addition, a general and comprehensive policy paper might result from a synthesis of practices and the discovery of the instrument of implementation at the lower levels of an organizational hierarchy. In 1961, for example, the document 'Regulation of the Tasks in State-owned Enterprises' (known as the 'Seventy Articles') was worked out on the basis of policy precedents of the 1950s and some fragmented but effective practices found in the later phases of the Great Leap Forward (see Chapter 3).

Policy-makers do not 'respond' to their environment, and do not make adjustments to policy output on the basis of feedback in a mechanical way, as is suggested by the cybernetic model of policy-making. Prominent in this analysis are the policy-makers' perceptions and interpretations of their situations and problems. Charles O. Jones suggests that events in society are interpreted in different ways by different people at different times.[9] The perception of a situation also might differ from the reality and practice. With reference to the adoption of a policy-making model at a particular historical juncture in China, we find that the approach which ought to be utilized officially does not necessarily result in that which is actually pursued. The former refers to a normative model of policy-making while the latter is concerned with a descriptive model.

In my analytical framework, there are three independent variables of relevance to the meta-policy-making stage which usually defines the approach to policy-making. These three variables are identified as ideology, organization, and politics. Ideology is a set ot action-oriented ideas. It often encompasses the ultimate direction which a society should pursue. It also defines and legitimizes the role of

Fig. 1 The Policy-making Model in China

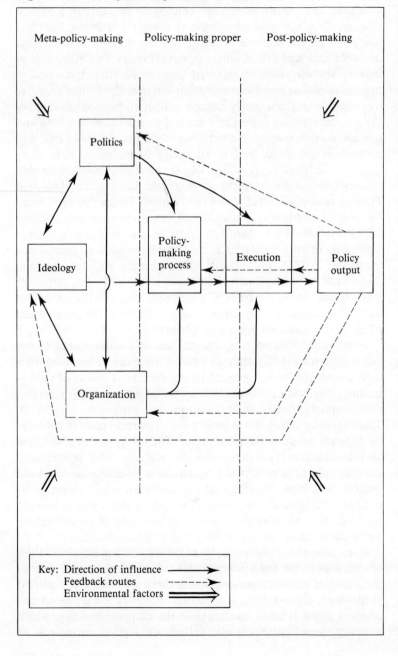

policy-makers as well as the relationships of political institutions to the society. Organization refers to an accumulation of formal requisites which sustain activities and interactions of organizational members beyond the level of the face-to-face relationship. These requisites include a formal hierarchy, the division of labour, the defined spheres of competence, functional specialization, motivation, public property, differentiated incentives, and written messages. They are often listed as requisites of the Weberian 'ideal type' of State bureaucracy. Politics is concerned with attempts to maintain and allocate power at both the élite and the societal level, for example, in factionalism, power struggles, civil strife, and so on.

These three independent variables are comparable to, but not identical with, the terms 'preferences', 'technology', and 'participation' in the 'garbage can model' of organizational choice.[10] In other words, ideology involves the process of defining policy premises and policy objectives; organization is taken to mean the tools for the implementation of objectives; politics concerns the roles, relationships, and modes of participation of policy-actors. While acknowledging that these three independent variables are, conceptually and theoretically, autonomous yet interconnected spheres of human activity at the meta-policy-making stage, the author will, for the present leave aside consideration of the relationships among them. The author will demonstrate in subsequent chapters that these three independent variables could be regarded as 'windows', the opening of which is contingent upon unspecified historical factors. The question is therefore raised as to whether it is true that the policy-making process in China resembles the 'garbage can model', or 'organized anarchy'. When, where, and how does an opportunity for choice emerge? Under what circumstances do these independent variables become activated and functional? What are the sequential patterns, if any, among these variables in the actual process of policy-making?

This book broadly agrees with the theoretical conclusion of the 'garbage can model' as regards the policy-making process and organizational choice. The author will argue that the policy-making process in China and elsewhere tends to take a discernible pattern, and that such a pattern might be shaped by ideology, politics, and organization under certain historical circumstances. This study also suggests, however, that not all of the independent variables would be activated and available in a given policy-making situation. The purposes of policy are often fragmented and not fully expressed; the organizational means and other resources are not always available, and are frequently in short supply; and the participation of policy-actors in the policy-making process tends to be fluid, changing and taking place outside the formal hierarchy and division of labour. In philosophical terms, it is believed that policy-makers have a general propensity to rationalize their choice and to bring order to the public sphere, but such an intention can only go as far as the limits of their intellectual abilities and the means and resources available in a given situation. Furthermore, political activity is an autonomous sphere, governed by its own laws. It is only related to policy-making occasionally, for example, as an intended result or as a by-product. Policy-making need not always be politicized, much less factional.

TWO THEORETICAL DIMENSIONS

The policy-making process in China may be analysed with two theoretical dimensions and three approaches. The two theoretical dimensions are the synoptic and the strategic. Both are conceptually borrowed from Charles E. Lindblom (see Appendix 1). The synoptic dimension includes two policy-making approaches, the administrative and the preceptoral, which alternated during Mao's era (1949–76). The post-Mao era (from 1977 to 1984) witnessed a transformation from the synoptic dimension to the strategic dimension and the ascendancy of the economic approach. The strategic dimension includes only one approach, that is, the economic approach.

The three policy-making approaches referred to above are parallel to, but not identical with, Dorothy J. Solinger's classification of three 'tendencies', that is, the 'bureaucrat', the 'radical', and the 'marketeer'. Solinger's study is mainly concerned with the relationship of value orientations and political forces to the changing pattern of policy output in the commercial sector in the PRC. In Solinger's version of the 'tendencies model', 'tendencies' refer to the value orientations to which the policy-actors adhere.[11] In this author's framework, value orientations and political forces are generally regarded as two of the three independent variables at the meta-policy-making stage of the policy-making system. From a theoretical perspective, Solinger fails to confront the issue of how the policy-making process, through value orientations, political forces, and other independent variables, is converted into policy outputs. This process is the theme of the present book, and the types of policy-making approach are regarded as characterizing such a process.

For analytical purposes it is appropriate to re-examine the two theoretical dimensions formulated by Lindblom, as they underline the three policy-making approaches in the Chinese historical context. Lindblom, from a mainly normative perspective, proposes that in the synoptic model (Model I), policy-makers should expect guidance from their intellectual faculties in evaluating and choosing policy alternatives. This is accomplished through a rational comprehensive review of all alternatives; policy-actors should be capable of foreseeing all consequences of each alternative; and should have full control over policy consequences. In the strategic model (Model II), policy-makers should be guided by their volition (that is, their preference and tangible interests). They are said to be 'short-sighted' because they cannot afford to project the present situation into the long-term future and to see all alternatives and all of their consequences. Thus they can only make policy in an 'incremental' and 'disjointed' manner and take successive steps to compare existing ways with limited new options. These successive comparisons are due to the limits of their intellectual faculties and the costs entailed in such a search.[12]

The synoptic model is parallel to Weber's view of policy-makers in an organizational context. He takes organizational goals and value premises as given. He places emphasis on rationality in terms of the 'superiority of scientific knowledge'. The uncertainty of environmental factors and the unintended consequences of organizational decisions are no longer relevant to his analysis of State bureaucracy.[13] Herbert A. Simon proposes a modification to the position represented by Weber: on the one hand, he considers value premises to be relevant to the choices of organizational objectives. On the other, he accepts that 'rationality' is bounded by psychological constraints, limited information and resources, and the unintended consequences of decisions.[14] According to Richard H. Hall, implicit in Weber's 'ideal type' is a 'closed system' of policy-making which is insulated from environmental influence. The post-Weberian authors, however, tend to adopt an 'open system' by taking the environmental factors into consideration.[15]

The strategic model is rooted in the policy-making theory of business firms and in the market economy. Richard M. Cyert and James G. March have suggested that participants (such as investors, managers, and labour unions) develop policies mainly through the formation of coalitions, a process which is guided by short-sighted preference. Therefore a 'consensus' on a given policy issue is a manifestation of the common or parallel interests of participants involved in the policy-making process. There might be a minority of opponents to the consensus, but these can be co-opted through 'side payments' given to them.[16]

Amitai Etzioni focuses principally upon the normative level of analysis and proposes another theoretical formulation in terms of the 'mixed scanning strategy'. This policy-making strategy differentiates contextuating (or fundamental) decisions from bit (or item) decisions. The former are made through an exploration of the main alternatives, as seen by the policy-maker in his conception of fundamental goals, with the details and specifications being omitted. The latter are made incrementally but within the context set by the fundamental and comprehensive perspectives.[17] It is noteworthy that Etzioni uses the scope of policy perspective (for example, macro versus micro) as a basic criterion for establishing his analytical scheme. Lindblom underscores the difference between 'theory' and volition (or preference) to construct his two theoretical models of policy-making.

Lindblom suggests, in general, that the democratic political system mainly employs the strategic model, and that the Socialist countries rely heavily upon the synoptic model. Mindful of Lindblom's position, it is appropriate also to state that the synoptic model is conventionally employed in the core of the public functions and that the strategic model is applied to the economic sector in Western societies. In contrast, within the Socialist countries of the Stalinist tradition, the synoptic model is adopted not only in the governmental arena, but in the economic sphere as well.

Anthony Downs suggests, from the vantage-point of organization theory, that in reality the State bureaucracy assumes an important role in allocating the non-marketable benefit and the indivisible cost of defence, law and order, and the protection of the fundamental rights of citizens, and so on.[18] This is true for both Socialist and democratic political systems. The historical development of planning and positive government indicates that the policy-making process in the West has increasingly been guided by a long-term perspective and a comprehensive review of alternatives.[19] In addition, preference (or interest) as such is not simply taken as a value-free category, but in most cases is taken as the 'claim' or 'rights', the allocation of which is guided by a legitimizing ideology,[20] and therefore by a synoptic perspective.

Interestingly enough, Adam Smith, who supposedly followed the logic of the strategic model, identified three duties of the State, and they cannot be reduced to the preference (or tangible interest) of each individual. These three duties are: the protection of the society from violence and invasion from another independent State, the protection of every member of society from injustice or oppression by other members, and the erection and maintenance of public works and public institutions.[21] In performing these three duties senior policy-makers must assume a synoptic perspective of policy-making. This is because the benefit and cost pertaining to these duties cannot be attributed to any individual or small group of individuals. Thus policy-making cannot be guided by 'preference' or tangible interest, as it is in the case of the strategic model.

In a Socialist political system, the State is expected to assume an exceedingly large role in the economic sphere, and in doing so, its policy-making should be guided by 'theory', rather than the 'preference' of the individual. In a democratic society, however, where market forces dominate in the economic arena, the role of the State in the public sector is visibly smaller than its Socialist counterpart, but not infrequently it is 'synoptic'. Of course the former leans toward the synoptic model of policy-making and the latter in general approximates the strategic model, given that no pure type of either exists in reality.

The Administrative Approach versus the Preceptoral Approach

In the Chinese context, the synoptic model may include two approaches: the administrative and the preceptoral. Both underscore the importance of theoretical knowledge in policy-making, and assign an omnipotent and omniscient role to the policy-makers. Modelled on the Soviet system of a command economy, the administrative approach represents the ideal of the planner's sovereignty in the developmental process. It presupposes that the central planners are able to formulate a rational comprehensive plan imposing full control over every phase of implementation. In addition, it relies heavily upon administrative instruments such as laws and regulations, experts, and material incentives to enforce policies. According to Lindblom, the preceptoral approach is characteristic of the Maoist model of policy-making as it depends upon persuasion, political indoctrination, amateur generalists, and mass mobilization to implement policies.[22]

The administrative approach toward policy-making is based upon scientific rationality, and is essential for modernization. The preceptoral approach gives priority to the Maoist notion of 'class struggle' in order to initiate and actualize social transformation. The former entails a particular organizational form in terms of the State bureaucracy, such as the emphasis on hierarchy, centralization, and discipline, while the latter stresses the movement-oriented Party, decentralization, participation and, to a certain extent, the spontaneity of the masses. In extreme situations, the latter also promotes the direct link between the top leaders and the masses, bypassing the intermediate echelons. The supreme leader is considered to possess moral excellence and the quality of extra-rationality. To highlight the differences between the two approaches, a graphic illustration is given in Table 1.

Sharing the theoretical weakness of the synoptic dimension, both the administrative and the preceptoral approaches of policy-making tend to overestimate the intellectual faculties and the actual capacities of policy-makers. Consequently, both approaches tend to increase the unintended consequences of policy. In other words, no matter which approach has been adopted in a given period, policy-actors have found themselves in a situation where they could neither formulate the 'right' policies adequately, because of the lack of coherence in their ideology, nor predicate and control the policy consequences fully, due to their limited intellectual faculties and the relative scarcity of information and resources.

The preceptoral approach tends to be the more unstable because its implementation is often allied with various untested and unreliable instruments such as political indoctrination, mass mobilization, and moral appeals, and it also frequently lacks operational goals and objective criteria for evaluating performance. Consequently, the preceptoral approach tends to run aground before receiving a full opportunity for implementation. Because of the chaos and crises which result, it is very often replaced by the administrative approach (see Chapters 3 and 5).

The Ascendancy of the Economic Approach

In the preceding pages, the synoptic dimension with its two approaches is considered to be normative, addressing itself to the

Table 1 The Administrative Approach versus the Preceptoral Approach

Analytical Dimensions	Approaches	
	Administrative	Preceptoral
1. Ideological perspective	(a) Imperative of modernization (b) Scientific rationality	(a) Priority of class struggle in society (b) Moral ideal
2. The perceived role of the policy-maker	(a) Sovereign planner	(a) Charismatic leader
3. Nature of theoretical knowledge	(a) Scientific calculable ingredients	(a) Moral rationality plus extra-rational elements
4. Organizational form	(a) State bureaucracy (b) Hierarchy (c) Centralization (d) Discipline	(a) Movement-oriented party (b) Direct link between the supreme leader and the led (c) Decentralization (c) Populism and spontaneity
5. Instrument of implementation	(a) Central planning (b) Regulation (c) Material incentives (d) Expert professionals	(a) Management by objectives (b) Mobilization (c) Non-material incentives (d) Amateur generalists (cadres and masses)

question of what is officially expected in the policy-making process. This means that the normative level and the descriptive level of policy-making are not always congruent with each other. To narrow the gap between the normative expectation and the reality, policy-actors can adjust the policy-making approaches in both functional and dysfunctional directions. The adjustments are functional to the extent that they contribute to the effectiveness of a policy-making approach. They are dysfunctional in the sense that they frustrate the intents of the original design. Again, the forms of adjustments in the administrative and preceptoral approaches differ, but they may be compared by means of an analysis of four areas, namely, goals, organization, management, and politics (see Appendix 2).

One should not underestimate the ability of Chinese policy-makers to make adjustments with positive results, and also to remedy the shortcomings inherent within a given policy-making approach. In the administrative approach, for instance, policy-makers could achieve remedies through an emphasis upon research and investigation, observance of the law of economy, and 'seeking truth from facts' in the process of goal formation. They could also introduce decentralization and administrative simplification in the organizational arena. They could strengthen financial accountability, administrative discipline, differentiated incentives, and the role of experts in the managerial arena. Finally they could attempt to strike a proper balance of interests among the central élite, local authorities, basic units, and individual producers, on the basis of the rule of law. There are a great many possible remedies also available to the preceptoral approach, for example, consultation with the masses (that is, the mass-line), the practice of criticism and self-criticism, the effective direct link from the top to the bottom, the dispatch of work-teams, the effective mobilization of human resources, and so on. In addition the two policy-making approaches might be associated with some unintended and undesirable adjustments, including 'commandism', 'bureaucratism', and the excessive concentration of formal authority in the administrative approach; the personality cult; the invincibility of class struggle; and the 'anarchist' tendency in the preceptoral approach.

Functional and dysfunctional adjustments to each of the two policy-making approaches cover a relatively broad range of possibilities (see Appendix 2). Overall, this book suggests that Chinese policy-makers cannot entirely overcome the fundamental deficiencies of the synoptic model with its two approaches. It assumes, therefore, that by trial and error or even by a systematic analysis, Chinese policy-makers would eventually find a viable direction of reform (for example, decentralization, market socialism, economic levers, the autonomy of production units, the free association of individual producers, the emphasis on tangible interests, and so on) leading to the economic approach which is rooted in the theoretical dimension of the strategic model.

The main arguments for the highly probable pressure to retreat from the administrative approach in the Chinese case are threefold. First, the State apparatus appears to be neither efficient nor effective in directly organizing and managing economic activity, and it is also deficient in the allocation of marketable benefits and divisible costs. Second, Socialist States, especially those which have evolved under the strong influence of the Stalinist model, tend to assume an extremely large role within the economic sphere in the theoretical perspective of the synoptic model. Third, the deficiencies inherent within the synoptic model would become amplified in Socialist systems due to the magnitude and complexity of the problems in economic policy-making within the Party-State. These deficiencies are closely associated with the issue of the proper mix between the measurable economic value and the non-measurable 'common good', the delays and obstacles in information flow, cost accounting, and the evaluation of performance in a gigantic State organization, the lack of an effective and sensitive incentive structure, the unclear delineation of responsibility, the problems of innovation and risk-taking, and the dilemma between life-long job tenure and the necessary rotation and mobility of the work-force. Such deficiencies are most pronounced in the industrial sector, where the State, in most socialist countries including China, plays an exceedingly large role.

Theoretically, a transformation from the administrative approach of policy-making to the economic approach would be easier than that from the preceptoral approach to the economic approach. Both the administrative approach and the economic approach are rooted in scientific rationality in terms of the relationship between means and ends, although the former represents rationality from a macro level while the latter focuses upon rationality in a micro perspective. Both approaches rely upon similar organizational and managerial tools, for example, regulatory control, differentiated incentives, and the role of expert-professionals.

The administrative approach contains an obstacle to development towards the economic approach, however, since the ideological reorientation of 'seeking truth from facts' and 'the observance of the law of economy' may undermine the assumption of the infallibility of the policy-maker within the Party-State. The official position of the Chinese Communist Party (CCP) suggests unequivocally that the truth is perceived by the minds of the top policy-makers and that the law is discovered by the Party-State. This view differs from that implicit in the economic approach, namely that social reality is interpreted and understood by all decision-makers intersubjectively — according to their different points of view and interaction between them.[23] Thus 'the truth', as such, may have many faces, depending on who the observer is. The CCP has not renounced its four basic premises — Marxism, Leninism, and Mao Zedong's thought, the Socialist road, the dictatorship of the proletariat, and the leadership of the Party. However, only one 'truth' is tolerated at any one time, namely, the one propounded by the top policy-makers. Therefore the future of economic reform cannot be predicted with great certainty unless it can be demonstrated that the afore-mentioned epistemological problems have been solved.

SUMMARY

The chapters which follow are divided into three parts. Part I deals with the early origins of industrial management at both the macro level and the micro level. Part II focuses on Mao's period. Part III is devoted to an analysis of trends in the post-Mao period.

A summary of the major thrust of the arguments in subsequent chapters may assist the reader.

(a) On the basis of experience in North-east China, the top Chinese leaders adopted a synoptic model of policy-making from 1949 to 1978.

(b) The synoptic model with its two approaches (administrative and preceptoral) tended to produce, and in many instances amplified, the unintended consequences of policy on industrial management.

(c) Generally, the two policy-making approaches were applied alternately, in response to the unintended consequences created by the other, until 1978.

(d) The preceptoral approach specifically created chaos and political and institutional disintegration, and was likely to run aground as soon as it was introduced; policy-makers tended to return to the administrative approach as a fall-back position (as, for example, in the Great Leap Forward and the Cultural Revolution).

(e) Remedial adjustments were frequently made to the synoptic model (in either of the two approaches), but these could not totally eliminate the deficiencies inherent in this policy-making model.

(f) Fundamentally, the tendency toward the strategic model (or the economic approach) of policy-making emerged as a response to the synoptic model and the unintended consequences allied with it, first on a limited scale during the Great Leap Forward, and later with increasing salience after the death of Mao Zedong.

(g) The change in policy-making approaches is dictated by three 'windows': ideology, organization, and politics, the opening of which depends upon unspecified historical situations.

PART I
THE EARLY ORIGINS

PART I
THE EARLY ORIGINS

2. The Origins of China's Industrial Management, 1949-1955

THE origins of China's industrial management system can be examined in two time periods. Between 1948 and 1952, a command economy and a system of rationalized industrial management developed in North-east China. In the years 1953 to 1955, the First Five-year Plan was introduced, the State Council with its powerful economic ministries was built, and the pattern of the planned economy and industrial management spread throughout China as most of industry became nationalized.

On the whole these two periods were marked by the development of the 'administrative policy-making approach'. Features of this approach include an emphasis upon modernization, the role of policy-actors as sovereign planners, a stress upon scientific rationality and calculation, a reliance upon the State bureaucracy for central planning, regulatory control, material incentives, and the maximum use of expert-professionals. From the post-Weberian perspective, such a process can be described as 'rationalizing without full rationalization' at the institutional level: the very process of rationalizing itself generated irrationality, inefficiency, and uncontrolled behaviour, all of which warrant controlling countermeasures. It is therefore suggested in this book that the tensions which accompanied the rationalizing process were derived not so much from the lack of the requisites for a modern and rational organization as from the intrinsic characteristics of the administrative approach (for example, its unintended consequences). Such tensions were aggravated especially in circumstances when the policy-makers were assigned an exceedingly large role.

THE RISE OF THE COMMAND ECONOMY

The command economy was established in the North-east Administrative Region (AR) during the period 1950-1, and was followed by the introduction of the Soviet model of planning during the First Five-year Plan (1953-7). The command economy is characterized by two features, central planning and public ownership, which represent a major perspective of macro-rationality. The early impetus towards an administered economy seemed necessary because of the deterioration of the economy following the war. In addition, the administrative approach appeared to be effective.

The rise of the command economy in North-east China was characterized by a transformation from a lower form of 'State capitalism' (a contract-oriented planning system) to a higher form (a target-oriented planning system). The contract-oriented planning system arose from the need for direct State intervention to assist industrial enterprises which were nearly bankrupt. The State provided contracts as well as material supply in order to maintain production. The target-oriented system was concerned with comprehensive economic planning on the basis of targets and balancing of materials. In fact, the North-east AR was among the few areas at the time ready for such a transformation. Although Shanghai had developed a relatively modern economy, it did not complete a similar change towards the fully fledged command economy until 1956, because it had a very large private enterprise sector.[1]

The leadership in North-east China, particularly Gao Gang, expressed considerable reservations about comprehensive economic planning. First, Gao maintained the philosophical notion which recognized the intellectual limits of policy-makers. He asserted, 'We are not God, and we cannot work out a perfect plan'. Second, he was aware of the difficulties, such as the lack of experience and statistical data, as well as the complexity of co-ordinating government units at different levels of the hierarchy, in different economic sectors, in different branches of industries, and in different localities.[2] Consequently, the regional leadership relied upon a loosely co-ordinated contractual relationship to manage the economy, and did not deal with the question of an annual plan for industrial enterprises until 1951. Such a contractual network provided economic links between various economic sectors, and between different types and branches of industries. This network encompassed functional links between supplies, production, and sales. During this time, enterprise units were grouped according to their products. In each functional area a managing bureau was responsible for management and control over each group of industrial enterprises. If the bureau carried out any planning at all, it had to enforce this planning through many separate contracts signed with the various enterprise units.[3]

This lower form of 'State capitalism' existed until mid-1951, when the Financial and Economic Committee of the Central People's

Government (CPG) promulgated 'control figures' for industrial production. The central industrial ministries and the AR were thus required to assign production targets to the enterprise units under their jurisdiction on the basis of the 'control figures' assigned to them.[4] Each group of enterprises was then required to formulate annual production, cost, and labour plans and submit them to the higher echelons (that is, the industrial ministries or bureaux) for review and approval. During the same period, procedures for making annual plans 'from the bottom to the top' and 'from the top to the bottom' were introduced and standardized.[5] There were frequent consultations and exchanges of information at various levels of the hierarchy. Moreover, a centralized system of supplying raw materials was established.[6] These developments brought the command economy of the North-east AR into the institutional framework of central planning which was set up by the CPG in 1951.

There were, however, inherent limitations on the extent to which the supervising authorities could impose annual plans at the enterprise level. This was partly attributable to the lack of modern organizational requisites. For example, when enterprises experienced a 'slow beginning and rushed ending' in implementing their monthly operational plans, the difficulties were at the time attributed to the inadequate preparation of blueprints, the lack of raw materials, the failure to adjust machines and equipment properly, and the poor handling of semi-finished products.[7] Also workshops were not able to produce consistently in accordance with a fixed monthly schedule, perhaps because of a lack of primary statistics and established work norms, or because of poor planning in job assignments, or for both of these reasons.[8]

The target-oriented planning system, which aimed to assign an extremely large role to policy-makers, represented a high degree of centralization. This system, however, entailed a counter-productive tendency towards irrationality, inefficiency, and uncontrolled elements. The target-oriented planning system is based upon the supposed capacity of policy-makers to ensure the accurate calculation of production input and output, as well as the supply of materials needed by a multitude of enterprise units. One cannot, moreover, expect enterprises to comply fully with the commands of a central planner, because they have their own interests and concerns, as well as a tendency to deviate from the intentions of the central planner.

Many incidents in North-east China suggest, for instance, that in making an annual production plan, enterprise units set up 'ambushes' (*maifu*), that is, they concealed their actual production capacity in order to ensure that the annual plan would appear to have been easily fulfilled.[9] The falsification of records and reports concerning production was a major problem in China's developing command economy. The case of Rubber Factory No. 4, under the jurisdiction of the Light Industry Ministry, revealed that the factory managed to acquire the title of 'model factory' and 'advanced factory' for production and for making savings, in both 1951 and 1952, through the falsification of statistical tables and reports.[10] This type of 'unintended consequence' resulted from the difficulties of working out an objective criterion for assessing the actual capacity of an enterprise, and for setting reasonable production targets. Frequently the supervising authorities increased production targets while enterprise units countered by lowering targets.

In order to cope with the 'unintended consequences' of the rationalizing process at the enterprise level, in 1951 the supervising authorities began to introduce the mobilizational approach, which allowed workers to participate in the formulation of annual plans and the supervision of their enforcement. In extreme cases, when production fell behind schedule, the 'commando approach' was employed to intensify production and to recover from delays in the production schedule. This approach relied heavily on overtime work, and frequently the job was done at the expense of the workers' health and damage to the equipment. A survey of press reports in the years 1951–3 indicates that workers' participation in planning was extensive.[11] Certainly the regional leadership also adopted some more conventional approaches for enforcing the annual plans, through the introduction of the responsibility system, the improvement of equipment and technology, the use of 'advanced work methods', devising new wage systems, technical training, and political indoctrination.

THE DEVELOPMENT OF THE ACCOUNTING SYSTEM

In the years 1948–51, a highly centralized accounting system for fixed assets and working capital was built up to facilitate the take-over, through registration and recovery, of State property;[12] this was followed by economic recovery and finally by the rationalization of industrial management in the North-east AR[13] and in the entire country.[14] The process started as a temporary measure,[15] but turned into a lasting corner-stone of the system of State ownership in a Socialist framework. This new system had two important features. First, every unit involved was given independent accounting status. That is, it was given responsibility for balancing its own income and disbursements. All transactions were made on the basis of contracts controlled by plans. Copies of these plans were submitted to the bank and higher supervising authorities for review. Second, no contracting party was permitted to engage in cash transactions: deals were handled through the transfer of accounts by the bank. In addition, the amount of cash which each unit was allowed to retain could not exceed the amount in daily use. In this new accounting system, enterprise units were therefore subject to close scrutiny and supervision by the bank and the higher authorities, in so far as the allocation of resources and working capital was concerned.[16]

After the completion of tedious groundwork in auditing and in estimating working capital,[17] and the introduction of independent accounting status for enterprise units, there still remained the problems of correctly delineating the financial responsibility of enterprise units, and of enhancing incentives for them to fulfil annual plans and contracts. During 1949 and 1950, the newly developed accounting system was plagued with a 'supply system mentality': State-run enterprises were only required to fulfil production quotas in accordance with the contracts which they had signed with their respective bureaux. This did not enable them to derive much benefit from the savings and the improvements in product quality which they had made. All surplus materials were returned to the contracting bureaux. The pricing system did not permit the differentiation of good quality raw materials and final products from bad.[18] The new accounting system was not sensitive enough to detect improvements in the utilization of equipment and facilities and the maximization of the use of working hours in State-run enterprises. Consequently, the enterprise accounting system was reconstructed and strengthened in 1951 with the following features:

(a) instead of being based on contracting, it was characterized by annual plans, the central allocation of resources and working capital, the independent accounting status of enterprises, and the settlement of accounts through the bank;

(b) enterprise units assumed financial responsibility for remitting profits and depreciation fees to higher supervising bureaux;

(c) a factory director's fund was given to enterprises in proportion to their fulfilment and over-fulfilment of various plans, in order to increase their concern with managerial performance and to increase the circulation of working capital.[19]

The introduction of the planning procedure and the accounting system to the enterprise level was supplemented by the campaign approach of the mass movements of the early 1950s. As William Brugger noted, the New Record Movement during the second half of 1949 and early 1950[20] was actually an integral part of a much larger effort to rationalize work norms, focusing on working hours, equipment utilization, and material consumption. In June 1950, Gao Gang, after assessing the achievements of the New Record Movement, suggested that it was able to change workers' attitudes of 'loafing on the foreign job' (*mo yanggong*) or 'soldiering' (in Frederick Taylor's term), and could significantly increase labour intensity.[21]

Nevertheless the campaign approach was not immune from its own 'unintended consequences'. Gao Gang pointed out that it tended to drive industrial workers beyond their physical limits and generated considerable grievances, especially when enterprise managers were required to respond to pressures imposed by the movement.[22] To remedy this, the Regional People's Government prohibited excessive overtime work.[23] Furthermore the movement contributed significantly to a deterioration in product quality, and the violation of technical and safety procedures. This resulted in numerous accidents and mechanical failures.[24] Consequently, after the New Record Movement in 1949 and 1950, the policy emphasis moved from the campaign approach to an institutional approach, focusing on the establishment of 'reasonable norms' on the basis of scientific methods.[25]

ONE-MAN MANAGEMENT IN NORTH-EAST CHINA

The rationalizing process was not confined to State machinery wielding economic power over the enterprise level, but extended down to the enterprise and workshop levels. It likewise produced unintended consequences and triggered continuous cycles of renewed control. The case of 'one-man management' illustrates this process and the tensions mentioned above.

One-man management was introduced to North-east China on an

informal basis immediately after the CCP's take-over of the region in 1948. The system was subsequently formalized when the First Party Congress of the CCP of the North-east AR was convened in March 1950. Explaining the need for the system, Gao Gang offered two reasons. Firstly, on the basis of the separation of the State apparatus from the Party organization, the factory director should not be made responsible to the Party Committee.[26] According to Gao Gang, the factory director is the representative of the State at the enterprise level, while the Party Committee is a voluntary political association. Secondly, is was necessary to delineate responsibility clearly, in order to ensure the fulfilment of production plans, and to allow for personnel specialization, as well as to increase motivation.[27] The resolution of the North-east Party Bureau, as approved by the Central Committee (presumably the Department of Industry and Transport) in May 1951, emphasized that the factory director was entrusted by the State with the management and control of the means of production and working capital. He was also granted exclusive power over production and administrative tasks.[28]

In the context of interlocking hierarchies, the factory director (or corporation manager) was given exclusive authority over all managerial functions.[29] Basically, 'one-man management' follows the principle of 'unity of command' as suggested by classical management theory.[30] The factory directors were the 'line officers'. They were in charge of the operation and performance in the field. They were also made directly responsible to their superiors at the bureau and ministerial level. They, in turn, had command over the 'line officers' at the level below (that is, workshop directors).[31]

One-man management was frequently interpreted as an integral part of the so-called 'responsibility system'. Under this system's conceptual umbrella, a distinction was made between the 'administrative responsibility system' and the 'production responsibility system'. The former was concerned with the administrative operations and functions of the factory director and his subordinate line officers within an enterprise. The latter was established for specific functional areas, which included: the production responsibility system, the technological responsibility system, the maintenance responsibility system, the work-post responsibility system, and the quality inspection system, and so on.

The formal role of the Party Committee was at the time confined to the so-called 'supervision and guarantee' (*jiandu yu baozheng*) of economic and administrative work. More specifically, this included the following functions: (a) striving for the fulfilment and then the over-fulfilment of annual plans through mass mobilization; (b) initiating periodical checks and supervision over the enforcement of the policies, directives, regulations, and laws of the State and the Party; (c) promoting supervision by a form of managerial democracy, for example, a congress of workers and staff or a factory management committee; (d) training and promoting enterprise personnel and carrying out security clearances; and (e) combating the violation of laws and discipline as well as 'bureaucratism'.[32]

Some informal arrangements were made, however, to remedy the rigid division of labour between the factory director and the Party Secretary, as, for example, in consultations between the two in 'head-knocking meetings' (*pengtouhui*),[33] and in efforts by the factory director to keep the Party Secretary informed.[34] Evidence indicates that not all factory directors were Party members at the time. If they were Party members, however, they were advised to join the Party Committee and were subject to the Party's discipline. They were also required to report on their jobs in the Party Committee.[35]

In line with what is called the post-Weberian perspective, the North-east AR leadership devised very sophisticated mechanisms for checking the 'authoritarianism' of factory directors.[36] For instance, both the chief accountant system and the chief engineer system were designed to provide 'independent control officers' directly appointed by the State in the areas of accounting and technology. These were two crucial functional areas at the enterprise level.[37] These officers were made responsible not only to the factory director, but also to the supervising bureau or ministry at the level above. All important documents and papers had to be endorsed jointly by the factory director and a control officer (the chief accountant or the chief engineer) before they could acquire legal effect. Scattered evidence indicates that in the early 1950s, these officers were appointed not only in North-east China, but also in areas throughout the rest of China.[38]

The establishment of factory management committees added yet another check upon the power of factory directors. These committees were given the power to discuss, but not necessarily the power to make decisions, at the enterprise level. In North-east China, this committee system was supplementary to one-man management, and was intended to perform consultative and supervisory functions. It was therefore not a sovereign decision-making body at the enterprise level, as William Brugger noted. These committees included both ex-officio members, such as the chief engineer and the union chairman, and ordinary members who were appointed or were elected by the workers and staff. Although the factory director could veto a decision of the committee, he was required to report and explain his decision to the supervising authorities at the higher level.[39]

The congress of workers and staff was another instrument of 'renewed control' in the post-Weberian sense. The factory director and his subordinates were required to report to the congress on a monthly and seasonal basis regarding production, capital investment, welfare and wages, personnel management, and so on. The congress was a collective entity, having a definite voice in the use of the 'factory director's fund' (a portion of the profit derived from the fulfilment and over-fulfilment of annual plans). In addition, it acted as a 'board of management' over the various welfare schemes, amenities, and collective facilities of the factory.[40]

During the year 1950, an approach which Harry Harding called 'internal remedialism'[41] was also adopted: like the rest of the country, North-east China launched a Party Rectification Campaign, which stressed political study, criticism, and self-criticism, with , the objectives of raising political consciousness, overcoming 'bureaucratism', 'commandism', arrogance, and self-satisfaction, and improving relationships with the people. In addition, 'external remedialism'[42] was practised in the *sanfan* and *wufan* (the 'three-antis' and 'five-antis') campaigns in late 1951 and early 1952. The 'three-antis' campaign was intended to combat corruption, wastefulness, and 'bureaucratism' among Party cadres and State officials. The 'five-antis' campaign was directed against industrialists and business-men who were allegedly guilty of violating the law in terms of the following five 'poisons': bribery, tax evasion, theft of State property, cheating on government contracts, and stealing State economic information. The *sanfan* and *wufan* campaigns, which were supposedly directed against capitalists, were perhaps less relevant to North-east China since that region had only a small number of private enterprises.[43]

POLITICAL CONTROVERSY OVER ONE-MAN MANAGEMENT

Political controversy over the system of one-man management started with the issue of whether the CPG and the Central Committee had taken a formal position on the subject prior to 1956. The available evidence is contradictory. A formal policy regarding the system of one-man management in North-east China was approved in the name of the Central Committee, as noted above. Moreover, at the national level, the Textiles Industry Ministry decided on 25 December 1950 to establish an administrative responsibility system for managers and other related staff. Also, on 28 May 1953, the Heavy Industry Ministry issued a directive which stressed the implementation of both the technical and the administrative responsibility systems.[44] The implementation of one-man management acquired fresh impetus in 1953, but the policy was not fully consolidated in the following two years. A document which was issued in the name of the Central Committee in October 1955 stated that 'the party organization within the enterprises shall seriously assist, estabish and consolidate one-man management, and in the meantime it shall educate all personnel in observing administrative discipline and the order to enterprises'.[45]

It is, therefore, odd to discover that Mao Zedong claimed he was not aware of decisions taken prior to 1956 by the Central Committee, the central ministries, and local units with reference to 'one-man management'. In April 1956 Mao stated that 'some matters have neither been decided upon by the Centre nor by the localities. However, it was adopted. The issue of one-man management was discussed by the Centre only after it was raised by [Li] Xuefeng [presumably during 1956]'.[46] Mao added that the development of the Soviet style of one-man management, together with the relationship between the centre and the localities, could be discussed further, because 'both the Politburo and the State Council have not yet made any decisions'.[47] Li Xuefeng, Head of the Department of Transport and Industry of the Central Committee, in his major speech to the Eighth Party Congress in September 1956, failed to mention the decisions previously made at both the Party and the ministerial level.[48] In view of this contradictory evidence, a likely explanation is that Mao Zedong in fact did not know of decisions on one-man management which had been taken by several subunits of the CPG Administrative Council and the Central Committee, given his preoccupation with other priorities, and the fragmentary nature of policy-making at the time.

As a number of authors have pointed out, one-man management was adopted in only a few localities and a few ministries from 1949 to 1955.[49] It was impossible to implement the system throughout

China, since the pace of political consolidation and economic recovery varied significantly in different areas. It is also worth noting that, in September 1948, the Central Committee made its first decisions on strengthening the Party Committee.[50] This was necessitated by the shift of emphasis from the rural environment to the urban setting. The previous emphasis upon party leadership was not consistent with the change to a new leadership style, and a new method of work, namely, one-man management.

Another difficulty in introducing one-man management was attributable to resistance from local Party organizations. According to an editorial in the People's Daily, published on 16 May 1954, Party men in general believed that since there was a need for the Party organization to exercise leadership over economic tasks, the Party apparatus should directly manage industry. Moreover, the Party organization should assume control when the administrative machinery could not function effectively and when problems could not be solved in time. On the whole, the editorial recommended one-man management in order to overcome 'individualism' and to tighten discipline in organizational life.[51]

Wang Renzhong, the First Secretary of the Party Committee of Hubei province indicated in the Eighth Party Congress in 1956 that there had been intense debate over whether the 'party collective and unified leadership' should replace 'one-man management' in Hubei. Wang argued for collective leadership by the Party Committee on the grounds that it had been an effective policy for many years, and was a legacy of the long-term revolutionary war. He also mentioned that the introduction of one-man management in the province from 1953 to early 1955 resulted in chaos in production, strained relations between the factory director and the Party Committee, and generated considerable grievances among the subordinate staff.[52] Wang suggested that the provincial Party Committee of Hubei took the lead in returning to the 'Party's collective leadership system' in early 1955 in accordance with a resolution on strengthening Party leadership in industry, passed by the Fourth Plenum of the Seventh Party Congress in February 1954.[53]

In the Eighth Party Congress, Li Xuefeng spoke against one-man management, stressing the need for the Party's collective leadership and the mass-line. In addition, he cited reasons opposing 'bureaucratism and commandism', as well as those against 'capitalist managerial thought', which was represented by one-man management.[54] Li's speech set the official tone on this issue for approximately two decades, from 1956 to 1976, and his view probably reflected Mao's position. During the Congress, Li evaded the issue of the separation between the Party and the State, a crucial point made by Gao Gang.

From a post-Weberian perspective, Anthony Downs' proposition concerning the structural tendency of a 'monitoring agency' (for example, the Party apparatus) to replace an 'operating agency' (the factory director) is pertinent to the issue of one-man management.[55] In other words, when stressing the functions of 'supervision and guarantee' by the Party, the Party Committee was given a licence to encroach upon the jurisdiction of the factory director and finally to replace the factory director, in an inherently unstable structure of 'parallel hierarchies'.

THE AUTHORITY-CENTRED EMPLOYMENT SYSTEM

In the early years of the PRC, the rationalizing process also penetrated the areas of labour management, the employment system, and the remunerative system. Some elements of organic State socialism clearly took hold despite the orientation toward rationalization, efficiency, and productivity. The term 'organic State socialism' here refers to the web of rights and obligations, featuring egalitarianism, collectivism, the community of shared benefit within organizational units (danwei), and concerning the 'neighbourly' relationship among organizational units. They are sanctioned by State laws and enforced by political institutions.

There are two systems of employment that are conceptually parallel to the administrative and economic approaches to policy-making, namely, the authority centred and the market centred respectively. The former is characterized by the exercise of State authority, co-ordination by planning, group orientation, and the life-tenure system. The latter concerns the interaction between employers and employees, co-ordination through contracts, individual orientation, and limited tenure. Policy-makers in North-east China were first committed to authority-centred employment as a result of their concern about employment problems and the need for a relief policy after the war. Also, during the various labour movements since the 1920s the CCP had repeatedly pledged to protect the employment rights of the working class. A further justification for State intervention was the rational utilization of industrial manpower, as embodied in the concept of central planning and implemented in the First Five-year Plan.

During the early 1950s, two policies provided an institutional base for the life-tenure system in State-run enterprises. The first was the decision of the CPG Administrative Council, on 8 August 1952, to hold each enterprise unit responsible for surplus labour resulting from managerial reforms, improvements in labour productivity, and the prohibition against dismissing workers (except for authorized shutdowns and work stoppages). This decision also entitled workers to re-employment, when the assets and equipment of a unit were transferred to, or combined with, another enterprise.[56] The second policy precedent concerned the protection of workers and staff against arbitrary dismissal. This protection was afforded by the 1954 'Outline of Labour Regulations Within State-owned Enterprises', which required that dismissals be reviewed and approved by higher echelons of the State.[57]

Early CCP policy neither tolerated the temporary worker system, nor permitted the hiring of workers on a temporary basis for any type of permanent job. In 1952, a measure of the CPG Administrative Council required temporary workers who had assumed regular production duty to change to positions as formal or preparatory workers in all State and private enterprises. From then until 1956, temporary workers were employed strictly for temporary jobs.[58] The hiring of permanent workers (under the so-called fixed employment system) meant that the State was committed not only to a full employment policy, but also to the concept of the worker's inalienable right to his job and other related benefits. This ideological commitment has been held firmly in spite of the imperative for efficiency, productivity, and economy ever since the PRC's early years.

THE STANDARDIZATION OF THE SYSTEM OF REMUNERATION

While the authority-centred employment system was evolving, the standardization of the remuneration system began in North-east China and spread gradually throughout China. Prior to mid-1950, the regional leadership in North-east China allowed various provinces and municipalities, as well as several industrial sectors, discretion to tailor their wage system to local needs. A work-point system coexisted with the supply system for a short period before 1950. Brugger has noted that a majority of mining and industrial enterprises and government offices began to adopt a work-point system, in which the earnings of workers, staff, and officials were tied to a standard-of-living index which took 1946 as the baseline. At the same time, the supply system remained applicable to cadres who were transferred from the old military and government establishments to civilian and industrial posts. In selected areas, such as the municipalities of Lushun and Dalian, the development of a standard system of remuneration was ahead of the regional schedule. They adopted a seven-grade wage system for blue-collar workers, with progressive differentials between the work points.[59]

The achievement of regional economic stabilization in 1950 made work points and the cost-of-living index irrelevant. The regional government was then in a position to introduce a new wage system with built-in adjustments to different local situations, various industrial branches, and supervising bureaux.[60] Gao Gang supported this new wage structure, together with the economic accounting system, as a weapon against the influence of the 'supply system'. He suggested, with a deep concern for productivity and efficiency, that for a long period many cadres and officials had lived, and in the 1950s still lived, by the supply system, under which differentials of treatment depended upon factors such as seniority, status, and physical strength, which did not directly reflect work contributions. Consequently, lazy cadres and officials would be well provided for regardless of the amount and quality of work they had completed. This system has been accurately described in the cliché, 'work or not, still half a catty of rice'.[61] Another guiding principle of the wage reforms in 1950 and 1951 was that the interests of individual workers should be integrated with those of the State in accordance with the principle, 'to each according to his labour; more pay for more work'.[62]

On 19 June 1950, the North-east People's Government increased the wages and salaries of workers and technicians by an average of 8 per cent above the 1949 level and substituted an eight-grade wage system for the 39-point system which had been adopted in specific enterprises and regions. The new wage system was structured exclusively on the basis of technical competence. There was also a substantial increase in both the income floor and the ceiling for technicians and engineers, in order to attract more technical personnel and to encourage technical study and training.[63] The salary and wage committees of various departments and bureaux were instructed to employ technical standards in place of 'simple democratic evaluation' in determining grades at the enterprise level.[64]

The main difficulty in standardizing the remuneration system lay in the sheer complexity and volume of work required for its extension to the entire economy at the regional level. It would be impossible to formulate within a short period of time the technical standards on which the new wage system throughout North-east China was based. In cases where standardization was successful, objective technical standards were formulated before workers were evaluated and classified. Whenever workers disagreed about their grades, they could refer to objective technical standards. However, whenever a subjective criterion was used for determining grades (such as attitudes toward work), disputes and dissatisfaction occurred. Consequently, these tensions among workers registered in an increase in applications for transfer and resignations, and the rate of absenteeism rose.[65]

The Central People's Government followed closely behind the regional government in North-east China in achieving the standardization of wage and salary schemes. This was done in two phases. The first phase began in 1952 with an emphasis upon the standardization of the work-point system, in which the earnings of industrial employees were tied to the standard-of-living index (which was similar to that used in North-east China). Officials and cadres who had been remunerated according to the supply system were then paid increasingly through monetary payment rather than payment in kind. The second phase, which began in June 1956, included an eight-grade wage system plus a form of monetary payment to replace the work-point system, coupled with a subsidy system and a standard salary system for staff members on the basis of their duties.[66]

Benefiting from the early North-east Chinese experience, the national wage reform of 1956 was governed by four principles: (a) the establishment of a unified and rational wage system and the elimination of 'egalitarianism' in the wage system within each branch of industry; (b) greater differentiation between types of jobs, as well as their physical intensity; (c) the establishment of a standard salary system for managerial personnel, including engineers and technicians, on the basis of job classifications; and (d) the incorporation of old wage systems into new schemes, taking wage increases into consideration.[67] Moreover, there was an emphasis on technical standards, and greater recognition was given to skills and technical competence. For example, there was a wage increase of 8 per cent for first-grade workers (the lowest grade), but 18 per cent for eighth-grade skilled workers. In some localities, higher-grade engineers and technicians were allowed a salary increase of 36 per cent.[68]

As a part of the overall rationalizing tendency, the piece-rate wage was first implemented in North-east China and then extended throughout the country, beginning with the first phase of national wage reform in 1952. In North-east China, the piece-rate wage system started in light industry and other selected industries employing sizeable numbers of unskilled workers, on the basis of a formal policy announced on 17 April 1951. The pace for extending the system was dictated by the development of production routines, the establishment of work norms and technical standards, and the steady supply of raw materials. Also, due to the nature of their jobs, technicians and workshop directors (line managers) were mainly paid an hourly time-rate wage plus bonuses, rather than a piece-rate wage.[69]

At the national level it was estimated that by the end of 1955 the piece-rate wage was implemented among 43.9 per cent of the industrial workers in selected industries such as coal, steel construction, and food processing — all of which were labour intensive. The 1956 national wage reforms resulted in an increase in the piece-rate wage, from 32.3 per cent to 42 per cent of the total wages bill during the First Five-year Plan (1953–7).[70] The bonus system began formally in 1952, in accordance with a policy paper formulated during a conference convened by the Financial and Economic Commission. In 1956 the State Council stressed the need for a bonus system in selected managerial functions such as new products, the saving of fuel and raw materials, the improvement of product quality, and some cases of over-fulfilment of production quotas. [71] Both the piece-rate wage and the bonus system suffered from ideological and political disruption which started in 1957.

LABOUR INSURANCE AND COLLECTIVE WELFARE

As early as 1 April 1949, a workers' insurance system was introduced to State-owned enterprises in North-east China. The insurance system, which was mainly funded by enterprise units, financed retired workers' homes, hospitals, and day-care centres. By 1950, 600,000 workers and 1.5 million members of workers' families had benefited from the scheme.[72] It took about two years (from 1 April 1949 to 26 February 1951) for the Ministry of Labour of the CPG and the All China Federation of Labour Unions, working together, to formulate a labour insurance law to provide retirement pensions, relief in sickness and accidents, and paid maternity leave. In addition, the law provided medical benefits, day-care facilities, and subsidies to workers and staff who supported large families.[73] Also, a part of the previous price subsidy (including payment in kind, such as grain, cloth, fuel, edible oil, and salt) was incorporated into the welfare and fringe benefit system at the enterprise level.[74]

The basic reasons for the early development of this insurance system were threefold. First, it was a part of the legacy of the labour movement led by the CCP which had fought for labour legislation since 1922. Second, the new wage system did not cover many areas of workers' needs in daily life which the supply system had provided for. Among these were retirement, disablement, illness, and accidents. A social insurance system was therefore required to close the gaps created by the change to the new wage system.[75] Third, the financial strength of the State was such that it could afford the stability and continuity of such welfare and insurance schemes. Joyce Kallgren noted that in the PRC's early years the State played an important role in meeting these urgent needs, especially in cases where it seemed likely that alternative courses of action would probably result in social and political chaos. According to Kallgren, these welfare programmes 'not only reflect the utopian quality of Marxist thought but also symbolize the Party's acceptance of the welfare functions of the [S]tate.'[76]

The 1951 Labour Insurance Regulation took into consideration the financial status of sponsoring units. It was implemented in mining and industrial enterprises with more than 100 workers and staff, and with labour unions which had an adequate administrative apparatus. It proposed that enterprises in mines, industry, and transport should be given first priority in implementation, followed by the banking system.[77]

The collective welfare system defined the community of shared benefits at the enterprise level. This system was further strengthened by an early version of the profit-retention system, which was tied to the fulfilment and over-fulfilment of annual plans. As early as 1950, when the New Record Movement was launched in North-east China, a labour union was permitted to claim a share of the factory director's fund on behalf of workers and staff, when production plans were fulfilled or over-fulfilled, and when production costs were reduced. This share of the fund was then used for the expansion of amenities and welfare facilities, such as schools and nurseries for the children of employees, clinics, canteens, public baths, and sports and recreational facilities.[78]

During these early years, the contribution of the collective welfare system to the real income of workers and staff members was considerable. By 1953 collective forms of remuneration provided by the State, labour unions, or enterprises comprised a substantial proportion of workers' incomes, up to an estimated 17 per cent in some key industries.[79] It is therefore clear that the development and growth of labour insurance and collective welfare during China's early years marked the development of another aspect of organic State socialism with an emphasis upon the collective, indirect, and diffuse forms of remuneration.

NON-MATERIAL INCENTIVES

The controversy over material incentives as opposed to non-material incentives began very early in the PRC's history, and centred on the relative weights of the two and on the operational definition of the latter. During the period 1949–55, questions arose as to whether ideological indoctrination should take precedence over material benefits when the motivational problems of industrial workers were being dealt with. In the West, there was an established view on these questions, Abraham Maslow's analysis of the hierarchy of needs. This analysis states that members of an organization do not normally respond to incentives of a higher order (for example, recognition, sense of fulfilment, and altruistic values) until the needs of the lower order (such as food and shelter) are satisfied.[80]

The view of some observers in China appears congruent with Maslow's view. For instance, Deng Zihui, the Third Secretary of the Central-South Bureau of the Central Committee, CCP, delivered a report to the General Regional Labour Union, noting that there were strains between political and economic interests, between long-term and short-term interests, and between the interests of the whole and those of the parts. He explained that 'since industrial workers are materialistic it is not practical to talk about politics, culture, care-taking and a beautiful future in a subjectivist perspective while allowing their stomachs to remain empty'.[81] (Translation supplied.) A contrary opinion was that of Lai Ruoyu, who observed in 1953 that 'when workers realize that their immediate interests and the interests of the parts should be subordinate to their long-term interest and the interest of the whole, they will be able to fight bravely for their beautiful future'. He added: 'this means a significant raising of their political consciousness'.[82]

It is appropriate to equate non-material incentives (which are generally called 'political work' by the CCP) with the concepts discussed by the Human Relations School in the West. Reinhard Bendix has suggested that the Human Relations School has its 'totalitarian' implications through its embrace of all aspects of human activities that are directly and indirectly related to industrial life.[83] Chinese managers, in fact, possess a much wider range of managerial tools than their Western counterparts, covering the areas from the Scientific Management School to the Human Relations School. They might even move beyond their Japanese colleagues in collectivizing not only the functions of the work-place but also workers' activities outside working hours. Such 'totalitarian' management breeds a total dependency of workers and employees on the factory organization. Andrew Walder's use of the term 'organized dependency' in general provides a valid analysis of the relationship of the enterprise to the worker.[84] This pattern was first seen in the mass-oriented managerial style in North-east China in the period 1949–55, which was intended to manipulate and control all facets of industrial workers' lives.

Three waves of mass campaigns from 1948 to 1952 may serve as a good illustration of 'totalitarian management'. The first wave, from November 1948 to October 1949, centred on political consolidation, the establishment of new managerial organizations, and democratic reforms. The second wave, from October 1949 to July 1951, stressed production reforms. The third wave, from August 1951 to 1952, emphasized the discovery of the potential of enterprises, the practice of savings and improvements in productivity, and the introduction of annual plans.[85] The mass-oriented management style was not immune from its inherent limitations. These included the monopolization of power by trade unions in the election and appointment of labour leaders, in committee work, and in the consultation process.[86]

Some issues regarding non-material incentives arose from 'contextual factors' (for example, political, economic, social, and cultural). First, the regional leadership found it difficult to overcome hostility towards staff members who had had ties with the old regime, in spite of a series of directives and measures introduced in April 1950 and May 1954.[87] Second, old staff members could not easily adapt to a democratic type of management and accept command by Party cadres who lacked managerial and technical competence.[88] Because of a shortage of technical personnel, the regional leadership endeavoured to improve their remuneration, and to promote workers to managerial ranks.[89] Third, attacks on 'traditionalism', together with the abolition of the gang-boss system, encouraged an attitude of defiance by young workers towards veteran workers and dampened the motivation of young workers to learn from veteran workers. Subsequently, the North-east AR leadership restructured the old apprenticeship system by drawing up 'contracts' to be signed between senior workers and unskilled workers in order to upgrade technical manpower and to improve labour discipline.[90] Finally, the call for efficiency and productivity tended to intensify industrial work, especially during the First Five-year Plan, placing additional strains on industrial workers, which were manifested in an increasing incidence of absenteeism, slowdowns, lateness, and a high transfer rate. Under these circumstances, political indoctrination and education were employed as a substitute for what could not be resolved through material incentives.[91]

ORGANIZATIONAL AND IDEOLOGICAL FACTORS

It is germane for us to return to an analysis of meta-policy-making as well as those independent variables which had a bearing upon the ascendancy of the administrative approach during the early years of the PRC from 1949 to 1955. An excellent opportunity to shape this approach emerged immediately after the Civil War, when the top policy-makers were under pressure to restore order to the economy and to maintain the political regime. Mao stated early in 1949 that 'only when production in the cities is restored and developed, and when consumer-cities are transferred into producer-cities, can the people's political power be consolidated'.[92] In fact, the regional leaders in North-east China who first confronted the problem of economic recovery were not given many choices: the infrastructure for a modern industrial complex and the framework of an administered economy had taken shape in North-east China during a period of one decade prior to the CCP's take-over in 1948. It was therefore convenient to make full use of this organizational advantage.

It is worth noting that the Japanese administration implemented two five-year plans between 1937 and 1946.[93] The available data suggest that the manufacturing industry of the region sustained a very high growth rate even after the outbreak of the war — of approximately 34 per cent from 1935 to 1940.[94] Immediately after the Civil War in 1949, the industrial sector of the region contributed 74 per cent of the total national product value.[95] Furthermore, North-east China benefited until 1953 from the Japanese engineers and managers retained until that date.[96] In addition, benefits came from technical assistance provided by the Soviet Union after the signing of the Sino-Soviet Treaty of Friendship, Alliance and Mutual Assistance in February 1950.[97]

Moreover, the CCP's top policy-actors had been accustomed to working with an enormous, complex, and centralized organization since the beginning of the Yenan period. Deng Xiaoping has testified that there was an overall tendency towards centralization of power within the CCP from 1941, through the establishment of the Party Committee system, the report system, the approval procedure, and organizational streamlining.[98] In addition, by the end of the Civil War, the CCP had become experienced in handling the problems of co-ordinating and organizing military operations on a grand scale (that is , involving over one million men). The foregoing analysis suggests that the administered economy, coupled with scientific enterprise management, evolved from a situation in which the existing organization (including its resources, know-how, and skilled manpower) was looking for a policy objective.[99]

The ideological 'window' seemed to be only half open, in that ideological considerations had only a limited impact on the formation of the administrative approach in the period 1949–55. There appears to have been no coherent and well-articulated view guiding the establishment of the command economy and rational enterprise management. Mao Zedong mentioned retrospectively that, during the early years, Chinese policy-makers learned much from the Soviet Union in the fields of planning, heavy industry, and statistical work. The Soviet systems were accepted without much critical reflection because, in Mao's words, 'we did not have experience!'[100] Gao Gang, as previously mentioned, did not feel entirely comfortable with the rapid establishment of target-centred planning in North-east China because an unrealistically large role was assigned to central planners, and there were also other difficulties. Yet the sequence of events leading to a full-fledged command economy did not wait for an articulated ideology. This does not mean that ideology has little relevance. At least some aspects of industrial management policy were affected by ideological considerations, such as the debate over the relative weight of the Party and the State in one-man management, the controversy regarding material and non-material incentives, issues related to life-tenure employment, and the prohibition against employing temporary workers.

At a higher level of ideological articulation, however, it did not seem that a 'line struggle' was involved in the ascendancy of the administrative approach in the North-east AR from 1948 to 1953. Deng Xiaoping, who was in charge of the purge of Gao Gang and Rao Shushi, has consistently maintained the distinction between factional activity and policy issues; Deng never regarded Gao and Rao as ideologically wrong in terms of their policy.[101] Mao Zedong's statement made in 1956, immediately following Gao's purge, confirmed the distinction between the political (factional) and policy (ideological) dimensions of the case. Mao encouraged officials and cadres to discuss policy questions without the fear of being suspected of 'factional activity'. A specific example of this was the destructive type of factional activity which occurred during the Gao–Rao incident.[102] The official record shows that Gao was not purged because of ideological differences with Mao or any other leaders.

POLITICS AND POLICY-MAKING

The political 'window' appeared half open at three levels: the top leadership level, the bureaucratic level, and the societal level. To begin with, the rise of the administrative approach prior to 1955 was not associated with attempts to maintain and reallocate power at the top leadership level, for several reasons.

First, the policy-makers of the North-east AR were left with almost full discretionary power to handle industrial management policy during the early years of the PRC, not only because of the preoccupation of the central policy-actors with political and military policies of greater importance, but also because of the different agendas and time schedules of the regional governments.[103] North-east China was one of the few ARs which were ready to undertake 'economic construction', owing to its early take-over. Second, as a procedural matter, the ARs were given the prerogative of consulting with the Party centre; the duty of carrying out trial-implementation and testing of national policy; tailoring the central policy to suit local needs; and providing policy proposals in an entirely new area.[104] In fact, North-east China was a forerunner in enterprise management policy and set policy precedents which were, in many cases, incorporated into national policies.[105] Third, the North-east AR enjoyed considerable autonomy over industrial management, in accordance with the 'Organic Law of Regional Government Councils' (dated 16 December 1949) and other laws and directives of the Central People's Government.[106] Legally speaking, 'an independent kingdom' was permissible within such a quasi-federal framework. At the time industrial policy was important in North-east China, but had not yet been elevated to the national level.

At first glance, this case study does not appear to reveal a definite pattern through which policy-makers entered into and found an exit from the policy-making process. For example, the transformation from contract-centred planning to target-centred planning in North-east China involved the regional policy-actors first. Later, the Financial and Economic Commission accelerated the pace of development, requiring the introduction of 'control figures' in 1951. In the case of one-man management, for instance, Gao Gang and the North-east AR clearly took the lead. A number of ministries and local governments subsequently made similar decisions in their respective jurisdictions. Relevant departments of the Central Committee, CCP, later endorsed the policy of one-man management (October 1955). Mao Zedong's entry into the issue of one-man management in April 1956 reflected much inconsistency and a lack of co-ordination in this area of the CCP's policy-making.

In spite of the fluidity of participation in policy-making, one salient tendency was that the high-level administrators who had been associated with the building of the early version of the administrative approach found their way into the planning apparatus and economic ministries of the Government Administrative Council (restructured as the State Council in 1954). Gao Gang was appointed Director of the State Planning Commission in December 1952 and Li Fu-chun succeeded Gao after the latter's purge. Li was a member of the decision-making team from North-east China. Wang Hefeng, Jia

Tofu, and Ma Hong were also all in the original North-east AR policy group. Chen Yun, who later chaired the powerful Financial and Economic Commission, had his North-east China connection as well. The 'colonization' of the planning and managerial sections of the top leadership structure by the North-east group sheds considerable light on the perpetuation of the administrative approach in subsequent periods.

Political factors were also activated at the institutional and the societal level, when the issues of power-sharing and distributive justice were raised in the mid-1950s. For instance, the abolition of one-man management and the strengthening of the Party's collective leadership system in 1956 were notable by-products of the re-alignment of political forces within the bureaucratic framework.

At the societal level, disputes over a fair share of power and material benefits highlighted the tension between industrial workers and managerial staff. It is noteworthy that during these early years the PRC adopted the 'autocratic model', in which government authorities imposed an effective land reform, securing the support of the peasantry, and mobilizing industrial workers and the urban poor through economic equality and distributive justice.[107] The 'autocratic model', however, was not compatible with the imperative for economic growth and efficiency in North-east China. Thus considerable limits were imposed upon the further expansion of workers' participation, and an effort was made to discourage hostility and discrimination against middle-class professionals. For the sake of efficiency, successive reforms entitled managerial personnel to large salary increments as their managerial responsibility increased.

SUMMARY AND IMPLICATIONS

This case study of North-east China has examined the rise of the administrative approach of policy-making from 1949 to 1955. This process was characterized by centralization, regularization, standardization, and an increase in State control over major functional areas of industrial life. The pattern of industrial management was shaped by an extension of the rationalization of organization from the State level down to the enterprise level. The key feature, therefore, of China's industrial management was its authority orientation, in contrast to the market orientation of its Western counterparts. More specifically, such a pattern of industrial management can be viewed as (a) a highly rationalized and centralized system, and (b) an organic State socialism with both material and non-material incentives. According to Franz Schurmann, the former is 'technical organization' while the latter generally concerns 'human organization'.[108] Chong-wook Chung further identifies the foregoing two dimensions in terms of the Soviet model and the Japanese model respectively. The synthesis between the two, Chung suggests, is due to the adoption of the Japanese model from 1948 to 1953, and the Soviet model from 1950 onwards.[109]

The rise of the administrative policy-making approach can be explained by the demonstrable superiority of the legal bureaucratic form of organization during the crisis of an economic recovery, which is characterized by an inflationary spiral, high unemployment rates, factory stoppages, and numerous bankruptcies. Each step towards the pure administrative approach tended to produce apparent, if not real, results in terms of an increase in production, but not necessarily an improvement in efficiency. Many of the adverse consequences of this approach (for example, high costs and waste) might have been concealed, for the progress of economic recovery was measured favourably against a very low starting point — the ruin and devastation created by the war and the accompanying chaos in the recovery period. Consequently, the top policy-makers felt encouraged to assume an ever larger role, from the initial policy of unified procurement and sales, through contract-centred planning, public-private joint ownership and, finally, the full-fledged command economy. As suggested in Chapter 1, the Weberian 'ideal type', which defines the organizational structure of an administered economy, is inherently 'synoptic' from the policy-making perspective. The case of North-east China adequately fits this observation.

This book suggests that the nature and sources of the tensions allied with the ascendancy of the administrative policy-making approach during these early years of the PRC can be re-examined in the post-Weberian perspective.[110] This perspective highlights the phenomenon of the so-called 'unintended consequences' in organizational life (such as irrationality, inefficiency, and uncontrolled elements) of an intendedly rational structure. Such unintended consequences result from the 'bounded rationality' of decision-makers and the difficulty of insulating an organization from the uncertainty of environmental factors. Very often organizational activity is marked, according to the post-Weberian perspective, by a cycle of purposive control, unanticipated results, and renewed control — as shown in our foregoing analysis of industrial organization in North-east China.

Existing studies of North-east China by Franz Schurmann, Stephen Andors, and William Brugger attribute the aforementioned tensions to the lack of the requisites for scientific and rational forms of industrial organization (for instance, the lack of managerial know-how, trained personnel, the so-called 'resource gap', and so on).[111] As an alternative, this author suggests that these tensions are mainly derived from the unintended consequences inherent in the rationalizing process itself. These unintended consequences in turn produced renewed control measures such as the early version of the profit-retention system, parallel hierarchies, factory committees, independent officers, congresses of workers and staff, as well as 'internal remedialism' (for example, the Party Rectification Campaign of 1950, criticism and self-criticism, and so on) and 'external remedialism' (the 'three-antis' and 'five-antis' campaigns). Indeed, all the features mentioned above have had a profound and lasting impact upon the basic pattern of policy-making in the PRC since its earliest days.

PART II
MAO'S PERIOD

3. The Passage to the Great Leap Forward, 1956-1960

THIS chapter is devoted to an analysis of the evolution of alternative policy-making approaches from the Eighth Party Congress in 1956 to the conclusion of the Great Leap Forward in 1960. This period has generally been regarded as the radical phase of the PRC's political history. A more detailed analysis, however, reveals at least three different policy-making approaches, which collectively contributed to the devastating failure of the Great Leap Forward. These three approaches were supposed to cope with the unintended consequences of the administrative approach of the preceding period (1949–55).

First, Chinese policy-makers modified the administrative approach by introducing a decentralized command economy which alleviated the heavy workload of central planners and delegated administrative and financial power to the local level. The second endeavour represents the trend, albeit limited, towards an economic approach, by reducing State intervention in the economic sphere and by expanding enterprise autonomy (by such means as the profit-retention policy, the increase of enterprise control over working capital, and the responsibility system of capital investment). The third policy-making tendency was shown in the rise of the preceptoral approach in two short periods: the second half of 1958, and from September 1959 to the end of 1960.

OPPORTUNITIES FOR CHOICE

This chapter begins with a discussion of the rise of opportunities for choice which warranted the Chinese policy-actors' search for alternative policy-making approaches. We shall then analyse each of the three alternatives in turn, and finally examine the issues of 'meta-policy-making'.

From 1948, when North-east China was taken over by the CCP, the policy-makers worked with different time schedules, agendas, and priorities. One Chinese analyst, for example, states that 'economic reconstruction was carried out in the Northeast region in 1950, while at the same time land reform was carried out in East China, the Central-South [Region] and the Northwest [Region], and the bandit suppression, anti-despot, rent reduction and deposit refund campaigns were carried out in the Southwest [Region]'.[1] The issues of economic development and industrial management did not emerge as a policy focus of national importance until the introduction of the First Five-year Plan in 1953, and questions concerning the fundamental deficiencies of the administrative approach were not raised until 1955.

China scholars suggest that the unintended consequences of the administrative approach during the early and middle 1950s planted the seeds of the political and ideological discord which was to last for more than two decades.[2] This view is confirmed by the top Chinese policy-makers who made similar diagnoses but recommended divergent remedies. Premier Zhou Enlai suggested, for example, in the First National People's Congress (NPC) in September 1954, that there were many shortcomings in the planning process. He mentioned inaccurate forecasting, a lack of comprehensiveness, a lack of consistency and co-ordination, poor management and organization, low efficiency and poor labour discipline, low product quality, and frequent accidents in the industrial sector.[3] Later, when proposing the Second Five-year Plan during the Eighth Party Congress in 1956, Zhou identified the problems of central planning in terms of frequent changes, long delays, the inadequate inventory of materials, false projections, and the lack of financial control.[4]

Chen Yun, in his address to the Eighth Party Congress, identified the limited capacity of central planners to formulate targets and collect accurate statistical returns from enterprises.[5] An expert on socialist economies, Thomas G. Rawski, made a keen observation on the 'tautness' inherent in the target-centred planning system in the period 1953–7. Rawski cited the withholding and falsification of information by enterprises, the resistance to excessive output targets, unexpected changes by upper echelons in the balance between the goals and means of production, the existence of excessive slack, the disproportionate attention to output volume, the cycle of alternate intervals of relaxation and storming, and so on. He found these problems to be comparable to those in the Soviet model.[6]

The issues of over-concentration of power and economic over-management, which were crucial to the relationship between the central and the local levels, figured prominently in a series of speeches and discussions, including those made during the Eighth Party Congress in 1956. Deng Xiaoping felt that this centralization was not limited to Party affairs but was also manifest in administrative functions and economic tasks. On the one hand, local and lower echelons were not given an opportunity for consultation or for demonstrating their initiative and creativity. On the other hand, the central authorities frequently made arbitrary decisions without regard to local variations. They usually issued far too many regulations and were not sensitive to the difficulties of implementation.[7] Liu Shaoqi suggested likewise that given the sheer size of the country, the monopolization of power by the central authorities was not possible. China's diversity required some delegation of power to local levels in order that the policies could be tailored to specific situations at the provincial, municipal, county, and administrative village levels.[8] Zhou Enlai stressed that local units were closer to enterprises and the masses, and were therefore in a better position to deal more effectively with actual situations.[9]

The problem of an over-managed economy was compounded by the abolition of the administrative regions (ARs) in 1954. Prior to 1954, the governmental structure constituted a 'tall hierarchy'[10] with three tiers: the Central People's Government, the administrative regions, and the provinces and municipalities. After 1954, the top policy-makers found themselves in a 'flat hierarchy'[11] with two tiers, where numerous uncoordinated ministries and commissions confronted more than 30 local units. In other words, bureaucratic complexity and rigidity was, by 1956, already two years old. Although the abolition of the ARs was accomplished smoothly through the promotion of the regional leaders to the central level, it was likely that the institutional and political sides of the issue were far too sensitive to be mentioned explicitly in speeches at that time.

THE ORIGIN OF A DECENTRALIZED COMMAND ECONOMY[12]

The rise of the decentralized command economy is closely associated with the formulation and execution of the famous policy paper, 'On the Ten Great Relationships' (referred to hereafter as the 'Ten Relationships'). This policy paper enumerated ten relationships in which problems could develop: those between (1) heavy industry, light industry, and agriculture, (2) coastal industry and inland industry, (3) economic construction and defence, (4) the State, the production unit, and the individual producer, (5) the centre and the localities, (6) the Han race and ethnic minorities, (7) the Party and the non-party, (8) revolutionaries and counter-revolutionaries, (9) 'right' and 'wrong'; and (10) in foreign relations.[13] The first three concerned the balancing of capital investment across different regions and economic sectors; the last five referred mainly to political categories.

We are mainly concerned here with the fifth relationship, that between the central level and the local level, and we will also analyse the fourth set of relationships, the balancing of interests between the central government, local units, enterprises, and individual producers. Using relatively simplified terms, Franz Schurmann refers to the latter as Decentralization I and the former as Decentralization II.[14] It is understood that the question of decentralization involves the hierarchical levels, specific functional arenas, and time periods. It is noteworthy that the implementation of the 'Ten Relationships' was subsequently restricted mainly to Decentralization I and II, especially in the financial sphere.

The formulation and implementation of the policy paper, the 'Ten Relationships', was quite fluid. At least three policy-making groups entered into the policy arena: the first group included Liu Shaoqi, Mao Zedong, and Bo Yibo, largely during the stage when a broad consensus was forged (1955–6); the second group involved Zhou Enlai, Chen Yun, and other vice-premiers (most likely including Bo Yibo) during the period 1956–7; the third group were the ministers involved in the execution of the policy in the period 1958–61.

Bo Yibo's recent revelation states that the policy paper arose spontaneously from interaction between himself, Liu Shaoqi, and Mao Zedong. In the second half of 1955, Liu Shaoqi, the Party's Vice-Chairman, summoned — through Bo — several ministerial officials for briefing sessions and fact-finding meetings. Many questions were raised with regard to the application of the Soviet model. Bo later duly informed Mao Zedong, Chairman of the Party. Mao's response to Bo was enthusiastic, and he requested that similar briefings and discussions be organized for himself.[15] By the end of 1955 Mao had attended several gatherings arranged by Bo of 34 ministers at the central level (including those of industry, agriculture, transport, commerce, and finance).[16] Mao ultimately manoeuvred his way into the economic and management policy domain through his 'summing up' of these briefings, and he maintained a significant influence while he was drafting the final form of the policy paper, the 'Ten Relationships'.

According to Mao, his speech on the 'Ten Relationships' in

December 1955 was intended to illustrate the contrast between the Chinese and the Soviet systems. It is most likely that this contrast included the issue of centralization and decentralization.[17] Mao was probably not aware of the fact that, as early as 1953, the Soviet Union had made similar attempts to introduce various forms of decentralization.[18] Focusing upon the weakness of the command economy, Mao pointed out that several dozen ministries and commissions had the power to issue directives and regulations to the provincial and municipal levels. In some cases the Party centre and even the State Council were not informed about these decisions. Local governments were overburdened both by uncoordinated policies imposed from above, and also by requests for numerous statistical reports.[19]

In Mao's view, after the provinces and municipalities emerged as policy-making centres, they developed their own policy priorities and interests. It became imperative to delineate their respective jurisdictions, and to recognize their interests, not only on the grounds of effective policy-making, but also to ensure that they would have the motivation for making decisions.[20] Accordingly, Mao proposed that the central ministries should heed the views expressed by the local authorities; that some legislative power be distributed to the provinces and municipalities; and that local interests be consulted prior to the implementation of a national policy.[21] This proposal, in general, followed the precedents and past practices established before the abolition of ARs in 1954. Most of Mao's views were echoed by Liu Shaoqi, Zhou Enlai, and Deng Xiaoping, among others, in the Eighth Party Congress in September 1956, as mentioned above.

From May to August 1956, immediately after the circulation of Mao's policy paper of 25 April 1956, the 'Ten Relationships',[22] Premier Zhou Enlai sponsored and organized the National Conference on Institutional Reform. During the Eighth Party Congress in September, a draft of the 'Resolution on the Reform of the Administrative System' was formulated and made available to all units in order to solicit their comments and opinions.[23] Zhou's 'Report on the Proposal of the Second Five Year Plan' in the Eighth Party Congress outlined several key points concerning the jurisdictions of the central and local levels; the scope of authority of the local governmental units in planning, finance, enterprise, material supply, and personnel; the decentralization of industrial enterprises to the local levels; the improvement of the system of dual command over enterprises; the centralized control of planning and financial indicators by the State Council rather that by separate ministries; and the discretionary power of local units over planning and manpower quotas. Zhou suggested that the State Council should prepare the decentralization scheme in the remaining part of 1956, initiate a trial implementation in 1957, and extend the scheme gradually throughout the country, starting in the Second Five-year Plan in 1958.[24]

The trial implementation of decentralization took place first in the civilian machine-building sector in early 1957. It was based on the 'Regulation concerning Changes in the Present Managerial System', which was promulgated by the First Ministry of Machine-building on 10 May 1957. The document granted wider discretion to the enterprise level, by reducing the seven evaluating indicators to four. Some of the rights over sales and pricing were delegated to the enterprise level and the powers of enterprises over profit-sharing, enterprise funds, renovation funds, personnel, wages, and organizational structure were expanded.[25]

Chen Yun was given an important role in sponsoring the drafting of a series of policy papers on the process of implementing both Decentralization I and II, including the 'Regulation for the Improvement of Industrial Management', and several other papers covering other areas such as commerce and finance.[26] These documents were promulgated in November 1957 after having been approved by the Standing Committee of the NPC at its Eighty-fourth Session. Chen delivered a keynote speech on decentralization to the Third Plenum of the Eighth Party Congress in September 1957, in which he stressed that the decentralization measures might create some unintended consequences in terms of the loss of central control, the relaxation of financial discipline, and the possible problems arising from profit-sharing between the central and local levels.[27] These observations unfortunately materialized in the Great Leap Forward.

In March, April, and May 1958 rulings were made on the scope and implementaton of the decentralization schemes.[28] These rulings were in line with the November 1957 regulation of the State Council.[29] This incorporated the key features of the May 1957 documents of the First Ministry of Machine-building, mentioned above, regarding decentralization from the State to the enterprise level, including a decrease in the number of mandatory indicators from twelve to four.[30] The 1957 decentralization regulation was in fact implemented more quickly than was originally intended. It is most likely that this was due to the pressure generated at the local and enterprise levels for greater financial autonomy, a point which will be dealt with later.

From November 1957 to June 1958, control over approximately 80 per cent of the enterprise units under the jurisdiction of the industrial ministries at the central level was reportedly transferred 'downward' to the local level. The only exceptions were enterprises which either required particularly sophisticated technology or were extremely large in scale and experimental in nature. Several local governments were not equipped, managerially and administratively, to take control of the decentralized enterprises since, for example, they lacked trained personnel. Thus the implementation of decentralization was postponed.[31] In September 1958, the Central Committee, CCP, and the State Council jointly promulgated another document which redefined the scope of powers, the supplies of materials, the sources of revenue, and the allocation of funds, capital, and manpower, in the relationship between the State Council and the local authorities.[32]

A LIMITED TENDENCY TOWARDS A STRATEGIC MODEL

Another element of Mao's concern in the 'Ten Relationships' was decentralization from the State to the enterprise level. At the time Mao admitted that, until the results of further investigations were known, it was not clear how power should be apportioned to the central, local, and enterprise levels. According to Mao, production units would be able to gain initiatives if autonomy were granted to them. One crucial point, in line with the economic approach in policy-making, that came out of the policy paper is that 'interest' in its tangible and material form can provide a guide for formulating policy. Mao emphasized the need for balancing the interests of the State, production units, and individual workers and staff members. Regarding enterprise autonomy, Mao stated, 'It is improper to centralize all power to the centre, provinces and municipalities without giving enterprises some power, discretion and some *interest*' (italics added; translation supplied).[33]

After Mao's paper, the 'Ten Relationships', was made available to the Party members, Liu Shaoqi spoke about the issue of interest and motivation in relation to the autonomy and size of the industrial organization, during his visits to Shijingshan Iron and Steel Works and Shijingshan Power-station in July 1957. Liu suggested that State ownership (or ownership by the people) was too abstract a concept, not to say impractical, to be operational. He recommended that the locus of decision-making should therefore be delegated to the hierarchical level where the impact of the decisions could be directly felt and where the effects on the interests of workers and staff could be tangibly identified.[34]

Liu was among those who promoted organic State socialism, a legacy left by the experiences of North-east China. During the same visit to Shijingshan he emphasized the importance of encouraging efficient enterprise units by means of collective forms of remuneration, collective welfare, and amenities. He envisaged that enterprises could run operations which would benefit the community, such as hospitals, schools, day-care centres, theatres, stores, banks, and farms.[35] He personally initiated the pilot programmes for self-financed housing projects for workers and staff in the Xiangjiang Machine-building Factory,[36] the bonus system in the Qishuyan Plant in Jiangsu, and the welfare system in Shijingshan Power-station, which were endorsed by Mao late in 1958.[37] Liu agreed with Mao that labour productivity could be raised by improving the working conditions and collective welfare of the workers.[38]

The general tendency of organic State socialism towards egalitarianism and the group-oriented remunerative system was reflected in the structuring of the bonus system and the piece-rate wage. In May 1957, the State Council decided to stop bonus payments to cadres, administrators, managers, and factory directors. After the initial chaos of the Great Leap Forward, the bonus system was partially restored at the end of 1959 in the form of the group-oriented 'comprehensive bonus', which was based upon a number of performance indicators.[39] The percentage of industrial workers who earned piece-rate wages rose from 32 per cent to 42 per cent of all workers by the end of the First Five-year Plan in 1957. This increase, however, was significantly undermined by the Great Leap Forward, representing a drop from 14 per cent of all industrial workers in 1959 to 5 per cent in 1960.[40]

After the November 1957 decentralizion regulation was introduced, a number of subsidiary programmes regarding profit retention, the supply of working capital, and capital investment were launched. The State Council first promulgated the 'Several Regulations concerning the Implementation of the Enterprise Profit-retention System' on 22 May 1958, on the basis of the 1954 profit-retention policy and its 1956 amendment by the Ministry of Finance. The 1958 profit-retention policy differed from the earlier versions, in that it took the enterprise unit as a basic accounting unit in calculating the share of profits retained by an enterprise, whereas the 1954 and 1956 versions took the supervising ministries or bureaux as the basic accounting units. Under the 1958 policy, enterprise units were entitled to a fixed portion of retained profits on the the basis of the fulfilment and over-fulfilment of annual profit plans. Under the earlier policies, a fixed percentage of retained profit was allocated to supervising ministries or bureaux, for example, 40 per cent, and the remainder was returned to the State Treasury.[41]

Another supplementary regulation concerned the supply of working capital to the enterprise level. Prior to 1959, enterprise units obtained their working capital from two sources: through direct financial appropriations by various levels of government, which carried no interest charges (also called self-owned working capital); and from bank loans which required the payment of interest. As from January 1959, the full amount of working capital at the enterprise level had to be allocated through the banking system. Financial departments at various levels appropriated funds indirectly through the banks, and delegated the power of financial management to the banks. The new regulation of January 1959 stipulated that enterprise units were required to pay interest charges on the full amount of working capital under their control.[42]

For a variety of reasons, the new managerial system for working capital was relatively short-lived, lasting from January 1959 to June 1961. First, the financial departments were reluctant to make budgetary appropriations of working capital and entrust them to the banking system, for in doing so they would lose a substantial proportion of their financial power. Second, while the financial departments were deprived of managerial power over working capital, the banking system was not yet ready to supervise the use of working capital at the enterprise level. Third, enterprise units were not sufficiently concerned about the efficient use of working capital because they were not market oriented and bankruptcy was not a threat. In addition, there was a tendency to convert capital into fixed assets in order to gain additional production capacity. Consequently, as from July 1961 it was necessary for the State Council to return to the old system, which appropriated 80 per cent of the working capital through financial departments and allocated the remaining 20 per cent through the banking system.[43]

The innovation of a 'responsibility system of capital investment' (*touzi baogan*) was introduced to the Shijingshan Iron and Steel Corporation in December 1957 under Liu Shaoqi's sponsorship. It was endorsed by Mao Zedong in 1958, with the justification that it allowed full play to 'activism' in the enterprise units.[44] The State Council accordingly promulgated a new regulation on 5 July 1958, giving broad discretion in capital investment to the enterprise level. Enterprise units were permitted to expand the scale of their investment projects under the following conditions: (a) there should be no decrease in the designed capacity; (b) the ceiling of State appropriations should be observed; (c) deadlines for construction should be met; and (d) no funds should be diverted for non-production-oriented facilities. The system reportedly lasted from July 1958 to December 1963 when it was officially abolished,[45] although it is likely that the system was stopped in early 1961, when the retrenchment policy was in force.

These reform-oriented programmes and regulations aggravated the economic imbalance during the Great Leap Forward for the following reasons. First, the decentralization of jurisdiction over industrial enterprises from the central to the local level was too drastic: while local governments certainly welcomed decentralization for the opportunity it gave them to gain a large share of revenue and resources, not all of them were managerially equipped to take over enterprises that had been transferred downward. Second, the responsibility system of capital investment encouraged local administrators and enterprise management to expand their production capacity and compete for scarce resources. As a result, a large amount of working capital was frozen in the form of fixed assets which did not really increase efficiency, productivity, profits, or product quality. Third, the profit-retention system and the supply of bank loans were equally responsible for an unnecessary accumulation of fixed assets, since enterprises were given more money to spend with minimal financial liability.

Various authors have noted that the over-extension of capital investment, derived from extra-budgetary funds, was partly responsible for the economic imbalance during the Great Leap Forward.[46] Parris Chang estimates that at the beginning of 1958 extra-budgetary income in general amounted to about 20 to 30 per cent of the budgetary revenues of local authorities at all levels.[47]

Table 2 The Total Investment in Capital Construction, 1953–1965

Year	Investment in Capital Construction (100 million *yuan*) Total	State Budget Investment	State Budget Investment as Percentage of Total Investment
1953	80.01	65.06	81.3
1954	80.62	74.98	82.7
1955	93.02	86.32	92.8
1956	148.02	139.86	94.5
1957	138.29	126.45	91.4
1958	266.29	214.40	80.3
1959	344.65	267.00	77.5
1960	384.07	297.13	77.4
1961	123.37	89.82	72.8
1962	67.62	56.61	83.7
1963	94.62	80.69	85.7
1964	138.69	118.53	85.5
1965	170.89	154.37	90.3

Source: State Statistical Bureau of the PRC, *Statistical Yearbook of China 1981* (Hong Kong, Economic Information and Agency, 1982), p. 299.

During the years 1958–61, when the three programmes described above were committed, the proportion of State budgetary investment registered a substantial decrease (to below 80 per cent). This meant that the State lost much of its control over the direction of the national economy. The statistics provided by the PRC clearly indicate this trend (see Table 2 above), although we are unable to isolate the impact of each programme.

These four programmes marked a tendency towards an economic approach to policy-making in which policy formulation and execution were guided by tangible interest ('preference' or 'volition' in Charles E. Lindblom's terms), and which co-ordinated the interaction between many actors (central and local units, enterprises, staff members, and workers). This tendency was promoted by Mao Zedong, Liu Shaoqi, Chen Yun, Zhou Enlai, and Bo Yibo, each playing his role as he saw fit. The tendency was short-lived and limited in its scale, but it was among the earliest attempts to remedy the administrative approach for organizational and managerial considerations. Another attempt was the Maoist preceptoral approach, which was formulated from a moral and political perspective, and entailed a charisma-inspired and mass-oriented style of industrial management.

THE POLITICIZATION OF THE ENTERPRISE MANAGEMENT POLICY

The mass-oriented style of industrial management can be traced back to the early experiences in North-east China. Mao Zedong did not start to promote a similar idea until 1956, but his view was shared by other top Chinese leaders. Anticipating the Eighth Party Congress scheduled for September 1956, Mao spoke of anti-bureaucratism and the inadequacy of the Soviet model of development and Soviet forms of organization, and also spoke about the controversy over one-man management. He stated in April that 'most of our systems stem from the Soviet Union, but they are rigid and the men [who work under them] are very restricted'. He then proposed that the new Party constitution should incorporate the idea of the mass-line as well as the dialectical relationship between discipline and creativity.[48] In the same Congress, Deng Xiaoping echoed Mao's view on the mass-line, suggesting that there was a need to carry out the mass-line thoroughly and overcome bureaucratism.[49] Liu Shaoqi focused upon the adverse effects of bureaucratism, asserting that 'it would hinder the democratic life of the country, the development of productivity and the progress of Socialist enterprises'.[50] In order to carry out the mass-line, a congress of the representatives of workers and staff, which had first been practised in North-east China, was reintroduced in 1957.

Mao's views on the mass-oriented style of industrial management were shared by Liu Shaoqi. The proposal to reform the outdated and irrational rules and regulations was originally formulated by Liu Shaoqi in consultation with local cadres and officials; it was subsequently incorporated into Article 23 of the policy paper entitled 'The Sixty Articles on Work Methods'. Article 23 states:

a majority of regulations and systems which have been accumulated for the past eight years are still applicable. Owing, however, to the fact that a considerable number of them have become obstacles to raising the activism of the masses and to the development of productivity, they must either be revised or abolished.[51] (Translation supplied.)

In Article 22 of the policy paper, Mao Zedong presented for the first time his formulation of the relationship between 'redness' (ideological purity) and 'expertise', and between politics and vocation: 'on the one hand, [we] oppose politicians without substance, and on the other hand [we] oppose practitioners who lose their correct sense of direction'. In a radical tone, Mao made the now famous assertion that 'ideology and politics are in command, and are also the soul [in all types of tasks]'.[52] Subsequently, in the Second Plenum of the Eighth Party Congress in May 1957, Mao argued that 'laymen' should take over command from 'experts' because each individual could at best master only one or two trades; he was merely able to be an expert in one or two functional areas, and therefore he was a 'layman' in the remaining areas.[53] Mao also commented on the slogan advocated by Stalin (that is, 'cadres determine everything and technology determines everything'), suggesting that these slogans were partial and did not assign a proper place to politics.[54] Liu Shaoqi echoed Mao's view in his talks with the Soviet Minister of Foreign Trade in 1958. He, however, proposed replacing the slogan 'technology determines everything' with 'mechanization, semi-mechanization, automation and semi-automation',[55] a mass campaign which was then vigorously promoted by Bo Yibo.[56]

Evidence suggests that Mao's initiation of a mass-oriented managerial style was closely associated with an acute sense of his own 'performance gap' in the policy arena of industrial management and economy. For instance, in January 1958 he implicitly suggested that, due to other important preoccupations (such as revolution and agriculture), he had not been able to pay adequate attention to such matters as industry.[57] He added in May 1958,

I didn't know about industry. I knew nothing about it. Yet I don't believe that industry is beyond my reach. Thus I talked to those who were in charge of industry. At the beginning I could not come to a grasp of it, but after several years of learning, I am able to know it. After all it is no big deal ...[58] (Translation supplied.)

Mao made similar statements in September 1958 and July 1959.[59] According to Michael C. Oksenberg, Mao's dominance over a given issue depended very much on his confidence and competence in a particular subject.[60] Yet in the context of the Great Leap Forward, Mao compensated for his inadequacy by demonstrating more intensely his ability to handle the issue. Mao provided the following justification for his intervention in promoting mass-oriented industrial management:

From the very beginning, there has been abundant activism and creativity among the working people. They were not emancipated in the past because of the oppression of the old system. They are liberated now and are ready to explode. . .
   In the past many people considered industry as something beyond reach and very mysterious. They regarded industrialization as no easy task. On the whole, they looked at industry in a very, very superstitious way.[61] (Translation supplied.)

The ministries and commissions of the State Council subsequently accommodated Mao's position on the need for 'revolution' in industrial management. The First Ministry of Machine-building, for example, issued a circular on 25 June 1958 on the decentralization of jurisdiction over 195 (out of approximately 460) regulations and systems which had been set up since 1949. Enterprises were given discretion to readopt or revise any of the 195 as they considered appropriate. Industrial enterprises were advised to simplify procedures and rules regarding financial and economic matters, and to be cautious in revising technical procedures and regulations.[62]

Without consulting the State Council, Mao impatiently took the implementation of the mass-oriented managerial style into his own hands by endorsing the radical models put forth by Wang Hefeng, the Party Secretary of Heilongjiang province, in early 1958. These models were based on the experiences of Qinghua Instrument Factory and Jianhua Machinery Works in the 'two participations and one reform' (that is, cadres' participation in manual labour, workers' participation in management, and the reform of unreasonable regulations and systems).[63] In November 1958, the experiences of these two factories were supplemented by a 'three-in-one' combination of cadres, workers, and technical personnel in technical innovations in a pilot scheme at the Changchun First Automobile Factory. This marked the completion of the formula of 'two participations, one reform and a three-in-one combination [that is, the participation of cadres, workers, and technicians in a technical innovation team]',[64] the key elements of the basic model of the Anshan Iron and Steel Company, established in 1960.

To support Mao's position, Li Xuefeng, Director of the Department of Industry and Transport of the Central Committee, published an article in *Red Flag* in August 1958. Li drew attention to the contrast between the opposite views of enterprise management: one view was that in managing a highly centralized modern enterprise, one could rely entirely upon engineers, technicians, and cadres with excellent managerial and technological skills, as well as upon 'scientific' rules and regulations; the other was a managerial system based upon the mass-line.[65] In addition, Ke Qingshi, then Mayor of Shanghai Municipality, was among those who supported Mao on the issue of the mass-line in industry in Autumn 1958.[66] During the same period (September 1958), Mao toured several provinces in the Yangtze River Valley. He presumably lobbied for additional support from provincial leaders for his mass-line formula. Following the tour, Mao gave the explanation that:

Up to the present, we still have some comrades who are unwilling to launch large-scale mass movements; they regard mass movements on the industrial front as irregular and debase them as 'rural work style' and 'guerrilla mentality'. This is obviously wrong.[67] (Translation supplied.)

On the basis of the available material, it is extremely difficult to document who registered opposition to Mao's view of a large-scale mass movement. Chung inconclusively identified Bo Yibo and Wang Heshou (Minister of the Metallurgical Industry) as opponents of Mao's mass-movement policy.[68] Red Guard publications[69] and official sources[70] make contradictory statements about Bo Yibo's stand on the mass movement. The author cannot identify any faction who actively opposed Mao's view.

Taking an incriminatory tone, an article published in *Red Flag* in November 1958 criticized the 'indulgent' style of management in large-scale enterprises, the use of foreign methods, an emphasis on administrative commands, and the practice of 'one-man management', as well as a reliance upon a minority of 'experts', material incentives, and excessive and unnecessary regulations and systems. The article also repudiated the so-called 'theory of the uniqueness of industry'. Implicitly arguing against the Maoist position, this theory held that mass movements should be limited to political revolution, rural work, and small enterprises, and could not be extended to economic construction, management work, and large enterprises.[71] The foregoing controversy marked the rise of the Maoist form of 'political symbolism', bringing the policy disputes over enterprise management to a higher level of theoretical abstraction, and treating the basic nature of the disputes in terms of the 'line struggle'.

THE MINISTERIAL RESPONSE TO THE CRISIS

From the last months of 1958 until July 1959 (during the Lushan Conference), Mao became aware of the excesses of the Great Leap Forward in the preceding year. As a result, he relaxed his radical policy before still another cycle of radicalization. In November 1958, he explained that the road to Communism was one requiring gradual steps. He suggested that while self-sufficiency was being developed, commodity exchange in the rural area should remain intact. He also stressed the need to ensure that central planning was reliable and balanced, although the activism of the masses should not be frustrated. He suggested that industrial management was more complicated than agricultural production, and that therefore the former should be carefully handled.[72] He also admitted in December 1958 that he had committed mistakes, for example the setting of unattainable targets for steel production (10.7 million tons). In February 1959, he even admitted his ignorance of central planning and the proportional development of the economy, which in part had led to the economic imbalance:

Surely we have had many shortcomings and mistakes. [We] have paid attention to one aspect of [the economic problem] but tended to neglect other aspects. This has resulted in the waste of manpower, tensions in the supply of non-staple foods, and has created a scarcity of raw materials for light industry. In addition, the transport system has lost its balance and capital construction has been over-extended. All these are our mistakes. Just like inexperienced little children who play with fire, we feel hurt only after having touched it. When we work in economic construction, we are as inexperienced as little children. [We] wage a war against the globe, but we do not know enough of the strategy. [We] should squarely confront these shortcomings and mistakes.[73] (Translation supplied.)

The Chinese policy-makers were compelled to take decisions not only because of the crises created by economic imbalance and the paralysis of the central planning apparatus, but also because of the political tensions associated with the Great Leap Forward. Mao pointed out in the Sixth Plenum of the Eighth Party Congress in December 1958 that since 1957, the provincial leadership was split regarding the policies of the Great Leap Forward and the alienation of the Party leadership from the people.[74] The renewal of centralized control appeared to be the only logical alternative under the circumstances.

As suggested in Chapter 1, the preceptoral policy-making approach shares a common intellectual root with the administrative approach. It should come as no surprise that an ultra-leftist-leaning leader such as Ke Qingshi could readily shift to the line of reasoning characteristic of the administrative approach by advocating the view of 'the whole country as a chessboard' in the crisis of late 1958 and early 1959. While on previous occasions Ke had been a champion of the preceptoral approach (featuring the personality cult, politics in command, the Party leadership, and mass-oriented management), he was the first person to signal the return from the charismatic leadership style of Mao Zedong to the sovereignty of the planner — see his retrospective justification given in his *Red Flag* article (16 February 1959):

The whole country as a chessboard is by no means a new problem. The Party centre and comrade Mao Zedong have taught us from the very beginning that we must come to grips with the overall situation and the standpoint of six billion people; we must handle correctly the relationship between the whole and the parts, between the key and ordinary points, and between the centralized leadership and hierarchical management, no matter whether conducting class production struggle, no matter what kind of jobs, making plans, managing business or in deliberation.[75] (Translation supplied.)

One week later, on 24 February 1959, an editorial appeared in the *People's Daily* entitled 'On the Whole Country as A Chessboard'. This editorial suggested that, in spite of the previous policy advocated by the Party centre regarding the simultaneous development of sectors and branches of the economy, it is consistent to insist on planned and proportional development to mobilize all concerned. The editorial underscores the centralized leadership and the unified arrangements in the fields of capital investment, the manufacturing of major products, the supply of raw materials, as well as the allocation of the means of production and consumer goods. Newly appointed as Director of the State Construction Commission, Chen Yun, in a lengthy article published in the issue of *Red Flag* of 1 March, provided a detailed blueprint for readjusting and reorganizing capital investment in the industrial sector, stressing the need to establish priorities and to recentralize at the national level, and criticizing 'departmentalism' and self-sufficiency at the local level.[76]

Accordingly, in the spirit of rationalizing organization, Deng Xiaoping set the tone for restoring order to enterprise management. In a conference on industry held by the Shanghai Party Committee on 20 February 1959, Deng emphasized that both 'construction' and 'destruction' were needed for the reform of regulations and systems.[77] He intended to stop the indiscriminate abolition of regulations and systems, the relaxation of discipline, and increasing violations of rules and regulations in the mass campaigns in the industrial sector. Deng's view was echoed by *Red Flag* in its February issue and an editorial in the *People's Daily* on 15 March 1959.

In early 1959 the central ministries and commissions started to point to the undesirable consequences of the campaign approach and to adopt a series of directives and regulations designed to end the chaotic situation which the Great Leap Forward had created at the enterprise level: for example, the policy paper concerning cost control and cost-planning by the State Planning Commission and the Ministry of Finance in March 1959;[78] the directive on quality control by the First Ministry of Machine-building in April 1959;[79] and the directive regarding the restoration of an equipment maintenance system by the First Ministry of Machine-building in June 1959.[80] In addition, a national conference on the task of cost-accounting was convened in July 1959.[81] Evidence also suggests that local financial departments endeavoured to strengthen economic accounting, cost analysis, and inventory control.[82] Overall, these directives and regulations constituted the prelude to a full-scale return to the administrative approach which began in 1961.

ANOTHER CYCLE OF POLICY RADICALIZATION

The famous Lushan Conference, held from July to September 1959, was a relatively long session marked by sharp disagreements between Mao Zedong and Peng Dehuai. A survey of formal speeches and informal conversations from November 1958 to July 1959 illustrates that Mao made virtually the same points that Peng raised in the Lushan Conference, if not more: for example, the need to correct 'leftist deviation', the need to strengthen and restore planning and co-ordination, adherence to the law of value, distribution according to labour, and above all, the importance of 'seeking truth from facts'. Both Liu Shaoqi and Bo Yibo testified retrospectively that Mao had raised the same points as Peng.[83] Li Rui, a close friend of Zhou Xiaozhou who was purged with Peng, revealed that Peng delivered his 'letter of opinions' after he had discovered Mao's similar position through a conversation with Zhou Xiaozhou. Zhou was then serving as Mao's secretary.[84] Mao changed his mind suddenly, probably because he considered that, unless he acted against Peng Dehuai, his political career would have been in jeopardy.

Peng's main criticism at the Lushan Conference concerned agricultural policy and the people's communes. The development of more radical policies in the industrial sector after this conference was a by-product of the political conflict between Mao and Peng, because it hardened Mao's radical position and silenced those who assumed a moderate position. Mao in fact went so far as to threaten to wage a civil war in order to force the top CCP leaders to go along with him in purging Peng.[85] It can hardly be said that Mao and Peng had an adversarial relationship on an equal footing. Rather, they had a clash of opinions on matters relating to a crisis. It is interesting to note that Peng Dehuai himself stated that there was no conspiracy or factional activity in the Lushan Conference.[86]

Immediately following the Lushan Conference, a radical tone appeared again in newspapers and throughout the mass media regarding the issue of the mass-line in enterprise management. An article published in *Liberation Daily* in November 1959 asserted, for example, that there was a 'struggle' between two viewpoints and two kinds of methods for reforming regulations and systems, during the mass movements in 1958. It added that in many enterprises bourgeois ideological influence was still strong and most managerial and technical personnel had not been 'remoulded'.[87]

The issue of the mass-line in industrial management continued to become politicized in early 1960. At this time Mao made his point explicit by endorsing the 'Constitution of the Anshan Iron and Steel Corporation'. This was a report on the experience of managerial revolution in the Corporation written by the Party Committee of Anshan Municipality in Liaoning province. Mao alleged that his ideas of technical revolution, mass movement, and 'two participations, one reform, and three-in-one combination' were opposed by some unidentified figures within the Party and the State, as was his view of 'politics in command' even prior to 1959. In an exaggerated tone Mao suggested that there were people advocating 'one-man management' and treating the Soviet model of the Magnitogorski Iron and Steel Combine as something 'sacred'. It was not until 1959 that there was a change of attitude concerning the mass movements, 'one-man management', and the Magnitogorski model of industrial management.[88]

Yang Shijie published another article in the *People's Daily* on 11 February 1960, treating the mass-line controversy (or mass movements) as a 'struggle of two kinds of thoughts and of two lines'. Yang politicized managerial issues from the perspective of a 'two-line struggle', suggesting that they reflected two opposite and antagonistic classes in the State apparatus, as well as society. Yang sharply attacked the type of industrial management which excessively stressed the importance of the infrastructure at the expense of the superstructure, by, for example, an over-emphasis on modern equipment and facilities, experts, technological know-how, material incentives, and standard operating procedures.[89]

Mao's view of the 'Anshan Constitution' did not generate much enthusiasm among his pragmatic colleagues. According to a 'confession' by Wu Lengxi (then Director of the New China News Agency), the *People's Daily* wrote a number of commentaries publicizing the 'Anshan Constitution' immediately after Mao endorsed it in March 1960. Approximately three months later, in June 1960, when the Shanghai Conference was convened, Wu asked Deng Xiaoping how to make a further effort to publicize the 'Anshan Constitution'. Deng replied that they had to concentrate on anti-revisionist work, namely, Sino-Soviet polemics. In short, Deng said, 'there is no hurry in dealing with the Anshan Constitution; besides, the Anshan Constitution itself still has a lot of problems'.[90] This circumstantial evidence suggests that the 'Anshan Constitution' was set aside by Deng Xiaoping and probably other Party leaders at the time. It was not officially approved by the Central Committee under Hua Guofeng's administration in March 1977.[91]

THE PATTERN OF META-POLICY-MAKING

Our discussion shows that all three independent variables (ideology, organization, and politics) were activated in changing and developing the policy-making alternatives during the period 1956–60. It is germane to analyse the explicit relationship of the independent variables to the policy-making process during this period.

The ideological variable became relevant to the policy-making process during the period 1956–60 in terms of defining its general context and also in the choice of specific models of industrial management. First of all, the controversy over the relative importance of class struggle and economic construction which started in the Eighth Party Congress in 1956 remained unresolved and this considerably prolonged the recurrent tendency towards the preceptoral approach to policy-making. The political report delivered by Liu Shaoqi and the Party's resolution on the same report assigned top priority to economic construction in the Eighth Party Congress, and this entailed a general leaning towards the administrative approach. The Party resolution read: 'the contradiction of the proletariat of our nation with the bourgeoisie has been basically solved'. It added, 'under the circumstances where the Socialist system of our country had already been established, the essence of the contradiction is that between the advanced Socialist system and the backward production forces'.[92] Nevertheless Mao Zedong registered his reservations on the above position immediately afterwards. For instance, in October 1957 at the Third Plenum of the Eighth Party Congress, he asserted that the class contradictions had yet to be solved in the economic and political arena, if not in the areas of the political regime and ownership.[93] Mao's reservations foreshadowed the continuous tensions and conflicts in the decision-making process in the two decades up to 1976 and beyond.

As a component of the preceptoral approach, the Maoist ideology of industrial management was not completely consolidated, but its impact was visible and largely negative. For example, with the support and encouragement of Mao Zedong, the formula of 'two participations, one reform, and a three-in-one combination' was tried and promoted at the height of the Great Leap Forward in 1958; and the 'Anshan Constitution' took shape in early 1960. This mass-oriented managerial style evolved from the conflicts between ideological purity and expertise, material incentives and non-material incentives, the mass-line and professionally oriented management, and regulatory control and a mobilizational approach.

Organizational factors were relevant to the rise of the preceptoral approach during the years 1956–60. This approach was largely conditional upon the saliency of the cult of personality and the weakness of institutional authority, as well as upon the strong legacy of the movement-oriented Party and the relatively underdeveloped State apparatus.

Taking the first of these factors, this was a difficult period of transition from personal authority to institutional authority. There was widespread criticism of the worship and deification of individual leaders, and Mao Zedong's thought was therefore deleted from the revised Party constitution in 1956 as a guiding principle having equal status with Marxism and Leninism. This was done, according to Deng Xiaoping, in view of the CCP's tradition of collective leadership, the resolution of the Twentieth Party Congress of the Soviet Communist Party, and the Marxist position.[94] None the less, Mao Zedong's personality cult was promoted during the Great Leap Forward, especially after the fall of Peng Dehuai.

Second, as from 1956, the Party leadership (in fact, the Party secretary's leadership) gained power at the expense of the representatives of the State such as managers or factory directors. This tendency strengthened the preceptoral approach in countering the emphasis on the State apparatus which the pragmatic leaders advocated. For example, Liu Shaoqi stressed the need to establish 'the most democratic, efficient, and solid State'.[95] Deng Xiaoping emphasized the distinction between the administrative role of the State and the political leadership of the Party during the Eighth Party Congress.

Third, the provinces and municipalities had been a major locus of power prior to the decentralization decree of November 1957. A series of decentralization measures and regulations recognized the provinces and cities, in retrospect, as the major tiers of power after the abolition of the ARs in 1954. These local units (the provinces, the municipalities, and the special districts or counties) provided the institutional footholds for the Party men (the Party secretaries) to promote the Maoist model of industrial management. Dwight Perkins has suggested that it was this group of Party men who took the lion's share of power which was then transferred 'downward' from the central to the local level.[96]

The political 'window' was thrown wide open during the period 1956–60. At the top level of leadership, Mao Zedong was motivated politically to establish his control in several new policy arenas, and to prevent the erosion of his influence as a result of the change in the task environment. After 1949 Mao Zedong suggested that what had been familiar in the past had to be discarded, and what had been unfamiliar had to be learned afresh.[97] As shown above, Mao was slow in making the necessary adjustments to his leadership as the basis of power was transfered from rural areas and guerrilla warfare to cities and economic construction.[98] To maintain his authority, Mao was compelled to take policy initiatives and to demonstrate that they were workable.

Mao was not entirely successful, however, in preventing the erosion of his power which occurred as a result of his proposal for a division of the top leadership into 'two fronts' at the end of 1953.[99] He then came under pressure to step down, in accordance with a proposal to rotate the party chairmanship.[100] The 'two-front' leadership team was actually twofold. On the one hand, Mao could minimize the possible exposure of his weaknesses and avoid the burden of day-to-day policy-making and administration by remaining on the 'second front'. He could intervene at will when he chose to interpret an issue as ideological and of great importance. On the other hand, the 'first-front' leaders would be given control over the Party and State apparatus as well as over information and implementation. This would enable them to accumulate considerable power. Consequently, the 'two-front' arrangement led to the loss of his power. As he put it, 'the big power fell apart' (da quan pang lo). According to Mao, the Cultural Revolution can be attributed to his proposal of the 'two-front' leadership team, and he implied that the delegation of so much power to the 'first front' was not his intention, and that he therefore was forced to recover his lost power somehow.[101]

Overall, the radical policies of the Great Leap Forward are largely attributable to a process through which Mao's political motive (namely the maintenance of his power) was searching for an ideology (for example, the 'class struggle' in industrial management) and for an appropriate organizational means of implementation (such as the formulae and methods represented by the Anshan Constitution). However, the chaos and crisis that this created warranted the reimposition of central control and therefore the restoration of the administrative approach.

Nevertheless, Mao was only able to gather a small group of protégés (such as Ke Qingshih and Li Xuefang), but not a well-organized 'faction' in the true sense of the word. Without relying on a faction, Mao was still able to impart a direction to industrial management policy through the use of a 'bypassing device' at three levels:[102] he could secure Zhou Enlai's compliance by appealing directly to Zhou's deputies, that is, the ministerial ranking officials; he was able to push his decentralization proposal by rallying the support of local party and government leaders and bypassing the central units; and he introduced mass-oriented management by bypassing the managerial class and directly mobilizing the mass who felt that they were deprived and pushed aside in the rapid process of routinization and bureaucratization which was allied with the rise of the administrative approach. This is taken as 'indirect manipulation' as well, that is, influencing others through manipulating their environment.[103]

CONCLUDING REMARKS

The foregoing analysis has focused on the evolution of three policy-making tendencies during the years 1956–60: the rise of a decentralized command economy, a limited movement towards the economic approach, and mass-oriented industrial management during two periods (the first half of 1958 and from September 1959 to the end of 1960). This book suggests that the crisis and chaos created by the preceptoral approach tended to require policy-makers to return to the administrative approach, and takes the radical phases of the Great Leap Forward as illustrating this. Although both approaches were rooted in a common assumption of the omniscience and omnipotence of top policy-makers, the administrative approach appears to have been more reliable and effective than the preceptoral approach in the crisis. Furthermore, the oscillation between the two approaches was largely due to difficulties of adjustment, in a post-revolutionary society, with regard to such issues as the relevance of the class struggle, the cult of personality, the role of a movement-oriented Party, and the 'revolutionary' managerial style.

4. The Post-Leap Trends in Policy-making, 1961–1966

THE post-Leap period (1961–6) witnessed three policy-making trends. Two were considered pragmatic since they included, firstly, a process of economic readjustment and industrial reorganization followed by the establishment of 'socialist trusts' and, secondly, the codification of previous experience and practice of industrial management in the drafting of the 'Regulation of Tasks in State-owned Industrial Enterprises' (cited hereafter as the 'Seventy Articles'). This chapter analyses these two trends. The third policy-making trend concerned the rise of the Daqing model of enterprise management, the analysis of which must consider its radical orientation, and it will therefore receive attention in the following chapter, where it will be treated as a prelude to the Cultural Revolution.

The process of economic readjustment, which is subsumed under the administrative approach, is concerned with redirecting the flow of investment and financial appropriation to efficient and profitable sectors, branches, and units of the economy. The term 'industrial reorganization' refers to a wide range of policy themes, including the realignment of contractual relationships between enterprises, loose forms of technical co-ordination among production units, the reorganization of industrial bureaux, and the establishment of specialized corporations. This process was also known as 'specialization and [inter-enterprise] co-ordination'. Both economic adjustment and industrial reorganization are intrinsic parts of the framework of central planning and State ownership.

ECONOMIC READJUSTMENT IN THE POST-LEAP PERIOD

The policy of economic readjustment and industrial reorganization was dictated by a sense of crisis, which provided considerable unity among the top leaders.[1] After 1962, when the sense of crisis subsided, rationalization became the main tenet in economic policy-making. Following Mao Zedong's call for 'research and investigation' and a 'summary of experience' in the early 1960s,[2] Liu Shaoqi took the lead in promoting the retrenchment policy of the post-Leap period. As early as 1956, two years before the crisis, Liu Shaoqi had cautioned against the structural tendency towards over-capitalization.[3] This tendency was accentuated during the Great Leap Forward and, in the post-Leap period, the policy of economic readjustment and industrial reorganization was mainly concerned with over-capitalization, especially as regards non-budgeted items at the local level.

The need for economic readjustment was first pointed out by Ke Qingshi and then elaborated by Chen Yun in February 1959. At the Lushan Conference in July 1959, Mao suggested that basic construction be curtailed immediately. Again, at the Pei-dai-he Conference in July–August 1960, the Central Committee (CC) approved a proposal by Li Fuchun and Bo Yibo for economic readjustment in the transport and industrial sector to start in late 1960, and this was subsequently incorporated into the programme of 'readjustment, consolidation, enrichment and improvement', passed by the Ninth Plenum of the Eighth Party Congress in January 1961. A further attempt was made in May 1961 to identify measures to reduce the number of industrial workers and staff members.[4]

The 'Directive of the Central Committee, CCP, concerning the Current Industrial Problems', dated 15 September 1961 (cited hereafter as the 'Directive'), identified the following difficulties to be overcome: economic imbalance resulting from excessively high production targets and the unrealistic pace of growth in the industrial sector; inefficient capital investment and abnormal industrial production; chaos and confusion in managerial tasks (such as the abolition of responsibility systems, damage to equipment and facilities, the decline in labour productivity, the deterioration of product quality, over-staffing, and the breakdown of co-ordination between enterprises); excessive workloads; and 'commandism' by supervising departments.[5]

In view of the over-capitalization at local government level, and the inability of the central authorities to deal with the economic situation, the 'Directive' attributed the failure of the Great Leap Forward to the lack of an overall perspective (*quanju guandian*) and the neglect of research and investigation. Accordingly, it recommended the following: more realistic targets for industrial production and capital investment should be set, allowing adequate scope (*yudi*) for their fulfilment; all the key production plans and investment projects must be assured of material supply; the successive increase of production targets from one level down to another must be avoided; extra-budgetary investment projects ought to be halted; the administrative allocation of material and the transfer of facilities and equipment should be strictly observed; the control of financial departments over working capital should be restored.[6]

The 'Directive' also suggested that central planning required conscious effort, and should not wait for balancing to evolve in a spontaneous and uncoordinated fashion. In addition, the 'Directive' emphasized the need for centralization of power in the areas of manpower, finance, and material supply. In due course, the CC, CCP, and the regional Party bureaux were given the power to centralize and take over all key enterprises whose products were oriented towards the national market.[7]

INDUSTRIAL REORGANIZATION IN THE EARLY 1960S

The previous experience of the top leaders of the CCP in the period of economic recovery and massive nationalization of industry, which started in 1953, equipped them to handle the policy of economic readjustment and industrial reorganization. However, as Zhou Enlai stated clearly in 1957, the industrial reorganization policy of the Second Five-year Plan had an entirely different focus.[8] There were two main themes in industrial reorganization during the post-Leap period: the first was to remedy economic imbalance and the second was to rationalize industrial management.

In order to remedy economic imbalance, Zhou Enlai actively implemented the 'Directive'. With the aim of effecting 'transfer, merger, closure and stoppage', a priority list of factories was formulated on the basis of an investigation into the supply of raw materials, fuel, and/or energy sources, a survey of markets, and an examination of the actual situation at the factory level. Factories which were efficient in terms of low consumption of raw materials and energy, low production costs, high productivity with high product quality, and a broad product mix were assigned a high priority and those which were inefficient and unprofitable were scheduled for closure. The priority list covered various branches of industry and different localities. In the meantime, Zhou Enlai conducted a pilot programme of 'transfer, merger, closure and stoppage' in North-east China among factories run by both industrial and non-industrial ministries.[9]

Liu Shaoqi emphasized the centralization policy in his report to the Enlarged Central Work Conference on 27 January 1962, saying that he felt too much power had been delegated to the local level, and that this had resulted in a fragmentation of power in the post-Leap period. He therefore recommended the recentralization of power to the central and regional bureau levels so that all human, material, and financial resources could be centrally allocated from the perspective of the whole situation (*quanju*). He made the following specific demands: (a) key industries with nation-wide sales should be centrally controlled; (b) local investment projects should be incorporated into national projects; (c) local production plans should be integrated with national production plans; and (d) State plans for labour allocation, material supply, revenue, loans and cash, working capital, and exports ought to be strictly enforced.[10]

The Financial and Economic Group of the Central Committee met in the West Chamber of Zhongnanhai, the headquarters of the CC, CCP, in February 1962, when Liu Shaoqi, Deng Xiaoping, and Chen Yun participated in the formulation of the 'Report on the Readjustment Plan for 1962'. On the basis of this meeting, the CC, CCP, promulgated the 'Six Articles on Banking' (dated 10 March 1962) and the 'Six Articles on Finance' (dated 21 April 1962), in order to tighten control over funds and financial management at the enterprise level.[11] On 31 May 1962 the CC, CCP, endorsed a report by the State Planning Commission which stressed the need for financial management and an approval procedure for medium- and large-scale construction projects. In May and June 1962, 19,000 inefficient and unprofitable factories were either stopped and closed down or transferred and merged, by reducing or stopping their supply of raw materials, fuel and electricity, working capital, and wages, and by food rationing. The Office of Readjustment of the State Planning Commission was chiefly responsible for the execution of this policy.[12] It had taken four years, since the first attempt in 1959, to find an effective way to implement this policy.

The second theme of industrial reorganization was rationalization. This was related to the policy of 'specialization and [inter-enterprise] co-ordination' as set out in the 'Seventy Articles' which were drafted by Bo Yibo and sponsored by Deng Xiaoping in September 1961. Taking a long-term perspective beyond the immediate crisis created by the Great Leap Forward, the 'Seventy Articles' suggested that enterprises should be co-ordinated according to national plans and that their material supply should be arranged through fixed supply stations.[13] In addition, the policy paper stipulated that whenever two enterprises found it feasible and necessary to establish direct links they should build up a relationship of economic co-ordination, a quasi-contractual relationship. Whenever direct links were not feasible they should take steps to merge several factories into one specialized corporation, taking into consideration production requirements and marketing and distribution advantages.[14]

The policy of 'specialization and [inter-enterprise] co-ordination' addressed itself to three interrelated problems. The first concerned the tendency to strive for self-sufficiency at the enterprise level, because of the uncertainty over the production quotas and material supply norms set by higher authorities, as well as the relative advantages in hoarding equipment and materials. Second, the policy sought to remedy the problem of conflicts of authority (termed 'multiple-headed administration' and 'dispersion of leadership'), and to facilitate the economic co-ordination of production across different jurisdictions, both vertically (ministerial) and horizontally (local).[15] The third issue was the pressure for managerial and technical rationalization because this usually improved the rate of utilization of equipment and facilities.[16]

The aim of the specialization and co-ordination policy in the 1960s was to build groups of 'small but specialized' and 'medium but specialized' factories to participate in different ways and at different stages of the production process. In Shanghai, for example, planners and decision-makers approached the issue of 'specialization and co-ordination' from the viewpoint of 'networks' consisting of a group of enterprises which covered the final stage of production, that is, the manufacturing and assembly of final products. The core of each network was surrounded by a group of subsidiary factories which specialized in parts and components as well as technical processing. The latter were in turn supported by still another group of subsidiary factories which mainly provided industrial services.[17] The model case of Changzhou municipality, which took shape as early as 1959, was based upon the idea of 'networks' or 'dragon systems' of co-ordination among mutually connected factories. They were formed by means of administrative intervention from the higher echelons as well as by voluntary negotiation between participating units.[18]

By the middle of 1965, five types of specialized industry had emerged from the experiments in industrial reorganization in Shanghai, Tianjin, and other major cities. The first type specialized according to the final product, as in the case of Tianjin in 1965. The second type specialized in semi-final products such as parts and components, as in the case of both Shanghai and Tianjin. The third type of specialized production involved technical processes such as casting, forging, and electroplating, and developed through the regrouping of workshops, which had previously belonged to established enterprises, into new specialized factories. The fourth type, found in Shanghai, related to supplementary technical and industrial services, such as equipment maintenance, the renovation of equipment and facilities, making instruments and tools, and physical and chemical tests. The fifth type was the so-called 'socialist trust' which was reorganized to carry out a range of interconnected functions, from the extraction and processing of raw materials, through the production of parts and components, the building of main bodies, and the assembly process, to distribution and marketing.[19]

THE RISE OF 'SOCIALIST TRUSTS'

The 'socialist trust', which was based upon the policy of 'specialization and [inter-enterprise] co-ordination', was one step forward from the 'network' or 'dragon system' found in Shanghai and Changzhou municipalities. A 'socialist trust' roughly embraced the factories which were normally included in a 'network' of specialization and co-ordination, and was likely to have a further extension of backward and forward linkages (to extraction and marketing respectively). In a managerial and organizational sense, a 'socialist trust' enjoyed a high degree of autonomy in relation to the central ministries and the local bureaux. The functional areas of a 'specialized corporation' were approximately equal to those of an industrial bureau at either the central or the local level. A 'socialist trust' or a 'specialized corporation' was organized on the basis of one line of products.

The organization of twelve 'socialist trusts' began in late 1963, but it was not until August 1964 that this experiment was formally endorsed by the Party centre. Among these 'socialist trusts', nine were on a national scale and three were regional. These groups of corporations were organized on the basis of four major functional categories: (a) joint corporations or general plants for manufacturing entire sets of machinery or automobiles, for instance, the Automobile

Industrial Corporation or the Textile Machinery Corporation; (b) specialized corporations organized according to type of product — for example, the Rubber Industrial Corporation or the Pharmaceutical Industrial Corporation; (c) enterprises whose functions centred on a single product at various stages of production, for example, the Aluminium Corporation or the Tobacco Industrial Corporation; and (d) enterprises requiring a high degree of centralization in order to use natural resources more efficiently, for instance, the Beijing-Tianjin-Tanggu Power Corporation and the East China Coal Industrial Corporation.[20]

Moving beyond the immediate concern in the early 1960s of economic readjustment, Liu Shaoqi soon addressed the fundamental weaknesses of the administrative approach. In a document promoting the 'socialist trusts', Liu stated, 'at present, our way [of running the economy] is that all offices and bureaux at the municipal and provincial levels and ministries at the central level intervene in the economy. This is an extra-economic way'. He also stated, 'this is a feudalistic way'. He felt that, since these ministries, bureaux, and offices were all administrative apparatuses, this was an administrative approach to running enterprises,[21] whereas he regarded the socialist trust as an economic approach.

Bo Yibo also pointed out the problems inherent in the administrative approach: the conflicting jurisdictions of the departments and bureaux and the inconsistencies in policy; the dispersion of managerial power and the fragmentation of decision-making; the unwieldy size of the bureaucracy and the multiple levels of the hierarchy; wastefulness and inefficiency; and the orientation of industrial management towards authority rather than markets.[22] The pilot schemes of socialist trusts were guided by the 'Report of Opinions concerning the Socialist Trusts in Industry and Transport'. This document was drafted by the Party group of the State Economic Commission headed by Bo Yibo and was later endorsed by the Party centre (presumably under Deng Xiaoping and Peng Zhen) in August 1964.[23]

The merit of the socialist trust lay in the economic principles and rationality that it entailed. Liu commented that these pilot schemes 'should follow economic principles and take rationality into consideration. Overall, [our objective] is to improve quality, increase variety, lower costs, raise labour productivity and improve technology.'[24] On the same occasion, Deng Xiaoping stated: 'to organize "trusts", all that we want are these advantages. Otherwise, if quality cannot be upgraded, variety cannot be broadened and technology cannot be improved, there is no point in having it [a socialist trust].'[25]

In spite of the repeated emphasis on the shortcomings of the administrative approach the socialist trust proposal was not able to move far beyond the administrative approach nor had it developed into a genuine economic approach by the middle 1960s. None the less, Liu Shaoqi expressed his desire to recommend an economic approach, to restructure the role of the State in a socialist economy, and to minimize State intervention:

Isn't it better to let the Party and Government at the central level and those at the local level be detached? They can take a position transcendent to the corporations and the tensions among them. Isn't it good to serve as arbitrators rather than as involved parties whenever problems emerge?[26]

The author is not in a position to assess the economic success or failure of the socialist trust experiment, since the experiment was short-lived, and the material available for both the post-Leap period and the post-Mao era is limited.[27] The material also tends to be biased because the experiment occurred during the phase of policy promotion (that is, it received extra support from the top leaders). For example, Deng Xiaoping ordered that the 'socialist trusts' be given preferential treatment by means of a generous 'profit-retention system' in order to make them look good.[28]

The original version of the 'socialist trusts' had two basic faults: the over-concentration of power in the headquarters at the corporation level, at the expense of participating factories or enterprises; and the creation of monopolies of certain products at the national level.[29] Both problems were addressed by Liu Shaoqi, who required not only a high degree of organization and efficiency at the intra-enterprise level, but also a greater degree of co-ordination and planning at the inter-enterprise level.[30] In the China Pharmaceutical Corporation, for instance, the production and distribution of medicines which were outside the distribution network of the corporation were banned, and those heads of production units and their superiors who lent support to such production or distribution were penalized. This corporation was formed from the application of the policy of 'closures, stoppages, mergers and transfers' to 100 of the 283 pharmaceutical factories throughout China.[31]

THE POLITICIZATION OF 'SOCIALIST TRUSTS'

The 'socialist trusts' were controversial from the beginning. Firstly, the formation of 'socialist trusts' aggravated the existing tension between the ministerial and local levels in the post-Leap period, whereas the highly centralized structure of the corporations was intended to curtail the power of local authorities. Believing in the sovereignty of the planner, Liu Shaoqi insisted upon organizing socialist trusts on a national scale, and opposed the option of regional socialist trusts. Liu stated that, in order to take advantage of the economies of scale, 'if we mean to stress planning, monopoly is needed' and 'there should be one [corporation] for each line of business at the national level'.[32] In spite of Liu's claim that the policy followed an 'economic approach', it was implemented in an 'administrative' and heavy-handed manner, and tended to alienate local leaders and enterprise units.

There were good reasons for the reluctance of enterprise units, especially those of an auxiliary nature, to accept the new structure of the socialist trusts. They found that the trusts were inconvenient, downgraded the organizational status of incorporated units, and forced them into a dependent role. Auxiliary units were instructed to give up their original assignment and to manufacture simpler products and components or to transfer their better equipment and personnel to core factories or corporations, but most resisted these instructions.[33]

In addition, the socialist trusts experiment adversely affected the supply of some commodities. At the Tianjin People's Pharmaceutical Factory, the establishment of the trust resulted in the reduction of the number of medicines produced from 100 to only five profitable lines. The net result was a curtailment in the variety and supply of needed products because of an increasing degree of monopoly.[34] Another example was the organization of the tobacco corporation under the Ministry of Light Industry in 1965. Local Party secretaries and peasants in Henan complained that the corporation purchased only top quality tobacco at an unreasonably low price, leaving the low grade tobacco for the localities and the peasants to handle. None the less, Li Xiannian, the Minister of Finance, continued to support Liu's policy, in order to protect the revenue sources of central government.[35]

In addition, local authorities were very concerned with the possible depletion of their revenues and the weakening of their control over resources. In Zigong municipality in Sichuan province, 70 per cent of the revenue was derived from the salt industry. When the salt trust was organized, the municipality found that its financial resources were cut substantially.[36] Another instance occurred when the First Ministry of Machine-building planned to organize a tractor corporation in 1964 and prepared to take several factories from the jurisdiction of Liaoning province. During the consultation process, the Party Committee in Liaoning province requested that the province be allowed to retain one tractor factory for automobile manufacturing. However, Liu told the Party Secretary of Liaoning province: 'This factory must be taken over. You are not permitted to manufacture automobiles, but I am!'[37] Local authorities also lost much of their control over the supply of materials as a result of the loss of their jurisdiction over certain types of enterprise.[38]

Socialist trusts added further to the controversy over administrative centralization, when the issue of the separation between the Party and the State was raised again. Until the establishment of socialist trusts, local Party organizations had been given a certain share of power in an arrangement called 'dual command'. However, the formation of socialist trusts required a transfer of power within the Party organizations from the local and provincial levels to the corporation level.[39] This meant that local Party Committees lost a substantial amount of power over enterprise units and the economic sector.

In order to implement the separation of the State from the Party, during this period Liu, Deng, and Bo attempted to streamline the Party hierarchy. Liu felt that for many years local Party Committees should have taken charge of Party affairs but had failed to do so.[40] He therefore advocated that the management of socialist trusts should take over the Party's tasks of organization and supervision. Deng said specifically that 'those [Party] organizations in the enterprises under the direct jurisdiction of ministries on the industrial and transport front should be subject to ministerial commands'.[41] Bo saw the problem as a need to settle the issue of 'multiple-headed leadership',[42] that is, mainly as a problem of disorganization and of conflicts over jurisdiction which had been caused by the expansion of the functions and structure of the governmental bureaucracy since the 1950s.

In order to implement Liu's and Deng's views on the reorganization of the Party apparatus in the economic sector, Bo Yibo took two major steps in 1955. First, he initiated a policy to build a Party Committee for the whole industrial and transport front, taking advantage of Mao Zedong's call to learn from the People's Liberation Army (PLA) and to establish political departments within economic organizations. The Party Committee for the whole industry and transport front was led by the 'Party Group' of the State Economic Commission whose director at the time was Bo Yibo. Party Committees were also established at the ministerial level to replace the 'Party Groups', which were in turn given control over Party Committees at the enterprise level. The new system replaced the former command hierarchy running down from the Central Committee to local Party Committees and enterprise Party Committees.[43]

Bo Yibo's second step was to sponsor the drafting of the 'Regulations for Political Work in Industry and Transport', which required all enterprises under direct ministerial jurisdiction to sever their organizational ties with local Party organizations. Above the existing political departments, which were ministerially based, a new tier of political departments was added to the whole industry and transport front.[44] The regulations also required that jurisdiction over corporate Party affairs and the youth leagues should be transferred to political departments. Trade unions were also to be placed under the command of the newly founded Party Committees at the ministerial level. Moreover, administrators at the corporation level were given a monopoly over major managerial policy at the expense of the Party Committee.[45]

POLITICS AT THE TOP LEADERSHIP LEVEL

There is no evidence that the attempts of Liu Shaoqi, Deng Xiaoping, and Bo Yibo to streamline and reorganize the Party apparatus in the economic arena were politically motivated. However the policy-actors directly involved provided different interpretations of the situation. For example, Zhou Enlai mentioned Bo Yibo's desire for power in merging the State Economic Commission, the State Planning Commission, and the State Construction Commission into a new unit, and making himself the head of the new unit. Zhou hinted that Mao Zedong was aware of Bo's motives and therefore appointed Yu Qiuli as Vice-Director of the State Planning Commission in order to assist Li Fuchun and frustrate Bo's wishes.[46]

Zhou's handling of this case indicates his reservations about the subject. He subtly referred the document drafted by the Party Group of the State Economic Commission, and entitled the 'Report on Trial Organization of the Trusts in Transport and Industry', to Chen Boda for his comments. Chen raised some objections on Mao's behalf to the formation of socialist trusts at the national level, drawing attention to the need to mobilize local initiatives. Chen preferred that regional 'trusts' be retained.[47] When Bo Yibo later conveyed Chen's views to Liu, the latter said, 'Go and ask Chen Boda what he means by "regional"! The trusts are meant to be highly centralized and monopolized. You [Bo Yibo] go back and write a report to me. I shall endorse it regardless of what he says.'[48] In retrospect, it appears that Chen Boda's views were similar to those held by Mao.

Some background information is needed in order to appreciate both the tension between Mao and Liu on the question of socialist trusts and the showdown forced by Mao in early 1966. The foregoing analysis has indicated that Mao and Liu agreed on the need for a balanced sharing of power and interest between the central and local governments. Liu, however, appeared much less accommodating than Mao in making concessions to local governments. This resulted partly from his view of the need for a strong centralized State in this crisis, and partly from his preference for the macro-rational administered economy in the post-Leap period. Liu's difference of opinion with Mao surfaced in the Enlarged Work Conference of the CC, CCP, in January 1962. In his speech to the Conference Liu asserted that the central government should possess the authority to appropriate the products and profits of local enterprises, even if those local enterprises were built by local government investment. In Liu's words, 'State ownership should not be converted into local ownership.' Mao responded to Liu's statement instantly, saying, 'Local interests should be taken care of too!' Thereupon Liu retracted his statement, expressing his sympathy for the feelings of the local units and proposing a division of labour among levels of government. None the less he insisted on the need to consider the entire situation (quanju) and the whole people (quanmin), thus implying an even greater centralization of power.[49]

Four years later, during the Enlarged Conference of the Politburo, Mao referred to the socialist trusts in a speech on 20 March 1966, saying, 'the central ministries in transport and industry should practise the "republic with a nominal king", that is, the central ministries should exercise nominal authority to allow the local level to have more substantial authority'.[50] He felt that the central government had taken over too many factories from the local level and therefore recommended that all these factories should be returned to their original government units.[51] When the Cultural Revolution picked up momentum in the second half of 1966, the pilot programme for socialist trusts was halted and subsequently, at the height of the Cultural Revolution, was subject to severe attack.

THE INITIATION AND FORMULATION OF THE 'SEVENTY ARTICLES'

The 'Seventy Articles' were formulated during the same period as the policy of economic readjustment and industrial reorganization. Mao admitted that up to 1960 the CCP leaders, including himself, had tended to administer the economy by means of subjective feelings and rough estimates of the situation, and that the country had suffered and paid dearly for this. He therefore proposed to conduct systematic 'research and investigation' of the period from 1949 to 1960, saying, 'there cannot be concrete policy without research and investigation'.[52] Mao even criticized Deng Xiaoping at the Guangzhou Conference in early 1961 for failing to carry out any 'research and investigation'.[53]

The 'research and investigation' was intended to provide an explanation of why the CCP had needed to change from the radical phase to the retrenchment phase in the post-Leap period. Summarizing the achievements of the CCP's top policy-makers by the 1960s, Mao stated that '[after all,] for a long period after advocating the general line of Socialist construction, we did not have time and it was also impossible to formulate a systematic and coherent body of guidelines, policy, and measures, because of a lack of experience'.[54] Therefore, it was expected that there would be obstacles and both positive and negative lessons before a correct direction could be found. According to Mao,

Overall, our Party does not have sufficient knowledge about the Socialist construction. [Thus] for a long time to come, [we must] accumulate experience and study it diligently so that we would be able to deepen our understanding of it and come to grips with its law. [We must] strive hard and seriously *investigate* and *research* it.[55] (Emphasis added; translation supplied.)

The process of research and investigation was intended as an exercise which would lead to the 'summing up' of experience, and the subsequent drafting of policy papers in various functional areas.

Mao himself sponsored in-depth investigation and research in the policy area where he felt confident and then drafted the policy paper, 'the Sixty Articles on Tasks in Agriculture'.[56] In the industrial arena, however, several field investigation projects were being mounted and various units, such as the Party Secretariat and the State Planning Commission, were involved.[57]

The investigation team led by Li Fuchun, Director of the State Planning Commission, was originally expected to play a fundamental part in drafting a policy paper on enterprise management. As soon as Li Fuchun's field investigation was concluded in June 1961, however, he was assigned to other tasks.[58] The Party Secretariat then asked Bo Yibo to synthesize all the research and investigation material and prepare a draft of a policy paper which was later known as the 'Seventy Articles'.[59] The Red Guard sources hint that the change from Li Fuchun to Bo Yibo was a result of the factional struggle of Mao Zedong against Deng Xiaoping and Liu Shaoqi,[60] but the author has no evidence from which to confirm this point.

Early versions of the 'Seventy Articles' became available by June 1961 and were drafted on the basis of Li Fuchun's investigation report in Beijing (which was written up by Ma Hong, Mei Xing, and others).[61] The Red Guard sources suggest that copies of the drafts of the 'Seventy Articles' were distributed to factory directors and managers for comments while the Shenyang urban survey was being conducted in July 1961.[62] Immediately afterwards, a final draft was submitted to the Party Secretariat, and Deng Xiaoping held meetings within the Secretariat and revised the draft, section by section, and chapter by chapter.[63] The 'Seventy Articles' were discussed and approved by the CC, CCP, in Lushan in September 1961, together with the draft of the 'Directive on Current Industrial Problems'.[64] There is no evidence to suggest that Mao expressed any reservations on either document at this time.

Incorporated into the 'Seventy Articles' were both a sense of crisis and a rationalizing approach. Since the rationalizing approach was employed to remedy the chaos created by the Great Leap Forward, it is inevitable that some aspects of previous Maoist policy were subject to criticism. Liu Shaoqi, for instance, stated in a conference in July 1961, 'The call to dare to think, to try, as well as to destroy and construct in a big way, and the abolition of many reasonable regulations and systems, among others have made the State suffer, the Party suffer, you [participants of the conference] suffer and the people suffer too.' Deng commented in 1961 that, 'At present, there are tensions in production relationships, the Party-mass relationship, the cadre-mass relationship and in ownership relations.' He believed that the people wanted stability, and that, therefore, in his words, 'chaos had to be rectified'. Furthermore, some of the shortcomings of the Great Leap Forward, such as mass movements, ritualism, and amateurism, were to be remedied.[65]

Bo Yibo gave the most accurate and comprehensive description of the policy perspective of the 'Seventy Articles' from which it is worth quoting at length:

Our management of industrial enterprises cannot be more chaotic than it is at present. Industrial enterprises have slipped into a half-planned or unplanned situation with the relaxation of the responsibility system. In the management of production, science is not respected and orders are given blindly. Product quality is deteriorating and economic accounting is in the worst shape ever. In addition, there have been increases in cost, and enterprises have suffered losses. In the system of distribution, the principle of 'distribution according to labour' is not being followed, but egalitarianism is [practised]. In the mass movements, there have been a big shake-up and a big noise, and the delicate work of thought has not been done. Administrative tasks are monopolized by the Party. The power of industrial management is dispersed and co-operation between enterprises has been disrupted. Therefore, when we draft the regulation [the 'Seventy Articles'] [our] direction and intention to solve this problem should be made explicit.[66] (Translation supplied.)

THE IMPLEMENTATION OF THE 'SEVENTY ARTICLES'

The 'Seventy Articles' provide comprehensive coverage of all major aspects of enterprise management. These include: planning management, technology management, labour management, wages, bonuses, and welfare, accounting and finance, economic co-ordination, responsibility systems, and so on. They define the nature, objectives, and organizing principles of the enterprise and its relationship with the supervising authorities and other enterprises. They also recommend measures for running State-owned enterprises.[67]

Several features of the 'Seventy Articles' were intended to deal with the adverse consequences of the politicized and mass-oriented managerial style of the Great Leap Forward. For instance, industrial enterprises were redefined as 'economic organizations' rather than political organizations, stressing their objectives in terms of the fulfilment and over-fulfilment of the State plan. In addition, the purpose of political work was reduced to 'the fulfilment of production plans in a better way'. The study of Mao's work, Marxism, and Leninism was toned down by stressing 'voluntary participation', and curtailing the hours devoted to political study. Technicians and functional staff were also given immunity from political indoctrination by treating them as an 'integral part of the working class'.[68]

As mentioned earlier, the 'Anshan Constitution', which represents the most advanced formulation of Mao Zedong's views on industrial management, was set aside by Deng Xiaoping in 1960 (see Chapter 3, p. 68). Yet it would be inappropriate to suggest that Mao was in conflict with the pragmatic leaders in the post-Leap period. In drafting the 'Seventy Articles', they made 'differential adjustments' in Mao's position: the political ingredients of the 'Anshan Constitution' were retained, but modified. For instance, a fresh effort was made to institutionalize the cadres' participation in manual labour; an attempt was made to accommodate workers' participation in managerial functions through an institutionalized, rather than a mobilizational, channel (the congress of the representatives of workers and staff); and a 'technical revolution' was conducted through the programme of 'mechanization, semi-mechanization, automation and semi-automation'[69] which was sponsored by Bo Yibo (see p. 61).

After 1961, the following dimensions of enterprise management were stressed during the implementation of the 'Seventy Articles':

(a) strengthening the planning procedure, but leaving enough room (*yudi*) for enterprises to fulfil their annual plans without sacrificing product quality and product costs;[70]

(b) abolishing the profit-retention system, but providing enterprises with a modest incentive scheme, which was tied to the total wage bill;[71]

(c) improving the supply of raw materials at both macro and micro levels through the promotion of 'economic contracts' and inter-enterprise co-ordination;[72]

(d) strengthening the power and office of the factory director to keep the State and the Party separate, but not weakening the collective leadership of the Party Committee;[73]

(e) restoring the technology responsibility system and the office of chief engineer, coupled with a renewed emphasis on quality control;[74]

(f) reaffirming specialized and professional accounting through the establishment of the chief accountant system while retaining some aspects of mass accounting;[75]

(g) a partial return to the piece-rate wage system, from 10 per cent of the total number of workers in 1961, to 13.8 per cent in 1962, and 19.9 per cent in 1963, in addition to the existing time-rate and welfare system; a limited restoration of the bonus system, from 2.9 per cent of the total wage bill to 5.9 per cent;[76]

(h) promotion of the employment of contractual and seasonal workers.[77]

THE ROLES OF THE TOP CCP LEADERS

The 'Seventy Articles', which reflect a synoptic perspective, were the product of a comprehensive review of past practices, and recommended the 'best' ways to manage state-owned enterprises. However they do not appear to have been implemented by one central co-ordinator, or even a tightly knit group of co-ordinators. The involvement of the policy-actors was dictated very much by their own interests and areas of competence, and to a lesser extent by their official positions and responsibilities. There was no fixed assignment of duties, but as the focus of attention changed, the policy-actors seem to have participated in successive phases of the implementation process in a more or less spontaneous fashion.

As mentioned above, Zhou Enlai and Chen Yun were involved in the early phase of industrial reorganization which was stipulated in the 'Seventy Articles'. Liu Shaoqi, in his own right, and together with Li Xiannian, Minister of Finance, sponsored a regulation concerning finance and accounting at the enterprise level in November 1962.[78] Liu was also instrumental in consolidating the system of seasonal and contractual workers and strengthening the collective welfare system.[79] Deng Xiaoping intervened in the functional area of the administrative and production responsibility systems at the enterprise level. In addition, Bo Yibo was identified as having sponsored the drafting of a regulation for the technology responsibility system in 1963.[80]

The legitimacy of carrying out the 'Seventy Articles' may be questioned, in view of Mao Zedong's reservations on the policy paper, which began to become evident in 1962. In addition, the Sino-Soviet dispute in the early 1960s imposed ideological constraints upon the implementation of the policy paper. Many articles and commentaries attacking the domestic policy of the Soviet Union and Yugoslavia at this time could be read as an implicit criticism of the Chinese policy of economic and managerial restructuring.[81]

As Secretary General of the Party Secretariat, Deng Xiaoping shouldered the political responsibility for implementing the policy paper. According to Red Guard publications, when the 'Seventy Articles' were released for comment, they were challenged as negating the 'three flags' (the general line of Socialist transformation, the Great Leap Forward, and the people's commune), as well as negating the Party's leadership and opposing the concepts of politics in command and the mass movement. Subsequently Deng forbade further discussion of the policy paper and instructed that it should not be revised for three years even if its rationale was questioned.[82]

It was Bo Yibo who spearheaded the trial implementation and conducted pilot schemes of the 'Seventy Articles'. Bo gave instructions that in enterprise units which were undertaking pilot schemes, the 'Seventy Articles' had to be read in public and no omission or revision was permitted. Bo also required that all central ministries of transport and industry should assign officials of a rank equivalent to or higher than a deputy minister to take direct responsibility for the trial implementation of the 'Seventy Articles'. They were also requested to form a special task force for the purpose of investigation and implementation. Over 200 enterprises were selected for the first pilot schemes of the 'Seventy Articles'.[83]

Bo chose the coal industry for the start of a pilot scheme to implement the key provision of 'five fixes and five guarantees' of the 'Seventy Articles' in October 1961.[84] The annual plans for enterprises set production capacity which was fixed in relation to five factors: (a) product design and the scale of production; (b) the number of personnel; (c) quotas for consumption and sources of raw materials, fuel, energy, and tools; (d) fixed assets and liquid capital; and (e) the relationship of economic contracts. The 'five guarantees' referred to the five obligations of enterprises to the State, which covered a guarantee for product mix, quantity and quality, the size of the total wage bill, the fulfilment of cost plans, profit remittances, and the length of time for the depreciation of equipment (the 'Seventy Articles', Article 7).[85] The 'five fixes' and 'five guarantees' were implemented as follows. The first task was to undertake basic inventory-taking and financial auditing. Scattered evidence indicates that this was carried out throughout China in 1962. Second, it was necessary to investigate and compile data on the production capacity of each factory and its sub-units and individual workers, as well as on various links in the production process and on sets of equipment. Third, norms had to be set for each factory and its sub-units as well as for each link in the production process and each set of equipment.[86] A survey of the regulations and directives issued by both the CC, CCP, and the State Council suggests that the 'Seventy Articles' were implemented intensively and covered a wide range of issues within a relatively short time span, from late 1961 to 1966.

THE TENSION ARISING FROM THE REVISION PROCESS

During the post-Leap period a rift developed between Mao Zedong on the second front and Liu Shaoqi, Deng Xiaoping, Chen Yun, Peng Zhen, and Bo Yibo on the first front, although it is likely that the Red Guard sources exaggerated the degree of this rift. The difference of opinion became apparent when the consequences of the Great Leap Forward were being assessed and remedial policies to deal with the crisis situation were being formulated. Mao remained silent on the 'Seventy Articles' at this stage of their formulation, and only later began to register his reservations and to request their revision.

In 1961 and 1962, the first-front leaders were required to confront the failure of the Great Leap Forward, for which they were held partly responsible. It was, however, also inevitable that Mao's share of the responsibility should be assessed, although implicitly in most cases. Thus Mao's credibility was also at stake. For instance, at the 'Pleasure View Chamber' (*chang guanlou*) in Beijing, Administrative Secretary Peng Zhen, with the knowledge of Liu Shaoqi, initiated a comprehensive review of all the important directives and regulations issued during the Great Leap Forward. It was here that mistakes were attributed to Mao.[87] Subsequently, at the end of January 1962, the

Enlarged Work Conference of the Central Committee was convened, and the issue of political responsibility was once again raised. The Red Guard publications, however, suggest that Mao was able to avert another career crisis by successful manoeuvring and with the support of Zhou Enlai and Lin Biao. The Red Guard sources may overstate the politicization of the 'West Chamber' conference convened at Zhongnanhai, the headquarters of the CC, CCP, in February 1962, for its main focus was on financial investment and monetary policies after the Great Leap Forward. None the less, some critical remarks at the conference might have been implicitly directed towards Mao Zedong.[88]

In this atmosphere of tension and inadequate communication, Mao suggested in the Tenth Plenum of the Eighth Party Congress (held in September 1962) that the 'Seventy Articles' should be revised. Deng Xiaoping's response was that since they had been implemented for so short a period, time was needed to observe the results. Three years later, in a conference in early 1965, Mao explained that most other policy papers, such as the 'Sixty Articles on the Tasks in Agriculture', 'Sixty Articles on Higher Education', and 'Forty Articles on Scientific Research Work', were to be revised as a matter of routine, and that therefore the revision of the 'Seventy Articles' should not be treated as an exception. Accordingly, Mao set a date for this revision, and Deng and Bo began the work in March 1965.[89]

While revising the 'Seventy Articles', both Deng and Bo kept to the original version as closely as possible. Deng believed that there were many useful parts in the old 'Seventy Articles' which could be retained. Bo Yibo stated that his guiding principle in drafting the 'Seventy Articles' had been to rectify chaos, and that this historical role needed reaffirmation. In his report to the Central Committee on 16 May 1965, Bo Yibo made it clear that he did not intend to make fundamental changes in the document, explaining that 'the principles of managerial work and the leadership system in the "Seventy Articles" were not only applicable then, they will also be applicable from now on'.[90]

On a number of occasions, Bo Yibo cast doubts upon the general applicability of Mao Zedong's thought to enterprise management. In a forum held to revise the 'Seventy Articles', Bo suggested that Mao's style of work in Daqing was not applicable to all problem-solving, and that over-simplication and vulgarization of Mao's thought should be avoided. In another forum held in Beijing in June 1965, it was suggested that Mao Zedong's thought, together with

Marxism and Leninism, should be explicitly mentioned as the guiding principles of enterprise management. Bo Yibo answered, however, that Marxism, Leninism, and Mao Zedong's thought should not be mentioned in a ritualistic way. When another speaker referred to the need for reliance upon the masses, Bo cited Deng's opposition to shouting slogans without giving substance. As a result, the suggestion was rejected.[91]

By September 1965, Bo had finished revising the 'Seventy Articles' and issued the new version to key enterprises and related units at the central and local levels in order to solicit opinions. He made preparations to implement the new version after the Conference on Industry and Transport, which was to be convened in 1966. However, the Cultural Revolution was launched in May 1966 and this prevented the new version of the 'Seventy Articles' from being put into practice.[92] In retrospect it appears that, despite this setback, the basic orientation and, in some cases, the specific provisions of the 'Seventy Articles' had outlived their opponents.

IDEOLOGY AND ORGANIZATION

The remainder of this chapter will examine the relationship of some independent variables to the ascendancy of the administrative approach. To begin with, several ideological factors were involved in the new policy-making approach in the post-Leap period. First, Mao Zedong withdrew from his position on 'subjective dynamism' which had warranted the rise of the preceptoral approach. ('Subjective dynamism' here refers to those ambitious attempts to test the upper limits of the country's economic potential. It also involves a 'wave' style of planning in which the utmost effort is put into the surge forward, and this is followed by consolidation.)[93] In discussing the 'dynamic balancing' in economic planning, Mao stated: 'it does not seem to have had big chaos; even if it were the case, it would return to normalcy after chaos'.[94] The adverse consequences of the Great Leap Forward, however, changed the guiding philosophy of policy-making to the need for 'planned and proportional development' on the basis of 'seeking truth from facts' and the 'law of economy'. This change signalled a transition from charismatic leadership to the sovereignty of the planner, both of which approaches are based upon an assumption of the omniscience and omnipotence of policy-makers.

Second, the development towards a decentralized economy created unintended consequences and even economic crisis (such as the loss of revenue sources, non-budgeted investment, the employment of unnecessary manpower, the illegal diversion of material supplies, deficit, and high inflation). The views of the 'whole country as a chessboard' and of 'the sum and the parts' were intended to discourage excessive local independence at the expense of central planning. Third, the notion of 'class struggle' lost its saliency in the formulation of enterprise management policy (for example, in the questions of material incentives, regulatory control, and expert-oriented management). This permitted the return to professionally oriented management, which was codified by the 'Seventy Articles'.

Owing to constraints imposed by organizational factors, the restoration of the administrative policy-making approach, especially in economic readjustment, involved a long delay, and the anticipated consistency between ends and means was lacking. Generally, there was a firm institutional foundation for the return of the administrative approach, in the newly established State Council (1954) and the Party Secretariat (1956), the central planning apparatus and State ownership, the tested methods of industrial reorganization, and scientific management at the enterprise level. Nevertheless the central policy-makers needed to find specific organizational means in order to cope with the over-extension of unbudgeted investment and to reclaim jurisdiction over key industries from local units. Some effective measures were subsequently developed by Zhou Enlai in his pilot scheme of 'closure, transfer, merger and stoppage' in North-east China in late 1960, and financial control was recommended by Chen Yun in February 1962. The development of these organizational means was crucial to the implementation of economic readjustment.

In the second phase of industrial reorganization, the socialist trust (which enjoyed relative independence from the State) was introduced on an experimental basis. It was designed to overcome the effects of 'territoriality', such as the lack of lateral co-ordination, mutual hostility among localities, struggles between local units for resources and markets, and endeavours to control industrial enterprises and thus to control revenues and investment funds. All of these effects were achieved at the expense of macro-rationality. The embryo socialist trust was not a full-fledged economic entity, relying upon economic leverage and markets, because it still retained the characteristics of a monopoly and administrative co-ordination.

Efforts were made to achieve better co-ordination through the establishment of Party Committees and political departments in various echelons of the industrial hierarchy, but this again was basically an administrative approach.

THE POLITICS OF POLICY-MAKING

In the political arena, participation in policy-making was fluid. In many instances the policy-actors had the opportunity to find their roles quite spontaneously, in a process of 'mutual adjustment'. Several groups of policy-makers participated in the successive phases of formulating and executing the 'Seventy Articles': research and investigation was authorized by Mao and conducted by Li Fuchun among others; the document was drafted by Bo Yibo and Deng Xiaoping; factory directors were consulted in Shenyang; the top Party leaders gave their approval at the Lushan Conference in September 1961; and finally various aspects of the 'Seventy Articles' were implemented by many policy-makers, such as Liu Shaoqi, Zhou Enlai, Bo Yibo, Deng Xiaoping, Chen Yun, and Li Xiannian.

The policy of economic readjustment, which was built upon a crisis orientation and consensus, was authorized by Mao Zedong and was actively shaped by Liu Shaoqi, Zhou Enlai, and Chen Yun. The controversial socialist trusts were initiated by Liu Shaoqi and Bo Yibo, with support from Deng Xiaoping. Zhou Enlai expressed some reservations because of the anticipated opposition from Mao Zedong. Mao was able to terminate the socialist trust programme by employing a 'bypassing device' and 'indirect manipulation', as noted previously. At the Enlarged Conference of the Politburo in April 1966, which included most subordinate local party leaders, Mao requested the return of industrial enterprises to local government units. This made it difficult for Liu Shaoqi and Bo Yibo to alter the course of events.

Overall, the ascendancy of the administrative approach was facilitated by the rise of Liu Shaoqi and other first-front leaders whose positions were strengthened by the establishment of the State Council and the Party Secretariat. The power of the first-front leaders increased when they were called upon to save the country from the crisis of the Great Leap Forward. They demonstrated that they were fully capable of handling the difficult situation. Liu Shaoqi was appointed as the State Chairman in April 1959 and proved the effectiveness of his leadership in enforcing the policies of economic readjustment and recentralization. He therefore emerged not only as the first among equals in relation to the other first-front policy-makers but also as parallel to Mao Zedong who was on the second front. Potentially, Liu was then in a position to replace Mao as the supreme leader.

On the whole, participation in policy-making at the top leadership level was fluid, but need not have been shapeless (that is, having no discernible pattern) during the post-Leap period. In general it reflected the division of labour between the first and second fronts. Pragmatic leaders on the first front, such as Liu Shaoqi, Zhou Enlai, Deng Xiaoping, and Chen Yun acted upon specific problems and implementation, while Mao Zedong on the second front tended to play a principal role in handling the broad question of the crisis over legitimacy, authorizing the fundamental change in the direction of policy, and balancing the interests of various groups (for example, the centre and the locality, the Party and the administrator, the leader and the led, the expert and the non-expert). Overall, policy-actors' participation in policy implementation was often conditional upon their formal duties and jurisdictions; and opinion on policy formulation was frequently based upon the credentials and competence of a policy-maker, as evaluated and recognized in a collegial context.

SUMMARY

This chapter has been devoted to an analysis of the return to the administrative approach in the industrial sector during the post-Leap period, 1961–6. As Charles E. Lindblom puts it, the synoptic model (or the administrative approach) is 'a powerful thumb without fingers',[95] being effective in restoring order to the national economy within a short time span, but limited in maximizing efficiency.

Above all, this author has examined the process of the formation of routines and consolidation in the post-Leap period. In the author's analytical framework, the economic approach and the preceptoral approach (that is, Maoist radicalism) are taken as responses to the administrative approach. For the development of a radical policy approach, we shall, in the next chapter, turn to the rise of the Daqing model, as well as to the Cultural Revolution.

5. Policy Radicalization: The Daqing Model and the Cultural Revolution, 1963-1972

THE Cultural Revolution is generally regarded as a process of policy radicalization. It is also associated with the rise of the preceptoral policy-making approach, in which Mao Zedong's thought became the guide and Mao's direct link to the masses was emphasized. However, the preceptoral policy-making approach was not applied consistently throughout the Cultural Revolution (1966 to 1969), but, rather, alternated with the administrative approach in three cycles: the anti-economism campaign in 1967, the seizure of power in enterprises in the years 1967-8, and the 'struggle, criticism, and transformation' period of 1968-70. Each phase concluded with the imposition of a centralized control structure which emphasized regulations, responsibility systems, discipline, the role of experts, and material incentives.

The charisma-inspired, mass-oriented style of industrial management of the Cultural Revolution had its roots in the radical version of the Daqing model which took shape during the period 1963-6. An analysis of the evolution of the Daqing model will therefore serve as a convenient introduction to industrial management policy during the Cultural Revolution by establishing the conceptual link between the two.

THE RISE OF THE DAQING MODEL

During its evolution, the Daqing model was influenced by both 'pragmatic' and 'leftist' leaders, and their contributions may be seen in the characteristics of the model. It went through a pragmatic phase from 1960 to 1962, and a radical phase from 1963 until the end of the Cultural Revolution.

The Daqing construction project officially began in 1960 after one year of preparation. From 1960 to 1962, the Daqing model incorporated four salient features. Firstly, it was organized along the lines of the Yenan type of military industry.[1] Because China was isolated from the outside world by the Soviet withdrawal of economic and technical assistance and the United States economic blockade, which was still in force after the Korean War, the Daqing industrial complex was required to manufacture crucially needed products, such as petroleum, and to substitute for imports of oil, regardless of cost and efficiency. Secondly, Yu Qiuli, who was in charge of the Daqing project, introduced the style of leadership and organization of the People's Liberation Army (PLA) because he had a PLA background and a majority of the technical and managerial personnel had been recruited from the PLA's engineering corps (in addition to engineers, technicians, professors, students, and workers from 37 other units).[2] Consequently, the Daqing model emphasized the PLA style of organizational discipline[3] and political work, including the institutional forms of political offices and departments,[4] and the principle of democracy in three areas (political, productive, and economic).

Thirdly, as from September 1961, the Daqing oilfield adopted many features of the 'Seventy Articles' when Yu Qiuli formulated the 'Regulation on the Work of Petroleum Industry', which defined the oil industry as production oriented (rather than politically oriented, as dictated by Mao). In Yu's view, 'production is the core of all our tasks and the concentrated expression of all the work [confronting the oil industry]'.[5] Furthermore, at the beginning of 1965, Yu initiated a pilot scheme of socialist trusts in the petroleum industry.[6] The Daqing model stressed organizational rectification, production responsibility systems, and scientific methods of management, along the lines of the 'Seventy Articles'.[7] Finally, owing to the influence from 1961 to 1966 of Liu Shaoqi's ideas on organic State socialism, collective welfare and community-building also figured prominently in the Daqing model.[8] For Daqing Liu advocated the integration of industry and agriculture, manual labour and intellectual work, and countryside and city; the process of community-building thus acquired the flavour of nineteenth-century Utopian Socialism.[9]

Mao's involvement with Daqing began in 1963 as part of his effort to regain his political influence within the State Council. He endorsed the Daqing model in order to reassert his control over the functional areas of industry, mining, and transport. He stated in December 1963 that 'among dozens of ministries, several of them have cadres whose performance and work style have been excellent, for instance, the Petroleum Ministry. [Yet in the past], other ministries could not see it [the merits of the Daqing experience] at all. They would never go there to seek advice, study or investigate it'.[10] (Translation supplied.) Subsequently, Yu Qiuli started to adjust his position to

Mao's view, and the Daqing model began to lean towards a 'radical' direction.

Under the influence of radicalism generated during the Socialist Education Movement in 1963, there was a greater emphasis on 'revolutionizing' management at Daqing. Managerial work was to have three orientations: towards the masses, the lower echelons, and production. In addition, to stress the direct relationship between staff functions and production, staff functions — including political work, production control, the supply of materials, scientific research and experiments, and the provision of amenities — were to be performed 'on the spot'.[11] One should not exaggerate the unique 'revolutionary' features of the management of Daqing oilfield, however, as other 'revisionist' leaders adopted similar industrial management policies at this time. Some examples are Bo Yibo's model of the Qiqiha'er Locomotive and Carriage Works[12] and Li Xiannian's policy of three orientations in accounting management.

Another example of 'revolutionizing' management was the 'three-three system' in cadre assignments: one-third of the cadres were to be in offices, one-third were to form an investigation team, and another third were to be assigned to the lower units. There was also to be a division of labour between the first and second 'fronts'. The 'first front' cadres were responsible for operational and routine functions while the 'second front' cadres dealt with staff functions and consisted of a political department, a production office, and a 'livelihood' office. Cadres were required to give up their privileges in housing, in children's education, and in life-style.[13] In August 1964, Daqing oilfield, like other enterprise units, started to implement the system of participation by cadres in physical work, through the arrangement known as 'three fixes and one substitute', whereby the function, time, and posting of a job were fixed and one cadre was substituted for one worker in a given shift.[14]

By 1964, Mao Zedong's view on 'revolutionary' industrial management was fully developed. In his radical stand on the class struggle in the 'superstructure', especially in the bureaucracy, Mao stated that 'the bureaucrat[ic] class on the one hand, and the working class together with the poor and lower-middle peasants on the other, are two classes sharply antagonistic to each other'.[15] In contrast to the pragmatic view of an enterprise as basically an economic organization, Mao stressed its political role, saying that 'management itself is a matter of Socialist education'.[16] He stated:

If the managerial staff do not go down to the [production] teams in workshops, practise 'three togethernesses' [with workers], and treat workers as teachers and learn [from them] one or several trades, they will end up in a fierce life-long class struggle with the working class. Eventually they as the bourgeois class will be defeated by the working class. Management will not be put into order if they do not learn some skills and stay laymen for a long period of time. It won't do if one wishes to enlighten others but himself remains unfamiliar with the situation.[17] (Translation supplied.)

BO YIBO'S ALTERNATIVE MODEL

Bo Yibo introduced the model of the Qiqiha'er Locomotive and Carriage Works in the year 1964–5, as an alternative means of revolutionizing enterprise management.[18] The core ideas of 'the Qiqiha'er model' could be found as early as April 1964 when the campaign of 'learning from the PLA' was launched. In military terms, the workshops, work sections, shifts, and teams were treated as the 'first front' of production, and the functional departments were taken as the 'second front'.[19] As the orientation was towards production, the lower echelons, and the masses, the functional departments were required to serve the needs of the 'first front' personnel and to strengthen their logistical functions.[20]

The Qiqiha'er model attacked problems of 'bureaucratism', such as procedural complexity, the overlapping of departmental functions, tedious and unnecessary rules and regulations, the proliferation of meetings, and large amounts of paperwork. Following the slogan 'crack troops and simple administration', an attempt was made to streamline the operations and structure of the functional departments. Problems that could be solved by one managerial staff member or one functional department were not to be referred to another staff member or department. Overlapping functional areas were to be minimized. By participating in manual labour cadres and staff were able to acquire the same level of competence as skilled workers in workshops.[21]

The Qiqiha'er model also stressed the overall reorganization of workshops[22] and centralized management, especially of materials inventory and cost-accounting in functional departments. As a result, funds and resources were made available for the use of needy workshops.[23] But this 'centralist' tendency was balanced by an orientation towards service in the workplace in the following functional areas: supply of materials, provision of blueprints and technical specifications, and payment of wages directly to shifts and teams. The abolition of work districts also simplified workshop organization.[24] There is evidence that the model was emulated in other factories.[25] Even during the Cultural Revolution it was treated as a positive lesson in 'managerial revolution'.[26]

Like the two patterns of industrial bureaucracy, empirically based upon the gypsum mine and its surface plant, which were described by Alvin Gouldner,[27] the Daqing and Qiqiha'er models show the relative success of organizational simplification, although in two entirely different settings on the eve of the Cultural Revolution. While Daqing oilfield decentralized power from its staff organization to its line organization (the work sites and oil wells), Qiqiha'er centralized power from the line organization (the workshops) to the staff organization (the functional departments). At the Qiqiha'er Locomotive and Carriage Works the use of advanced and integrated technology and the imperative of a continuous production process required close managerial and technical co-ordination between the functional departments, but had less effect in the individual workshops. At the Daqing oilfield, however, drilling sites or oil wells were spread out over a large geographical area and were much more independent functionally and managerially than their counterparts (the workshops) in manufacturing industries. In factories like the Qiqiha'er Locomotive and Carriage Works, where technical and managerial functions were integrated at the enterprise level, it was difficult to simplify the functional departments.[28] The manufacturing units of Daqing (the refinery and the chemical fertilizer factory) later adopted a much more centralized structure of command than that of the oilfield proper,[29] with an elaborate division of labour in the functional departments, making the Daqing case in this respect comparable with the Qiqiha'er model.

In theoretical terms, the Daqing model is applicable to the mining and construction industries while the Qiqiha'er model is better suited to the manufacturing sector. According to Andrew G. Walder, organic or participative structures of management tend to be predominant where the technological environment is not stable, as, for example, in the construction industry.[30] This also appears to be the case for the Daqing model. In contrast, more mechanistic structures represented by Weber's ideal type work better in routine and predictable technological and environmental conditions, [31] such as those found in the Qiqiha'er model.

THE ATTACK ON THE STATE COUNCIL

The Cultural Revolution started at the Central Committee Work Conference of September–October 1965, when Mao Zedong first raised the question of Wu Han's historical play, *Hairui's Dismissal from Office*, but the central leaders evaded the issue at the time. It was not until late in 1966 that political change moved from educational and cultural circles to the economic and industrial sphere. The State Council, which was strategically placed at the centre of the national economy, therefore bore the brunt of the frontal assault launched by the ultra-leftist leaders, such as Lin Biao, Chen Boda, Jiang Qing, Zhang Chunqiao and Yao Wenyuan.

It is reasonable to suggest, as Thomas W. Robinson does, that during the Cultural Revolution the State Council operated as a 'political arena'.[32] This situation could be partly attributed to the fact that Zhou Enlai allowed himself to be dictated to by any group of leaders who were in a position of strength. Zhou stated that 'the Cultural Revolution Small Group was Mao Zedong's general staff; the Military Affairs Commission was the headquarters of the Cultural Revolution; and the State Council served as an executive arm.'[33] Zhou's accommodating posture did not mean, however, that he was willing to give up his foothold in the State Council.

As a prelude to the Cultural Revolution, Mao attempted in mid-1964 to expand his influence over the State Council by restructuring and strengthening the State Planning Commission, which was headed by Li Fuchun. Firstly, the enlargement of its membership from 18 to 23 enabled Mao to place Chen Boda, his trusted protégé, in the Commission.[34] Furthermore, in November 1965, Mao personally recommended the appointment of Yu Qiuli as Deputy Director of the Commission, to assist the ageing Li Fuchun. Zhou Enlai stated that this was done in order to frustrate Bo Yibo's ambition for power.[35] Secondly, some of the powers of other commissions and ministries (including the Ministry of Finance, which was headed by Li Xiannian)[36] were transferred to the State Planning Commission in 1964. Thirdly, in August 1966, eight ministries which had originally been under the State Economic Commission, which was chaired by Bo Yibo, were transferred to the jurisdiction of the State Planning Commission.[37]

As Mao was encroaching further upon the domain of the State Council, the ultra-leftist leaders such as Lin Biao, Chen Boda, and Jiang Qing attacked Zhou Enlai and the State Council indirectly through an assault on Yu Qiuli. They are said to have mobilized the Red Guards to storm the Daqing Construction Exhibition in Beijing seven times in October 1966.[38] They blamed Yu Qiuli, Liu Shaoqi, Deng Xiaoping, and Bo Yibo[39] for arranging the Exhibition with a 'revisionist' theme.[40]

None the less, Yu Qiuli enjoyed the support not only of Zhou Enlai, but also of Mao Zedong. In November 1966, Chen Boda completed a report on the problems of enterprise management and formulated a policy paper, known as the 'Twelve Articles' or the 'Cultural Revolution in Mining and Industrial Enterprises (Draft)'. Mao was not satisfied with the policy paper and instructed Chen to send it to Yu for comments and revisions. Yu criticized and substantially revised the policy paper, which was later known as the 'Fifteen Articles'.[41]

But Lin Biao opposed Yu over the 'Fifteen Articles', insisting, in December 1966, that the scope of the Cultural Revolution should be larger in mining and industrial enterprises than in culture and education. Lin said, 'the problems of mining and industrial enterprises are in no way less than those in the cultural and educational departments. [In fact] they are more important than those in the cultural and educational departments.'[42] Yu did not incorporate Lin's view into the policy paper, however, and Lin therefore raised the issue and criticized Yu in a meeting of the Standing Committee of the Politburo. Zhou tried to mediate by asking Yu to make a self-criticism and to communicate Lin's view to the lower echelons.[43]

Circumstantial evidence indicates that the paper, the 'Fifteen Articles', was probably not implemented because of the unexpected 'anti-economism' campaign which took place in early 1967. None the less, Yu Qiuli's conflict with the ultra-leftist leaders filtered down to the mass level through the mobilization of Red Guard groups and the manipulation of the mass movement.[44]

Subsequently Zhou Enlai was forced to take the side of Yu Qiuli in order to resist the pressure of the ultra-leftists in the State Council. From January 1967 until 1968, Zhou, on at least four occasions, spoke openly in defence of Yu. On 10 January 1967, he defended Yu on the grounds that Yu had made important contributions to the building of Daqing oilfield, and that Mao had personally recommended his promotion to the State Planning Commission.[45] Zhou's true intention in defending Yu was revealed on 7 April 1968, when he stated that the function of central planning and the function of the Ministry of Foreign Affairs should not stop. At the time Yu was in charge of planning and Zhou took personal responsibility for foreign affairs.

ZHOU ENLAI'S DEFENCE OF THE STATE COUNCIL

In April 1968, Zhou instructed the State Planning Commission to carry out its duties with a clear order of priorities and in the light of the drastic reduction in the functions of the State Council. 'Otherwise,' said Zhou, 'it won't be nice if all the business halts after two [more] years of revolution.'[46] Zhou's reliance upon Yu probably derived from the fact that the latter was trusted by and indispensable to Mao Zedong. Both Yu and Gu Mu were in charge of Mao's pet project, the 'third front military construction'.[47] Li Xiannian was among the few who assisted Zhou to maintain the minimum, but continuous, functioning of the State Council and to take charge of finance and transportation.[48]

Under pressure from Mao, Zhou took pre-emptive action by voluntarily reducing the size of the State Planning Commission from approximately 6,000 members to 50. The new unit, called the 'Little State Planning Commission' (xiao ji wei), was in operation from 1968 to 1972. It was still headed by Yu Qiuli, who was supervised by two representatives elected by the 'rebel groups' within the Commission.[49] Mao, however, did not seem fully confident about Zhou's arrangements, so he again appointed Chen Boda and Gu Mu, among others, to be 'advisers' to the 'Little State Planning Commission'.[50]

As from 26 January 1967, military control was imposed progressively on the central ministries and commissions and the bureaux and offices under the direct jurisdiction of the State Council. Donald W. Klein's study of the attacks on the State Council up to mid-February 1968 indicates that, in a sample of 366 ministers and vice-ministers, 182 were criticized and, of 49 ministers, 34 were attacked.[51] By July 1969, 44 of the 80 units within the State Council were under some form of military control and, in the later stages of the 'revolution', were reorganized under revolutionary committees.[52] During the so-called 'January Storm' in early 1967, Zhou intervened on behalf of numerous ministers, including Chen

Yi, Li Xiannian, Yao Yilin, and Lu Zhengchao, as well as several vice-premiers, such as Tan Zhenglin, Li Fuchun, and Xie Fuzhi.[53] Zhou Enlai's strategy in defending the State Council was to take the matter of the 'seizure of power' firmly in his own hands in January 1967. He concurred in Mao's instruction to seize power in the State Council, but resisted ultra-leftist attempts by proposing a 'supervision formula'. He also advocated 'making revolution within the original units'. Both proposals allowed cadres and officials to stay in power within their own units, but subjected them to some form of supervision and criticism by the 'rebel groups'. Zhou proposed a five-category classification of officials, with each category liable to some form of disciplinary action.[54] Zhou's efforts to 'cleanse' the State Council left the ultra-leftist group with no excuse to intervene.[54]

Zhou Enlai was, however, also subject to abuse and pressure from Mao Zedong and the ultra-leftist group. For instance Mao requested Zhou to reduce his personal staff from 20 to 5.[55] In order to survive, Zhou made himself and the State Council indispensable by curing the paralysis of the railway and transport systems, and maintaining the operation of production units at an acceptable level. From early 1967 until 1968, Zhou Enlai and Li Xiannian were preoccupied with settling the labour disputes, factional rivalries, and managerial problems of the railways and harbours. Zhou personally intervened on 17 January 1968, stopping the Red Guards from seizing large quantities of ammunition and supplies destined for Vietnam.[56] On 12 May 1968, Zhou gave detailed instructions for restoring order to several key railway centres, including Shenyang, Zhengzhou, and Liuzhou. He also issued directives for settling the problems of harbours in Shanghai, Qingdao, Dalian, and Xinhuangdao.[57]

A different issue which the ultra-leftist leaders also exploited to attack the State Council was that of seasonal-contract workers. According to Red Guard publications, the system of seasonal-contract workers (or temporary workers) was originally borrowed from the Soviet Union after Ma Wenrui, the Minister of Labour, went there on a tour of investigation with Lai Ruoyu, the Chairman of the All-China Trade Union, in 1956.[58] Upon their recommendation, Liu Shaoqi initiated pilot schemes of the policy during the Great Leap Forward, when 20,000,000 temporary workers were employed.[59] The system was subsequently incorporated into the 'Seventy Articles' in 1961. To implement the 'Seventy Articles', the

State Council promulgated the 'Provisional Regulations Concerning the Employment of Temporary Workers and Staff in the State-owned Enterprises' in October 1962.[60]

The political controversy over the system of seasonal-contract workers can best be appreciated in the context of the disagreements between Zhou Enlai and the State Council officials on the one hand, and Lin Biao, Chen Boda, and the Gang of Four on the other. Circumstantial evidence suggests that the latter appeared to take advantage of the petitions, rallies, and demonstrations of the seasonal-contract workers and apprentices in order to put pressure on Zhou Enlai. Jiang Qing seems to have intended to encourage and even provoke the seasonal-contract workers and apprentices to make 'revolution' when she held a meeting with their representatives in the Great Hall of the People on 26 November 1966.[61]

As a result, seasonal-contract workers and apprentices flooded into the major cities, including Beijing, to stage protests and demonstrations.[62] Zhou Enlai was able to avert the ultra-leftist attack on him by making use of a decision of the Cultural Revolution Small Group to postpone the issues of wages, welfare, and promotion. Subsequently all organizations of seasonal-contract workers were declared illegal and they were ordered to stop their activities.[63] In 1971, however, after the Cultural Revolution, the State Council had to make concessions by converting temporary workers who had assumed regular duties into permanent workers, with the result that the percentage of temporary workers among all industrial workers fell from 12–14 per cent to 6 per cent.[64]

THE ANTI-ECONOMISM CAMPAIGN

Enterprise units were immune from the disturbances of political mobilization for over 50 days until Mao Zedong's return to Beijing on 18 July 1966, and the passage of the 'Sixteen-point Resolution' on 8 August 1966.[65] To reiterate the relevant points of the Resolution (namely, Points 12, 13, and 14), *People's Daily* published an editorial on 7 September which was entitled 'Grasp Revolution and Promote Production'. This emphasized that during the first year of the Third Five-year Plan, all peasants, workers, and scientific and technical staff should insist on staying at their posts. In the cities, the Socialist Education Movement was to continue, without a change of format. In addition, the Red Guards were not to interfere with political activities and managerial performance in enterprises.[66]

The 'Sixteen-point Resolution' contained ambiguities, so that both the Party and enterprise leaders tended to interpret it in terms of its emphasis on production and discipline. For instance, workers' spare time was filled with endless rounds of meetings to discuss the problems of production and daily life. Workers who wished to exchange 'revolutionary experiences' were transferred from day to night shift or from one workshop to another so as to make it difficult for them to organize political activities. When workers did go to visit other factories or to file petitions to the higher echelons of authority they were charged with 'wrecking production' and undermining the 'Sixteen-point Resolution'.[67] For a short period, enterprise leaders acted upon their own initiative and were able to resist the pressure from rebel workers.

The so-called 'economism' which surfaced at the end of 1966 and in January 1967 referred generally to workers' demands for some immediate economic benefits, such as promotion, back-pay, wage increases, and bonuses, as well as the grievances of the seasonal-contract workers. To a lesser extent, it was concerned with the requests from workers for leave and travelling expenses and from 'rebel organizations' for funds and facilities. When local authorities and enterprise cadres were attacked and discredited, they could not resist the workers' pressure and this resulted in some chaos.[68] The official explanation of the rise of 'economism' was that the 'capitalist powerholders' at the local and enterprise levels exploited the issue of 'economism' in order to divert the Cultural Revolution and to shield themselves from attack by the Red Guards and the 'rebel workers'.[69] The evidence cited above, however, does not show that enterprises, cadres, and managers had any such preconceived plan.

A news bulletin issued by the New China New Agency (NCNA) on 16 January 1967 indicated that the Shanghai Municipal Party Committee had 'conspired' to interrupt water and electricity supplies, transport, and harbour works in mid-December 1966. The NCNA alleged that the Party Committee in Shanghai had attempted to bribe workers with State funds, by means of promotions and wage increases, by issuing subsidies, and by increasing welfare benefits. Workers' travels to exchange Cultural Revolution experiences were subsidized.[70] The bulletin also confirms the claim made in Raymond Wylie's study of Shanghai dockworkers that stevedoring services were suspended until 8 January 1971, as a result of massive absenteeism among dockworkers.[71]

It is understandable that cadres and officials found requests from rebel organizations for funds, facilities, and housing in the name of 'revolution' even more difficult to resist than requests from individuals. There were reports of banks paying money to Red Guard organizations and the 'revolutionary rebels' upon request.[72] There were also isolated seizures of houses by rebel-group leaders.[73] This tendency appears to have spread to the agricultural sector as well, where it was reported that communal grain reserves, public monies, and property were divided up by the peasant households.[74]

When local authorities and enterprise cadres found it difficult to cope with the pressure of the mass movements they tried to evade their responsibility by referring workers' demands and grievances to Beijing for a sympathetic hearing and satisfactory settlement.[75] This increased the workload of the Party and the central government, but may not have represented organized resistance, despite an alleged conspiracy to 'transfer contradictions upward' to Beijing.

It is interesting that the top CCP leaders, from the 'ultra-leftists' to the 'revisionists' appear to have been united on the issue of 'economism'. For instance, 34 'rebel organizations' in Shanghai, led by Zhang Chunqiao and Wang Hongwen, put forth an 'urgent notice' on 9 January 1967 which encouraged industrial workers to stay at their posts and over-fulfil the annual plans. In addition, it recommended that travel permits should be revoked, expenditure accounts should be frozen, and the settlement of wage adjustment, back-pay, and welfare issues should be postponed. It also prohibited the occupation of public property and facilities, as well as robbery, theft, and violence.[76] On 18 January 1967, the finance and trade system, presumably under a 'capitalist roader', Li Xiannian, issued another urgent telegram of the same nature, and also made comprehensive rulings on many issues, including the duties of accounting personnel and cashiers, taxation and revenues, wages, bonuses and welfare, the property and funds confiscated by the Red Guards, banking procedures and the banking system, the restoration of harbour services, and the protection of State property.[77]

At the ideological level, the anti-economism campaign marked a return from short-lived syndicalism to Leninism. An article in *People's Daily* on 17 January 1967 suggested that trade unionism, as part of the tendency towards 'economism', led the workers' movement in the wrong direction by waging an economic struggle and avoiding direct assaults on the capitalist system. The article also criticized 'economism' for encouraging spontaneity in the workers' movement, and for opposing a revolutionary movement guided by revolutionary theory (and presumably by the Party).[78] Anti-economism thus entailed the restoration of established political institutions (the State and the Party), as the representatives of the workers' interests, and of their role in fulfilling long-term economic objectives. An article published in *Guangming Daily* stated:

After the proletariat has seized political power, the counter-revolutionary revisionist will display material incentives and induce the masses not to pay any attention to the interests of the State, the collective interests and the long-range interests but to chase after personal, temporary economic interests, thereby making people lose their revolutionary will to fight for communism.[79]

The Cultural Revolution started with an anti-establishment theme, but the anti-economism campaign indicated a renewed emphasis on established political institutions, including both the Party and the State. Until this point, Mao's name was closely associated with attacks on those who held power within the top echelons of the Party, but, paradoxically, his view was cited in retrospect to lend legitimacy to the leadership role of the Party:

Serving the people wholeheartedly and not divorcing ourselves from the masses for a single moment; proceeding from the interests of the people and not from the interests of an individual or a small clique; and being responsible simultaneously to the people and to the leadership organs of the Party; all this is our point of departure.[80]

THE SEIZURE OF POWER IN ENTERPRISES

Until the anti-economism campaign, the Cultural Revolution appeared to develop in a spontaneous manner, but the seizure of power that followed was directed by Mao Zedong through Zhang Chunqiao and other ultra-leftist leaders. It seems that Zhou Enlai, Yu Qiuli, and other leaders in the State Council were bypassed in this phase, and local and enterprise authorities bore the brunt of the attacks by rebel workers and Red Guards. Mao's policy-making style is characterized by Harry Harding, Jr. as a 'dogmatic mass-line', in which he authorized a course of action identified as 'correct' and steered the mass movement through feedback and policy modification.[81]

In January 1967, Shanghai again took the lead, by setting the pace for the seizure of power at various levels of the State and Party hierarchies throughout the country. Zhang Chunqiao's retrospective account states that, when he and Wang Hongwen were successfully counter-attacking 'economism' in January 1967, they reported to Mao on the seizure of power in Shanghai.[82] Mao, however, did not specify which organizational form the seizure of power in the Shanghai municipality should take, and this omission later became the source of his difference with Zhang and Wang.

Zhang Chunqiao and Wang Hongwen did not violate the 'Sixteen-point Resolution' entirely because some of its provisions appeared to give them licence to adopt a commune type of organization. For instance, Point 4 suggested that during the Cultural Revolution the masses should liberate themselves and nobody should monopolize and replace the role of the masses. Furthermore, the masses should be trusted and relied upon, and due respect should be given to mass initiative. There should be no worry about causing chaos. In addition, Point 5 suggested that the focus of the Cultural Revolution was the rectification of the 'capitalist roaders' within the Party, although it added a qualification that more than 95 per cent of the cadres should be united in Mao's revolutionary cause.[83]

The broad and vague provisions of the 'Sixteen-point Resolution' allowed very flexible interpretations of issues, including the commune type of organization. Consequently, Zhang and Wang established the Shanghai commune on the basis of 25 Red Guard and rebel-worker organizations, with other units joining later in January 1967.[84] The form of this Shanghai commune was, however, contrary to the Leninist view of a proletarian political regime, because it stressed spontaneity and failed to specify a definite role for the Party. On 12 February 1967, therefore, Mao had to intervene, asking, 'If a change to the commune occurs, what are we going to do about the Party?' Thus he suggested that, no matter what its name, the commune should have a Party and should not be a substitute for the Party. In addition, he registered his reservations over the anarchistic and ultra-leftist tendencies of 'doubting everything, and bringing down everything'.[85]

During the same period, the commune type of organization was also tried out in enterprises. On 27 December 1966, a Revolutionary Production Committee was first advocated and subsequently established in the Shanghai Glassware Machinery Plant. The committee members were elected by the workers themselves. The industrial workers were given the power to elect, recall, or replace the committee members, in contrast to the past practice whereby cadres and managerial personnel were appointed by the higher echelons. The managerial staff were redesignated as 'service personnel', eliminating such titles as 'chief' or 'director', in order to remove social differentiation between the bureaucrats and the masses.[86]

Despite their divergence of views, Mao Zedong and the ultra-leftist leaders such as Zhang Chunqiao and Wang Hungwen shared an anti-establishment sentiment, namely, an opposition to the functional departments. Mao retrospectively justified the seizure of power in enterprises after more than two years of chaos and turbulence when he spoke at the First Plenum of the Ninth Party Congress in April 1969:

It seemed there was no alternative but to make the Great Cultural Revolution, because this foundation of ours was not sound enough. According to my observations, still in a considerable number of enterprises, if not all or a majority of them, leadership was not in the hands of genuine Marxists and the masses of workers. In the past, there was no lack of good people among those who had command over factories. There were good people among the Party Secretaries, Deputy secretaries and members of the Party Committees. There were also good people among the Branch Party secretaries. However in the past they followed Liu Shaoqi's line, which was no more than what was called material incentives, profit in command, the bonus [system], reluctance to promote the proletarian politics, etc.[87] (Translation supplied.)

THE HEILONGJIANG MODEL OF 'TRIPLE COMBINATION'

Within approximately one month, however, the commune type of 'revolutionary production committee' in Shanghai was superseded by Heilongjiang's experience of the 'triple combination to seize power', which incorporated rebel workers and military representatives, as well as 'revolutionary cadres'.[88] As from 10 February 1967, the Heilongjiang model was publicized in the mass media throughout the country. The main theme of the experience was that those who held power in enterprises should not be challenged and replaced indiscriminately.[89] By the end of the same month, the organizations of rebel workers and Red Guards in Shanghai had adjusted their position and accepted the organizational form of a 'triple combination', coupled with an emphasis on Party policy and the State law, as well as the principle of 'making revolution and promoting production.'[90]

An administrative approach to policy-making reasserted itself during the seizure of power in enterprises. This featured a renewed emphasis on labour discipline, the established authority, planning, and rationalizing methods in industrial management. The Central Committee, CCP, and the State Council promulgated the 'Ten-Article Regulation on Grasping Revolution and Promoting Production' in early March 1967.[91] In addition, the former issued another policy paper directly to workers and staff members in industrial and mining enterprises on 18 March 1967.[92] Finally, the Congress of Revolutionary Workers and Staff in Beijing passed a resolution on 22 March 1967.[93] All three policy papers focused on the need to strengthen managerial authority, the fulfilment and over-fulfilment of production plans, the importance of quality control, the reduction of waste and costs, the improvement of efficiency and labour productivity, the making of savings on raw materials and fuel consumption, and so on.

In line with the formula of 'making revolution within the original units' which was recommended by Zhou Enlai, measures were taken to discourage 'rebel groups' and workers from engaging in political activities outside their established units as from March 1967. For example, at the Shanghai Steel Tube Works there were originally six revolutionary organizations which drew their members from various workshops, teams, and shifts and organized all kinds of political activities irrespective of work units. Many of these activities were therefore not co-ordinated with the units' production schedules. When the pressure for restoring order increased, these rebel organizations had to be recombined and adjusted in order to fit the boundaries of the established units.[94] Similarly, rebel organizations above the enterprise level were also regrouped according to particular branches of industry as, for example, in the widely reported case of the Bureau of Electronic Meters and Communication Equipment in Shanghai,[95] and in other cases at the national level.[96]

In response to the 'unintended consequences' of the simplification of functional departments and the downward transfer of cadres to the workshops from August 1967 to April 1968, attempts were also made to improve the morale of cadres and managerial staff. There is evidence that many purged cadres at the middle management level were reinstated,[97] since the promoted cadres or 'rebels' were not sufficiently competent and experienced to handle day-to-day managerial functions.[98] The reinstatement of purged cadres was in part a result of their demand for a 'reversal of verdicts' during the period from Summer 1967 to Spring 1968 when, as noted by Lin Biao, the progress of the Cultural Revolution slowed down.[99] The seizure of power in enterprises and the restoration of the old managerial systems and the purged personnel were basically concluded in Summer 1968, when the last two revolutionary committees were established in Tibet and Xinjiang.

'STRUGGLE, CRITICISM, AND TRANSFORMATION'

The 'struggle, criticism, and transformation' campaign was the last effort of Mao Zedong and the ultra-leftist leaders to 'revolutionize' the administrative structure and enterprise management before the conclusion of the Cultural Revolution. It was launched by Zhang Chunqiao, Yao Wenyuan, and Wang Hongwen in early 1968 in Shanghai, where it met with limited success.[100] It appears that both the Central Committee of the CCP and the State Council were bypassed. The campaign did not gain momentum until July 1968 when *People's Daily* conveyed Mao Zedong's message concerning the need to revolutionize the leadership team at both the government and enterprise levels.

The revolutionary committees at all levels were required to practise unified leadership, eliminate overlapping jurisdictions, streamline organizational structure, and maintain closer ties with the masses. These tasks were to be carried out on the basis of the model experience of Ling Bao county.[101] A close examination of the recommended changes in industrial organization reveals that the campaign was very similar to the process of 'learning from Daqing in Industry' which was launched during the Socialist Education Movement in the period 1963–6.

Yao Wenyuan published an article entitled 'The Working Class Must Take Full Command' in the second issue of the *Red Flag* in

August 1968, in which he urged the 'working class' to break the resistance of the 'bourgeois elements', to smash 'independent kingdoms', and to co-operate with the PLA in order to correct all erroneous tendencies and to settle various difficult and unsolved problems. Yao specifically recommended strengthening the revolutionary committees in enterprise units, conducting ideological debate and criticism, rectifying the Party and cleansing the rank and file, streamlining administrative organs, reforming 'unreasonable' regulations and systems, and transferring managerial staff to the production floor. The term used to summarize these principles was 'struggle, criticism, and transformation'.[102]

A long-term recommendation was made that training programmes should be restructured in order to cultivate a new breed of managerial and technical staff along the lines of 'the Polytechnics of Shanghai Lathe Works'.[103] In the short term, the 'Anshan Constitution' was advocated once again. Existing managerial systems and regulations were reviewed, with particular attention being paid to problems within workshops, the lack of communication with workers, and the constraints imposed on workers' participation. In addition, managerial systems were criticized for putting too much emphasis on professional work and undue reliance upon control and supervision.[104]

The policies and regulations proposed by the 'Seventy Articles' in the period 1961–6 were condemned. Liu Shaoqi was blamed, in very exaggerated language, for the policy of placing 'profit in command' and for advocating the 'closure of factories if no profit is made'. Specific provisions of the 'Seventy Articles', such as the 'five fixes' and the 'enterprise fund', were criticized, as was the principle of 'more work, more pay'. Differentiated incentives (that is, profits and bonuses) were in general regarded as undesirable in that they fostered wild speculation, unhealthy competition, poor product quality, and industrial secrecy, as well as creating a privileged class within the managerial stratum.[105]

Showing a general lack of understanding and appreciation of managerial functions, the critics singled out 'crimes' such as the unwieldy size of management, redundant staff, unnecessary meetings, and excessive paperwork, as part of their general attack on 'bureaucratism' (with reference to elements like 'red tape', 'passing the buck', and 'departmentalism'). Moreover, much criticism was directed at authoritarian leadership styles, such as the practice of 'control, check, fine, suppression, and [wage] deduction'.[106] The technology responsibility system, however, suffered the most severe condemnation. At the Shanghai Electrical Machinery Works, the chief engineer system was criticized as a system where 'the design department legislates laws, the technical inspection department enforces laws, and workers obey laws'. As a result, functional departments in charge of technology were abolished and replaced by a three-in-one research group.[107] A new form of organization known as the workers' investigation group was developed and played a role in identifying problems in the managerial system.[108]

The 'struggle, criticism, and transformation' movement lasted from August 1968 until the following year. At the Ninth Party Congress in April 1969, Lin Biao continued to push the movement into all spheres, including factories, communes, and schools, and to legitimize it in terms of the 'two-line struggle'. The 'two-line struggle' argument suggested that during the previous 17 years enterprise management policy had oscillated between bourgeois and proletarian 'lines' in four phases. Phase I was the period from 1949 to 1957, when expert-oriented management was installed, with an emphasis on material incentives and regulatory controls. Phase II, from 1958 to 1960, was represented by Mao Zedong's position in which he stressed the leading role of the workers, the importance of political ideology, and the commanding role of the Party. Phase III, which occurred in the early 1960s, resurrected the practices and policies of Phase I and witnessed the implementation of the 'Seventy Articles'. Finally, Phase IV, which commenced in 1966, was a revival of Mao's position during Phase II.[109]

This image of a 'line struggle' at the enterprise level presupposes the existence of two fully articulated and contradictory views of enterprise management before the Cultural Revolution. It also implies that there was an organized opposition which conspired against Mao Zedong, thus warranting the counter-attack staged by Mao. In retrospect it seems that, in 1969, when doubts as to the results of the Cultural Revolution were being expressed, 'political symbolism' which focused on the 'line struggle' lent legitimacy to the 'struggle, criticism, and transformation' campaign, and served to articulate the grievances of workers in the hierarchical structure of enterprises.[110]

THE RETURN OF THE STATE PLANNING COMMISSION

On balance, the radical phase of 'struggle, criticism, and transformation' tended to founder when difficult questions of managerial functions were addressed. Indiscriminate attacks on managerial staff and functional departments tended to result in the disruption of normal industrial operations such as the scheduling of production, regular experimental work, technical procedures, design work, and safety factors.[111] Moreover, reforms of outdated and unreasonable regulations and systems were frustrated for they frequently fell within the jurisdiction of higher authorities. On 1 July 1969, an investigation of a timber factory in suburban Beijing was reported in *Red Flag* with an editor's note cautioning against a careless approach to the reform of regulations and systems. Article 23 of the 'Sixty Articles on Work Methods' (January 1958) suggested that when an important issue of national significance was involved, recommendations of regulatory reform should first be made to the higher echelons. Only after their approval was given could the reform be carried out on an experimental basis. The article also emphasized that regulations and systems for industrial management should be evaluated in both a positive and a negative light, and not simply attacked indiscriminately.[112]

In the second half of 1969, the problem of morale among cadres and managerial staff reappeared. The theme of careful and delicate political indoctrination of cadres was stressed, and the 'liberation' of cadres appeared on the agenda.[113] *People's Daily* published an editorial entitled 'Pay Attention to Work Methods' on 5 November 1969, as a reminder to avoid 'ritualism' in ideological work,[114] that is, the adoption of new procedures without any change in the thinking of the people involved.

After the Second Plenum of the Eighth Party Congress in August–September 1970, the strain between Mao Zedong and Lin Biao intensified[115] and undermined the ultra-leftist leaders' capacity to promote their policy. In the meantime, the 'struggle, criticism, and transformation' approach, which was based upon the radical version of the Daqing model of the mid-1960s, was proving unworkable.

When the National Conference on Planning was convened in February–March 1970, for example, Mao continued to press for an overall change of economic institutions at the macro level. However, his intervention was largely counter-productive. The 'Outline of the Fourth Five-year Plan', formulated after the National Conference, produced, first of all, a drastic decentralization of jurisdiction over industry to the local level. The number of centrally controlled enterprises was reduced from 10,533 (46.9 per cent of the total product value of the State sector) to slightly more than 500 (8 per cent of the total product value). Secondly, there was a large-scale devolution of financial power, material supply, and capital investment to the local level through the 'big contracting-out' (da bao gan) arrangement. Thirdly, the taxation, credit, and wage systems were simplified. These changes weakened central planning considerably, disrupted the economy, and lowered economic efficiency and labour productivity.[116]

In June 1970 Mao Zedong authorized the establishment of the Revolutionary Committee of the State Planning Commission, which was formed by merging the personnel of nine old units, including the old State Planning Commission, the State Economic Commission, the Office of Transport and Industry of the State Council, the State Statistical Bureau, the Ministry of Labour, and the State Pricing Bureau. This new unit had 610 staff members or about 11.6 per cent of the number working in the State Planning Commission before 1967.[117] In September 1970, the State Planning Commission first attempted to establish its legitimate presence by publishing a radical article which emphasized the mass-line, the principle of self-reliance, the use of indigenous methods, the full play of local initiatives, and revolutionary management of the Daqing type.[118] Subsequently the Commission implemented a recovery-oriented policy of inventory-taking and account-auditing.[119] Yu Qiuli's position became secure with his appointment as Director of the State Planning Commission, presumably in September–October 1972.[120]

After the death of Lin Biao in September 1971,[121] Mao Zedong indicated his willingness to support Zhou Enlai in carrying out national economic tasks. Zhou pointed out the need for rectification in a conference of the State Planning Commission on 5 December 1971. Subsequently, the policy paper, 'The Summary of the National Conference on Planning for 1972', was drafted. The policy paper stressed the need for effective central planning, enterprise rectification, the restoration of the production responsibility system, the revival of rules and regulations, a change in the cadre policy, and so on. Because of opposition by Jiang Qing and Zhang Chunqiao, however, Zhou did not submit the policy to Mao.[122] In October 1972 the State Planning Commission drafted another policy paper, 'The Regulation of Unified Planning and Economic Management', in order to provide remedies to the problems caused by drastic decentralization after 1970, the uncontrolled expansion of capital investment, weaknesses in the wage system, deficiencies in the enterprise leadership system (that is, the Revolutionary Committees), and so on. The policy paper made 10 recommendations for improving the management system. It was presented to the National Conference on Planning in January 1973, but had to be withdrawn because of Zhang Chunqiao's opposition, although it was supported by representatives from 28 provinces, cities, and municipalities.[123] None the less Zhou Enlai, with assistance from Yu Qiuli, was able to carry out enterprise rectification on his own until Deng Xiaoping returned to the political scene and provided a fresh initiative, a topic to be discussed in the next chapter.

THE POLITICAL DIMENSION OF THE CULTURAL REVOLUTION

This chapter has analysed the rise of the preceptoral approach to policy-making from 1963 to early 1972, with special focus on the Cultural Revolution. In terms of substantive policy, the Daqing model probably contained more concrete proposals for revolutionizing industrial management than the alternative programmes recommended by Maoists. My analysis of the whole range of issues pertaining to industrial management suggests that the Cultural Revolution did not present any new and viable alternatives.

Overall, political and ideological conditions during the Cultural Revolution were probably conducive to the rise of the preceptoral approach to policy-making. The Cultural Revolution can be taken as a process through which political motives looked for an ideological premise and then for viable organizational means. The search ended in failure not so much for lack of an articulated ideology, but because the organizational means were unavailable.

The position of the first-front leaders was strengthened because the State Council and the Party Secretariat were effective in formulating and implementing the retrenchment policy during the post-Leap period. Liu Shaoqi's influence expanded as a result of his appointment as State Chairman in 1959 and his demonstrated competence in providing effective leadership and solutions to the crises created by the Great Leap Forward. To maintain his foothold in policy-making Mao was compelled to make his impact felt in industrial management and economic policy, first in promoting the Daqing model in 1963, then in restructuring the State Planning Commission in mid-1964, and finally in opposing the socialist trusts in 1966.

In the second half of 1966, the ultra-leftist leaders mobilized the Red Guards and rebel groups to attack the State Council, paralysing it and opening the door for charismatic leadership to enter into industrial management policy. Subsequently, policy direction was dictated by Mao Zedong's manoeuvring, in playing one group against another at the top leadership level, the institutional level, and the societal level, and in selecting the proper course of action among competing alternatives.

Mao was similarly careful to avoid a situation where he could be 'captured' by any individual or faction. For instance, he instructed that Chen Boda's policy paper on the Cultural Revolution should be sent to Yu Qiuli for revision, but he did not accept Yu's revised version either. Instead, in late 1966, he adopted Lin Biao's idea that the Cultural Revolution should expand to the enterprise level with a broader scope of attack. In the anti-economism phase of early 1967, although he did not follow Jiang Qing's move to mobilize seasonal-contract workers, he insisted on the overall mobilization of workers to seize power at the enterprise level. He authorized the seizure of power in Shanghai, but he did not endorse Zhang Chunqiao's specific format of commune-type organizations. Instead he endorsed the Heilongjiang experience of 'triple combination' as the model for the revolutionary committees. When the 'struggle, criticism, and transformation' campaign, which was initiated by Yao Wenyuan, ran aground in 1969, Mao began to allow the return of the State Planning Commission in early 1970 in order to curtail the extreme activities of the ultra-leftists. By the end of the Cultural Revolution, factional rivalry between the 'pragmatic' leaders and the Gang of Four became institutionalized in a check-and-balance system controlled by Mao Zedong.

THE DISCREPANCY BETWEEN THE RADICAL VISION AND THE REALITY

Ideological change also led to the ascension of the preceptoral approach to policy-making. Mao Zedong and the ultra-leftist leaders expressed views in support of the importance of charismatic leadership, class struggle, and mass-oriented activity. For instance, at the Enlarged Conference of the Politburo on 18 May 1966, Lin Biao pointed out the danger of restoring bourgeois dominance in a socialist country, and also the possibility of a *coup d'état* at the top leadership level of the CCP. Envisaging the final struggle between the proletariat and the bourgeoisie, Lin explained the centrality of Mao Zedong in the Cultural Revolution in terms of the 'genius theory', that is, the view that Mao had creatively developed Marxist dialectics during his long revolutionary experience.[124]

At the Work Conference of the Central Committee on 25 October 1966, Lin Biao suggested that there was a mass dimension to the political movement (the Cultural Revolution) which was inspired and launched by Mao Zedong himself, saying: 'Only the Great Marxist leaders such as Mao Zedong with his rich experience in [class struggle] and deep wisdom in Marxism and Leninism dared to launch a mass movement so revolutionary that it shocked the whole nation and the world'. Furthermore, from a long-term perspective, Lin added, ideological tasks were of paramount importance because of the enormous impact they had on the social, political, and economic development of the country. Finally, Lin asserted that the leaders of various units should have faith in the masses and not be afraid of the chaos created by the Cultural Revolution, in view of its overall merits in promoting revolutionary change.[125]

Mao and Lin Biao both believed that policy should be derived from a final and definite answer to the question of social development as a whole. Once that question is settled, they considered, all other problems can be solved. As Mao stated in 1971:

Whether the political and ideological line is correct or not determines everything [concerning policy]. The correctness of the Party's line means everything. If we do not have people, we shall get them; if we do not have guns, we shall get them; if we do not have political power, we shall get it. However, if the [political] line is incorrect we will lose everything we have. The line is [the] key link. Once the key link is grasped, everything will be in order.[126] (Translation supplied.)

Mao Zedong believed that he was the one who could discover the correct 'line' and the 'key link'. Lin Biao did not challenge this view when he promoted the 'genius theory'. In 1971, Mao provided a retrospective justification for the political conflicts with his opponents since the founding of the Party in the 1920s, enumerating ten 'line-struggles', from Chen Duxiu, Li Lisan, Luo Zhanglong, Wang Ming, Zhang Guotao, Gao Gang, and Rao Shushi to Peng Dehuai, Liu Shaoqi, and Lin Biao. On each occasion, Mao was on the correct side and his opponents were on the incorrect side. In his words, 'I have always been insistent in so far as the question of "line" and principle is concerned; I will never make concessions with regard to the important principles.'[127]

Professor Tsou Tang describes the political system which arose from the Cultural Revolution as 'revolutionary-"feudal" totalitarianism'.[128] The term 'revolutionary' here refers to the all-encompassing scope of the political and social transformation intended by Mao Zedong's platform. The term 'feudal' stresses the organizing element of personalized authority (or 'charisma'), which includes the cult of personality, patron/client relationships, and the embryonic form of rival factions which became increasingly institutionalized from 1966. This author suggests that the so-called 'revolutionary-"feudal" totalitarianism' can be appreciated in terms of the preceptoral policy-making approach, and that the movement 'back from the brink of the feudal-revolutionary totalitarianism' (as Tsou expresses it) was dictated by the alternation between the administrative and preceptoral approaches.

CONCLUDING REMARKS

The rise of the preceptoral approach was associated with the need to move away from the established political institutions (that is, those subsumed under the administrative approach), but it did not provide an effective and viable alternative. The attack on the State Council therefore moved the policy-making locus to the local Party organizations; the attack on the local Party organizations made the rebel organizations and the Red Guards into the organizational arms of Mao Zedong; and the deficiencies of the rebel organizations made it essential to rely first upon the military units and later upon the workers' propaganda teams. In the final phase, Mao's split with Lin

Biao, together with the abuses associated with the military units, made the return of the State Council (especially the State Planning Commission) an almost inevitable result of the entire process. The consolidation of the preceptoral approach would have required a corresponding organizational means; in the absence of such means the approach had to be abandoned.

This explains why, although the preceptoral approach was introduced during three phases — the anti-economism campaign in early 1967, the seizure of power during the period 1967 to July 1968, and the 'criticism, struggle, and transformation' campaign of August 1968 to early 1970 — each phase concluded with the renewed imposition of the administrative approach. We shall turn to the transition to the post-Mao period in the next chapter, where we shall consider the consolidation of the administrative approach.

PART III
THE TRANSITION TO
THE POST-MAO ERA

6. Deng Xiaoping's Policy of Enterprise Management, 1973-1984

THE next four chapters will focus on the changing modes of policy-making in the transition to the post-Mao era. The present chapter will be devoted to an analysis of industrial management at the enterprise level; Chapter 7 will focus on the managerial role of the ministries and bureaux, and on the problems of industrial reorganization; Chapter 8 will discuss the policy of enterprise autonomy in the post-Mao era; Chapter 9 will analyse the feedback to the enterprise autonomy policy and the subsequent attempts to propose an innovative alternative (that is, the tax-for-profit schemes).

During the decade from 1973 to 1984, Deng Xiaoping played a key role in facilitating the restoration of the administrative approach to policy-making and in strengthening the pragmatic policy tendency in enterprise management. Not only did he consolidate the framework of central planning and state ownership, but he also contributed to the return to a managerial structure in enterprises which was close to the Weberian 'ideal type' of organization (having a strong leadership team, responsibility systems, rules and regulations, a role for 'experts' or professional managers, a concern with technology, and differentiated incentives).

The policy tendency represented by Deng was embodied in two documents, the 'Twenty Articles' of 1975, and the 'Thirty Articles' of 1978. Both provided a codification of China's managerial experience and laid the foundations for the modernization of industry in the transition to the post-Mao era. Deng was able to forge a consensus and give a clear direction to enterprise management policy in 1975. Subsequently this policy was implemented through two phases of 'rectification' of industrial management: the period 1977-9 and the period 1980-4.

THE CONTROVERSY OVER THE 'TWENTY ARTICLES'

Deng Xiaoping's return to the political scene in April 1973 tended to strengthen the pragmatic group. After regaining his membership in the Politburo in August 1973, Deng rose rapidly in the hierarchy of power, from First Vice-premier, to Acting Premier of the State Council, and then to Director of the General Staff Department of the PLA by early 1975. From 1973 to 1974, however, Deng Xiaoping remained largely inactive in the area of industrial management while Yu Qiuli held responsibility in this area. Deng's entry into this area resulted from some complex developments in the field of meta-policy-making which will be examined later in this chapter.

As Acting Premier from January to November 1975, Deng Xiaoping sponsored the formulation of three major policy papers (known as the 'three poisonous weeds' after his downfall). Of these three, the 'Twenty Articles' (or 'Some Problems in Accelerating Industrial Development') addressed industrial management.[1] The formulation of this paper started with some *ad hoc* and fragmented decisions, and led to a comprehensive review of industrial policy. The pattern of policy-making was similar to what Amitai Etzioni calls a 'mixed scanning strategy', namely, a combination of a series of 'bit decisions' with a comprehensive review.[2] Deng played the role of 'troubleshooter' by organizing a series of meetings, including the Conference on Railways in March 1975 and the Conference on Steel Manufacturing in May 1975.[3] It was reported that a number of problems were solved. As a result, various departments and units requested a 'summary of experiences' and a more comprehensive approach to the problems of industrial development.[4] Accordingly Deng took a personal initiative, saying that 'it is inadequate' (*bu xing*) to solve problems on a piecemeal basis; '[problems] should be considered in a comprehensive fashion when investigating the long term plan.'[5]

The core ideas of the 'Twenty Articles' stemmed directly from a decision concerning 'The Task of Strengthening the Railways' made by the Central Committee of the CCP in early 1975. The decision was taken in the light of numerous major incidents throughout China in the preceding year involving trains. These were caused partly by a lack of discipline, and partly by factionalism within the railway system, local government, and Party organizations. When there was a deadlock in these factional rivalries, some factions would resort to stopping trains, thus forcing the central authorities to intervene and settle the disputes in their favour. After this pattern had developed, the Central Committee of the CCP realized the need to deal with the problem systematically. Deng Xiaoping found that the railways, which had a capacity of 55,000 carloads per day, operated at a level of 40,000 carloads per day, or approximately 27 per cent below capacity. According to Deng, the Central Committee of the CCP, probably including Mao, deemed it necessary to establish regulations and systems, and to strengthen organizational discipline.[6]

On the basis of this experience in streamlining railway management, Deng Xiaoping called for organizational 'rectification' (*zheng dun*) throughout state-owned enterprises on 5 March 1975, in a speech to a group of local party secretaries in charge of industries. Deng also pointed out that under the slogan 'grasp revolution, promote production' cadres would only tackle 'revolution', but dared not deal with 'production', a practice expressed in the cliché, 'safe in grasping revolution, dangerous in promoting production'. Although the performance of the agricultural sector was acceptable at that time, the industrial sector was far below capacity, especially in 1974.[7] Deng considered that the 'whole thing is a mess',[8] and that the overall situation (*quanju*) warranted a systematic comprehensive solution, together with long-term projections to the end of the century.[9]

The formulation of the 'Twenty Articles' was also guided by some policy precedents and tested programmes of enterprise management dating from the 1960s. An article by Gong Xiaowen (a writing group for the Gang of Four) was correct in suggesting that the policy paper 'was just a reprint of the discredited "Seventy Articles"'. Deng's supporters also stated that the 'document [the "Twenty Articles"] was basically a substitute for the "Seventy Articles" of the past'. Deng admitted on two occasions, in 1967 and 1972, that he did not follow Mao's line in drafting the 'Seventy Articles'. Yet in August to October 1975 when the 'Twenty Articles' were being drafted, he still insisted on the relevance of the 'Seventy Articles': 'in Industry there is a regulation [the "Seventy Articles"]. It needs revision but not abolition.' He added: 'the "Seventy Articles" is still good and also useful. The [Party] centre has not abolished it.'[10]

Deng's contributions could be further pinpointed in terms of the specific contents of this policy paper, for example, the need for regulations and systems, the importance of discipline for dealing with factionalism,[11] the need to strengthen enterprise leadership and improve employees' motivation, the management of technical manpower,[12] the questions of industrial safety and quality control,[13] technological transfer, and compensation trade.[14] All of these ideas and instructions were explicitly given by Deng Xiaoping during the formulation of the policy paper from August to October 1975. The available evidence indicates that the State Planning Commission, headed by Yu Qiuli, was responsible for drafting the 'Twenty Articles',[15] which underwent six major revisions and 32 minor modifications. Deng made extensive comments on at least three versions.[16]

In the process of formulating the policy paper, 20 'responsible comrades' of enterprise units and 12 high cadres of Party committees at the provincial level were consulted. In October 1975, the State Planning Commission reported that the policy paper was ready for submission to the Politburo, the Central Committee, and the National Planning Conference for discussion. At this point, however, Yao Wenyuan said that he had not seen the draft of the 'Twenty Articles' himself, and that 'it was still premature to submit the draft to the Politburo yet'.[17] In November of the same year, the factional rivalry erupted into the open. Thus the draft of the 'Twenty Articles' did not reach the top level of leadership for approval until after the downfall of the Gang of Four.

The policy paper, the 'Twenty Articles', which reflected a society rent by factions after the Cultural Revolution and the Lin Biao incident (see Chapter 5, pp. 115–18), was intended to tackle the problems created by the influx of new recruits into all kinds of organizations, especially industrial enterprises. The problems were aggravated as the Gang of Four worked against time to build a power base and prepare for a showdown with Deng Xiaoping. The document, taking an integrated approach to industrial management policy, dealt with a number of issues at the macro level: the relationship between industry and agriculture, the domestic and export economies, construction projects and capital investment, central planning, science and technology, and so on.[18]

The 'Twenty Articles' outlined the conventional method of management of industrial enterprises. This included the restoration of standard procedures for annual plans, a policy of industrial reorganization, inter-enterprise co-ordination, and regional co-operation.[19] The paper focused on managment at the enterprise level, recommending that the director responsibility system should be strengthened under the collective leadership of the Party committee, and that the role of functional departments should be emphasized.[20] In practice, this meant a revival of the chief engineer system and the chief accountant system.[21] It also called for the reintroduction of production responsibility systems as well as the re-establishment of rules and regulations. The importance of technology and research and the role of technical personnel were also stressed.[22]

The formulation of the 'Twenty Articles' was nevertheless constrained by political and ideological pressure from Mao Zedong and the ultra-leftist group. With reference to the restoration of material incentives, the document reaffirmed both Maoist policy and organic State Socialism: the wages of low-income workers had to be raised so as to reduce wage differentials gradually. It also suggested improvements to the collective welfare system, by such means as canteen facilities, day-care centres, health clinics, and maternity benefits. Though it did not go so far as to propose the return of bonus payments and piece-rate wages, the policy paper made the ideological point that the structure of incentives should be based on the principle of 'to each according to work'; and the possible limit to the notion of 'bourgeois rights' should be determined by the existing moral and material conditions of the masses. In this context, the notion of 'bourgeois rights' is concerned with the legal claims of individuals and groups in the allocation of the fruits of labour according to labour input rather than wants; it is taken as a remnant of a bourgeois political regime which has survived the Socialist transformation of an economy. In the Chinese Communists' view, 'bourgeois rights' should be eliminated only when a society is morally and materially ready to develop into a full-fledged Communist society, that is, having a general abundance of goods, an appreciation of the intrinsic value of work, and dedication to the public interest. In other words, the emphasis on non-material incentives (such as political consciousness, social recognition, and achievement orientation) should be synchronized with the higher level of economic growth and affluence, and improvements in education and culture. The policy paper also touched upon participation by workers in making and implementing annual plans, and in improving rules and regulations.[23]

SWINGS TO LEFT AND RIGHT

Deng Xiaoping began his fall into disgrace in November 1975 and was stripped of all his responsibilities after the death of Zhou Enlai and the Tien-an-men incident of April 1976. Before Deng's fall, and after his return in July 1977, industrial management policy swung to left and right, in two consecutive phases. The first phase was marked by a leftward swing, which emphasized the radical elements of the Daqing model and restored the 'Anshan Constitution'. The second phase was characterized by the revival of the main themes of the 'Twenty Articles', as well as the ideological controversies over material incentives, the objectives of enterprise management, and the criticism of 'military communism'.

Immediately after the fall of the Gang of Four, the Politburo, headed by Hua Guofeng, endorsed Mao's 'Anshan Constitution' on 22 March 1977, exactly 17 years after Mao wrote it.[24] When the 'National Conference on Learning from Daqing in Industry' was convened in April 1977, Hua Guofeng, taking an ultra-leftist tone, repeated Mao's view that the 'class struggle' should be the key link in all the tasks that were confronting the nation, and that the revolutionizing of the superstructure must continue because some production relations were still not compatible with the productive forces or the economic base.

However the Conference also had a pragmatic orientation. Yu Qiuli's speech stressed themes which were related to Deng's three policy papers of 1975, including the 'Twenty Articles'. Yu emphasized the need for enterprise rectification and the consolidation of enterprise leadership teams; the need for ministerial control and central planning; the re-establishment of managerial systems in planning, material supply, finance, labour, technology, and equipment at the enterprise level; concern with the livelihood of staff and workers; and the importance of the role of experts and of technical training.[25] Song Zhenming, Director of the Revolutionary Committee and Party Secretary of Daqing, called attention to the need to strengthen managerial systems and to tighten up industrial discipline.[26]

Yu recommended that, in implementing and extending the Daqing model, six standards for evaluating and comparing results could be used: (a) the study of Marxism, Leninism, and Mao Zedong thought, and an insistence on the Socialist path of development; (b) an effective leadership team based upon a combination of veteran, middle-aged, and younger cadres; (c) a well-disciplined body of workers and staff members; (d) scientific methods of management suited to the requirements of production and the needs of the masses; (e) the fulfilment of all economic and technical indicators for state plans and the achievement of high standards; and (f) the improvement of the livelihood of workers and staff.[27]

The so-called 'petroleum gang', composed of people who had been promoted as a result of their contribution to the success of the Daqing oilfield (Yu Qiuli, Kang Shi'en, and Song Zhenming), took full advantage of the 'Learning from Daqing in Industry' movement during 1977 and 1978. Yu Qiuli became a member of the Politburo at the end of 1977, while concurrently holding posts as Vice-Premier and Director of the State Planning Commission. Kang Xian took over the directorship of the newly restored State Economic Commission in early 1977 and was added to the list of Vice-Premiers of the State Council. Song Zhenming was promoted from Vice-Minister to Minister of the Petroleum Industry in 1977.

When Deng Xiaoping's return to power was confirmed on 21 July 1977 in the Third Plenum of the Tenth Party Congress, Yu was sensitive enough to detect a change in the political wind and diluted the ultra-leftist stance of the Daqing model. To do this, the State Planning Commission on 16 July 1977 publicly supported Deng Xiaoping in an article refuting the Gang of Four's assault on the 'Twenty Articles' of 1975.[28] The State Planning Commission also sponsored the publication of two books summarizing the Daqing experience from 1960 to 1978: *Investigation of the Political Economy of the Daqing Experience* and *Industrial Enterprise Management in Daqing*. Ma Hong served as advisor on the first book and as chief editor of the second. The two books set the tone of ideological reorientation with regard to enterprise management from July 1977 and beyond. (Ma Hong had worked closely with Deng Xiaoping and Bo Yibo in drafting the 'Seventy Articles' in 1961 — see Chapter 4.)

Yu Qiuli was not the only person who adjusted his policy stance and ideological position in the light of Deng's political return. Many writers who supported Deng went further than Yu and spoke openly on a number of controversial issues relating to enterprise management. These included material incentives and the objectives of enterprise management. In many cases they made explicit reference to views which Deng Xiaoping had expressed previously, mainly during 1975.

The wage system was one of the issues that Deng Xiaoping wished to bring to an open discussion forum, but he was unable to do so in 1975 because of political and ideological pressure. He said in private in 1975 that the principle of 'more pay for more work' should not be treated as a matter of 'bourgeois rights', and that piece-rate wages should be legalized.[29] In August 1975, a national conference on wages and labour was scheduled to propose a wage increase, but the move was aborted because of the Gang of Four's opposition.[30] No sooner was the return of Deng Xiaoping formally announced in August 1977 than an academic conference on the theme of 'to each according to his labour' was convened. The basic consensus of the conference was that wage differentials based upon the principle of 'to each according to his labour' did not entail any form of exploitation nor the restoration of a capitalist system in a Socialist context.[31] However the opposing 'leftist' view was also given considerable space in the press reports.[32]

By the end of 1977, the ideological debate on wages had shifted to an analysis of the 'concrete forms' of the wage system, such as the relative merits of time-rate versus piece-rate wages and of bonus systems.[33] At the Fifth National People's Congress in February–March 1978, Hua Guofeng urged central ministries to submit proposals for wage reform in consultation with local authorities. He suggested:

the staff and workers in State-owned enterprises should mainly adopt the time-rate system supplemented with the piece-rate system, as well as the time-rate combined with a bonus system. In addition, allowances should be made for those jobs requiring greater physical intensity and poor working conditions.[34] (Translation supplied.)

On 28 March 1978 Deng Xiaoping was given an opportunity to comment on a policy paper on the wage issue which had been drafted by the Political Research Office of the State Council. He reaffirmed the established policy that wage scales should be based upon the contribution of labour and technical competence rather than upon political attitudes.[35] In December 1978, Deng stated explicitly that the principle of 'more work, more pay' should apply to the majority of workers, recognizing that a minority of the 'politically conscious workers' could be motivated — temporarily — by something other than material incentives.[36]

The debate over the wage issue after Deng's return had the following main themes. Firstly, it was intended to legitimize the past efforts of Zhou Enlai and the State Council to restore the system of time-rate wages, piece-rate wages, and bonus systems (one example being Zhou Enlai's conflict with the Gang of Four over the introduction of piece-rate wages at Huangpu Harbour in October 1973).[37] Secondly, larger wage differentials were justified by economic growth and as an instrument of management.[38] Jiang Yiwei was one of the first authors to use such arguments.[39]

Moreover, the pragmatic leaders had not been able to define the objectives of enterprise management until Deng's return in July 1977. Before the death of Mao Zedong, both Zhou Enlai and Deng Xiaoping encountered resistance from the Gang of Four in their attempts to define these objectives in terms of profits and costs and economic accounting.[40] Deng felt considerable constraint in discussing the issue at a conference related to the 'Twenty Articles' on 4 October 1975, so he suggested that although 'profit in command' should not be explicitly mentioned, profit was still an important financial resource for the State.[41]

After the fall of Gang of Four, many authors tried to clarify the controversy over 'profit in command', but the arguments they used to justify profit were extremely circumscribed, citing, for example, 'Socialist economic accounting'[42] and the 'necessary accumulation' in a Socialist economy.[43] After the journal *Economic Research* resumed publication in January 1978, Ji Chongwei and Wang Zhenyuan wrote an article in April in which they distinguished between the 'profits of Socialist enterprises' and 'profit takes command', and between 'legal' and 'illegal' profit. They suggested that profit could be obtained legitimately by observing quality standards, reducing profit, increasing the range of products, and labour productivity.[44] It was not until October 1978 that Sun Yefang, who was among the first casualties of the Cultural Revolution, published an article suggesting that no matter what terms were used to describe profit (for example, 'accumulation' or 'cost'), it was an integral part of the material wealth produced by the staff and workers in the manufacturing sector. It was, therefore, perfectly legitimate to increase profits, which were a major indicator of the performance of enterprises.[45]

Once the 'forbidden zone' of the objectives of enterprise management was opened up, another issue, that of 'economic utility', emerged as a major topic in academic discussion. Sophisticated analyses on this topic were subsequently developed.[46] In view of the deficiencies of target-centred planning (production for the fulfilment of annual plans) a full discussion of the issue of contract-centred planning began in 1979. As a result, the principle of 'production based upon sales' became widely accepted.[47]

As noted above, Yu Qiuli and the 'petroleum gang' attempted to adjust their policy in response to the return of Deng Xiaoping, but they could not change their work style and ideological commitment quickly. For example, Song Zhenming, Minister of the Petroleum

Industry, admitted in his self-criticism after the sinking of the Bohai No. 1 Drilling Ship in 1980 that officials of the Petroleum Ministry tended to exaggerate 'will-power' in an effort to exceed physically feasible plans, and to emphasize revolution and sacrifice while neglecting the need for a strong scientific attitude. Song stated that 'in recent years, we have tended to substitute the subjective will for objective reality and to adopt some inappropriate measures regarding production and construction during past political campaigns.'[48] This resulted in situations where equipment and manpower were pushed beyond their limits.[49] In other words, the Daqing model was attacked as representing Mao's view of over-emphasizing will-power while neglecting the objective laws of economic development.[50]

For the first time the shortcomings of 'military communism' as a managerial style — stringent discipline and excessive egalitarianism as were found in the Daqing model of industry and the Dazhai model of agriculture — were openly attacked.[51] The mobilizational approach ('concentrating a superior force in the battle of annihilation') was also declared to be inappropriate to management and planning in construction projects.[52]

All of these criticisms appeared to point to the deficiencies of Mao's preceptoral approach in policy-making. In an article in *Economic Management* in 1981, Yan Fang identified these deficiencies as follows: (a) policy-makers' alienation from reality, ignorance of economic results, and lack of an analytical and calculating perspective; (b) the quest for speed at the expense of the efficient use of resources, the quality and variety of products, and essential maintenance; and (c) ritualism and the application of political campaigns to economic construction and industrial management.[53] These criticisms of 'military communism' and the over-emphasis on will-power marked the conclusion of the Maoist pattern of policy-making.

THE FORMULATION OF THE 'THIRTY ARTICLES'

Between late 1977 and April 1978, the formulation of the 'Thirty Articles' (or 'Decisions concerning Some Problems in the Acceleration of Industrial Development') represented the second phase in the restoration of the administrative approach to policy-making.[54] The policy-making process pertaining to this policy paper appears to have followed an incremental approach and to have adhered closely to policy precedents and tested past experiences. An editorial in *People's Daily* on 4 July 1978 summarized the origins and evolution of the policy paper, referring to the formulation and trial implementation of its predecessor, the 'Seventy Articles', as well as Mao's request for the revision of the document in the 1960s; the case of the 'Ten Articles' of 1972 (known as the 'Regulation of Unified Planning and Economic Management'), sponsored by Zhou Enlai; and the 'Twenty Articles', sponsored by Deng Xiaoping in 1975.[55]

It appeared that, in formulating the 'Thirty Articles', the State Planning Commission, headed by Yu Qiuli, made a 'differential adjustment' to both Hua Guofeng and Deng Xiaoping. In drafting the policy paper, the Commission seems to have deliberately avoided contradicting either Hua's or Deng's principles. On the one hand, the policy paper incorporated the ingredients of the 'Anshan Constitution', which had just been endorsed by the Central Committee under Hua's leadership on 22 March 1977. On the other hand, it adopted almost all of the major provisions of the 'Twenty Articles' advocated by Deng Xiaoping in 1975.

In fact, the 'Thirty Articles' were formulated after Deng Xiaoping's second return in July 1977, and the paper was first circulated within the Party on 20 April 1978,[56] giving Deng plenty of opportunities to make his views known and to provide input into the policy-making process. In October 1977, for example, at the Ninth National Congress of Labour Unions (the first held since the Cultural Revolution), Deng explicitly stated his policy stand on the modernizing role of the proletariat in large-scale socialized production, as well as the relationship of political consciousness to labour discipline.[57]

The 'Thirty Articles' adopted most of the provisions of the 'Twenty Articles' regarding the relationship of industry to the macroeconomic environment, covering the support given to agriculture, the development of transportation, fuel, raw materials, the strategic problems of energy and environmental protection, recycling, the export of mineral resources, and the importance of technology. Several provisions in the 'Thirty Articles' were derived directly from the 'Seventy Articles': the 'five fixes' and an enterprise fund, industrial reorganization, the policy of specialization and co-ordination, and distribution according to work.

The 'Thirty Articles' provided a comprehensive list of tasks to be completed in enterprise management, but it was not possible for the economic leaders in the State Council to carry them out simultaneously. Owing to the increasing influence of Deng Xiaoping, the implementation of the policy paper appears to have been concentrated selectively in the areas of concern to him, such as the re-establishment of responsibility systems,[58] the rebuilding of enterprise leadership teams,[59] the restoration of the chief engineer system and the chief accountant system, and the emphasis on the role of experts and technology.[60] Deng's emphasis coincided with Yu Qiuli's efforts to promote 'rectification' and 'Learning from Daqing in Industry'.

In addition, the 'Thirty Articles' marked a tendency towards a greater emphasis on material incentives, at a stage of economic development when workers and staff felt an urgent need to improve their material well-being. This renewed emphasis on material incentives was distorted by organic State Socialism, however, despite an awareness of the need to strengthen the link between differentiated incentives and efficiency and productivity. Thus, even though the six wage adjustments from 1977 to 1983 were explicitly intended to improve efficiency and labour productivity, the State in each case attempted to fulfil its obligations to workers and staff on other grounds, for example as compensating for the decline in living standards created by a wage freeze since the Great Leap Forward, counteracting inflationary pressure in the post-Mao era, and alleviating grievances amongst the lower-paid and more slowly adjusted categories, such as school teachers, administrative cadres, middle-aged intellectuals, and medical personnel.[61]

Moreover, egalitarian pressure and group orientation were strong after the restoration of bonus systems and piece-rate wages, which were intended to increase the differentials between various income groups and to provide full recognition for the individual's contribution. In May 1978 the State Council promulgated the 'Circular concerning the Implementation of the Bonus [System] and the Piece-rate Wages', restoring bonus systems and piece-rate wages in enterprise units which had completed 'rectification'. In November 1979, bonuses were restored for enterprises making savings on raw materials, fuel, and electricity (one of the original provisions of the 'Seventy Articles' in 1961). The 'Provisional Measure on the Piece-rate Wage in State-owned Enterprises' was promulgated in April 1980, following the conduct of pilot schemes during the previous two years.[62]

The development of bonus systems and piece-rate wages corrected the weaknesses of the system of supplementary wages (amounting to between 7 and 12 per cent of the total wage bill) which had been in force since 1963.[63] These weaknesses were manifest in tendencies described by the Chinese in terms such as 'absolute egalitarianism' and 'eating out of a big rice pot'. The implementation of bonus and wage regulations was distorted by pressure from organic State Socialism, namely, the efforts by the State and enterprises to fulfil their obligations to the individual and to ensure that each one received a share in the benefits. For example, the bonus system was abused throughout the period 1978–80 in order to supplement the wages of low-paid workers.[64] Many State-owned enterprises indiscriminately paid workers and staff 'new year bonuses' in cash or in kind. These payments sometimes exceeded two or three months' wages, and were often paid regardless of the performance of employees and enterprise units.[65]

After the circulation of the 'Thirty Articles', the policy-makers, especially at the central level, dealt with the problem of controlling the indiscriminate payment of bonuses. Deng Xiaoping, for example, registered his concern at a conference convened by the Central Committee on 16 January 1980.[66] In January 1981, the State Council imposed a ceiling on bonus payments: they should not exceed two months' wages or salary in normal circumstances, or three months' wages in exceptional cases. It required bonus payments to be tied closely to performance.[67] In relation to the total wage bill, bonuses have increased proportionately, accounting for from 3 to 5 per cent of total wages in the 1950s, 10 to 12 per cent in 1978, and an estimated 16 to 25 per cent during the years 1979 to 1984, when the policy of enterprise autonomy was in force.[68]

In line with the emphases in the 'Twenty Articles' and the 'Thirty Articles', organic State socialism brought about a large and steady expansion of collective welfare services and labour insurance in the post-Mao era. The total expenditure on labour insurance and welfare increased from RMB9.52 billion in 1952 to RMB153.82 billion in 1982. Collective welfare alone increased from 14 per cent of total wages in 1952 to 24 per cent in 1983. To make up for the slow increase in investment in public housing over the previous few years, expenditure by the State and enterprises on residential building as a proportion of the total expenditure on construction (productive and non-productive) increased from 6.1 per cent in the 1950s to 25.4 per cent in 1983.[69] The growth of collective welfare and labour insurance has tended to increase the proportion of dispersed, group-oriented, and indirect forms of remuneration.

TOWARDS ONE-MAN MANAGEMENT AND INDUSTRIAL DEMOCRACY

The policy of reorienting industrial management in the post-Mao period mainly took the form of repeated attempts to restore the policy precedents of the 1950s and 1960s, but very cautious steps to embark on entirely new policy alternatives were also taken. Even Deng Xiaoping, although one of the most powerful leaders at the forefront of the reforms, was not able to overcome organizational inertia and initiate entirely new policies outside the policy precedents, for example in the areas of enterprise managerial leadership and industrial democracy. In a speech entitled 'The Reform of the Leadership System of the Party and the State' to the Enlarged Conference of the Politburo on 18 August 1980. Deng recommended two policies which aimed to reorganize industrial management: (a) the vigorous implementation of collective leadership by the Party committee along with the responsibility system for individual administrators, and (b) the further extension of the congress of workers and staff. These two recommendations were made in view of the over-concentration of power within the Party and the State and the undesirable consequences stemming from this (such as bureaucratism, organizational rigidity, paternalism, extensive privileges, and the life-tenure employment system).[70]

With regard to Deng's first recommendation, Ma Hong reaffirmed the need to draw an institutional boundary between the Party apparatus and the enterprise unit. The former is a political structure, led by the Party committee, organized according to the principle of democratic centralism, and responsible for ideology and politics. The latter is an economic structure, organized according to the 'unity of command', and responsible for managerial and administrative functions. According to Ma, the previous practice of concentrating all managerial powers within the Party committee resulted in the personal rule of the Party secretary (or 'one-man management by the Party secretary'). This tended to weaken the Party's indispensable role in ideological and political work, impair democratic management by the workers, and undermine the unified command of the factory director over managerial functions. Furthermore, the dominance of the local Party organization tended to impede the full utilization of experts, the development of the responsibility system, and co-ordination across ministerial and regional boundaries.[71] Another article recommended that Party secretaries should not be permitted to assume posts as factory directors, that no administrative cadres, apart from a few high-ranking ones, should be incorporated into Party committees, and that a Party committee and a factory director should not share the same building.[72]

For the first time, a number of authors were given the opportunity to clarify the conceptual confusions and analyse the undesirable consequences of the criticisms and campaigns against 'one-man management' which arose after the Eighth Party Congress in 1956, the Great Leap Forward in 1958, and the Cultural Revolution during the 1960s. For instance, Wang Mengqui, in an article published in *Economic Research*, discussed Lenin's contribution to the shaping of one-man management in the Soviet context, and Lenin's position on the 'parliamentary model' of collective leadership.[73] Another author gave a relatively accurate analysis of the system of director responsibility (or 'one-man management') in its original version in North-east China during the period 1949–52, and the modifications introduced by the 'Seventy Articles' in 1961.[74]

In his speech to the Enlarged Conference of the Politburo on 18 August 1980, Deng Xiaoping proposed alternatives to the policy precedents concerning the system of factory director responsibility under the collective leadership of the Party committee (hereafter referred to as Party collective leadership). These alternatives included a board of trustees, a factory management board, and a factory director system under the joint committee.[75] However, these were deleted in the revised version of this speech which was included in *The Collected Essays of Deng Xiaoping*, published in 1983.[76] In the 'Provisional Regulations on the Task of the Enterprise Director in State-owned Enterprises', promulgated on 2 January 1982, the principle of Party collective leadership was retained. The Party committee was still given power over the formulation of policy regarding long-term and annual plans, and over major plans for technical renovation, wages, and technical education; it was also entrusted with power over the establishment, change, and abolition of major regulations and systems, as well as the reorganization of enterprises and the appointment of key administrators above the level of departments and workshops. The factory director was given exclusive power over the execution of policy and unified command over production and management.[77] In philosophy and in design, the 'Provisional Regulations' closely followed the practices of Northeast China during the period 1949–52 and the 'Seventy Articles' of 1961. Thus Deng's new proposals on the subject were set aside. Another policy that Deng Xiaoping promoted after 1980 was industrial democracy, an idea which he shared with Mao Zedong. Deng, however, was inclined towards an institutional form of workers' participation, such as the congress of staff and workers, while Mao advocated mass campaigns (see Chapter 3). The notion of industrial democracy — 'democratic self-government of the producers' — has deep intellectual roots in Marxism.[78] In his critique of the textbook, *Soviet Political Economy,* in 1961–2, Mao advocated the rights of producers in managing the affairs of the State, enterprises, culture, and education.[79] Ye Jianying took the same position at the First Session of the Fifth NPC in February–March 1978.[80]

As enterprises became more autonomous, as from 1979, their leaders became more powerful; thus democratic management was called for, in order to enhance the accountability of managerial leadership and the supervisory power of the workers.[81] It is surprising, however, that relatively few new features were added to the concrete arrangements for industrial democracy when the 'Provisional Regulations for the Congress of Staff and Workers in State-owned Industrial Enterprises' were promulgated on 13 July 1981.[82] Some issues remained unresolved, such as whether the labour union, a voluntary association, should be made the executive arm of the congress of workers and staff, which is regarded as an integral part of the management of enterprises.[83] Deng proposed several new alternatives to the existing system of Party collective leadership; others also made suggestions on modifying the congress of staff and workers. Both systems were tested in a series of pilot schemes sponsored by Ma Hong, Jiang Yiwei, and others connected with the Institute of Industrial Economics of China's Academy of Social Sciences. The available evidence does not indicate why Deng's proposals on these two subjects were dropped. Indeed, the 'Provisional Regulation of State-owned Industrial Enterprises' (dated April 1983) reaffirmed the structure of the factory regime of the early 1950s: the system of collective leadership by the Party committee, democratic management by the staff and workers, and administrative command by the factory director.[84]

THE SECOND PHASE OF RECTIFICATION

The theme of rectification was first advocated by the 'Twenty Articles' in 1975, but was put into practice in April 1977, when the 'National Conference on Learning from Daqing in Industry' was convened. From 1977 to 1984, the rectification of enterprise management went through two phases. According to Yuan Baohua, the first lasted from the fall of the Gang of Four in 1976 to the end of 1979, and was characterized as 'recovery-oriented rectification'. The second started in 1980, and was reform oriented.[85] Between these phases, in April 1979, the Central Committee Work Conference incorporated rectification as one of the four policy priorities of 'readjustment, reform, rectification and improvement'. Rectification, however, did not receive sufficient attention at the implementation level from the top CCP leadership until some considerable time later.

The State Economic Commission slowly began the second phase of rectification in early 1980, but it was delayed by the change of economic leadership after the exposure of the Bohai Drilling Ship incident in July 1980, and the promotion of Zhao Ziyang as Premier of the State Council in September. Rectification did not regain its momentum until the 'Conference on Enterprise Rectification' in July 1981 and the 'National Conference on Industry and Transport' in August 1981. On the basis of these two conferences, the State Economic Commission set six targets for rectification: (a) the building of strong managerial leadership teams manned by younger and technically qualified factory directors and deputy dirctors; (b) the establishment or improvement of the leadership system, reinforced by a congress of staff and workers; (c) the strengthening of the rank and file of staff and workers; (d) the establishment of systems of production responsibility, quality control, accounting, and training; (e) the fulfilment of State plans; and (f) the improvement of the collective welfare of staff and workers.[86]

Rectification began to be linked with economic reform in its second phase. The participants at the 'Conference on Enterprise Rectification' in July 1981 agreed that the establishment of responsibility systems and the strengthening of managerial leadership teams would enable enterprise units to overcome the problems of egalitarianism, to improve efficiency, and to increase financial returns.[87] In the Fourth Session of the Fifth NPC in November–December 1981, Zhao Ziyang stressed the need to introduce and improve the economic responsibility systems, to delegate power to the enterprise level, to give definite economic benefits to staff and workers, and to improve managerial and accounting systems. In addition, Zhao emphasized the need to improve the incentive system, to reduce costs, to upgrade product quality, and to enhance economic efficiency.[88]

In the first half of 1982, Zhao also authorized pilot schemes of rectification, to be carried out first in approximately 300 key industrial enterprises, with the entire task of rectification to be completed within two to three years. The task of rectification was accordingly assigned to central ministries and local industry bureaux, as well as to Party committees at the enterprise level.[89] The Central Committee and the State Council jointly announced the 'Decision to Carry out Total Rectification of State-owned Industrial Enterprises' on 2 January 1982,[90] for which the 'Report on Learning from Daqing in Industry', a paper drafted by the Party Group of the State Economic Commission, was distributed as the guideline.[91] A series of monthly conferences was organized subsequently by the Commission, from 1982 to 1984, in order to facilitate the 'exchange of experience' among cadres and officials at ministerial and local levels. The Commission estimated that, by August 1982, 9,155 enterprise units were undergoing rectification; they accounted for 55.9 per cent of national output value, 65.3 per cent of national remitted profit, and 58.4 per cent of State tax.[92]

Most provinces and municipalities started rectification in early 1982, and proceeded, group by group, to different enterprises. In 1983, after one year, the first group of rectified enterprises was ready for inspection and certification (*yan shou*). An enterprise would generally be subject to self-inspection, inspection by industrial bureaux, and finally selective inspection by the local economic commission.[93] In addition, enterprises which passed inspection would be rewarded in various forms, such as a higher percentage of profit retention, preferential tax rates, wage increases, and so on.[94] Yuan Baohua, the head of the Enterprise Rectification Leadership Group, indicated that, by the end of 1983, 1,163 (or 37 per cent) of 3,116 large and medium enterprises listed in the rectification plan had completed the task, and 7,388 (or 14.5 per cent) of 50,565 enterprises listed within the State budget had done so. Yuan estimated that 60 to 70 per cent of State-owned enterprises would be able to finish rectification by the end of 1984.[95]

During the decade from 1973 to 1984 Deng Xiaoping set the course for restoring the enterprise management policy of the 1950s and early 1960s, and laid a solid foundation for the return of the administrative approach in policy-making. In the next chapter, we shall turn to changes in policy above the enterprise level.

POLITICS AND POLICY IN THE POST-MAO ERA

Since the conclusion of the Cultural Revolution in 1970, and especially since the fall of the Gang of Four in 1976, meta-policy-making has, in general, contributed to the restoration of the administrative approach in policy-making. The consolidation of the administrative approach coincided with the first stage of economic reform (1979–83). It also laid the foundation for the evolution towards the economic approach in policy-making during the second stage of economic reform which started in 1984.

Three main phases of political development had some direct bearing upon the return of the administrative approach. These three phases were (a) the period 1973–6, which was marked by factional rivalry between the Gang of Four and Deng Xiaoping; (b) the period 1976–80, which featured the rise and fall of the transitional figure, Hua Guofeng; and (c) the period 1980–4 which was characterized by the dominance of Deng Xiaoping and his associates.

The first period, 1973–6, saw the slow restoration of the administrative approach in policy-making, part of which has been analysed above in connection with the return of Yu Qiuli and the State Planning Commission and Zhou Enlai's attempt to strengthen industrial management and economic planning during the early 1970s. This tentative rise of the administrative approach was blocked because of the rivalry between the two institutionalized factions, and the fall of Deng Xiaoping in November 1975. One of these factions was led by Zhou Enlai, Deng Xiaoping, and officials within the State Council; the other was the so-called 'Gang of Four'. Each was given a foothold at the institutional level and was assigned to a definite functional arena. Making use of Anthony Downs' terminology, we may view the relationship between the two as similar to that between an operating agency (consisting of the pragmatic leaders) and a monitoring agency (the Gang of Four) under a top controller (Mao Zedong). This power structure enabled Mao to minimize the distortion of the policy of the operating agency through the supervision of the monitoring agency.[96]

These two factions were institutionalized on the following bases: (a) the maintenance of a balance in appointments to key positions within the Party and the State; (b) a division of labour, with the pragmatic faction led by Zhou and Deng being in charge of the 'Four Modernizations' and the ultra-leftist faction being responsible for conducting the 'class struggle' (ideological criticism and evaluation); (c) a well-defined role for each, with the former having the power of initiation and the latter exercising the power of veto and reporting directly to Mao; and (d) support from well-defined constituencies (with the pragmatic leaders relying upon entrenched officials, veteran cadres, and professional and technical personnel, while the ultra-leftist leaders' power base comprised alienated elements of the establishment, young cadres, and those whom David Apter described generally as the 'scientific illiterate' — who do not share a scientific culture).[97]

The political and functional boundaries between the two factions were reaffirmed in late 1974 and early 1975 when the top Chinese policy-makers tried to implement Mao's 'three directives' and arrange Zhou Enlai's retirement.[98] In the second half of 1975, however, Deng Xiaoping started to encroach upon the Gang of Four's functional domain with the formulation of the three policy papers (later known as the 'three poisonous weeds'). This resulted in Mao Zedong's personal intervention in favour of the Gang of Four in the Qinghua University controversy in November.[99]

IDEOLOGY AS A POLITICAL TOOL

Hua Guofeng benefited from the anti-Deng Xiaoping campaign which began in early 1976. He was promoted by Mao Zedong to the position of Acting Premier on 3 February 1976 and to First Vice-chairman of the Party on 7 April 1976, immediately after the Tien-an-men Incident. After the arrest of the Gang of Four, he was appointed Acting Chairman of the Central Committee of the CCP and Chairman of the Military Affairs Commission (MAC) of the Central Committee, at an enlarged meeting of the Politburo on 7 October 1976. In addition, Hua Guofeng and Ye Jianying led a political campaign against the Gang of Four to expose their crimes of 'usurping the Party and State power', to investigate persons and facts related to the Four and, finally, to eliminate their ideological influence.[100]

In March 1977, Deng Xiaoping began to engineer his political come-back through a series of compromises with Hua Guofeng: Deng was able to reassume his strategic positions within the State, the Party and the Army, in exchange for the confirmation of the posts which Hua Guofeng had gained temporarily immediately after the fall of the Gang of Four. Thus Hua was able to hold concurrently the Chairmanship of the Party, the Chairmanship of the Military Affairs Commission (MAC) of the Party, and the Premiership of the State Council. Deng was reappointed as a member of the Standing Committee of the Politburo, Vice-chairman of the Party, Vice-chairman of the MAC, Vice-premier of the State Council, and Director of the General Staff Department of the PLA.

Hua Guofeng succeeded in keeping Deng Xiaoping in a subordinate position until the middle of 1978. To do this Hua insisted on a narrow interpretation of Mao Zedong's thought. This was termed the 'two whatevers': 'Whatever Mao says must be followed strictly; whatever policy was laid down by Mao must be carried out thoroughly.' Hua's stand therefore blocked Deng's move to improve his power position and prevented a change of policy and personnel. In addition Hua's associates resurrected the controversy over the 'two estimates', a view that prevailed during the Cultural Revolution, and which held that (a) the cadres and officials who had been promoted during the first 17 years, from 1949 to 1966, were undesirable and that (b) the policies which had been formulated and implemented during those years merited a critical re-evaluation. The 'two estimates' argument was employed to prevent or delay the 'reversal of verdicts' regarding purged cadres, potential allies, and supporters of Deng.

By the middle of 1978 the controversy over Mao's thought emerged as the most important question in the process of redefining the power relationship between Hua and Deng. Deng took this issue to an audience of military leaders at the Army Political Conference on 2 June 1978. He stressed that practice was the sole test for any policy or ideological stand. In his formulation of the principle of 'seeking truth from the facts' and 'practice as the sole criterion to verify the truth', he suggested that Mao's thought was not above this objective test, and therefore was subject to revisions. Any policy position could be right, so long as it proved to be workable.[101] Deng's position was reaffirmed in the Third Plenum of the Eleventh Party Congress at the end of 1978, which marked the beginning of the inexorable decline of Hua Guofeng and his supporters, from 1979 to 1980. The return to a full-fledged administrative approach to policy-making was hindered by political factors during the first phase (1973–6), and by the oscillation between left and right in the second phase (1976–80). In the first phase, Deng had to make 'differential adjustments' to Mao's position and impose self-restraint because of pressure from the Gang of Four. He consequently kept a low profile on such issues as piece-rate wages and the bonus system, as well as profit-guided management. In the second phase, after the fall of Deng in November 1975, Hua Guofeng and Yu Qiuli were able to steer policy towards the left by promoting the 'Anshan Constitution' and the radical tenets of the 'Daqing model'. However, as soon as the second return of Deng was confirmed in 1977, both Hua and Yu made 'differential adjustments' and gradually shifted policy in the direction favoured by Deng.

The third phase was marked by the dominance of Deng Xiaoping and his associates, whose efforts led to the consolidation of the administrative approach to policy-making, by means of the rectification of enterprise management, repeated attempts to enforce economic readjustment and industrial reorganization, and the centralization of jurisdiction over industry and financial power. The third phase also saw the rise of the economic approach to policy-making in the midst of economic reform. Although participation in policy-making during the third phase was fluid, and involved Hua Guofeng, Li Xiannian, Yu Qiuli, Chen Yun, and Zhao Ziyang, the overall direction of policy towards economic reform remained steady, in spite of various setbacks, unintended consequences, and short-term shifts of emphasis towards a policy of readjustment.

THE OPENING OF THE IDEOLOGICAL 'WINDOW'

The ideological 'window' was thrown open during the decline of the preceptoral approach and the ascent of the administrative approach to policy-making. This shift was marked by the waning of the cult of personality, the increasing importance of 'facts' as the basis of policy-making, and the diminishing role of ideology. Some of these features surfaced as early as 1975, one year before Mao's death. For instance, a key paragraph in the 'General Programme' of 1975 reads: 'We should know that there is no born genius in the world. Any leading cadre who is floating on the surface and divorced from practice cannot acquire the knowledge and ability to build Socialism.'[102]

After the death of Mao Zedong, Deng Xiaoping made a number of attempts to articulate a legitimizing ideology in order to redefine Mao's historical role and to justify the need for a pragmatic policy direction. These attempts were seen on at least three occasions: the Third Plenum of the Tenth Party Congress in July 1977, the Army Political Conference on 2 June 1978, and during the drafting of the 'Resolution on Several Questions concerning Party History since the Establishment of the PRC' from March 1980 to June 1981. However, the main thrust of his argument was first put forth in the 'General Programme' of 1975:

We must criticize idealist theories and *a priorism*, and persist in the materialist theory of reflection. Party committees at all levels should often carry out investigations, understand situations, and make concrete analyses. We must seek truth from facts and stand against reporting the good but not the bad. We advocate telling the truth [but] not lies.[103]

But Deng Xiaoping did not relinquish the belief in the infallibility of the Party and top policy-makers, an idea which was common to both the preceptoral and the administrative approaches to policy-making, and one from which the legitimacy of the regime derives. Thus, in Deng's words, 'Comrade Mao Zedong is not an isolated individual; he was our leader until his death. [We] should not exaggerate Comrade Mao Zedong's mistakes. If we do so, in painting Comrade Mao Zedong black, this would also mean painting our Party and State black...'.[104] (Translation supplied.)

Above all, the transfer from the preceptoral approach in policy-making to the administrative approach did not require the policy-makers to give up their omniscient and omnipotent role. Yuan Baohua, one of the Chinese central planners, believed that 'activities in production, technology and finance at the enterprise level should still be combined with requirements for the development of [the] Socialist economy through the State plan.'[105] Thus, the central planners still possessed the intellectual ability and the prerogative to discover and interpret these 'requirements' (or the 'economic law') on the basis of State ownership and central planning.[106]

This chapter has examined the organizational means at the enterprise level which enabled the return of the administrative approach. In general, the top policy-makers strengthened the institutional foundation of the administrative approach by relying upon know-how and methods developed in the early years (1949–52), the First Five-year Plan, and the post-Leap period. The next chapter will focus on the level above the enterprise unit and will analyse the centralization of industrial enterprises during the 1970s as well as the attempts to impose central control through the introduction of economic readjustment and the reorganization of industry. I would suggest that there were significant centralizing impulses, although there was an overall policy trend towards decentralization and enterprise autonomy, in addition to the use of economic levers and the development of a market-oriented economy.

SUMMARY

This chapter has examined the continual efforts to carry out enterprise rectification and the streamlining of management, which took place over one decade from 1973 to 1984, and which strengthened the institutional base of the administrative approach. In the post-Mao era, the issue of economic reform has received much publicity, but it was Deng Xiaoping's policy of enterprise management (also promoted by Yu Qiuli, Zhao Ziyang, and Yuan Bohua) which provided a solid foundation for the economic recovery from the Cultural Revolution and the Gang of Four era. Deng's policy also marked the completion of a full cycle from the administrative approach in the early years of China (1949–52), through the repeated but abortive attempts towards the preceptoral approach during the Maoist era (1956–76), and finally back to the administrative approach (as from 1977), before the trend towards an economic approach began in 1978.

7. Industrial Reorganization in the Post-Mao Era, 1977–1984

From 1977 to 1984, the programme of industrial reorganization at the macro level went through two distinct but overlapping phases. The first phase (1977–9) was recovery-oriented, and concentrated on regrouping enterprises and readjusting their economic relationships, by means of programmes of 'closure, stoppage, merger and transfer' which were applied to the less efficient enterprises and by the reallocation of resources to consumer-oriented industries. This phase tended to reinforce the administrative policy-making approach which was rooted in central planning and State ownership. The second phase (1980–4) was reform-oriented, and attempted to forge an economic network oriented toward markets. Thus it entailed the rise of the economic policy-making approach, and also suggested moves towards 'comprehensive urban reform'.

Industrial reorganization generally entails decentralization from central ministries and local bureaux to corporations and conglomerates, and centralization from factories to corporations. If such reorganization is reform-oriented, it also attempts to replace bureau-type enterprises with market-oriented management.

This chapter will first analyse the overall tendency of industrial reorganization and then focus upon two cases (one concerning heavy industry, the other pertaining to light industry) which highlight the impact of 'economic readjustment' and show that the crisis created by reform-oriented industrial reorganization led to a renewed tendency towards centralization. We will next consider the pilot schemes carried out in cities and localities that had implemented various forms of industrial organization, some as early as the 1950s and 1960s. Finally, we will examine industrial reorganization in the post-Mao era, looking at Changzhou, Sha municipality, and Chongqing, focusing particularly on comprehensive urban reform.

THE FIRST PHASE OF INDUSTRIAL REORGANIZATION

The term 'industrial reorganization' is used in various contexts with different shades of meaning. Firstly, industrial reorganization is often undertaken in order to form new economic ties among enterprise units (such as those relating to contracting and subcontracting, technical and administrative co-ordination, and 'economic associations' on the basis of contractual ties). Secondly, industrial reorganization is frequently intended to create new units of industrial production and distribution at various organizational levels. For example, several plants or factories (*gongchang*) may be incorporated into a general factory (*zongchang*) to take advantage of technical and managerial efficiency. At the economic and legal levels, industrial reorganization may form industrial corporations. These may include (a) specialized enterprises within a single trade or having common products and components or similar technical processes; (b) conglomerates of enterprises embracing different trades and products, but having some functional relationships in technical, production, and economic processes; and (c) socialist trusts formed on the basis of one product, incorporating several enterprises which are technically and managerially related, and having a monopoly in distribution.[1]

The first phase of industrial reorganization began after the fall of the Gang of Four. Its main features were codified in the 'Thirty Articles' of April 1978 and included (a) a loose form of contractual tie among several technically and functionally related enterprises or factories; (b) the 'dragon system' which linked a number of enterprises in a chain of technical processes, centring upon one category of products or services; (c) a processing centre containing several workshops or factories that performed similar technical functions, such as casting, heat treatment, repairs, the manufacture of tools and instruments, and so on; and (d) a conglomerate which incorporated a number of enterprises from different industrial and economic sectors, as well as from various administrative jurisdictions, provinces, and municipalities.[2]

Reorganization took place first in what were known as the 'five small industries' which were built prior to the Cultural Revolution. The five small industries (small steel factories, electricity plants, fertilizer factories, coal-mines, and cement works) were mainly rural-oriented. Their performance was quite poor, involving high production costs, low efficiency, low product quality, and high consumption of fuel, energy, and raw materials.[3] Of all the enterprises that exhibited losses in 1978, more than half were in the 'five small industries'. Three-quarters of the 1,400 small chemical-fertilizer factories in China were reportedly in deficit in the same year.[4] The implementation of the programme of 'closure and stoppage, merger and transfer' appears to have been rigorous. In Jilin province, for example, all small enterprises in these industries were either closed or merged with and transferred to other enterprise units, unless it could be shown that they had suffered only short-term losses, but had good long-term prospects.[5]

After the Central Committee Work Conference in April 1979, industrial reorganization was combined with a policy of economic adjustment: capital investment was curtailed, and high priority was given to light industry. Consequently, enterprise units in the machine-building sector which had suffered losses were closed down or merged. This took place at a time when production targets were being scaled down and the supply of fuels and raw materials was being reduced.[6] Enterprises which remained in operation necessarily produced less than their actual capacity and then found markets for their products entirely on their own.

In addition to having an orientation towards recovery, however, the first phase was guided by the goal of rationalizing relationships between enterprises. Accordingly command over enterprises was restructured from the viewpoint of macro-rationality and in terms of efficiency at the national, regional or sectoral level. Industrial reorganization was justified, firstly, in terms of the advantages to be derived from the economies of scale and the technical division of labour among various work units. Secondly, with its aims of specialization and co-ordination, it was regarded as an alternative means of not only developing more lateral working relations among enterprises but also reducing the total number of bureaux, offices, and ministries which could directly intervene in enterprise management.[7]

Thirdly, industrial reorganization was intended to attack a problem common to both 'big and comprehensive' and 'small and comprehensive' enterprises, namely, the tendency of each enterprise unit to be acquisitive and possessive towards its equipment and facilities at the expense of their utilization rate.[8] This problem was partly caused by the historical development of key industrial enterprises without support from an adequate number of auxiliary factories, as well as the 'third-front military construction projects' which stressed 'self-reliance' and independent manufacturing.[9]

Fourthly, the policy of industrial reorganization aimed to provide remedies to the problem of the 'territoriality' of economic activity, which was created by the administrative boundaries of ministries and localities and the vested interests that these administrative divisions fostered. There was a tendency for such bodies to erect artificial barriers to protect their own markets and raw material sources, thereby laying claim to the revenues and profits generated by the enterprises under their jurisdiction.[10] This was criticized as 'departmentalism' or the 'small producer's mentality'.[11] An editorial in the *People's Daily* suggested that 'comprehensive factories' would enable local cadres and officials to have at their disposal products manufactured in their own domain, regardless of cost, labour, and economic efficiency.[12] Audrey Donnithorne calls this the 'cellular economy'.[13]

Zheng Hai-hang, a Chinese analyst, suggested that the first phase of industrial reorganization was basically confined to the State-centred system of economic management. None the less, it alleviated the problems of multiple-headed command and factory 'comprehensiveness'; and it overcame 'territoriality' and revitalized the national economy. The main weaknesses of the State-centred system lay, however, in the concept of incorporating enterprise management into the State administration (*zhengqi heyi*), and in the role of the State as an 'enterprise writ large'. That is to say, the enterprise became an appendage of the State bureaucracy, and the State was regarded as a giant factory in which enterprises were simply workshops. The basic deficiencies of the State bureaucracy then tended to penetrate the corporations, leading to unified management by the headquarters of corporations, one single-tier accounting system, the 'six concentrations' of managerial powers, and a diffused and ineffective incentive system. The structure of specialized corporations, general factories, or conglomerates was likely to suffer from the separation of responsibility from power, their unwieldy size and bureaucratic complexity, and the jealousy of ministries and bureaux over their power.[14]

THE SECOND PHASE OF INDUSTRIAL REORGANIZATION

The second phase of industrial reorganization, which began in mid-1980, was reform-oriented. Its intention was to correct several basic faults of earlier policies (including some associated with socialist trusts which dated back to the mid-1960s). These faults included organizational difficulties (such as an over-concentration of power in corporate headquarters as compared with subsidiary factories, and monopolies in distribution), as well as a heavy-handed approach in forming conglomerates (for example, disregarding the interests of local governments and subsidiary enterprises).[15]

The State Council promulgated the 'Provisional Regulation of Promoting Economic Combinations' on 1 July 1980, and proposed basic changes in the methods of implementation. The forming of 'economic combinations' (ranging from a loosely co-ordinated form of contractual ties to a tightly knit conglomerate) should follow the principle of 'voluntarism and mutual benefit', and should avoid the heavy-handed approach 'from the top to the bottom'. It should also work gradually from easy cases of reorganization to the more difficult. Economic leverage (taxation, bank loans, and pricing) should be used to encourage the development of 'economic combinations'. When participating units were not ready for higher forms of organization (such as conglomerates) economic contracts should be used to forge economic combinations.[16]

The policy paper recommended that 'economic combinations' should take the form of a joint committee of representatives of the participating enterprises. It was considered that this organizational form should be flexible enough to encompass enterprises from different branches, localities, types of ownership systems and jurisdictions, while retaining existing channels of material supply, of marketing of commodities, and of administrative command. The policy paper also encouraged the development of a direct economic link between manufacturing centres and bases of material supply, and reduced the intermediary role of the departments of commerce, material supply, and sales. In general, the policy paper attempted to scale down State intervention and to make full use of the potential economic ties between enterprises, the development of which had previously been hindered by administrative hierarchies and ownership systems.[17]

The provisional regulation promulgated in July 1980 did not, however, seem capable of overcoming the organizational inertia and resistance which derived from the tendency towards 'territoriality' and 'self-reliance' (or 'comprehensiveness') of various administrative units. The State Council therefore promulgated another policy paper (entitled the 'Provisional Regulation of Developing and Promoting Socialist Competition') on 17 October 1980. Its main tenet was that each economic unit, sector, or region had its own natural advantages and disadvantages. The recognition of the uniqueness of each unit, sector, or region would provide a foundation for economic competition, an opportunity for co-operation, and an incentive to revitalize the economy. On the one hand, the market channel for commodities and material supply should expand further and the power of pricing should be decentralized. On the other hand, the administrative barriers of departments and localities should be destroyed: no department or locality should be permitted to monopolize the market for commodities and raw materials. The State should assume a mainly regulatory role, using economic leverage (such as pricing, taxation, loans, and interest), and employing indicative planning (through research and surveys, forecasting, and market management).[18]

In line with the two regulations referred to above the second phase of industrial reorganization proceeded steadily from 1980. By September 1981, a total of 1,983 conglomerates had been formed through the merging of 19,336 enterprises. These comprised 5.12 per cent of the total number of enterprises in the PRC. There was a higher proportion of conglomerates in the three major cities, Beijing, Shanghai, and Tianjin, where they amounted to approximately 30 per cent of the factories and enterprises in each city. There were also 3,400 integrated economic units with special forms, such as 'joint ventures', 'compensation trade' operations, 'technological co-operation agreements', and so on, which cut across regional and departmental boundaries, lines of trade and industries, and the ownership systems.[19] This policy trend has continued up to the time of writing.

Liao Jili analysed the policy-making philosophy of the second phase of industrial reorganization in terms of the need for a transformation from vertical linkage to horizontal linkage in economic management. Liao considered that horizontal linkage appeared mainly in the relationship of production to sales and marketing, as well as in commodity exchange. Horizontal linkage should ideally exist as a relationship of mutual benefit and competition among enterprise units. These were the basic ingredients of an enterprise-centred and market-oriented economy. Liao regarded vertical linkage (that is, the command of the State over enterprises) as undesirable, and a breeding ground for 'subjectivism', 'commandism', and the alienation of policy-making from reality.[20]

Horizontal linkage was intended to establish an important role for enterprise units in the economic system, enhancing their capacity to respond to changes in the market situation and varying social demands. It should also maximize economic utility with minimum costs. Liao considered industrial reorganization to be an effective instrument for promoting horizontal linkage. He envisaged the rise of an economic system in which enterprises would eventually become emancipated from departmental ownership (both ministerial and local), and become relatively independent producers in the field of commodity exchange. Industrial management would thus become market-oriented rather than authority-oriented.[21]

Liao was one of the first Chinese authors to suggest that the further development of horizontal linkage would contribute to the rise of economic centres, as substitutes for administrative centres in China's economy. These economic centres would emerge from natural economic networks, and would perform a variety of economic functions in industry, trade, monetary flow, pricing, science and technology, the exchange of information, and forecasting. These became the core ideas of the comprehensive urban economic reform which unfolded in late 1982 and reached its fruition in 1984. Bo Yibo, as a top policy-maker, stated in 1983 that comprehensive urban economic reform should foster economic networks centred on the cities and should remedy the problems associated with the State administration and vertical divisions, as well as geographical blockages imposed by local governments.[22] All of these views contained the basic elements of an economic policy-making approach, in which policy formulation is guided by preference (or tangible interest) and from a perspective of micro-rationality (for example, calculation and choice by enterprise units or by individual consumers). These views emerged strongly in the second phase of industrial reorganization.

INDUSTRIAL REORGANIZATION IN THE MACHINE-BUILDING SECTOR

The power to carry out industrial reorganization is derived from the direct command and management of ministries over enterprise units, and is, in turn, affected by cycles of centralization and decentralization, as in the five such cycles which occurred in the machine-building sector from 1952 to 1982.[23] The First Ministry of Machine-building (renamed the Ministry of Machinery in 1982 upon assuming responsibility for civilian machinery)[24] seemed to be generally in favour of central control over machine-building for such reasons as the economies of scale, the huge amount of investment involved, a product orientation towards national markets, and revenue implications for machinery products.[25] In retrospect, it seems that the cycles of decentralization were counter-productive in terms of quality control, labour productivity, cost reduction, overall efficiency, the improvement of product designs and technology, and control over capital investment. On the other hand, centralization led to bureaucratic rigidity and complexity and to the loss of autonomy and initiatives in the lower units of production.[26]

The machine-building sector was one of the earliest reported cases of industrial reorganization. The first pilot programmes were conducted in the automobile and agricultural machinery sectors in early 1978. Subsequently, the First Ministry of Machine-building convened the 'National Conference in Learning From Daqing in the Machine-building Industry' in August 1978, announcing a two-to-three-year plan of industrial reorganization to be carried out in Beijing, Shanghai, and Liaoning province (with Tianjin added the following year), and on a nation-wide scale within three to five years.[27]

The Ministry proposed three steps in industrial reorganization. The first step would establish specialized corporations and general factories along the same lines as existing industry in the provinces, municipalities, and autonomous regions. This would put a group of enterprises (or factories) under the unified command of one corporation (or a general factory) and thus solve the problem of 'multiple-headed leadership and dispersed management' by many ministries and bureaux in the machine-building industry. The second step was a further improvement in the division of labour and in co-ordination, on the basis of similar products and the standardization of prototype machines. The final step was the consolidation and development of specialization and co-ordination, with an emphasis on technical innovation which would raise the technological level for large-volume production.[28]

The Ministry made strenuous efforts to overcome the prevalent and serious problems in both 'small and comprehensive enterprises' and 'big and comprehensive enterprises', especially in such functions as casting, smelting, and heat-treatment.[29] A number of cases show that tangible results could be achieved by regrouping and incorporating technical processing jobs into larger and more efficient centres, as in Nanjing[30] and Tianjin.[31]

The policy of industrial reorganization began to receive a new impetus in 1979 from the policy of economic readjustment. The shortage of fuel and raw materials and the decrease in overall production had caused idleness in the production capacity of the machine-building sector. As a result, many machine-building enterprises were transferred or even closed down. Enterprises that wished to avoid 'closure and stoppage' found that they had no alternative but to accept merger and transfer.[32] Through the scaling down of production targets, many machine-building enterprises acquired *de facto* autonomy, that is, they formulated their own supplementary production plans and found a market for their own products. One such enterprise was the Niningjiang Lathe Factory in Sichuan which maintained an average output of 1,075 sets from 1979 to 1981, and relied mainly upon its own marketing channels; yet the annual production target set by the factory's superiors was about 200 sets.[33]

In the second phase of industrial reorganization, which began in 1980, the Ministry endeavoured to strengthen lateral economic ties between enterprise units and also to organize various conglomerates. By 1983, the number of conglomerates had reached 498. In addition, the Ministry initiated a pilot scheme of joint corporations of industry and commerce and entrusted them with the authority to conduct foreign trade: there were 32 such units in 1982 and 103 in 1983. Basically, all of these conglomerates followed the provisional regulation promulgated in July 1980, which promoted 'economic combinations'; they were organized into enterprises from different departments and localities.[34] Some of them were sponsored by the Ministry, but others were started by the participating enterprises.

During the second phase of industrial reorganization, a socialist-trust type of conglomerate was restored, despite its deficiencies, as found in the 1960s. Following the precedent of the China Automobile Industrial Corporation (1964–6), for example, a new conglomerate with the same name was started by the Second Automobile Manufacturing Works in 1978, endorsed by Hubei provincial authorities in 1979, and finally established in April 1981. This conglomerate was then named the Tung Fong Automobile Industrial Joint Corporation, embracing 66 factories and 113 components-and-parts factories in 18 provinces, cities, and autonomous regions.[35] It was subsequently absorbed into China's Automobile Industrial Corporation in May 1982.[36]

The China Automobile Industrial Corporation was organized on the basis of a report filed by the State Machine-building

Commission,[37] headed by Bo Yibo. It acquired the main features of a socialist trust, namely the monopolistic nature and a high concentration of managerial powers (in materials supplies, production, marketing, personnel, finance, and inventory control). The corporation modified the 1964–6 version, however, and achieved some organizational flexibility by building a network of relationships with subcontracted factories (in the areas of material supplies, the production of parts and components, marketing, and sales). It also maintained a profit-sharing scheme with subsidiary units when they were not ready to sever administrative ties with their supervising authorities. This corporation was managed by a board of trustees under the guidance of the newly established Ministry of Machinery, which had replaced the old General Bureau of Automobiles and incorporated almost all automobile factories and corporations in China.[38]

INDUSTRIAL REORGANIZATION IN THE LIGHT INDUSTRY SECTOR

The light industry sector benefited from economic readjustment after the Central Committee Work Conference in April 1979, while the machine-building industry suffered a severe cut in its financial appropriation and investment funds. At the National Conference of Planning in November 1979, the light industry sector was given 'six priorities': the supply of raw materials, fuel, and electricity, funds for renovations and technical reconstruction, the financing of capital investment and bank loans, foreign exchange, the importation of technology, and transport facilities. As a result, the total product value of the light industry sector rose by 14.3 per cent from 1979 to 1980, 10.6 per cent from 1980 to 1981, and 8 per cent from 1981 to 1982. The balance between light industry and heavy industry changed from a ratio of 43.7:56.3 in 1979 to 50.6:49.4 by 1982.[39]

Because of the wide variety of products in the light industry sector (which includes sugar, tobacco, paper, soap, salt, and matches, as well as chinaware, canned food, and leather products), the economic imperative to achieve economies of scale is not as strong as in the heavy industrial sector. The policy of industrial reorganization therefore emphasized the linking of production to marketing and export rather than the amalgamation of small units into large ones. In addition, after the Third Plenum of the Eleventh Party Congress in December 1978, the Ministry of Light Industry retained its role of providing policy directives and guidance as well as long-term planning, but allowed local governments to manage enterprise units and to co-ordinate key functions such as material supplies, marketing and sales, production, personnel, finance, and inventory. In the meantime, the Ministry went through a 'hiving-off' process, creating a number of new corporations to take charge of production and distribution directly.[40]

There were basically four types of management in light industry. The policy of industrial reorganization was tailored to the specific context of each type. The first type covered collectively owned enterprises within the second light industrial sector. This sector was reorganized according to the kinds of products and the lines of business within a single collective ownership system. The second type was a kind of specialized corporation providing services in research and development, overall planning, and the exchange of experiences, such as the Industrial Craft and Fine Art Corporation which was under the jurisdiction of the Ministry. The third type was a two-tier managerial system allowing both the Ministry and local governments to form corporations in the same functional area. The General Salt Corporation of China, established in February 1980, and the General Corporation of Light Industrial Machinery of China were two examples of this type of nationally oriented corporation. At this time also, corporations specializing in a single product were established at the local level. The fourth type was the monopoly type of corporation (or the socialist trust), such as the General Corporation of Tobacco which was established in January 1982.[41]

Like the machine-building sector, the light industry sector experienced an increase in State control and centralization, and a return to the administrative policy-making approach in response to the revenue crisis and the 'market anarchy' which began in 1980. The case described below fully illustrates the contention that reform-related crises tended to reinforce the restoration of the administrative policy-making approach.

Upon the recommendation of the Ministry of Light Industry in May 1981, and on the basis of attempts made in 1964 and 1978, the State Council authorized the establishment of the China General Corporation of Tobacco in January 1982. The Corporation was given power over the cultivation and procurement of tobacco and the production and distribution of tobacco products throughout the country.[42] In other words, the function of the Corporation was extended in both backward (namely, cultivation and procurement) and forward (that is, wholesale) directions. Furthermore, the Corporation was organized with a highly centralized structure, having the 'six concentrations' of power: in material supplies, production, sales, personnel, finance, and inventory.[43]

Although the General Corporation had a relatively large amount of power, local governments were still permitted to engage in the tobacco business and therefore to claim part of the revenue from the business. As from early 1983, competition between the central and the local levels for a share of the tobacco business became intense. Despite an increase in tobacco production of 10.8 per cent over the preceding year, both taxation and the profits remitted decreased substantially. In a total of 84 'budgetary' tobacco enterprises (that is, those whose income would be taken into account by the Ministry of Finance when calculating State revenues, as opposed to 'extra-budgetary' enterprises whose profits would be at the disposal of local governments), the rate of profit decreased by 10.8 per cent or 230 million *yuan*, and the number of enterprises registering a deficit rose from 14 to 23.[44]

In July 1983, a report filed by the State Pricing Bureau and the China General Corporation of Tobacco stressed that a substantial amount of tax and profit was being lost as a result of the price-cutting competition between budgetary and extra-budgetary tobacco enterprises. It therefore recommended a system of unified price control and planned production of tobacco.[45] Following this report, in September 1983, the State Council promulgated the 'Regulation of Tobacco Monopoly' which set up the State Tobacco Bureau and strengthened the monopolistic characteristics of the China General Corporation of Tobacco. This move was one step closer to the organizational form of a socialist trust, as originally proposed in the 1960s.[46] However, the implementation of the regulation encountered the same problems as were faced in the establishment of socialist trusts, namely, strong resistance from local governments. For approximately one year from September 1983, many local governments would not allow the transfer of jurisdiction over local tobacco industries to the China General Corporation of Tobacco. These local industries were subsidized by local governments and were allowed to compete with the Corporation through extraordinarily low prices. The State Council therefore requested the closure and stoppage of these local tobacco factories in July 1984.[47]

The foregoing analysis suggests that the restoration of the socialist-trust type of conglomerate was partly a response to 'anarchy' in the market-place. This was also true in the bicycle industry, where industrial reorganization was used to impose central control to curb overproduction during the years 1978–83.[48]

PILOT SCHEMES IN THE MAJOR CITIES AND PROVINCES

In China, each local government had direct command over and management of a number of industrial enterprises and could, therefore, carry out the task of industrial reorganization. During the post-Mao era, pilot schemes were conducted in several cities which had previously undergone industrial reorganization, including Shanghai, Beijing, Tianjian, and Liaoning.

Shanghai experienced several cycles of centralization and decentralization. After Mao's death, the Shanghai municipal authorities controlled a large number of industrial enterprises[49] compared with those under central control in the city. In addition, Shanghai maintained its prominence among China's industrial cities from the 1950s to the 1980s mainly by means of four major periods of industrial reorganization, in the years 1956–7, 1958–9, 1962–5, and, lastly, 1978–84 (that is, the post-Mao era).[50]

In the post-Mao era, Shanghai organized 42 industrial corporations which embraced 2,256 enterprise units under the jurisdiction of 12 industrial bureaux; they comprised 33 per cent of the enterprise units in the city, or two-thirds of the total product value in the industrial sector. They may be classified into four basic types. Firstly, there were specialized industrial corporations which were formed on the basis of similar types of products, work processes, technology, and parts and components; secondly, there were conglomerates organized on the basis of products which were technically related by extending both forward and backward linkages; thirdly, there were corporations which combined industrial production with marketing and trade; and fourthly, there were service-oriented corporations which carried out such functions as repairs and packing. Most of these corporations or conglomerates were administrative units which did not enjoy enterprise status (that is, they were not independent accounting units). There were no significant lateral ties between corporations from different bureaux and the division of labour between enterprises was restricted to enterprises within the same bureau. Industrial reorganization in the post-Mao era resulted in some adjustment in the balance between light industry and heavy industry, with a new ratio of 52.6:47.4 in 1981.[51] Shanghai's pilot schemes of industrial reorganization contain both new and old elements. The Shanghai Hua-sheng Electrical Fan General Factory, for instance, was formed in the period 1979–80 by incorporating three State-owned factories and six collectively owned factories into one entity through negotiation and contractual arrangements. The General Factory was considered to be readjustment-oriented since it entailed a change of emphasis of investment policy to consumer-oriented light industry. It was also reform-oriented in the sense that it accommodated two types of ownership system, broke administrative boundaries, and promoted a viable form of enterprise which was oriented towards market demand.[52]

There were, however, indications of 'regression' and of retreat from reform. The formation of the Gaoqiao Petroleum Chemical General Corporation, for example, was an attempt to establish a socialist trust. In 1981–2, eight technically related enterprises (plus one research institute), which had been administered by five ministries and four local bureaux, were incorporated into the newly founded Corporation through the direct and 'heavy-handed' intervention of the State Council. The General Corporation was formed in order to take full advantage of managerial and technical co-ordination among units which were geographically close to each other. It was given considerable monopoly over petroleum products within the area, and was organized with a high degree of concentration of managerial and technical powers.[53] In contrast, the China Nanjing Radio Corporation (formed in 1981) was established through a more moderate 'economic method', involving persuasion, negotiation, and voluntary participation; it incorporated 38 factories and one research institute into a relatively decentralized management structure.[54]

Shanghai was exemplary in forging inter-regional economic combinations through the development of compensation trade, joint ventures, and joint production, co-operation between supplies and sales, and the formation of conglomerates. By 1983, 240 similar projects were reported. Shanghai also provided 1,100 projects of technological transfers, 1,800 technical consultancy projects, and 1,500 new-product trials.[55] A joint venture between the Food Processing Industrial Corporation of Shanghai Light Industrial Bureau and Ming-sui county of Heilongjiang province to manufacture confectionery was launched in 1981. Within a profit-sharing scheme, the Shanghai bureau provided blueprints, technical training, recipes, the design of the assembly lines, the quality control procedure, and specialized equipment. The county provided floor space and raw materials. The factory had a production capacity of 4,000 tons, and an estimated annual profit of 2 million *yuan*.[56]

Industrial reorganization in Beijing began in April 1978, earlier than in most other localities, and concentrated upon economic readjustment. By the second half of 1979, 446 enterprise units were organized into 75 specialized corporations and general factories under the jurisdiction of the relevant industrial bureaux. At that time, the main emphasis was on the most marketable products (or well-known brand-names), such as sewing-machines, metal furniture, electronic appliances, calculators, television sets, and so on. Industrial reorganization in Beijing did not follow the linear development of increasing the size of a corporation, but, instead, some large corporations were divided and reorganized into small and efficient units.[57]

Liaoning province also organized socialist trusts in the 1960s. At that time, 12 industrial and transport corporations were formed, embracing 120 provincial enterprises and 88,000 employees (or 20 per cent of the total), and constituting 17 per cent of the total product value of the province.[58] After 1979, the province restored and established 162 specialized corporations, 65 general factories, 329 conglomerates, and 31 joint research and development centres.[59] The number of 'comprehensive factories' was also considerably reduced. For example, in the field of electronic machinery, the percentage of 'comprehensive factories' dropped from 80 per cent to 52 per cent; in the field of electronic plating, 78 out of 178 units were closed down. In Liaoning there was an emphasis on forming research and development centres in order to build a link between research activity and production.[60]

Tianjin was also one of the four experimental localities which dated back to the 1960s. In the early 1960s, Tianjin built a number of socialist trusts in the areas of machine tools, paper manufacturing, the dyeing and printing of textiles, and plastics. These socialist trusts were closed down during the Cultural Revolution but were gradually restored after 1970. Approximately 80 corporations of the bureau type were formed from 1978 onwards, and some of them were converted into socialist-trust type corporations. On the whole, Tianjin's case reflected a change in policy emphasis in the second phase of industrial organization after 1980, namely, towards implementation from the bottom to the top, the principle of voluntarism and mutual benefit, a decentralized management structure, and flexibility in incorporating enterprises from different administrative jurisdictions, ownership systems, and localities. Nevertheless, managerial power within a corporation still seemed highly centralized in the areas of production and profit-sharing.[61]

RECOVERY ORIENTATION IN CHANGZHOU

In the past, industrial reorganization in China focused mainly on the major cities and provinces, especially after the emergence of the reform-oriented socialist trusts in the mid-1960s. It is therefore important to analyse the recent extension of industrial reorganization to small and medium-sized cities. Incidentally, this policy figured prominently in pilot schemes in Changzhou municipality, Sha municipality, and Chongqing municipality. All three cities were later chosen as locations for the trial implementation of comprehensive urban economic reform in 1982. In general, industrial reorganization in Changzhou was recovery-oriented, along the policy lines of the 'Thirty Articles' (of April 1978); Sha municipality created a reform-oriented model for industrial reorganization; Chongqing was cited as successful in carrying out selected aspects of the urban reform policy.

Changzhou municipality was one of the earliest examples of a small city where industrial reorganization was carried out with marked success. In 1959, the Textile Industrial Bureau began to promote a policy of specialization and co-ordination among a group of textile enterprises, centring on the production of ruffled velvet cloth. A 'dragon system' of co-ordinated production processes for ruffled velvet cloth was formed in 1962 with tangible results in terms of improved products, a greater variety and volume of products, and an expansion in exports. As early as 1965, Changzhou municipal authorities attempted to form a specialized tractor corporation, but were forced to dismantle it during the Cultural Revolution. Subsequently, Changzhou's leadership maintained a loose but very effective form of specialized production and inter-enterprise co-ordination (the 'dragon system'), from which the new species of conglomerates developed.[62]

On the whole, industrial reorganization in Changzhou municipality passed through three stages. The first stage (1962–78) centred on the 'dragon system'. The second stage (1979–81) emphasized the establishment of industrial corporations of an administrative type. The third stage, from 1982, was a movement away from administrative corporations to enterprise types of corporations.[63]

The 'dragon system' was a form of economic and technical co-ordination among enterprises of independent legal and accounting status, organized through administrative intervention. The headquarters of each 'dragon system' was normally located in its main factory and was under the command of each supervising bureau. The headquarters mainly performed staff functions for the bureau, such as overall planning, technical advice, and service. When a 'dragon system' was organized across different branches of industry, the supervising bureau of the main line of production was required to appoint an official who would be responsible for operational control and co-ordination among several related factories.[64] The 'dragon system' in Changzhou was formed on the basis of three types of co-ordination, as well as a division of labour: (a) the production of components and parts and the assembly of whole sets of industrial products; (b) a sequence of related technical processes with each factory playing a part (for instance, synthetic fabrics, khaki cloth, printed cloth, and ruffled velvet cloth); and (c) the connected stages within one process, focusing on one type of raw material.[65]

The 'dragon system' provided new solutions to problems arising from co-ordination among enterprises from different jurisdictions and ownership systems. It allowed each participating unit to retain its ownership system, its jurisdiction, and its channel of financial remittance (that is, profit and tax). In addition, when collective-owned enterprises joined the 'dragon system', they were properly compensated for the equipment and facilities they provided. The 'dragon system' was further strengthened through preferential arrangements (such as avoiding double taxation of semi-finished products and final products; adjusting the internal pricing of semi-finished products within each stage of the co-ordinated process; and affording financial appropriation for large-scale technical renovation). In addition, the participating units were permitted to arrange supply contracts among themselves, bypassing the intermediary material supplies bureau.[66] It became increasingly difficult later to co-ordinate the 'dragon system' as a result of increasing complexity and differentiation, further diffusion in the manufacturing of parts and components, and tensions with regard to the fair allocation of funds, raw materials, and working capital.[67] The second stage of industrial reorganization in Changzhou municipality started in January 1979 after the municipal authorities decided to form a tractor corporation. Nine specialized corporations and 12 general factories were subsequently established, by the further consolidation of the 'dragon system'. These specialized corporations and general factories adopted the organizational design of a socialist trust — a high concentration of power and a monopoly over sales and marketing. As a result, the participating enterprises registered complaints about their reduced powers and role; the collective-owned enterprises also complained of a decrease in their retained profits and the loss of their rights over marketing, sales, and control of their development fund. These corporations and general factories were mainly administrative in nature, so the participating enterprises did not see the necessity of adding a new organizational tier between the industrial bureau and themselves.[68]

The third stage of industrial reorganization in Changzhou municipality began in 1982 with the conversion of six industrial bureaux into economically oriented conglomerates, specialized corporations, or branch-wide corporations. At the same time, a considerable share of power over such matters as personnel, planning and marketing, financial accounting, and organizational restructuring was delegated from the municipal level to the corporation level. Each subsidiary unit was given considerable autonomy; thus there were a two-tier accounting system and a two-tier management system.[69]

REFORM ORIENTATION IN SHA AND CHONGQING MUNICIPALITIES

Sha municipality in Hubei province had about half the population of Changzhou. It emerged as a new industrial city in the post-Leap period, and its industrial reorganization policy basically reflected the relevant provisions of the 'Seventy Articles' (of September 1961): (a) the readjustment of product designs and the organization of specialized production; (b) the establishment of fixed sources of material supplies; and (c) a streamlined network of co-ordinated production.[70] This industrial reorganization policy suffered from limitations imposed by the institutional framework of the command economy, namely: the over-centralization of power, resources, and equipment derived from the collective-owned units and branch factories tended to affect adversely the interests and activism of these co-opted units; unified management tended to lead to organizational rigidity and to dampen the effectiveness of differentiated incentives; and the administration of industrial production on the basis of jurisdiction accentuated artificial barriers to economic co-ordination and strengthened the tendency towards 'comprehensiveness' of factories in Sha municipality.[71]

The industrial reorganization policy of Sha municipality began to change in early 1979, focusing on well-known brands of products, and developed its production capacity by minimizing the scale of investment and avoiding the procurement of complete and expensive sets of equipment and facilities. As a result, the first group of six specialized corporations (or general factories) was formed. In the second half of 1979, a policy of profit retention was implemented in this first group of corporations. In addition, these corporations were given autonomy in the following areas: to make supplementary production plans, to market some of their products, to use retained funds, to decide internal pricing within each unit, to dismiss and promote middle-ranking personnel, and to restructure their organization.[72]

In the process of industrial reorganization, the Sha municipal authorities required that efficient enterprises should be given an opportunity for further development, and that the less efficient ones should be regrouped and merged in order to increase the range of marketable products and to improve the circulation of capital. In operational terms, this strategy meant a change of emphasis from basic construction to consumer products; a reorientation from major products to auxiliary parts, components, and technical services; a change to increased variety and small volumes of production whenever feasible; a change from procurement and supply by the State to the market allocation of materials; and a reorientation from the domestic market to exports.[73]

On the basis of their success in 1979, the Sha municipal authorities established a further 12 specialized corporations (or general factories) in the fields of velvet cloth, instruments and tools, apparel, food processing, chemical products, bicycles, towels, and bedsheets. In the meantime, they endeavoured to convert the bureau type of corporations into the enterprise type. Their favourable results encouraged the Hubei provincial authorities to decentralize command over nine enterprises to the municipal level in the first half of 1982.

After consolidation in the second half of the year, 15 corporations (or general factories) remained; these consisted of 66 per cent of the total number and 78 per cent of all employees, and represented 92 per cent of product value and 95 per cent of tax and profit in the six key branches of industry.[74]

Industrial reorganization in Sha municipality was notable for balancing the interests of major and subsidiary enterprises. Firstly, the contribution of subsidiary enterprises in providing fixed assets and working capital was duly recognized and translated into shares. Secondly, the realized profits to be distributed comprised two components: a fixed proportion of the profit of the preceding year; and increments calculated in relation to the number of employees (20 per cent), the size of funds contributed by each participating enterprise (30 per cent), and the size of the increased profit (50 per cent). Thus, material interest cemented the relationship between the corporation and its affiliated units.[75]

Chongqing municipality also launched a policy of industrial reorganization in the years 1979–80, focusing on the 'closure, stoppage, merger and transfer' of 250 small industrial enterprises. Thus, 126 conglomerates were established with some heavy-handed and much-criticized administrative intervention.[76] Chongqing, however, was successful in some categories of industrial reorganization. Firstly, the Chongqing Clock and Watch Industrial Corporation built a marketing network which cut across the administrative boundaries of the province. The corporation mainly resorted to loose forms of economic arrangement (such as sub-contracting, joint ventures, and the bartering of components and parts), and forged stable economic ties with 14 factories in the city and suburban districts and factories in other cities within the province and beyond.[77] Secondly, Chongqing achieved economic co-ordination between civilian and military industries, as in the conglomerate of motor-cycle factories built in 1979. This embraced military enterprises in the city and 111 subsidiary factories in the province. From 1979 to 1983, the conglomerate achieved an annual production volume of 150,000 motor cycles, or 60 per cent of the national total.[78]

CONCLUDING REMARKS

This chapter has analysed the two interconnected phases of industrial reorganization, focusing on variations of implementation in selected ministries and localities. The first phase was largely built upon the revival of the policy precedents and tested programmes of the 1950s and 1960s, including the socialist-trust type of conglomerates. This phase was relatively effective in improving rationality, efficiency, and control over industrial production, management, and distribution. Indicative of the second phase was the change to an emphasis on enterprise autonomy, market mechanisms, and the economic leverage of the State. In theoretical terms, the first phase may be taken as a remedial response to the unintended consequences of a highly centralized and intendedly rational system of economic management. Yet the first phase produced its own unintended consequences, and therefore warranted the search for a new alternative. This alternative was illustrated in the second phase, which exhibited all the distinguishing characteristics of comprehensive urban economic reform.

The second phase was marked by several changes in direction. The policy of reform-oriented industrial reorganization pointed towards an economy characterized by horizontal interactions between enterprise units and guided by market forces. It is not always possible, however, for policy-makers to rely upon the conventional means of an administered economy to forge a market-centred economy. In addition, the risks and crises associated with the policy of reform-oriented industrial reorganization tended to reinforce a tendency towards centralization. For example, when the State plunged into a financial crisis, as it did in 1979, centralization through the socialist-trust type of conglomerate produced immediate and tangible results in terms of economic stability (as in the cases of the China Automobile General Corporation and the China Tobacco General Corporation). It is not surprising that Chinese policy-makers were tempted to resort to the administrative approach to policy-making since the command economy was an effective and reliable instrument for mobilizing resources and since the direct command and management of enterprises guaranteed a safe and steady source of State revenue.

8. The Enterprise Autonomy Policy in the Post-Mao Era, 1978–1984[1]

FROM the early 1970s to the early 1980s the administrative policy-making approach became more salient, as the cases of enterprise rectification and industrial reorganization discussed in Chapters 6 and 7 showed. During the same period the fundamental deficiencies of the administrative approach warranted two forms of response: the remedial and the innovative. The former provided limited and piecemeal modifications to the existing framework of policy-making (namely, the enterprise autonomy policy). The latter represented an attempt to depart from existing methods (as in the 'tax-for-profit schemes').

The remedial response occurred mainly in the first stage of economic reform (1978–83) and the innovative response took place mainly in the second stage. The present chapter will analyse the remedial response, looking first at meta-policy-making in the reform era, and proceeding to examine the origin and development of various versions of the enterprise autonomy policy, especially in the financial arena. The next chapter will analyse the unintended consequences of the enterprise autonomy policy and the feedback pertaining to it, and will then examine the innovative 'tax-for-profit schemes'.

THE POLITICAL CONTEXT OF THE POLICY

The reform policies in the first and second stages were marked by conflicts regarding policy objectives, concrete reform programmes, and policy consequences. These conflicts were in part derived from variables pertaining to meta-policy-making, which were activated in the reform era.

Immediately after the fall of the Gang of Four, Li Xiannian was made responsible for economic policy at the top leadership level and Yu Qiuli (who was later promoted to the Politburo) was in charge of the implementation of economic policy through the State Planning Commission and the newly restored State Economic Commission. The rivalry between Hua Guofeng and Deng Xiaoping from 1977 to 1980 unintentionally produced two uncoordinated centres of power in the area of economic policy: one, which represented the entrenched State officials, was led by Yu Qiuli and was supported by Li Xiannian; they promoted the enterprise autonomy policy, but paradoxically with a 'leftist' work style (termed 'military communism', as noted earlier); the other group was led by Chen Yun and later by Zhao Ziyang, who entered the arena at the Third Plenum of the Eleventh Party Congress in December 1978.[2]

After the Central Committee Work Conference in April 1979, the Chinese Communist Party used the slogan 'readjustment, reform, rectification, and improvement' (*tiaozheng, gaige, zhengdun, tigao*) to summarize its overall policy direction.[3] There was immediate disagreement as to the relative weight to be given to readjustment and reform in this abbreviated platform. The enterprise autonomy policy was the core of economic reform from 1978 to 1983. It was promoted by an alignment of political groups which included officials of the State Council, local leaders, factory managers, and academics. The development of two power centres in economic policy partly explains why the enterprise autonomy policy advanced so quickly despite an urgent call for readjustment by the Politburo of the Central Committee during the years 1979 and 1980.

During the period 1978–83, Chen Yun, Zhao Ziyang, Deng Xiaoping, and Bo Yibo gradually obtained control over economic policy. Of particular significance in the rise of this new coalition were the entry of Chen Yun and the return of the Financial and Economic Commission (FEC). The FEC gained a substantial influence through the establishment of the Research Group for Economic Reform in June 1978, the Office of Economic Reform in May 1980, and the State Economic Reform Commission in May 1982.[4] Subsequently the Ministry of Finance moved to the forefront of economic reform, when the 'tax-for-profit schemes' became the prominent issue in China's economic reform and financial crises.

Ideological variables afforded legitimacy to the enterprise autonomy policy, but had little other influence on the formulation of the policy. They had a stronger influence on the 'tax-for-profit schemes' and the comprehensive urban reforms. A comprehensive theory of economic reform developed very quickly between 1978 and 1980 and removed ideological obstacles to economic reform which had been left by the Cultural Revolution. It did not, however, provide concrete programmes for implementing the enterprise autonomy policy. The analysis below illustrates the vast gap which existed between theories of reform and actual schemes to implement the enterprise autonomy policy.

Overall, the reform-oriented theoretical framework stressed that the roles assigned to Chinese policy-makers were extremely large and perhaps impossible to fulfil. Furthermore, it suggested, the State had been at fault in directly running industrial enterprises which involved marketable benefits and divisible costs. Nevertheless it did not go so far as to recommend a full-fledged market economy and the complete dismantling of central planning and State ownership. It did, however, suggest the possibility of a synthesis between planning and the market.

Hu Qiaomu was the first to provide a theoretical framework explaining why the intendedly rational system of the command economy had unintended consequences. Hu suggested that there had always been a sizeable sector of the economy which was neither planned nor rational. For instance, both agricultural production and industrial production were insufficient to meet the plans of the State, the demands of the people, and exports. There was a constant shortage of goods and raw materials, while fuel was also in short supply. Many products were not suitable for end-users, because of poor product mix, low quality, and incorrect specifications. As a result, waste and excessive stocks were common. Hu considered that attention was rarely paid to economic results in enterprise management; accounting systems were inadequately developed and there were few established norms for material consumption, working hours, and working capital; as a result, there were financial losses and much waste of manpower and raw materials; the relative cost of products was generally very high; work stoppages and overstaffing were frequent and productivity was low; finally, technological progress lagged behind that of the West.[5]

Many authors later echoed and elaborated upon Hu Qiaomu's views and identified the fundamental deficiencies of the 'purely administrative method' as follows:

(a) the extremely large and impossible role given to central planners in view of their limited intellectual ability to handle the planning process;[6] the overloaded communications network;[7] the complexity and sheer size of the country;[8] and the problem of the separation of power from information in a highly centralized command economy;[9]

(b) the inability of the State bureaucracy to manage industrial production directly, because it had an authority orientation rather than an economic[10] or market orientation;[11]

(c) a lack of sensitivity in the financial system of 'unified revenue and expenditure', which prevented the designation of economic responsibility over the use of resources and manpower, and was concomitant with the hoarding of materials and funds and the over-extension of capital investment;[12]

(d) the slowness and inaccuracy in providing differentiated incentives to efficient enterprises and individual producers,[13] and in building a direct link between material interest and performance.[14]

Chinese policy analysts now agree that many remedial responses to the unintended consequences of the administrative type of policy-making were inadequate. For example, they feel that several cycles of centralization and decentralization between the central and the local levels did not address the fundamental deficiencies of economic management at the macro level. In the relationships between the State and enterprise units, remedial responses such as the profit-retention policy and the contracting-out responsibility system of capital investment encouraged enterprises to comply with plans, but produced unintended consequences (such as the indiscriminate payment of wages and bonuses, the over-extension of capital investment, and a huge budgetary deficit). Conventional counter-measures to the undesirable consequences of highly rationalized enterprise management were also found to be inadequate (as in the case of parallel hierarchies, independent controllers, the congress of staff and workers, supervision through banks, investigation tours, and periodical audits and asset-takings). An incremental approach to implementation, by means of pilot schemes and policy experiments, bridged the gap between social reality and the exceedingly broad role of policy-makers, but still did not compensate fully for the basic weaknesses of the administrative type of policy-making.

Chinese policy analysts did not suggest that the administrative type of policy-making should be relinquished entirely. Hu Qiaomu asserted that the strength of the State-administered economy lay in its capacity to take full advantage of planning and rationality at both the micro and the macro level; the capitalist system, Hu said, enjoyed the advantages of planning and rationality only within an enterprise but suffered from anarchy and irrationality at the macro level. Hu therefore regarded economic reform as an attempt to find the appropriate institutional forms of the State that embody 'rationality' at the macro level. Hu argued that the concept of a planned economy was not itself at fault, but that economic laws had been violated.[15]

Some Chinese authors came very close to Amitai Etzioni's recommendation of a mixed scanning strategy of policy-making, or a combination of a comprehensive review and 'bit decisions'. As an alternative to the dilemmas posed by a mammoth centrally planned system, Liu Guogang and Zhao Renwei proposed an integration of central planning and the market by offering this metaphor: the former represents a macroscopic perspective from the top of a mountain, and the latter is a limited vision from a valley. A person on the mountain cannot see much detail, but does have a comprehensive picture of the whole situation, and someone in the valley cannot see the whole picture, but can see himself and the immediate surroundings clearly. Taking a theoretical perspective similar to Charles E. Lindblom's two policy-making models, Liu and Zhao added: 'The command apparatus of the society makes decisions with an emphasis on the general interest of society..., and the producers and consumers...in the market tend to stress individual and local interests.'[16] (Translation supplied.)

Chinese analysts also registered considerable reservations as to whether the policy-making process could be reduced to the mere interplay of material interests, as was suggested by the strategic model. For example, He Qianzhang cogently argued that central planning was not simply an aggregate of enterprise plans because, in his words, 'The basic units cannot understand the overall situation and frequently they merely consider their own interests'.[17] (Translation supplied.) In order to make managerial activities compatible with the needs of the society, he said, there was still much need for the State to co-ordinate economic activities nationally.

Ma Hong probably came closest to recommending that economic policy-making should involve the interaction of many policy actors. However, he did not deny the importance of the role of the State. According to Ma Hong, individual employees should be given the power to decide upon such matters as their own patterns of consumption and the selection of their professions. Enterprises should have autonomy regarding the use of their share of profits, sales and marketing, planning and production, and personnel management. At the macro level, however, the State should retain its role in the control of economic development, the scale of capital construction, and the living standards of the people.[18]

THE ENTERPRISE AUTONOMY POLICY 175

Authors writing on post-Mao China proposed a restructuring of the State but not 'a withering away of the State' in the economic sphere. The new role of the State could therefore be redefined as follows. Firstly, the form of central planning should change from mandatory to indicative planning, so that the State provided guidance and long-term forecasting but did not intervene directly.[19] Secondly, the State ownership system should be confined to the infrastructure of the economy, namely, transportation, harbours, and energy, among others and, in principle, government departments should not own or manage industrial enterprises directly.[20] Thirdly, the means of production should be reclassified as 'commodities', to be allocated through the market, and both enterprises and individuals should be entitled to derive their income from the means of production on the grounds of the concept of 'incomplete State ownership'.[21] Finally, the State's role in the economic sphere should be limited to the use of economic leverage through economic and financial measures (such as the control of credit, revenues and taxation, tariffs, the pricing mechanism, foreign exchange, and so on) rather than direct administrative means.[22]

The theories discussed above were not translated into workable policies or programmes during the first stage of economic reform because of the closure of the organizational 'window' (that is, the lack of know-how and the proper means for implementation). The first stage of economic reform can therefore be taken as a process through which articulated ideological premises (such as a reduction in State intervention, the use of economic leverage, and a market orientation) were in search of organizational means (that is, feasible programmes and schemes and means of implementation).

THE BROAD POLICY CONTEXT

It is germane here to examine the broad policy context within which the enterprise autonomy policy evolved during the post-Mao era. After the Third Plenum of the Eleventh Party Congress in December 1978 and the Central Committee's Work Conference in April 1979, the first priority in the CCP's policy slogan of 'readjustment, reform, rectification, and improvement' was given to readjustment, at Chen Yun's insistence. Probably because of a lack of co-ordination, the State Economic Commission initiated a reform-oriented policy of enterprise autonomy and at the same time this policy was implemented at a rapid and almost uncontrolled pace from 1979 to 1980.

Several top Chinese leaders supported Hu Qiaomu's views on reform (as mentioned above). Hua Guofeng, for instance, encouraged Hu to rewrite and publish the article, which was first presented as a lecture to the State Council in July 1978.[23] At a conference on economic reform sponsored by the State Council in September 1978, Li Xiannian (who was in charge of finance and economy in the Politburo) lent Hu strong support. Li echoed Hu's position, suggesting that the core problem of China's economic system was not merely a question of the proper allocation of power at various hierarchical levels, that is, centralization as opposed to decentralization, but it hinged on a movement away from the framework of the State-administered economy.[24]

It is not entirely appropriate to classify the Chinese policy-makers according to their views on the four positions of 'readjustment, reform, rectification, and improvement' because they were committed to these four positions in varying degrees and their priorities changed over time.[25] During the first stage of reform (1979–83), an increasingly articulate faction pressing for re-adjustment, which was headed by Chen Yun and Deng Xiaoping, was opposed by an amorphous group of central administrators, local officials, enterprise managers, and academic observers who promoted a policy of enterprise autonomy. In 1984, most of the 'adjusters' became 'reformers' during the introduction of comprehensive urban reforms.

In preparation for the Third Plenum of the Eleventh Party Congress in mid-December 1978, Deng Xiaoping delivered a speech which showed a change in emphasis in the diagnosis of the ills of China's economic system. While evading the question of whether the 'purely administrative method' was fundamentally deficient, Deng asserted that power within China's economic system was too centralized, and should therefore be decentralized. 'Otherwise', he said, 'neither would it [a highly centralized system] be favourable to the full play of activism of all four parties, that is, the State, the locality, the enterprise, and the worker; nor would it be favourable to the improvement of economic management and labour productivity.'[26] (Translation supplied.) The Communiqué of the Third Plenum of the Eleventh Party Congress basically reflected Deng's position, taking the issue of the over-concentration of power as the main theme, and playing down the deficiencies of the purely administrative method.[27] By late March 1979 Deng Xiaoping became aware of the seriousness of the economic imbalance and concluded that readjustment should be the overriding priority.[28] At this time Deng's position was closest to that of Chen Yun.

The enterprise autonomy policy was intended to delegate many managerial powers to the enterprise level (from plans for supplementary production, the supply of materials, personnel management, product design, exports and foreign currency, and marketing and distribution, to financial management). In each of these areas, however, the enterprise was given a very limited amount of power. Moreover, the delegation of this limited amount of power was subject to the pleasure and thus the approval of supervising units (such as a central ministry or a local bureau).[29] In addition, local government only carried out selectively the programmes and schemes of financial decentralization which were authorized by the State Economic Commission and the Ministry of Finance, among others. The State Council admitted retrospectively in a policy paper in May 1981 that 'with reference to the expansion of enterprise autonomy, [we] have so far implemented the profit retention policy, but reform in other areas has not yet materialized'.[30] (Translation supplied.)

It is difficult to classify the enterprise autonomy policy in terms of the concept of total versus partial reforms.[31] Overall, it may be taken as a 'partial' reform because its intended scope stayed very close to the existing framework of the command economy. Policy-actors at both the central and the local level became aware of the difficulties of implementation, which derived from a lack of synchronization and co-ordination, and the incompatibility of policies with the overall managerial structure. But they were unable to move away from an incremental approach because they could not anticipate and control the unintended consequences of the enterprise autonomy policy, such as the inequality of income among enterprise units, the over-extension of capital investment, and the depletion of revenue sources.[32]

In sharp contrast to the wide range of recommendations made by academic observers, both ministerial and local officials tended to narrow the scope of policy experiments, postpone policies which had greater unanticipated results, and confine their search for alternatives to tested policies. The schemes and programmes of the first stage of economic reform were repetitions — at a slower pace — of those originally advocated and implemented in the 1950s and early 1960s. To be precise, various schemes of the enterprise autonomy policy, which were formulated and implemented mainly during the period 1958 to 1961, were repeated in the six years from 1978 to 1983. Ministerial and local policy-actors were under pressure to produce tangible results and to minimize mistakes that were associated with any unintended consequences. As a result, they adopted an incremental approach to policy-making and were guided by feedback from each phase of implementation. In most cases they chose alternatives on the basis of a limited review of the existing pilot schemes.[33]

PROFIT-RETENTION SCHEMES

The earliest version of enterprise autonomy was put into practice in December 1978. It was concerned with the revival of 'enterprise funds' (a system dating back to the 1950s and 1960s),[34] and was based on Article 9 of the 'Thirty Articles', promulgated in July 1978.[35] The enterprise funds system allowed enterprises to have a share of up to 5 per cent of the total amount of wages, should all of the eight technical and economic indicators of the annual plan be fulfilled, and 3 per cent if only four major indicators (quantity, quality, variety, and profit) were achieved. This share of retained profits would be converted into an enterprise fund for the improvement of collective welfare facilities and for 'socialist emulation awards' and bonus payments for the enterprise.[36] The system of enterprise funds was intended to apply to all State-owned enterprises, but was later incorporated into many new schemes of profit retention.

In 1979 the State Council and its sub-units began to introduce two major versions of the profit-retention system to enterprise units which were able to make a profit. Both were derived from the profit-retention policies of the 1950s, especially the 1958 version (see Chapter 3). The first version was based upon one of five regulations promulgated by the State Council in July 1979, the effect of which was to increase incentives for State-owned enterprises, according to their performance. These five regulations gave enterprises modest discretionary powers in the areas of managerial and marketing functions, profit retention, depreciation funds, and the use of fixed capital and working capital.[37]

The drafting of the five regulations probably benefited from feedback from the pilot schemes which were conducted in various localities at the end of 1978. The State Economic Commission convened a meeting in March 1979 for 'summing up' the experience of the existing pilot schemes of the profit-retention system. In the meantime it decided to sponsor directly another eight pilot schemes in Shanghai, Tienjin, and Beijing.[38] The five regulations were submitted to the Work Conference of the Central Committee, CCP, in April 1979 and were subsequently endorsed in principle by the Central Committee. Finally, they were discussed by the Second Session of the Fifth NPC and approved by the State Council.[39]

To implement the five regulations, the State Economic Commission convened the National Conference on the Increase of Production and Savings in Industry in Chengdu in July 1979. At the conference, the Sichuan experiment was singled out as a model pilot project. A quick survey of the contemporary press reports suggests that the State Economic Commission also decided to authorize approximately 100 experimental enterprises in each province, major city, or autonomous region to implement the new profit-retention system. The State Economic Commission estimated that this first version of the profit-retention system would apply to 3,358 enterprise units or about 8 per cent of the total number of State-owned enterprises throughout the country. They constituted about one-third of the total output value and 40 per cent of realized profit.[40] The first version of the profit-retention system was based upon the 'total-sum method' of calculation: a share of the profits would be awarded to each enterprise unit in proportion to the total profit (that realized in a given baseline year).[41]

The change from the first to the second version of the profit-retention system was abrupt. The State Economic Commission and the Ministry of Finance jointly issued a circular on 22 January 1980 which altered the method of calculation from the 'total-sum method' to one which differentiated between the baseline year and the incremental part of the profit. Each enterprise unit would be awarded a sharply increased percentage of the retained profit when the realized profit exceeded the baseline. By various calculations, the baseline profit could be fixed in accordance with the sum of the realized profit of a given year or the average of several preceding years. This was called the 'fixed-comparison method'.

The second version of the profit-retention system was, however, based upon the 'circular-comparison method', with a shifting annual baseline. The amendments in the circular of January 1980 recommended that enterprise units would be entitled to a percentage of profits when they could reach the same level of profits as that of the preceding year; should the profit exceed that of the preceding year they were to become eligible for an additional share from the increased portion of annual profits, the ratio of which was adjusted for different branches of industry. The amount of retained profit given was in proportion to the fulfilment of major economic and technical indicators (quantity, quality, profits, contract, and so on).[42] This process was also described as 'whipping the galloping buffalo' (*bian da kuainiu*) and placed an additional pressure upon the most efficient and most productive enterprises.

Furthermore, the State Economic Commission and the Ministry of Finance responded to the superficially good results of the pilot schemes introduced between July 1979 and January 1980 by authorizing even more experimental units. By June 1980, it was estimated that 6,600 units were included. They constituted 16 per cent of the enterprises within the State budget, or double the number included in 1979. They provided 60 per cent of the total national product value and about 70 per cent of enterprise profits. In some localities, such as Shanghai and Tienjian, the experimental enterprises provided 80 per cent of the profits, and in Beijing 94 per cent.[43]

The State Economic Commission took about nine months to make the necessary adjustments to the second version.[44] In September 1980, the Commission submitted another policy paper, which permitted some ministries, bureaux, and localities to adopt the 'fixed-comparison method' (that is, a fixed baseline for a number of years) at their own discretion.[45] However, the State Economic Commission did not seem fully aware of the serious economic imbalance created by the profit-retention system at the time, thus recommending that 'each locality and department should further extend the task of expanding enterprise autonomy'.[46]

THE REFORMULATION OF THE ENTERPRISE AUTONOMY POLICY

It was two years before an attempt was made to implement the policy of readjustment, even though readjustment was given a clear priority in the Central Committee Work Conference as early as April 1979. Zhao Ziyang was appointed Premier of the State Council in September 1980, and he started the policy priority immediately after Hua Guofeng and Yu Qiuli stepped down. Another Work Conference of the Central Committee was convened in December

1980. To maintain the consistency and continuity of central policy, this Work Conference fully endorsed the economic reform which had taken place since the Third Plenum of the Eleventh Party Congress (in December 1978), but reiterated that readjustment should be the central priority of the economic task; reform should be subordinate to and supportive of readjustment.[47] The State Economic Commission and the newly established Office for Economic Reform sponsored the National Conference on the Reform of the Industrial System from 26 January to 12 March 1981. At this conference it was admitted that 'some units do not have an adequate understanding of the positive meaning of the guideline of readjustment, and readjustment has been encountering certain resistance'.[48] (Translation supplied.) It also suggested that the further extension of the enterprise autonomy policy should be halted, a decision which overturned the recommendation of the policy paper of September 1980 on the same subject.[49]

The enterprise autonomy policy went through a process of reformulation in the second half of 1981. It became known as the 'industrial production, economic responsibility system'.[50] This change was not only conceptual, but also theoretical. The concept of 'enterprise autonomy' was rooted in Mao's ideas of balancing the interests of the State, enterprises, and individual producers, and permitting 'full play to the activism' of basic units and individual producers. This concept was consistent with an economic policy-making approach in which a large number of participants interacted, and were guided by their tangible interests. In a very different perspective, the term 'responsibility' implies that the relationship between the State, enterprises, and individual producers should be hierarchical rather than economic in nature. Thus responsibility would determine the amount of power to be decentralized and the sum of the interests to be distributed within a mainly administrative framework. The reasons for strengthening the industrial production, economic responsibility system were given in another policy paper about one year later, in October 1982:

The implementation of the industrial production, economic responsibility system would facilitate some changes in the over-concentration of power within the managerial system of excessively rigid control, and enable enterprises to have certain managerial autonomy. It would put the principle of material interest in the relationship between the State, enterprises, and staff and workers in a proper perspective. To a certain extent, it would be able to overcome the weaknesses of egalitarianism and of 'eating rice out of a big pot', to mobilize activism among enterprises and enhance a sense of 'master' among staff and workers.[51] (Translation supplied.)

The profit-retention system remained the core of the reformulated enterprise autonomy policy — the industrial production, economic responsibility system. In its two major versions, the profit-retention system was intended to apply to enterprise units which were making a profit, enterprises of large and medium scale, and those which were State-owned. Because of variations in local situations and the existence of many types of industrial enterprise, local and central policy-makers had to develop new incentive schemes. By the second half of 1981, the broad concept of the economic responsibility system embraced the following empirical types:[52]

(a) the total-sum method of profit retention which was applicable to enterprises whose system of production was in order, which achieved their production target, and which had a stable rate of growth of profits;

(b) the differential-sum method of profit retention in which a higher percentage of profit was retained in cases where the planned profit was exceeded than in cases where it was simply fulfilled (whether the fulfilment was assessed by the fixed-comparison method or the circular-comparison method);

(c) profit retention on the basis of exceeding the profit plan only;

(d) the 'contracting-out' method in profit-making units or the profit-contract system (*lirun baogan*), which was based upon a contract negotiated between the State and enterprises; the latter being responsible for remitting an agreed amount of profit to the State while retaining the rest; in some cases, a progressive rate of profit-sharing was adopted when contracted enterprises had fulfilled the basic quota of profit remittance;

(e) the 'contracting-out' method in enterprises which had suffered losses (*kuisun baogan*), coupled with fixed subsidies and the retention of funds below the ceiling of the losses;

(f) the responsibility system for both profits and losses with no obligation to remit profits and no claim over subsidies to the State (this system applied in the collective-owned enterprises of the second light industry sector);

(g) tax-for-profit schemes, in which taxation was substituted for the remittance of profits, and enterprises paid tax, but retained all their profits.

Some enterprises changed from one method to another in the light of the relative advantages of each method and the particular situation of their own units. Yet they had to commit themselves to one method for a fixed period (usually three to five years). As a result, central and local policy-makers were not in a position to initiate new policies and programmes of profit retention before the experimental period concluded. Nevertheless, some tentative policies and pilot schemes were carried out — in the areas of depreciation funds, working capital, and capital investment — during the years 1979 to 1983 when the profit-retention policy was in force, and before the full-scale introduction of tax-for-profit schemes in 1984.

LOCAL PILOT SCHEMES

The foregoing analysis suggests that local authorities played a significant role in providing input for policy formulation and feedback regarding the implementation of the pilot schemes. The next logical point of analysis would be the pattern of interaction between the central and the local levels in the policy-making process in some selected places, for example, Sichuan, Guangdong, Shanghai, and Beijing.

The case of Sichuan province has received much publicity, but its role in initiating the enterprise autonomy policy should not be exaggerated. The pilot schemes in the province were among a national total of 3,358 schemes authorized directly or indirectly by the State Council.[53] The experiments in Sichuan can be appreciated in terms of what Dror calls the 'sequential decision model'.[54] That is to say, central policy-makers relied upon feedback from the pilot schemes in selected localities to guide the implementation of the enterprise autonomy policy throughout the country. In this respect, Sichuan provided three versions of the enterprise autonomy policy — called the 'small expansion', the 'medium expansion', and the 'big expansion' versions — which became the forerunners of similar versions elsewhere in China.

The 'small expansion' version was introduced on the basis of a policy paper known as the 'Fourteen Articles' which was issued by the Party group of the Provincial Economic Commission on 12 February 1979. The paper recommended the delegation of powers to enterprises. These powers included: a part in the planning of supplementary production above the State quota, a small share of power in sales and marketing, a limited power of discretion over exports and a share of foreign currency, a modest increase in depreciation funds, and a small amount of discretion over wages and bonuses. Most important of all, however, was the fact that experimental enterprises were given a claim to a share of retained profits. The 'medium expansion' version started in accordance with a circular known as the 'Twelve Articles', which was issued by the Provincial Party Committee on 22 December 1979. This version recommended an even greater delegation of powers to enterprises than did the 'small expansion' version. Both represented variants of the profit-retention system. The 'big expansion' version belongs to the category of 'tax-for-profit schemes' which will be dealt with in the next chapter.[55] Up to 1981, the 'small expansion' version included 100 industrial enterprises and 40 commercial units; the 'medium expansion' version consisted of 417 industrial enterprises and 250 commercial enterprises; and the 'big expansion' version included 29 units.[56]

In Sichuan province, the 'small expansion' version meant differentiating between fulfilment of and exceeding the annual plan. The enterprises participating in the pilot schemes were given an incentive fund of 8–12 per cent of the total wages and 3–5 per cent of the planned profit when they fulfilled the plan, plus 20–25 per cent of the profit when they exceeded the planned target. This version followed the 'circular-comparison method', whereby the profit realized in the preceding year was taken as the minimum profit target for the current year. The 'medium expansion' version changed the method of calculation to the 'total-sum method' in which experimental enterprises were given a fixed amount of the retained profit in proportion to the increment in their profit over the profit level of the baseline year (1979). The percentage of retained profit was fixed for three years from 1979 to 1981.[57] As noted above, the July 1979 version of the profit-retention policy of the State Council followed the 'total-sum method' (and in particular, its subcategory, the 'fixed-comparison method'), and the January 1980 version adopted the 'circular-comparison method'.

Other provinces which were chosen to carry out pilot schemes were expected to follow central policies and directives with considerably less leeway than Sichuan province was allowed. Guangdong province, for example, did not begin to implement the profit-retention system until late August 1979, one and a-half months after the State Council had promulgated its profit-retention regulations in July 1979. The first group of approximately 100 enterprise units carried out the central policy of profit retention on the basis of the 'fixed-comparison method'. The remaining units underwent the reform in terms of the restoration of 'enterprise funds'. Guangdong province does not, however, seem to have changed to the 'circular-comparison method' of calculation, as required by the State Council's policy paper of January 1980. The provincial authorities permitted the supervising bureaux to control production targets and levels of retained profits for the most efficient enterprises, in order to avoid a sharp increase in the baseline for the profit plan and to minimize disincentives.[58] On the whole, the Guangdong leadership appears to have given first priority to economic readjustment, as proposed by the Work Conference of the Central Committee in April 1979, and did not respond to the call of the State Economic Commission for further expansion of the profit-retention system.

The State-owned enterprises at county level in Guangdong province were not at first subject to the influence of central policy. Consequently, the provincial policy-makers had considerable scope for policy innovation when they began to formulate the Qingyuan model of profit retention, and institutional reform which centred on the County Economic Committee, in late 1978. In spite of controversy and opposition, the Qingyuan experiment was later endorsed by Xi Zhongxun, the First Secretary of the Provincial Party Committee. By November 1979, 507 State-owned, county-level enterprises in 33 counties in Guangdong had carried out the Qingyuan scheme.[59] The Qingyuan model was also endorsed by the central policy-makers and introduced in about 125 counties throughout China by early 1981.[60]

In Shanghai, the profit-retention system was first introduced in three enterprises in April 1979. After July 1979, the system expanded to include an additional 103 enterprises on the basis of the 'total-sum method' (the first version authorized by the State Council). The municipal authorities responded to the State Council's profit-retention policy of January 1980 (the second version) and changed to the 'circular-comparison method'. This change met resistance among the participating units. They devoted their efforts to the maintenance of equipment, rather than to an increase of production, for fear of facing higher targets in the following year. As a result, the output value in the industrial sector dropped by 2.5 per cent in the second half of 1980. This was partly attributed to a reduction in the financial appropriation to heavy industry in the city. But Shanghai did not return to the first version of the profit-retention system until September 1980, when the State Council became aware of the deficiency of the 'circular-comparison method'.[61]

Shanghai developed a new system of profit retention in 1979, by taking the industrial bureau rather than the enterprise as the basic unit of calculation in two industrial bureaux: the Textile Managing Bureau and the Metallurgic Industrial Bureau.[62] In the former, 90.5 per cent of the realized profit was remitted to the State and 9.5 per cent was to be retained by the bureau.[63] In the latter, an amount equal to the 1978 baseline profit was to be remitted to the State; when the realized profit exceeded the 1978 baseline profit, 60 per cent was to be remitted to the State and 40 per cent was to be retained by the bureau.[64] The two bureaux were permitted to adopt this system on the basis of the 'total-sum method' for a five-year period. The main advantage of this system was that the bureau was given a chance to make adjustments in the distribution of profit among the enterprises which it supervised and to minimize inequalities derived from unreasonable pricing systems, and differentials due to endowment factors.[65] This bureau-centred system of profit retention was extended to 11 major industrial bureaux, embracing 1,839 enterprise units, by 1982. In the commercial sector, 3,800 enterprises in the city were also incorporated into the bureau-centred profit-retention system, as from 1979.[66] This bureau-centred profit-retention system originated from a similar version approved and promulgated by the State Council in 1955.[67]

Beijing began its pilot scheme of profit retention in three selected enterprises, and in the second half of 1979 the pilot scheme was expanded to embrace 100 units. In the first half of 1980, the profit-retention system was extended to 366 enterprises, or 76 per cent of the total. However, Beijing did not experience the disturbance, felt elsewhere, of changing from the 'fixed-comparison method' to the 'circular-comparison method'. As in Guangdong, the calculation of the retained profit was controlled by the Municipal Economic Commission and the Bureau of Finance and Taxation, as from 1980. This allowed the municipal authorities some discretion to adjust profit-retention schemes and to avoid disincentives to efficient and productive factories. Beijing also adopted the bureau-centred profit-retention system in a number of enterprise units.[68]

The foregoing analysis suggests that the central policy-makers set the pace for the expansion of the enterprise autonomy policy, but that local authorities were given considerable discretion as regards following their recommendations. For example, Guangdong did not increase the number of experimental enterprises beyond the original group of about 100, while Sichuan and Beijing extended the pilot schemes to about 350–400 enterprises. Also, considerable discretion was given to local authorities in amending the schemes and formats suggested by the central authorities. For example, in certain categories of industry, Shanghai and Beijing took the bureau rather than the enterprise as the unit of calculation, a system which dated back to 1955. Guangdong province initiated the profit-retention system and institutional reform at the county level. Sichuan province always introduced versions of the profit-retention system more quickly than other localities. Of course, the State Council was in a position to monitor the results of pilot schemes in Sichuan and to make adjustments accordingly.

THE MANAGEMENT OF WORKING CAPITAL AND FIXED ASSETS

In relation to China's annual State budget of approximately 100,000 million *yuan*, working capital and fixed assets constitute a very large sum, the efficient use of which is crucial to economic growth in the PRC. Working capital amounts to 300,000 million *yuan*. Annual investment in fixed assets is valued at 80,000 million *yuan*.[69] These two areas received the attention of the central policy-makers in July 1979, when the five regulations of enterprise autonomy were promulgated. All of these regulations were proposed and implemented on the basis of the policy precedents of the 1950s and 1960s.

The managerial problem of working capital was not effectively dealt with until the enterprise autonomy and the profit-retention systems were carried out in 1980. The delay was partly due to the need to complete the groundwork for 'inventory-taking and asset-auditing'. During 1980, the State Council, together with local units, were able to complete an assessment of working capital and to fix norms for each State-owned enterprise. On the basis of these, the State Council started to increase financial responsibility for the amount of working capital in the enterprise's possession, either through the collection of fees or the charging of bank interest. The main purpose was to economize in the use of working capital in the form of money, stock, production (or semi-finished products), and commodities (that is, the finished products), and to shorten the period of circulation of working capital.[70]

The State Economic Commission, the Ministry of Finance, and the People's Bank of China jointly issued a policy paper on 9 December 1982, calling for the strengthening of the management of working capital. It noted that working capital had increased by 12.8 per cent in each 100 *yuan* of product value from 1965 to 1981. Taking State-owned enterprises in the industrial, commercial, and transport sectors as a whole, it reported that the total amount of working capital was 317,500 million *yuan* (or 35,000 million *yuan* worth of stock in excess of the norm stipulated by the State). It was estimated in 1981 that 13,000 million *yuan* of stock would be reported as spoiled because of lengthy storage and technical and economic depreciation.[71] The policy paper therefore recommended the following:

(a) strengthening production planning and improving the balance between production and distribution;

(b) strictly prohibiting non-planned capital investment so as to minimize proportionally the use of working capital;

(c) increasing the channels of circulation of commodities and expanding the volume of sales;

(d) fixing a date for the disposal of material stock through the reclassification of rejects or reductions in prices;

(e) financial units and supervising authorities should establish the norms for working capital as well as for the supervisory system.[72]

The idea of employing economic leverage to maximize the use of working capital was first seen in one of the five regulations announced in July 1979 (entitled the 'Provisional Regulations of Bank Loans for the Full Quota of Working Capital in State-owned Industrial Enterprises'). Yet the State Council took no further action until it endorsed the policy paper concerning the change to unified management of working capital by the People's Bank which took effect on 25 June 1983. It proposed an agenda for carrying out the pilot schemes in selected provinces and municipalities, and in chosen branches of industry, projecting that it would require two years for the system to be implemented, group by group, throughout the country.[73]

On the basis of a 'two-track' system (namely, financial appropriation and bank loans), increases in working capital from 1979 to

1983 were mainly supplied by bank loans (about 82 per cent), and a smaller proportion was appropriated by the financial departments (18 per cent). Therefore, the change to a system requiring the 'full quota' to be supplied by bank loans simply recognized the existing trend.[74]

With regard to the financial management of fixed assets (equipment and facilities), most Chinese academic observers agreed that renovation should be more effective than capital investment in producing tangible economic results, at least in the short term. They also accepted that an 'intensive' approach (that is, maximizing the efficiency of the existing equipment and facilities) should enjoy a higher priority than an 'extensive' one (that is, the further expansion of capital investment), especially during economic readjustment. They therefore advocated an increase in funding for renovation projects in order to enhance 'intensity'. A simple increase in funding for renovation could not, however, solve the problem of the inefficient use of fixed assets.[75] On the basis of the Shanghai case, one author suggested that funds for technical renovation had actually increased after the introduction of economic reform, but that the economic returns of using the funds had not improved.[76]

Addressing the difficulties mentioned above, the State Council issued a policy paper on 21 June 1980, calling for increased funding for technical renovation, and also placing emphases upon: (a) energy-conserving projects, (b) the light, textile, and handicraft industries, (c) the transportation system, and (d) projects for improving product quality and product mix, and for increasing consumer goods and export commodities. It also attempted to ensure a steady supply of funds for renovation through the following means: an adjustment of the depreciation rate, the use of retained profits and bank loans, financial appropriations by central and local governments, and fund-raising activities by the enterprise units involved. In addition, it urged an improvement in the planning and management of renovation projects, and in financial supervision by related departments and banks.[77]

In the area of capital investment, the State Council authorized pilot schemes of financing capital investment through bank loans as early as August 1979. For approximately one year, from 1979 to 1980, 619 entirely new construction projects were introduced throughout the country, relying upon the loan contracts signed with the People's Bank. The amount of the bank loans was estimated at 3,200 million *yuan*. Moreover, 8,400 million *yuan* in loans were made available to about 900 existing capital investment projects. The State Council decided that, as from 1981, enterprises which had implemented independent accounting systems and were capable of returning the money borrowed should depend mainly upon bank loans to launch their capital investment projects. It also recommended that State-budgeted funds for capital investment should be appropriated to basic construction units through construction banks rather than departments of finance at various levels. The construction banks should then manage the funds and provide loans to the enterprises in accordance with the capital investment plans of the State and the specific guidelines and conditions set by the State.[78]

In 1981 and 1982, the State Council was preoccupied with the problem of the over-extension and redundancy of capital investments. It took no new initiative until March 1983 when the 'contracting-out' system of economic responsibility was introduced. The system was aimed at overcoming the disincentives for construction units and enterprises to shorten construction periods, improve quality, reduce construction costs, and increase economic returns. It recommended that construction units would be entitled to retain 50 per cent of the funds saved in accordance with the authorized budget. Such retained funds would be divided into three: 60 per cent for the Enterprise Development Fund, 20 per cent for the Collective Welfare Fund, and 20 per cent for wage increases.[79]

In addition, the system would award retained funds to enterprise units, provided that the latter met the required stipulations in the following areas: the scale of construction, the total investment ceiling, the completion deadline, the standard of economic returns, and the amount of inter-enterprise co-ordination.[80] This system can be traced back to a similar system that existed during the years 1958–60, which incorporated an amendment to discourage any expansion in the scale of construction through the financial sources provided by enterprise units and local government (see Chapter 3). On balance, enterprise units would be able to obtain more power than was available in the centrally planned and controlled system of previous capital investment projects.

SUMMARY AND IMPLICATIONS

As mentioned in Chapters 1 and 2, the structure and characteristics of the administered economy can be defined not only in terms of its design and intention (or 'organizational logic'), but also in terms of the counter-measures taken to cope with its unintended consequences. According to Nicos Mouzelis, the post-Weberian perspective of organization theory features a cycle of control, unanticipated results, and renewed control.[81] The enterprise autonomy policy can therefore be taken as one form of renewed control device embedded in the intendedly rational structure of the command economy. This policy was intended to ensure that deviation by enterprises was minimized and that their compliance with plans increased.

Overall, the central policy-actors exhibited a keen concern with the uncertainty regarding the outcome of alternative policies and were under pressure to produce tangible results without fundamentally altering the existing system. They were cautiously bound by the policy precedents and tested schemes of the 1950s and 1960s and also made limited modification as a result of feedback from pilot schemes. The uncontrolled pace and unintended consequences of policy resulted partly from the fallibility of policy-makers and the 'bounded' rationality of the policy-making process, and partly from the 'territoriality' of China's industrial management. The latter aspect was shown in the attempts of local authorities and enterprise units to maximize their retained profits as well as in their attempts to convert retained profits and funds into capital investment and to protect their markets and sources of raw materials.

The next chapter will systematically examine the unintended consequences of the first stage of economic reform and the new departures introduced in the second stage.

9. The Unintended Consequences of Reform and the Tax-for-profit Schemes, 1980–1984[1]

THIS chapter has a theoretical connection with the last chapter, and makes the assumption that reform in a State-administered economy tends to produce unintended consequences. The top Chinese policymakers had two options for coping with these unintended consequences: one was to attempt to reimpose central control and therefore to return to the command economy. The other was to search for an innovative path to break the vicious cycle from reform, to unanticipated results, to the reimposition of central control. This chapter provides a detailed analysis of the unintended consequences of the enterprise autonomy policy (and of the other forms of financial decentralization), the reimposition of central control, and the innovative departure from the command economy by the substitution of taxation instead of the remittance of profits (known as 'tax-for-profit' schemes).

The issue of the unintended consequences of reform and the reintroduction of central control is a part of the post-Weberian framework. This framework suggests that any attempt at rationalization is inherently inadequate and that it is difficult, if not entirely impossible, to eliminate the residual area of irrationality, so that a further cycle of rationalization must occur. This chapter intends to substantiate the above observations by conducting an empirical investigation of a series of interactions between central policy-makers and local and enterprise units, in the arena of financial decentralization.

THE UNINTENDED CONSEQUENCES OF FINANCIAL DECENTRALIZATION

During the reform era most of the unintended consequences took place in the financial arena; they were mainly the result of the tendency towards financial decentralization (including the enterprise autonomy policy) to the local and enterprise levels; and they were similar to those which occurred in the industrial sector during the

Great Leap Forward. From 1979 to 1984 the unintended consequences of financial decentralization included the following issues: (a) the over-extension of capital investment, (b) the depletion of the sources of central revenue, and (c) the perceived danger of excessive expenditure on wage increases, welfare, and housing. This chapter will examine each of these issues.

There was an uncontrolled expansion of capital investment (including capital construction and renovation) on four occasions: in the years 1958, 1970, 1978, and 1982; each was marked by a sudden increase of capital investment, of about 10,000–12,000 million *yuan* over the preceding year, accompanied by high ratios relative to the GNP and the State budget.[2] The pattern of over-extension of capital investment in the post-Mao period differed from that of Mao's period in one important respect. The former was associated with a drastic rise in extra-budgetary capital investment, which was sponsored by local and enterprise units. The percentage of extra-budgetary investment within the national total rose from 20 per cent in 1979 to 38 per cent in 1980, 43 per cent in 1981, and 50 per cent in 1982 (see Table 3). Two major and reinforcing factors were responsible for the uncontrolled expansion of extra-budgetary capital investment: the introduction of a revenue-sharing policy between the central and local levels in February 1980, and the profit-retention system, which began on a large scale in 1979 and 1980.

The revenue-sharing system was introduced upon the recommendation of the Financial and Economic Commission (FEC) of the State Council. On the basis of feedback from the pilot schemes in Jiangsu and Sichuan which began in 1979, the State Council promulgated the 'Circular of Adopting Financial Management of the Classification of Revenue and Expenditure and Contracting-out according to Hierarchy' on 1 February 1980.[3] It decided to allow local governments a share of revenue which would be derived mainly from profit and from defined categories of taxation of enterprises under their jurisdiction. Local governments were only required to remit a fixed percentage of additional revenue to the State treasury and could keep the remainder for new expenditure when the minimum quota of revenue collection had been fulfilled. Local governments which had been in deficit would be given another portion of industrial and commercial tax and a fixed amount of subsidy.[4]

The trial implementation of the revenue-sharing system began in Sichuan and later spread to other provinces.[5] This system was applicable to almost all provinces and localities, although there were

Table 3 The Total Investment in Fixed Assets, 1976–1982 (100 million *yuan*)

| Year | Grand Total | Investment in Capital Construction | | State Budget Investment as a Percentage of Total Investment | Extra-budgetary Investment as a Percentage of Total Investment* |
		Total	State Budget Investment		
1976	523.94	376.44	310.93	83	17
1977	548.30	382.37	312.35	82	18
1978	668.72	500.99	417.37	83	17
1979	699.36	523.48	418.57	80	20
1980	745.90	558.89	349.27	62	38
1981	667.51	442.91	251.56	57	43
1982	845.31	555.53	276.67	50	50

* Calculation by the author.

Notes: 1. The statistics on investment in fixed assets cover only investment by State-owned units. In 1982, investment by collective units, cities, and towns in fixed assets was 17.4 billion *yuan* and investment by urban and rural individuals in housing construction was 18.1 billion *yuan*.

2. As some changes to the planning and scope of statistics of investment in capital construction were made in 1982, the relevant figures for the preceding years have been adjusted to render the data comparable.

Source: State Statistical Bureau of the PRC, *Statistical Yearbook of China 1983* (Hong Kong, Economic Information and Agency, 1983), p. 323.

exceptions. For instance, Shanghai, Tianjin, and Beijing were still required to follow the old system of 'unified revenue and expenditure' in order to ensure the income of the central government; Guangdong and Fujian were given flexibility under a so-called 'special policy and flexible measures' relating to revenue and expenditure: the former was required to remit a fixed sum to the central government, and the latter was given a fixed amount of subsidy by the central government.[6]

The 'Circular' accentuated the tendency towards 'territoriality' among local governments. It added substantial incentives for them to increase their revenue by expanding the profit-retention system in the enterprises under their jurisdiction. In order to protect their sources of revenue, they began to inject their available funds into capital investment projects so as to be able to claim a share of the retained profits from these new projects. To maintain a favourable profit rate, they tried to erect economic barriers to prevent material resources flowing from their jurisdiction to other locations, and to protect their market for commodities from 'invasion' by the other localities. Even when locally controlled enterprises were not efficient or productive, they could be immune from competition with efficient and productive units in other localities. After 1979, central policy encouraged the channelling of locally sponsored capital investment into the light industry sector and consumer products — a tendency that was not necessarily undesirable in itself.[7]

There have been differences of opinion as to whether financial decentralization to the local and enterprise level contributed to the expansion of capital investment, especially extra-budgetary investment. The official position is that there was a direct linkage between the two. Zhao Ziyang suggested as early as March 1980 that enterprise units tended to acquire more working capital than was economically justifiable, because the profit-retention system created loopholes, and there was also a dangerous tendency to over-stretch capital investment and to pay excessive wages and bonuses.[8] Wang Bingqian, Minister of Finance, put the case bluntly in early 1983, when he wrote that 'the expansion of enterprise financial power at the expense of the State revenue should no longer be tolerated; the encroachment of the State revenue through falsification of records should not be permitted'.[9] (Translation supplied.)

With regard to the question of why retained profit, working capital, and other available funds were often converted into capital investment, it was widely accepted that these monies cost next to nothing and that capital investment could improve production capacity and therefore the prospect of claiming a further share of any profit. The conversion of available funds (including retained profit) into capital investment was again facilitated by an increasing reliance upon bank loans in addition to direct financial appropriation to support investment projects. As a rule, 'bank loans' were charged a low rate of interest and were subject to very generous terms. Local and enterprise units found it to their advantage to convert available funds into capital investment.[10]

The enterprise autonomy policy and the 1980 revenue system were designed to provide remedies to the over-concentration of power and rigid financial management, and to allow local and enterprise units the necessary initiative and discretion to revitalize the economy. The further expansion of capital investment was, therefore, probably not a deviant tendency in itself, as China's financial analysts suggested.[11] However, the shortage of materials and energy, bottlenecks in transport facilities, redundancy in investment projects, poor product quality and high product costs, and many unwise and inefficient investment projects placed an extra strain on the national economy and created a considerable economic imbalance in terms of a high inflation rate and a deficit.

Another of the unintended consequences of economic reform concerned the depletion of State revenue. The PRC's official statistics indicate that there was a steady decline of financial revenue relative to national income, from 37.2 per cent in 1978, to 32.9 per cent in 1979, 28.3 per cent in 1980, 25.8 per cent in 1981, 25.4 per cent in 1982, and 25.9 per cent in 1983. In monetary terms, State revenue decreased from 112,110 million *yuan* in 1978, to 110,330 million *yuan* in 1979, 108,520 million *yuan* in 1980, and 108,950 million *yuan* in 1981. It did not return to the earlier levels until 1982 and 1983 when it rose to 112,400 and 124,900 million *yuan* respectively.[12] The State thus found it increasingly difficult to raise revenue through profit remittance and began to rely upon taxation leverage. State income (including a high percentage of profit) from industrial enterprises dropped from 39.3 per cent in 1978 to 31.9 per cent in 1983 in relation to total revenue.[13] More specifically, remitted profit, as a percentage of total realized profit decreased from 95 per cent in 1978 to 87 per cent in 1979, to 82 per cent in 1980, and 76 per cent in 1981.[14]

The relative decline of State revenue was compounded by an increase in expenditure on three major items: (a) the price subsidy to agricultural procurement,[15] (b) financial support for wage increases,[16] and (c) capital investment. The first two items were justified on other policy grounds, and the last item was in part attributed to extra-budgetary spending by local and enterprise units, as noted above. It was the State, however, that had to balance the overall budget, under the pressure of a steep increase in deficit from 1979 to 1983. The deficits in 1979 and 1980 broke the historical record: 17,060 million *yuan* and 12,750 million *yuan* respectively.[17] To alleviate the financial crisis, the central government cut centrally sponsored capital investment projects from 41,737 million *yuan* in 1978 to 25,156 million *yuan* in 1981, to 22,667 million *yuan* in 1982, and 34,576 million *yuan* in 1983.[18] The two most crucial areas, energy and transport, registered a decline of 10.9 per cent and 16 per cent in 1980, compared with the figures for 1978.[19]

THE REIMPOSITION OF CENTRAL CONTROL

To cope with the financial crisis, the State Council resorted to two basic approaches: one was the conventional administrative means of tightening financial control, and the other was innovative: the use of economic leverage, including the introduction of a new tax policy. In early 1981 the State Council promulgated a regulation to reduce the expenditure by enterprise management, in order to stop the depletion of profits and therefore of State revenue. It was estimated that administrative and managerial expenditure in State-owned enterprises was four times higher than that in ordinary administrative organs. Managerial expenditure was frequently incorporated in production costs.[20] Moreover, the Ministry of Finance launched a campaign against tax fraud and tax evasion in May 1981, and this continued until 1984. It was estimated that, in 1981 alone, tax evasion and tax fraud amounted to 1,300 million *yuan*. The cases reported included falsification of sales volumes, production costs, and the categories of taxable commodities, as well as other types of false accounts.[21]

In December 1981, the State Council decided to inspect the financial management of enterprises, and sent 1,200 inspection teams (with 7,600 members) throughout the country.[22] By April 1984, 26,800 inspection teams, with 190,000 members, were organized in 22 provinces, municipalities, and autonomous regions. Approximately one-third of the key enterprises and local administrative units were inspected by 1984. The main financial irregularities found were: (a) the falsification of cost accounting in order to reduce profit remittance (an estimated 1,200 million *yuan* or 34 per cent of the total); (b) tax evasion and tax fraud (an estimated 800 million *yuan* or 22 per cent); (c) the excessive payment of bonuses and subsidies, in cash and in kind; (d) the illegal transfer of profit into welfare funds; and (e) corruption and excessive expenditure on managerial fees.[23]

The State Council also enacted a number of new laws to prevent the depletion of State revenue. For instance, a regulation was promulgated in October 1982 to stop the increase in the number of unauthorized local taxes and levies being imposed upon enterprise units.[24] The 'Regulation on Cost Management in State-owned Enterprises' was promulgated on 5 March 1984 to standardize cost accounting, and thus to minimize the depletion of taxes and profit.[25] On the whole, taxation, a form of economic leverage, became an increasingly important source of State revenue from the commercial and industrial sector; this source provided 40.3 per cent of State revenue in 1978, 42.8 per cent in 1979, 46.2 per cent in 1980, 49.4 per cent in 1981, 53.4 per cent in 1982, and 51.6 per cent in 1983.[26]

In early 1981, the State Council started to respond to the over-extension of capital investment. The 'Regulation of the State Council concerning the Strengthening of Planning Management and Control of the Scale of Basic Construction' (dated 3 March 1981) required all capital construction projects, at both local and central levels, to be incorporated into the basic construction plans of the various responsible units, to be subjected to the approval of the State Planning Commission, and to be supervised by departments of finance and statistics at various hierarchical levels. These basic construction plans detailed financing, credits, material supply, and manpower. Local and central units were again urged to concentrate on renovation projects rather than on new construction projects.[27]

An example of the employment of economic leverage was the joint announcement by the Central Committee and the State Council in December 1982 of a new tax scheme for raising funds for energy and transport projects. The reasons for the scheme were that, while there was inadequate funding for key projects in energy and transport, such funds as were available were being dispersed too widely. That is to say, the demand for extra-budgetary funds for capital investment at the local, sectoral, and enterprise levels had exceeded the requirements of society and the limits of resources and energy. The new tax scheme aimed to curtail extra-budgetary capital investment, readjust the structure of investment, and alleviate the inadequacy of financing to investments in the transport and energy industries. The regulation stipulated that an annual tax of 10 per cent would have to be levied on enterprise income derived from extra-budgetary funds at all levels. The initial target was to raise 12,000 million *yuan* in the years 1983–5.[28]

The payment of excessive wages, bonuses, and subsidies in kind was seen as an unintended consequence of the profit-retention system (in its two versions) in 1979 and 1980. Since the wage scale and increments were more controlled and standardized than bonus payments and subsidies in kind, the latter received more attention than the former for the purpose of administrative control. After the Work Conference of the Central Committee in December 1980, the State Council promulgated a regulation in January 1981 to stop the indiscriminate payment of bonuses. This suggests that there were serious problems concerning uncontrolled payments of bonuses and excessive egalitarianism in the allocation of bonuses among staff and workers, as a result of the relaxation of the political education scheme and the lack of a managerial system. In addition, enterprise managers tended to use the payment of bonuses as the sole means of increasing the income of staff and workers, without trying to maximize productivity and economic efficiency. In some extreme cases, enterprise units raised commodity prices in order to reap illegal profits and, therefore, to pay handsome bonuses to their employees. The regulation set a ceiling equivalent to two months' wages for bonus payments (or three months' wages in extraordinary cases) and entrusted the ministries and local bureaux with the task of implementing the policy.[29] Furthermore, the State Council promulgated policy papers, regulations, and amendments on this subject in May 1981,[30] April 1982,[31] and April 1983.[32]

The enterprise autonomy policy was meant to give enterprise units greater financial power and thus more discretion to dispose of their income in line with the idea of 'to each according to his labour', that is, additional incentives for productive and efficient units and workers. Therefore a simple increase in bonus payments was not regarded as a deviant tendency in itself, as was an indiscriminate increase. None the less, State control over wages and bonuses remained a policy emphasis in the post-Mao era. The uncontrolled increase of wages, bonuses, and other kinds of payment was probably more apparent than real. First of all, there was a sharp increase in monetary wages from 1977, but real wages did not rise significantly, except for an increase of about 16 per cent in 1978–9 over the figure for 1977. The wage increase of 24 per cent between 1977 and 1980 took place after a long wage freeze between 1965 and 1977 (see Table 4). Moreover, the wage increase was not necessarily associated with economic reform. It is also worth noting that the increase in insurance and collective welfare from 1978 to 1983 was significant, at about 110 per cent (see Table 5).

The reimposition of central control over wages and bonuses during the years 1980–2 was not compatible with the overall direction of economic reform. The economic approach was devised to bypass the conventional administrative approach in April 1983, when the State Economic Commission, the Ministry of Labour and Personnel, and the Ministry of Finance jointly recommended a floating wage scale between the ceiling and the floor defined by the relevant central ministries and local bureaux.[33] A draft wage reform put forth by the Ministry of Labour and Personnel (dated 12 April 1984) emphasized the direct link between the floating wage scale and the enterprise bonus fund.[34] On the basis of this draft, the idea of a floating wage scale was drastically amended, and was further elaborated upon in two additional policy papers in April and May 1984. Direct control over wages and bonuses was finally relaxed when the State Council issued a new regulation employing taxation leverage in June 1984. Enterprises would be permitted to pay workers an extra two and a-half months' wages without tax; a tax of 30 per cent would be levied on extra wages of between two and a-half and four months' pay; and a tax of 100 per cent would be levied on extra wages of from four to six months' pay; and there would be a tax of 300 per cent on extra wages in excess of six months' pay. Accordingly, the ceiling for wage increases and the floor for wage reductions were cancelled.[35]

The slow growth in real wages reflected the partial success of the central policy-makers' objective of readjustment during the first stage of economic reform (1978–83). The central policy-makers were, however, less successful in increasing the differential in remuneration between more efficient enterprises and individuals and those that were less efficient, especially in the areas of bonuses, collective welfare, and labour insurance. The reason for this lay partly in the legacy of organic State Socialism which was reinforced in the post-Mao era. For example, the State strove to fulfil its economic

Table 4   The Average Wage of Staff and Workers in State-owned Units, 1976–1983

Year	Average Wage (*yuan*)	Index (1952 = 100)	
		Monetary Wage	Real Wage[1]
1976	605	135.7	112.1
1977	602	135.0	108.5
1978	644	144.4	115.2
1979	705	158.1	124.0
1980	803	180.0	131.2
1981	812	182.0	129.4
1982	836	187.4	130.7
1983	865	193.9	132.5

Note: 1. The increase in the cost of living prices has been deducted.

Source: The State Statistical Bureau of the PRC, *Statistical Yearbook of China 1984* (Hong Kong, Economic Information and Agency, 1984), p. 460.

Table 5   Labour Insurance and Welfare Funds Paid by State-owned Units, 1952–1983

Year	Labour Insurance and Welfare Funds (100 million *yuan*)	Percentage of Total Wage Bill (%)
1952	9.5	14.0
1957	27.9	17.9
1962	28.3	13.2
1978	66.9	14.3
1979	92.1	17.4
1980	116.0	18.4
1981	132.4	20.0
1982	153.8	21.7
1983	179.6	24.0

Source: The State Statistical Bureau of the PRC, *Statistical Yearbook of China 1984* (Hong Kong, Economic Information and Agency, 1984), p. 461.

obligation to its citizens by improving living standards, which had deteriorated as a result of a long wage freeze since the Great Leap

Forward. The State endeavoured to provide an equal share of benefits for enterprise units under the idea of the 'neighbourly relationship'. Each enterprise unit attempted to honour the notion of a share of material benefits for each employee in an entity which resembled an industrial commune. The proportional expansion of group-oriented, indirect, and diffuse forms of remuneration (such as labour insurance and collective welfare) also strengthened the tendency for enterprises to develop into communities with systems of shared benefits rather than remaining as purely production units. These communities were and still are sanctioned by a series of State regulations and policies. And last, but not the least, the question of the 'iron rice bowl' was not tackled until pilot schemes of the labour contract system were introduced in early 1980 and the 'Circular of Active Trial Implementation of the Labour Contract System' was promulgated by the Ministry of Labour and Personnel in February 1983.[36]

THE TAX-FOR-PROFIT SCHEMES: A BREAK AWAY FROM THE VICIOUS CYCLE

In the vicious cycle of reform, its unanticipated results, and the reimposition of central control, the substitution of taxation for profit remittance (hereafter referred to as the 'tax-for-profit' schemes) may be seen as an entirely new departure, pointing towards the economic policy-making approach. The earliest experimental 'tax-for-profit schemes' evolved from the policy towards collective-owned enterprises, over which the State had previously exercised indirect and mainly economic control. The pilot schemes of this system were reportedly carried out in Guanghai county in Hubei province in 1979. The experiment then spread to other localities under the auspices and guidance of the State Economic Commission, the Ministry of Finance, and local Party and government units.[37]

By August 1980, three basic versions of the 'tax-for-profit' schemes had developed: (a) the Sichuan version, which required experimental enterprises to pay three types of taxes in lieu of profit remittance (namely, industrial and commercial tax, a fixed-asset tax, and income tax);[38] (b) the Shanghai version, which stipulated that instead of remitting profits, the participating enterprises had to pay five taxes and two fees (including industrial and commercial tax, income tax, a fixed-asset fee, and a working-capital fee);[39] and (c) the Liuzhou version, under the sponsorship of the General Bureau of Taxation of the Ministry of Finance, required experimental units to pay value added tax, endowment tax, differential-income-adjustment tax, an enterprise income tax, and a working-capital fee.[40] After having fulfilled its financial obligation to the State, an enterprise unit would be given full discretion to dispose of its income and full responsibility for its profit and loss. In early August 1980, the State Economic Commission issued a circular requesting each local government to select one or two State-owned enterprises in which pilot schemes of the new system were to be conducted.[41]

The State Council requested Ma Hong, Director of the Industrial Economic Institute of China's Academy of Social Sciences, to convene a Conference on Theory and Practice of Reform of the Economic Institution from 16 to 25 April 1981. The consensus of the conference was that the 'tax-for-profit' scheme was 'an objective demand and inevitable tendency of economic reform; a major reform in the balancing of interests between the State and enterprises; and an important measure to employ economic leverage to manage the economy.' (Translation supplied.) The main advantages of the system were that: (a) an enterprise would be able to become a genuine and dynamic economic entity; (b) the bonds of the financial system of unified revenue and expenditure could be broken; and (c) the barrier of local boundaries could be eliminated to facilitate cross-regional economic co-operation.[42]

To mobilize support and public opinion, Ma Hong wrote an article which was published in *Economic Research*. In this he provided further elaboration of the rationale of the 'tax-for-profit' schemes. Ma considered that this new system would make enterprise units fully accountable for their performance and strengthen the link between the material interest of employees and the economic success (or failure) of enterprises. The new system would also compel enterprise units to compete for markets without the 'safety cushion' provided by the State in terms of planned purchases and sales, subsidies, and assured supplies of materials and fuel. Moreover, the new system would facilitate the improvement of management in enterprises and the development of purely economic ties among enterprises through contracts and markets.[43]

The Ministry of Finance appeared to be assuming an increasingly important role in implementing the new system, in collaboration with the State Economic Commission and the Office for Institutional Reform. By May 1981, the Ministry seemed to have the sole power to authorize the expansion of the new system. It was estimated that, from 1980 to 1981, some 270 enterprises carried out pilot 'tax-for-profit' schemes.[44] The number of experimental enterprises reached 456 units during the period 1981–3, when a large-scale extension of the policy was being actively contemplated.[45] There was, however, no definite evidence that the central leadership was committed to further extension of the system until Zhao Ziyang delivered the proposal for the Sixth Five-year Plan, at the Fifth Session of the Fifth NPC in November 1982.

In this proposal, Zhao suggested that 'tax-for-profit' schemes should be implemented in two steps. The first step would allow the coexistence of taxation and profit remittance, that is, the realized profit of enterprises would be subject to income tax and local tax, while a range of profit-sharing schemes between the State and enterprises would be applied to the amount of profit remaining after taxation. The second step would introduce a progressive scale of enterprise income tax on the basis of the amount of profit. According to Zhao, this new system would expand while the pricing system would remain basically intact for the coming three years.[46]

After some preliminary investigations of various alternatives, the Ministry of Finance and the Office for Institutional Reform formulated an initial draft of 'tax-for-profit' schemes to be conducted in Shanghai, Tianjin, and Jinan.[47] The draft was discussed at a national conference sponsored by the Ministry of Finance and attended by 320 representatives from financial bureaux, local taxation bureaux, ministries of the State Council, representatives of experimental enterprises, and researchers and scholars from various universities and research institutes. The results of the discussion were reported to Zhao Ziyang on 23 March 1983 and to the meeting of the State Council on 25 March 1983.[48] Accordingly, on 12 April 1983, the Ministry of the Finance promulgated the 'Provisional Measure concerning the Substitution of Taxation for Profit-remittance in State-owned Enterprises'.[49]

The pilot schemes conducted up to March 1983 presented the State Council with a choice of three systems: (a) the profit-retention system, in either of its versions; (b) the profit-contract system (or the 'contracting-out' responsibility system) of the Capital Iron and Steel Corporation; and (c) the 'tax-for-profit' schemes.[50]

The profit-retention system was excluded on the following grounds. Firstly, the multitude of profit-retention schemes and the inconsistencies between them enabled participating enterprises to

Table 6 The Growth Rate of Retained Profit, National Output Value, Average National Income, and State Revenue, 1979–1981 (per cent)

	1979	1980	1981
Retained profit	14.50	16.75	19.30
National output value	8.50	8.70	4.10
Average national income	7.00	6.90	3.00
State revenue	-1.60	-1.70	-1.90

Source: Yuan Yu-sheng, 'Zhengque chuli guojia yu qiya zhijian de lirun fenpei guanxi' ('Correctly Handling the Distribution of Profit between the State and Enterprises'), *Caijing kexue*, No. 3, 1983, p. 9.

claim excessively large shares of retained profits. As a consequence, the growth of retained profits exceeded the growth of national total output value and average income, and produced negative growth in State revenue (see Table 6). It was estimated that, during the four years from 1978 to 1982, 420,000 million *yuan* of profits were retained by enterprise units and the proportion retained was increasing (being 11.9 per cent in 1980, 13.2 per cent in 1981, and 15 per cent in 1982).[51] The experimental units tended to choose whatever scheme was to their advantage and, in some cases, they adopted more than one scheme as they saw fit. Secondly, the administrative work of designing a specific scheme for each participating unit was considerable; the constant disputes over the baseline profit and the appropriate increments in profit became a political burden when local governments were also involved. A third, and more serious, problem was that the multitude of schemes and the ambiguity in each permitted enterprise units to violate accounting rules and financial laws to increase costs illegally in order to reap a large retained profit. A fourth reason was that the State had difficulty in collecting tax on the profits derived from extra-budgetary investments (such as bank loans for technical renovation and an increase in fixed assets). Finally, local governments tended to collaborate with enterprises to resist the efforts of the State Council to take revenue and resources out of their jurisdiction, and to frustrate any attempt to form efficient conglomerates and forge viable economic ties across local boundaries.[52] In these endeavours, they were assisted by the revenue-sharing regulation promulgated in February 1980.

The profit-contract system was considered undesirable, not only because it favoured the idea of 'one scheme for one enterprise' but also because it depleted State revenue.[53] For example, a survey of 267 enterprise units which adopted this system in 1983 shows that the State was able to claim about 13 per cent of the incremental profit, while enterprise units retained about 71 per cent, and the other 15 per cent was earmarked for the return of profits derived from special loans or projects.[54] Like the profit-retention system, the profit-contract system entailed an enormous administrative workload in standardizing methods of calculation, and there were constant disputes over the appropriate baseline profit and the appropriate level of increments in profit.

THE NEW ROLE OF THE MINISTRY OF FINANCE

The working conference convened by the Ministry of Finance in March 1983 produced two opposing positions. On the one hand, the supervising bureaux of enterprises were concerned that their share of retained profits might be adversely affected by the new system. On the other hand, financial units believed that the new schemes might encroach upon State revenue. The Ministry of Finance acted more or less as an arbitrator, arguing that, from 1978 to 1983, the retained profits of enterprises had increased (from 11.9 in 1980, to 13.2 per cent in 1981, and to 15 per cent in 1982). The Ministry suggested that a balance ought to be maintained between the funds retained by enterprises and those remitted to the State. The Ministry ruled that the 'tax-for-profit' schemes should be implemented throughout the country. Wherever possible, enterprises which had started some form of tax schemes should convert them into the standardized schemes promulgated by the Ministry of Finance.[55]

The Ministry of Finance stipulated that all large and medium-sized State enterprises must pay income tax of 55 per cent of their realized profits. The remaining 45 per cent of the profits must be divided between the State and enterprises in accordance with one of the following schemes: (a) a progressive rate based on a profit contract, (b) a fixed rate of profit remittance, (c) a scheme of taxes adjusted according to endowment factors, or (d) a fixed amount of profit remittance based on the 'contracting-out' responsibility system (for large-scale or mining enterprises only). It became evident that the central authorities were able to ensure that a fixed percentage of revenue, 55 per cent of profits, was remitted to the State treasury, but the enterprises' share in the remaining 45 per cent of profit was tied to their performance.[56]

The 'tax-for-profit' schemes gained fresh momentum as soon as they were implemented on 1 June 1983. In August 1983, the State Council requested the Ministry of Finance to investigate the possibility of further expanding the system. Specialists and scholars were also consulted. In early 1984, comprehensive urban reform appeared to be under way, with pilot schemes being carried out in a number of localities. At the Second Session of the Sixth NPC in May 1984, Zhao Ziyang proposed that the second step of the 'tax-for-profit' scheme should be implemented.[57]

The central policy-makers must have been encouraged by the initial results of the first step: the profits of State-owned industrial enterprises in 1983 were 4,200 million *yuan* higher than those of 1982; the distribution ratio between the State and enterprises was also favourable (61.8 per cent for the State and 38.2 per cent for enterprises); and the amount of retained profit for all types of enterprises increased sharply (to 2,700 million *yuan*, or 28.2 per cent above that of 1982). A total of 107,145 enterprises in the industrial, commercial, and transport sectors were included in the new policy; they comprised 92.7 per cent of profit-making enterprises in those sectors.[58]

The Ministry of Finance convened the National Work Conference on the Second Step of the Substitution of Taxation for Profit Remittance at the end of June 1984. The Ministry decided to begin the second stage of the policy on 1 October 1984.[59] Enterprises would be allowed to retain all of their profits, after the payment of 11 kinds of tax and a new wage-increment tax. (Those 11 taxes were: product tax, value added tax, salt tax, sales tax, endowment tax, city construction tax, property tax, land tax, vehicle and ship tax, enterprise income tax, and adjustment tax.) The Ministry gave an extra allowance to small-scale profit-making enterprises, by permitting them to pay tax in accordance with an eight-grade progressive scheme. Small-scale enterprises were generally defined as those with fixed assets below 4 million *yuan* and profit below 3 million *yuan*.[60]

The full-fledged form of the 'tax-for-profit' schemes represented one of the most radical reform proposals advocated in recent years, and marked the beginning of a new era in the PRC's history of economic reform.

THE INTENDED SCOPE AND METHODS OF IMPLEMENTATION OF ECONOMIC REFORM

Analysts writing on the political economy of post-Mao China realize that the first stage of economic reform from 1978 to 1983 was slow and limited.[61] They have given a number of explanations as to why this was so.[62] The present empirical study affords some elaborations and qualifications to the explanations attempted so far. This author suggests that comprehensiveness does not automatically guarantee that a reform will succeed, and 'synchronization' does not necessarily eliminate all the major difficulties inherent in the implementation process.

First of all, with reference to the intended scope, total reform is probably superior to partial reform, given the assumption of the functional interdependency of the components in a State-administered economy. In theory, total reform requires policy-makers to be omniscient and omnipotent — to be able to analyse all problems accurately, to formulate new and workable solutions, and to control all aspects of implementation. With regard to the pace and method of implementation, synchronized reform is in theory better than incremental reform. It is clear, however, that the former would excessively tax the intellectual abilities and the limited resources of policy-actors. There are four possible modes of reform which take two dimensions (intended scope and implementation) into consideration (see Fig. 2).

The first stage of economic reform approximated Mode D in Fig. 2 (that is, partial-incremental reform), as demonstrated in the enterprise autonomy policy. Although this policy proposed that many categories of power were to be decentralized to the enterprise level, only a very limited amount of power in each category was actually given. It was obvious that the enterprise autonomy policy was intended, at the operational level, to provide remedial solutions to the existing framework of the command economy. Central policy-makers, being under pressure to produce tangible and reliable results, confined their research for policy alternatives to established precedents and past practice, while policy-actors at the local and enterprise level were concerned only with what they could gain immediately (such as retained profits and other funds). In the implementation process, both central and local policy-actors were guided by feedback from pilot schemes. They generally followed a policy of

Fig. 2   The Modes of a Reform Programme

Implementation Method	Intended Scope	
	Total	Partial
Synchronized	Mode A	Mode C
Incremental	Mode B	Mode D

'incrementalism', and their decision-making behaviour indicated a concern for areas of organizational risk, being marked by coalition formation, problematic search, uncertainty avoidance, and organizational learning (to use the terminology of Cyert and March).[63]

The second stage of economic reform was close to the total-incremental reform of Mode B in Fig. 2. When the 'tax-for-profit' schemes were combined with the 'comprehensive urban reform', the intended scope of the second stage was exceedingly large. The Central Committee of the CCP announced its epoch-making policy paper, the 'Resolution on the Reform of the Economic System' on 20 October 1984 after a series of pilot schemes conducted in 1983 and the first half of 1984.[64] Its recommendations included enterprise autonomy, the commodity economy, price reforms, the use of economic leverage, differentiated incentives, the separation of enterprise management from State administration, the overhauling of central planning, and a city-centred developmental strategy focusing on the expansion of markets.[65] After trial and error, the top policy-makers were forced to adopt an incremental approach in implementing the second stage of economic reform. The implementation of the October 1984 Resolution was postponed as a result of the existing energy crisis, a bottleneck in transportation, the relative scarcity of raw materials, excessive non-budgetary investments, and the limited financial power of the State. The

Chinese policy-makers again had to assume a reactive rather than a proactive posture to urgent problems, following an unanticipated relaxation of control over bank loans and wage payments, an unexpected expansion in the volume of currency, and spiralling increases in commodity prices.[66] In his 'Report of Government Work' of 27 March 1985, Premier Zhao Ziyang suggested that, within the context of the large and complex reforms proposed in 1984, and the limited economic and financial power of the State, Chinese policy-makers should anticipate the risks and difficulties to be encountered, and proceed step by step, adjusting to feedback and the results of the pilot schemes.[67]

SUMMARY AND IMPLICATIONS

This chapter and the last, focusing on the first stage of economic reform, have dealt mainly with a classic issue in the reform movements of Socialist countries, namely, the full cycle involving reform, unanticipated results, and renewed control. The problem has been analysed from a post-Weberian theoretical perspective. This chapter has been able to cover an innovative alternative to the command economy (the 'tax-for-profit' schemes) only briefly, because of the limited amount of data made available since 1983.

In general, one may regard the second stage of economic reform with guarded optimism because political and ideological factors seem to have favoured its implementation, even though the 'window' of organizational means has not been fully opened. After the death of Mao Zedong, nearly all the policy-makers had ideas of reform (such as enterprise autonomy, the use of economic leverage, and the increasing importance of markets), despite the change in the economic leadership from Li Xiannian, to Chen Yun, and finally to Zhao Ziyang. For a short time, 1979–83, readjustment was presented as a top priority and resulted in the reimposition of central control, but it eventually yielded to the imperative of reform.

In addition to providing an ideological critique of the fundamental weaknesses of the command economy (see Chapter 8), Chinese analysts have identified the shortcomings of specific institutional arrangements. Referring to the urgent need for the 'tax-for-profit' schemes, Han Shouzu, a Chinese economist, suggested, for instance, that the profit-remittance system, which was transplanted from the Soviet Union in 1949, was an integral component of the 'unified revenue and expenditure system' (*tongzhi tongshou zhidu*). This system required State-owned enterprises to remit all of their profits to the State treasury, and the State to disburse all the funds of enterprises. Enterprises units, regardless of individual effort, were excluded from sharing in the profits derived directly from their managerial performance; similarly they were not held responsible for their financial losses in the system which was known as 'eating out of a big rice pot' (*chi daguofan*).[68] In this respect, therefore, the 'tax-for-profit' schemes constituted a significant step towards the economic approach. This approach marked a transformation from a pattern of policy-making that was guided by theory and co-ordinated by authority to one that was guided by interest and co-ordinated by means of interaction (or coalition formation). Justification for the reform was based upon the balancing of the interests of the State, enterprises, and individuals, as well as upon the interaction of many policy-makers. The State was regarded as a participant, albeit a principal one, through the process of negotiation and compromise.

In terms of policy-making, Mode B, total-incremental reform, as adopted in the second stage of reform, might be successful. Not only would a comprehensive review enable policy-makers to see the interrelationship between components of the reform policy more clearly, to anticipate its results with the least uncertainty, and therefore to identify more viable alternatives for economic reform, but an incremental method of implementation (through pilot schemes and adjustment to feedback) would minimize the risks involved, given the relative scarcity of information and resources for the execution process. Nevertheless, the author's analysis of the ultimate direction of the reform cannot be conclusive, in view of the difficulties of developing a mixed economy — either from an administered economy or within a capitalist system — and of attaining the optimal balance between public and private sector. A consideration of such issues would warrant a separate treatment.

10. Conclusion

THE foregoing analysis suggests that the evolution of the policy-making system in the People's Republic of China during the period from 1949 to 1978 was marked by an alternation between the administrative approach and the preceptoral approach. The increasing saliency of the economic approach was seen in the transformation from the synoptic to the strategic model, which occurred on a limited scale during the Great Leap Forward (1958–60) and was later reinforced in the post-Mao era (in two stages) from 1978 to 1984. The entire process of development involved three policy-making approaches on two theoretical dimensions (that is, the administrative and preceptoral approaches on the synoptic dimension, and the economic approach on the strategic dimension).

This book has so far focused more on changes in the policy-making approach than on any tendency in policy outcomes which may be observable, even though the latter might sometimes reflect the former. Furthermore our study of policy-making approaches highlights the main characteristics of the actual policy-making process. Our findings suggest that, overall, the policy-making process in China has been not so much organized and articulated as suggested by either 'incrementalism' or 'rationalism'. Therefore it is entirely possible, as has been demonstrated in this book, for objectives to search for organizational means, and vice versa. Policy participation is fluid, but need not be shapeless. And it is not necessarily confined to the fomal hierarchy and official positions. Our rigid and well-charted outline of the reality of policy-making therefore yields to a blurred boundary and even to 'twisted' and 'distorted' images.

A REDEFINITION OF THE ROLE OF THE TOP POLICY-MAKERS

It is the opinion of this author that it would be untenable for Chinese leaders to confine their search for viable policy-making alternatives to an assumption that policy-makers are omniscient and omnipotent. Indeed, the role of a sovereign planner is as demanding as that of a charismatic leader, and neither is able to cope with the unintended consequences of an intendedly rational system in an over-managed society. In some cases the cure has been worse than the illness (for example, the economic imbalance created by the Great Leap Forward, the over-investment crises in the post-Mao era, and so on). There were altogether three periods during which the top Chinese leadership endeavoured to bridge the gap between the officially expected role of policy-makers and the reality. In the first period, 1949–57, the fundamental weaknesses of the administrative approach were attributed to imperfect methods and techniques, while the question of the limited intellectual ability and actual capacity of policy-makers was evaded. Zhou Enlai, for example, suggested in 1954 that the shortcomings in central planning were derived from inaccurate forecasting, a lack of comprehensiveness and consistency, inadequacy in the co-ordination and division of labour, and poor management and organization.[1] In 1956, he also mentioned frequent changes, false projections, long delays, and insufficient inventory and financial control.[2] Chen Yun pointed out that central planners were unable to formulate accurate and reasonable targets because of deficient statistical data and a lack of information regarding enterprise behaviour (see Chapter 3).

During the second period, which started with the Great Leap Forward in 1958, China's policy-makers became aware that irrationality, inefficiency, and uncontrolled elements might be perpetuated in a Socialist economic system for a relatively long period of time, but that they could in theory be eliminated. Mao Zedong thus suggested that policy-makers (unlike sages and prophets) are unable to act in an omniscient and omnipotent fashion to impose order and to direct the national economy in a perfectly balanced and proportional way, and to control fully the uncontrolled elements in policy-making (such as 'spontaneity' and 'lack of direction') and to observe the supposed 'law of economy' ('the kingdom of certainty' as he called it). Mao stated in 1959:

[A] Socialist society can, [in theory], maintain its balance [of economic development] through planning, but one cannot, therefore, deny that [in practice] it requires a process of understanding pertaining to what should be the 'necessary proportion' [of the economy].[3] (Translation supplied.)

Mao admitted that, in the short term, 'there is no natural-born sage; even reaching the stage of a Socialist society not all people can [instantaneously] turn into prophets'.[4] (Translation supplied.) In the long term, however, policy-makers will be able to gain full freedom (that is 'the kingdom of freedom') after they strive hard enough and have accumulated sufficient experience in the effort to discover the 'law of economy' which supposedly exists (that is, 'the kingdom of certainty').[5] In other words, Mao suggested that policy-makers (the ruling élite) would eventually find the correct answer to Socialist modernization, but not in the foreseeable future.

The third period coincided with the post-Mao era (1978–84). In 1978 Hu Qiaomu pointed to the half-planned and non-planned sectors of a planned economy and the basic inadequacy and weaknesses of State intervention in a Socialist society. It was realized that economic reform is not simply a matter of decentralization within the existing framework of a command economy, but a complete change from a State-administered economy to a market-oriented one. Although the Chinese politicians and ideologues were not ready to eliminate the role of the State in the spheres of production and distribution, they began to accept a diminution in State intervention (which was evident in such aspects as the smaller scope of the planned economy, indicative rather than mandatory planning, the employment of economic methods, taxation, interest and price policies, and the market mechanism) (see Chapter 9).

The CCP's top leadership had come a long way to be able to admit that the elements of uncertainty in the policy-making process placed limitations upon them. The 'Resolution on the Reform of the Economic System' of the Central Committee (dated 20 October 1984) cited Lenin's view that all-embracing and comprehensive planning amounted to a 'bureaucratic Utopia'. Thus, for a long time to come, the planning of the national economy is likely to remain a very broad and flexible outline. This does not alter the CCP's official view that policy-makers should in theory be able to discover the supposed 'law of economy' and guide economic development in the correct direction. From this viewpoint, policy-makers are infallible, and the 'ultimate truth' is still taken as the guide for policy-making.

Having a relatively well-defined objective of reform, the post-Mao leadership will still need to confront the formidable task of implementation in the context of a State-administered economy. In fact there is no easy choice between partial and total reform, and between incremental and synchronized implementation. A partial-incremental reform is extremely difficult because the change of one component (such as plans or targets) cannot be insulated from the other components (such as material supply, financing, marketing, pricing, or profit) in the gigantic and complex system of the command economy. Nor is a total-synchronized reform any easier, because it rests upon an assumption that policy-makers are infallible — that they are capable of anticipating and completely controlling the consequences of reform. As we have demonstrated in preceding chapters, both remedial and innovative responses to the fundamental deficiencies of the administrative approach in policy-making entailed risks and crises. The path towards a modified and an entirely reformed command economy is certainly very narrow.

THE VICIOUS CYCLE OF ALTERNATIVE APPROACHES

This empirical case study has suggested that the success of reform in a highly centralized and over-managed policy-making system depends upon an ultimate leap from the vicious cycle of alternative approaches in policy-making. This vicious cycle comprises the following phases: the rise of the administrative approach in the Stalinist tradition, the unintended consequences of the administrative approach, responses in terms of the preceptoral approach or the economic approach, or both, crises created by the responses, and the return to the administrative approach (see Fig. 3). According to Charles E. Lindblom, the administrative approach is a 'strong thumb without fingers', that is, it is powerful and effective, but not delicate enough.[6] Thus it is tempting for the top policy-makers to take the administrative approach as a fall-back position when they encounter setbacks and repercussions from either the preceptoral approach or the far-reaching reforms entailed by the economic approach.

A number of authors studying the Socialist political system have discerned this pattern of changes in the policy-making approach. For instance, David Lane has treated the divergent paths of political development in Socialist countries (such as the Yugoslav model, the Maoist model, and the Eastern European alternatives) as reactions to a 'perverted' form of Soviet Socialism or 'bureaucratic state capitalism'.[7] Focusing on institutional features, Alec Nove has detailed remedial responses to the fundamental weaknesses of the Soviet species of economic and managerial systems.[8] Jeremy Azrael has analysed the divergence among the Socialist countries in terms of 'varieties of de-Stalinization'.[9] Taking a similar approach, Maurice Meisner has focused on ideological responses to the rise of

Fig. 3   The Vicious Cycle of Policy-making Approaches

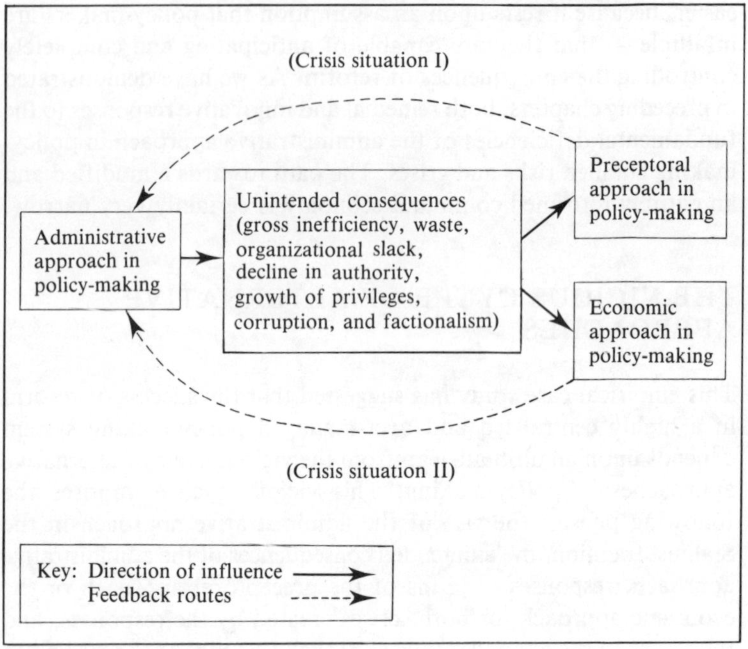

(Crisis situation I)

Administrative approach in policy-making

Unintended consequences (gross inefficiency, waste, organizational slack, decline in authority, growth of privileges, corruption, and factionalism)

Preceptoral approach in policy-making

Economic approach in policy-making

(Crisis situation II)

Key: Direction of influence ⟶
Feedback routes   ----->

the Socialist bureaucratic state in the PRC.[10] Harry Harding has discussed extensively the political and organizational remedies to the 'bureaucratic dilemma'.[11]

It is worth noting that the policy-makers' responses to the unintended consequences are partly subjective. The policy-makers in a Socialist country who take a moral and political perspective tend to adopt a preceptoral policy-making approach. Those who view the problems from an organizational and managerial angle are likely to formulate alternatives within the economic approach, that is, the strategic model. As previously demonstrated, the charisma-inspired and mass-oriented style of management during the Great Leap Forward and the Cultural Revolution illustrated the preceptoral approach constructed from a moral and political perspective. The enterprise autonomy policy and the 'tax-for-profit' schemes indicated the organizational and managerial orientation of the economic approach, albeit on a very limited scale (see Fig. 3).

It is appropriate to present two cases, the Soviet Union and Yugoslavia, in order to illustrate various difficulties which have been encountered in changing from the administrative policy-making approach to either the economic approach or the preceptoral approach. In general, Yugoslavia seems to have been more successful than the Soviet Union in moving towards the economic approach.

The rise of the administrative policy-making approach was closely allied with the process of rationalization, the formalization of routines, and the institutionalization which featured in the building of states in the modern era. The development of the Socialist states was no exception to such a process. Max Weber foresaw that 'Socialism would, in fact, require a still higher degree of formal bureaucratization than capitalism' when he wrote *Economy and Society* in 1911–13, long before the 'Russian experiment' took place.[12]

The evolution of the command economy was related to wars and crises in both the Soviet Union and China. Tracing the origins of central planning in the Soviet Union, E.H. Carr has suggested that Lenin's early exposure to a State-controlled economy in Germany during the First World War contributed significantly to the rise of 'State Capitalism' and 'War Socialism' in the Soviet Union after the Russian Revolution.[13] Lenin believed that Socialism was closely associated with war and State-building:

The dialectic history is such that the war, by enormously hastening the transformation of monopoly capital into state monopoly capital, has by that very means brought mankind enormously nearer to [S]ocialism.[14]

According to Alec Nove, Lenin concluded after the Revolution that 'if one took over the [S]tate, then one would achieve effective control over the cartelized industries.'[15] Furthermore, the political tradition of Imperial Russia was also selectively adopted: the various divisions of the Supreme Council of the National Economy after December 1917 closely corresponded to controls which had been devised by the Imperial Russian Government for wartime exigencies.

During the period of 'War Communism' from 1918 to 1920 all industrial concerns employing more than five workers were nationalized, and the attempt to administer industry along Socialist lines became the most important issue for Russian Communists. War and a State-administered economy are closely related, because a war crisis requires the total mobilization of an exhausted and ruined country and the imposition of central controls over production, regardless of costs. In the words of Benjamin Higgins, an American development economist, 'total war, like planning in the development of poor and stagnant economies, involves marked and discontinuous structural change and resource allocation without reference to the market.'[16]

In 1918, after the Revolution, Lenin attempted to introduce discipline and one-man management in industry, which led him briefly into Trotsky's camp on the issue of the 'militarization of labour'.[17] In E.H. Carr's words, the main lessons for industry which the Civil War drove home concerned the necessity for centralized control, direction, and planning, and the need for technical specialists and one-man responsibility in management, for the sake of efficiency. Under the pressure of the Civil War in December 1918, Lenin persuaded his followers to change from collegial administration to one-man management:

Collegiality, as the fundamental type of organization of the Soviet administration, represents something rudimentary, essential at the first stage when things have to be built anew. But once more or less stable forms are established, the transition to practical work is bound up with one-man management as the system which more than anything else guarantees the best utilization of human capacities and a real, not merely verbal, check on work done.[18]

The Stalinist model of a State-administered economy, inherited from Leninism, made provision for the unintended consequences of the formal structure (such as falsified records, organizational slack, distortions in product mix and in aggregate output, tampering with accounts, the informal practices of expediters, barter, the use of personal connection, and other deviations).[19] It was also characterized by remedial responses to the aforementioned deficiencies (in the form of parallel hierarchies,[20] 'independent controllers' such as chief accountants,[21] bypassing devices such as production conferences,[22] mass supervision practices,[23] periodical auditing, and bank supervision).

It was not until the Khrushchev era, after 1953, that the remedial responses began to develop in two distinct directions. The first direction, advocated by Nikita Khrushchev himself, focused on the decentralization of economic power from the ministerial level to the regional level,[24] and strengthened the direct link of the top political leadership with the masses,[25] workers' participation,[26] and community involvement in the policy process.[27] In spite of the Sino-Soviet polemics during the 1950s and 1960s, Khrushchev shared with Mao an anti-intellectual, anti-hierarchical, and anti-professional outlook (for instance, he proposed that manual labour should be a prerequisite for university admission).[28] Khrushchev's view of the policy-making approach approximated the preceptoral alternative advocated by the moral and political leadership in Mao's China.

The second type of remedial response followed an economic approach. In an article published in *Pravda* on 7 September 1962, Lieberman, one of the earliest advocates of economic reform in the USSR, stated that the basic criteria for success in the performance of an enterprise were that profits should be expressed as a percentage of the enterprise's capital, and that enterprise units should have the autonomy to formulate their own plans on orders negotiated with customers. Other authors developed Lieberman's view further by suggesting that, while planning was essential, the centre should be relieved of its intolerable burden of decision-making at the micro level. The reforming economists in the Soviet Union also had in mind some variants of the reforms introduced later in Hungary, and stressed the use of economic levers such as prices, credits, and markets in an essentially administered economy.[29] These reform ideas were still at the experimental stage at the time of Khrushchev's political demise.[30] Subsequently the proposals of both Khrushchev and Lieberman produced an impasse, because of their unanticipated results. Therefore the Soviet Union has not been able to transcend the framework of the command economy.

THE YUGOSLAV EXPERIENCE

Like China and the Eastern European countries,[31] Yugoslavia experimented with divergent paths towards Socialism as part of its search for a national identity and its critique of the Soviet system.[32] Yugoslavia had her own experience of a State-administered economy modelled after the Soviet Union. After the Second World War, when the First Five-year Plan was announced in 1945, the nationalization of the industrial sector eliminated all private enterprises except for the smallest service-oriented enterprises. All important policy-making was centralized in the hands of some 217 federal and republican ministries. These supervised the heads of industrial conglomerates, who in turn commanded the factory directors. This system compelled factories to operate on the basis of detailed annual or even shorter-term plans, rigidly fixed targets of production, buying and selling quotas, and norms for wages and profits. All investments were centrally controlled and the profits of enterprise units were funnelled into a central investment fund.[33]

According to the Yugoslav leader, Josip B. Tito, the factory directors, under pressure from centralized administrative planning, began to provide false underestimates of the capacity of enterprises, thereby enabling themselves to fulfil production plans more easily. They also showed less concern for efficiency and productivity.[34] Another author has suggested that the most typical 'distortions' in the Yugoslav economy included: careless attitudes towards the means of production; a decline in product quality and mix; and concealment of both technical and manpower potentialities.[35] The Yugoslav system was based mainly upon administrative discipline and various forms of moral and political pressure for the attainment of efficient economic activity. Yet the result was often contrary to the planners' original objectives:

The leading cadres of enterprises 'required' an even bigger amount of labour — both in the form of means of production and objects of production, and of active labour in the form of manpower — for no one bore the consequence of the latter, but only the responsibility for not fulfilling the plan...[36]

The Yugoslav diagnosis of the unintended consequences of the State-administered economy was that the role assigned to central planners was exceedingly large, even impossible; they did not have the knowledge or the capacity that they should have possessed in the policy-making process. Firstly, the Planning Commission lacked a clear understanding of the existing state of the economy and its basic units — the enterprises. In 1948, Tito complained of the absence of statistics. Kardelj also criticized the lack of precision in reports from enterprises to higher authorities. Secondly, even if the necessary data had been available, there were no economic criteria for evaluating the performance of enterprises or the economy. Very often the Planning Commission was bound by targets determined by the Party and the State leadership on the basis of their understanding of the Marxist philosophy of history, which could not be put into operation in the policy-making process. Thirdly, changing and complex legal provisions made it extremely difficult for those in authority to communicate their wishes down to the grassroots level, especially when speed was required. The flood of legal provisions caused so much confusion that, in 1952, only 150 out of 3,500 Acts could be enforced. Fourthly, the highly centralized structure of command stifled initiative at the lower levels, because those who made decisions which could improve quality were not rewarded. Ljubo Sirc noted that Kardelj himself eventually scorned this 'omnipotent' supervision: 'To make one person work, three persons were needed to supervise him.' Finally, the pricing system did not reflect the relative scarcity of resources.[37]

From an organizational and managerial perspective, Yugoslavia went much further than China in her decentralization policy in changing the economic system in the direction of market socialism, and in forming workers' councils.[38] The Yugoslav reforms were repeatedly pushed during the 1950s and 1960s, but suffered many setbacks, until they were superseded by the present system. Some of the reform programmes which China is now attempting may be found in Yugoslavia's efforts to promote the use of economic development, which took place as early as 1952, and featured the use of economic leverage such as taxation, interest rates, depreciation rates, and provisions for loans for capital investment, and so on.[39]

In his book, *The New Class*, Milovan Djilas provided a moral and political interpretation of the adverse consequences of the Soviet model. He attacked the 'closed Party circle', namely, the core or special stratum of the governing bureaucracy. According to Djilas, the new class of Communist functionaries obtained their privileged positions by using, enjoying, and disposing of almost all nationalized property. Although the managerial personnel of factories were not regarded as members of the new class, they were an integral part of the State bureaucracy which assisted the new class in controlling and appropriating State property.[40]

Dusan Popovic attacked managerial staff, whom he regarded as the social base upon which contemporary Statists seek to rely. He added that unskilled and semi-skilled labourers were dehumanized by being deprived of their rights, exploited by various economic or non-economic means, and placed at the bottom of the pyramid of Statist exploitation.[41] Taking the same moral tone, Adolf Dragicevic warned of a 'natural tendency' for technically co-ordinated power, vested in the hands of technical managerial staff, to degenerate into political and economic dominance over workers, and for managers to form a class to face the numerically greater, but more disorganized, mass of workers.[42] Accordingly, Yugoslavia's preceptoral policy-making approach adopted the participatory-management style of the workers' council, and emphasized the ideological role of the Party (or the Communist League) in bridging the gap between the top leaders and the masses.

In its version of the economic policy-making approach, Yugoslavia introduced extensive political and economic decentralization, and restructured the State ownership system. The latter was seen in 'social ownership' — the joint control exercised by local governments (communes and republics) and workers' councils at the enterprise level. In addition, economic institutions, such as banks, played an increasingly important role in the allocation of investment funds. The market therefore became the main instrument in the distribution of resources for production and consumption. 'Economic levers' were used extensively in Yugoslavia.

META-POLICY-MAKING IN THE SOCIALIST POLITICAL SYSTEM

It might be useful to conclude this study with a survey of various writers' analyses of meta-policy-making in industrial management policy in China. The present author shares with many other writers on China's policy-making process the assumption that three independent variables are relevant in the change from one decision-making approach to another, namely, politics, ideology, and organization (see Chapter 1). There have been three main approaches to the study of policy in China, each constructed on the basis of one of these independent variables.

A political approach takes policy output as a by-product of politics, be it patron-client networks, factional rivalry, or coalition formation. Studies of this type include Andrew J. Nathan's 'factionalism model',[43] Michael Oksenberg's focus on occupational groups,[44] Tsou Tang's formulation of the cleavage between the establishment and society,[45] and David Lampton's study of policy oscillations resulting from periodic outbursts.[46] The ideological approach focuses on doctrines and principles, and tends to assume that the CCP's policy flows automatically from its official ideology. It therefore assumes that there is always an articulated ideological position for each policy. Franz Schurmann,[47] Stephen Andors,[48] and Charles Bettelheim[49] are representatives of this approach to the study of industrial management. The organizational approach centres on the relationship of institutional and procedural variables to policy-making. Studies taking this approach include the works of John W. Lewis,[50] A. Doak Barnett,[51] Michael Oksenberg,[52] Parris Chang,[53] Kenneth Lieberthal,[54] Harry Harding,[55] Audrey Donnithorne,[56] and Nicholas Lardy.[57] In the arena of industrial management, Thomas Rawski[58] and William Brugger[59] mainly employ the organizational approach.

In the present study, the author proposes a different position, encompassing all three approaches, and asserts that the time frame in which each variable functions is important to our understanding of meta-policy-making. From the perspective of the so-called 'garbage can model', each independent variable is treated as a 'window', the opening or closing of which is contingent upon some specific historical conditions. There is no reason to suggest that all three are necessarily activated in each policy-making situation. Because the independent variables are sometimes only partially activated, the policy-making process does not always take place in a well-structured, coherent, and consistent fashion.

Indeed this book, like many other studies of policy-making, has moved away from the classical model of 'conservative rationalism', which has a clearly defined end, readily available means, perfect consistency between end and means, and a cohesive structure of policy participation (either by a single rational actor or a formal and well-organized policy-making entity).[60] This book borrows heavily from the theory of incrementalism in highlighting the use of pilot schemes, the role of past practices and policy precedents, limited modifications on the basis of experience, and adjustments as a result of feedback in the Chinese context.[61] The author basically subscribes to the incrementalism approach, as regards the limited availability of means (and other correlates such as bounded rationality, inconsistency between end and means, unintended consequences, and so on), but still has considerable reservations as to whether policy-makers should always possess a well-defined objective (such as profit-maximization for the rational economic man).

This book suggests that organizational means and policy participation might sometimes be irrelevant, and also that ideological premises might be entirely fragmented. The findings of this book tend to confirm the general perspective of the 'garbage can model' which proposes that the influence of independent variables, such as ideological premises (goal formation), organizational means (methods, know-how, and resources), and policy participation (the

Fig. 4   The Modes of the Policy-making Process

		Modes	
Variables	Rationalism	Incrementalism	Organized anarchism (garbage-can model)
Ideological premises	h	h	h/l
Organizational means	h	h/l	h/l
Policy participation	h	h/l	h/l

Key: h = high degree of articulation and availability
     l = low degree of articulation and availability

relationship of actors) is empirically open-ended.[62] One can draw up a theoretical model encompassing the three modes of the policy-making process on the basis of the relevance of the three independent variables (see Fig. 4).

This book has already demonstrated that the beginning of the command economy and one-man management in China did not involve a clearly defined ideological premise and was not politically motivated; it was built upon the existing planned economy and industrial complex left by the Japanese colonial administration. Thus it is entirely possible for the available organizational means to be in search of an ideological premise (such as Chinese Socialism) and a political motivation (as was provided by Gao Gang's quest for self-aggrandizement). Similarly, it is possible to have a well-defined doctrine in search of the organizational means for its implementation. For example, in the Cultural Revolution Mao Zedong had a well-defined doctrine for a charisma-inspired and mass-oriented management, but the Daqing model that Mao recommended was not a viable means for implementing it.

In addition, it often took a considerable time for a well-formulated doctrine to find the appropriate means. For instance, when the retrenchment policy was being carried out from 1959 to 1962, ideological premises such as 'the whole country as a chessboard' and the 'parts-and-sum' relationship did not find effective means of implementation for four years, until the West Chamber Conference. Furthermore, theories of economic reform were articulated in the period 1979–80, but viable formats (such as the 'tax-for-profit' schemes) were not found until after some false starts (as, for example, in the profit-retention system and the profit-contract system). Therefore one cannot rely upon the traditional view of consistency between the goal and the means in order to characterize the policy-making process in most, if not all, cases in the PRC.

To say that ideology is often irrelevant does not, however, mean that it has no bearing at all. On the one hand, this author is not willing to go as far as Charles E. Lindblom who proposed that ideology had no place in policy-making merely because of the difficulties of putting it into operation.[63] In some situations ideology appears to have provided guidance for policy-making. For example, the nationalization of industry, the collectivization of agriculture, and the establishment of extensive welfare networks and an insurance system were all influenced by the CCP's ideological commitments. On the other hand, this author does not assert that Chinese policy-makers always had such high principles as they claimed. They were not always blind to the moral implications and the practical feasibility of policy. This study has shown that they evaluated policy proposals and implementation on the basis of their intrinsic merits and practical results. They also evaluated their own performance in the policy-making process.

As regards policy-makers' participation in policy-making, several factors may be worthy of consideration. To begin with, policy-actors in the Chinese context required an institutional foothold in order to enter into a particular area of policy, be it membership of the Secretariat, membership of the Politburo, or ministership of the State Council. Moreover, it would be easier for a policy-actor to exert influence if he were assigned to a specific functional area on the basis of his established knowledge of and competence in this area. We may note, for example, Chen Yun's role in the decentralization policy (1957–62), Bo Yibo's role in the 'Seventy Articles' (1961–6), and Deng Xiaoping's role in enterprise rectification (1974–5).

Factional politics occasionally have a functional role in the policy-making process, although not in the exact manner suggested by the traditional formulation of a two-factional model. In fact, the question of whether there are always two clearly defined and well-organized factions in each policy-making situation is an empirical one. There have also been cases of non-factional and one-factional policy-making. Non-factional policy-making was seen in the formulation and implementation of the policy paper, 'On the Ten Great Relationships', in which each actor found his role through a series of mutual adjustments in a more or less spontaneous situation. One-factional policy-making was seen in the readjustment-versus-reform controversy in 1979–81, when Chen Yun, Deng Xiaoping, and others acted as a faction against an amorphous group of ministerial and local bureaucrats, enterprise units, and academic observers.

The two-factional models of policy-making are relevant in a limited number of cases. These include, for instance, the Cultural Revolution and its aftermath, in the period 1966–76 (that is, the period of rivalry between the pragmatic leaders and the ultra-leftist leaders under Mao Zedong). This author is of the opinion that the two-factional model cannot be applied to all cases of policy-making in the PRC. Nor is Jurgen Domes' concept of 'factionalization' always helpful because it presupposes the ultimate development of two factions.[64] But whether such a development will occur is an empirical question.

In the theoretical controversy over the 'factionalism model', Professors Andrew J. Nathan and Tsou Tang held the view that the types of political alignments of and the conflicts between the top Chinese leaders have changed over time rather then remaining constantly factional.[65] Professor Tsou cautioned against using our understanding of Chinese politics during one particular period as the basis for interpreting or reinterpreting the entire political history of the CCP.[66] The present study has not only confirmed the views of Tsou and Nathan, but added further qualifications to their observations.

Our concern in this book is with the relationship of politics (whether factional or non-factional) to changing policy outputs. This book has drawn distinctions at three analytical levels: the first is concerned with whether or not politics (that is, an attempt to maintain or allocate power) is activated in the policy-making process; the second level relates to the types of politics, namely, non-factional, one-factional, two-factional, or multi-factional; the third concerns the need to account for the process through which politics affects policy outcome, for example, in terms of intended results or by-products, and so on. The author's observation on the basis of this case study of policy-making suggests that politics may not always be relevant to policy-making and need not be factional. Although politics involves deliberate choice, as does policy-making, one cannot automatically assume that policy-actors always have opportunities for choice and the intellectual faculties for making policy, much less the necessary motivation, apparatus, and resources to enforce such choice. An over-estimate of policy-makers' motivation, intellect, resources, and capacity tends to inject too great an element of politics into the study of the policy-making process.

SUMMARY AND IMPLICATIONS

With the case history of one policy-making area this book has demonstrated that the fundamental deficiency in the synoptic model (including the administrative and preceptoral approaches) is derived from the official expectation that the policy maker, whether a sovereign planner or a charismatic leader, will play an omniscient and omnipotent role. The unrealistically large role envisaged does not match the reality of policy-making situations, where policy goals are often fragmented, diverse, and at best only partly articulated, while the organizational means are either absent or in short supply; and participation in such a process is fluid, ever-changing, and, in most cases, not fully structured. On the same synoptic dimension, therefore, the charismatic leader (who represents the preceptoral approach) is not an effective substitute for the sovereign planner (who represents the administrative approach).

The synoptic model involves a search for a policy-making model to alleviate the tension between the synoptic ideal and reality. The economic approach appears to be a viable alternative to the administrative approach or the preceptoral approach. In the PRC, the movement towards the economic approach first took place on a limited scale during the Great Leap Forward, and has gained fresh momentum in two consecutive stages in the post-Mao era. This book suggests that the Chinese policy-actors started their partial-incremental reform during the first stage (1978–83) and changed to total-incremental reform during the second stage (from 1984). During the second stage, the intended scope of the reform has been comprehensive, but its implementation has followed a step-by-step approach, thus comprising what Amitai Etzioni calls a 'mixed scanning' strategy which has a general direction, but which makes marginal adjustments according to feedback.[67]

This book has identified two basic types of movement towards the economic approach. One is remedial, in the sense that the economic reform (such as decentralization, enterprise autonomy, and profit-retention schemes) stays within the parameter of the command economy. At the institutional level, remedial reform is explained in terms of the cycle of purposive control, unanticipated results, and renewed control in the policy arena of industrial management. This explanation has been based upon the post-Weberian notion of imperfect rationalization, and has run parallel with Herbert A. Simon's view of 'bounded rationality' from a decision-making perspective. At the other end of the conceptual continuum, the second type is the innovative reform (such as the market-centred economy, the use of economic leverage, and the tax-for-profit schemes), entailing development towards the 'strategic model', in which policy-making is guided by volition, preference, and tangible interest, and is co-ordinated through interaction (such as bargaining, mutual adjustments, and coalition formation).

Last, but not least, it is germane for us to discuss the implications of this book's analysis as regards the 'tendencies model' in the study of the Socialist political system in general and Chinese politics in particular. The theoretical framework of policy-making differs from that of the 'tendencies model', but it is better able to account for the varying degrees of policy articulation and the unintended consequences of policy, which are noted but not explained by Franklyn Griffiths, who considers that 'tendencies' refer to:

pattern[s] of [value] articulation associated with a loose coalition of actors operating at different levels of the political structure, whose articulations tend in the same direction but who are *unlikely* to be fully aware of the common thrust and consequences of their activity [emphasis added].[68]

In both empirical and theoretical terms, the 'tendencies model' makes unwarranted assumptions. It highlights the phenomenon of a policy cycle or 'policy oscillations';[69] and it works, in a logically backward manner, to identify the value orientations and political forces which precede changes of policy output. However, such a model unrealistically assumes that each policy is intended, that its implementation is fully controlled, and that its consequences are anticipated. This book takes a contrasting position, treating the independent variables of policy-making (such as ideology, politics, and organization) as 'windows', a position which approximates the situation demonstrated in this case history of industrial management. To some extent, this book has dealt with unresolved issues concerning the application of the 'tendencies model' to Chinese politics, such as the 'caricatures' of Chinese politics and the 'two-line struggle', as identified by Harry Harding, Lowell Dittmer, and others.[70] The 'two-line struggle', with all of its correlates (such as the infallibility of the supreme leader, dogmatism, political symbolism, retrospective justification, and so on), is seen as a remedial adjustment in the preceptoral policy-making approach (see Appendix 2), as well as the crisis situation and responses in the cases of the Great Leap Forward and the Cultural Revolution (see pp. 60-9 and 113-15 respectively).

As suggested in Chapter 1, Dr Dorothy Solinger, in her work on commercial policy in the PRC, shows her awareness of the analytical distinction between the policy-making model and the 'tendencies model', but, while the author relies upon the former to study China's industrial management policy, Solinger employs the latter to analyse commercial policy in the PRC. She states that 'the trichotomy [that is, the tendencies of the "bureaucrat", the "radical", and the "marketeer"] on which this analysis rests *corresponds* to universal typologies set out in several influential studies' (emphasis added).[71] These 'universal typologies' of policy-making, which were mentioned but not used by Solinger, refer to the normative modes of policy formation and implementation which have been the central concern of this book. They include: (a) Amitai Etzioni's three power-means, coercive, normative, and remunerative; (b) the analysis by G. William Skinner and Edwin A. Winckler of the CCP's control over the Chinese peasantry; and, above all, (c) Charles E. Lindblom's three-fold pattern of policy-making.[72]

Although Solinger's research emphasizes the assumed linkages of value orientations and political alliances to changing policy output, in theoretical terms she fails to deal with the process of how ideology or politics are related to policy output. This book has attempted to identify the features of meta-policy-making and the characteristics of the policy-making system. The author has thereby been able to identify the dynamic process of policy formulation and the extent of its implementation, as well as the unintended consequences and subsequent adjustments, during the history of the PRC.

Appendices

APPENDIX 1   THE THEORETICAL DIMENSIONS OF THE POLICY-MAKING PROCESS

Dimensions	Model I (Synoptic Model. Root Method. Rational Comprehensive Approach)	Model II (Strategic Model. Branch Method. Successively Limited Comparison)
1. Criterion/criteria for the 'correct' decision	(a) Objectivity; absolute standard (b) To be discovered and can be discovered; final and definite answer (c) Quality of decision	(a) Intersubjectivity (b) Choice by agreement; approximation to the truth (c) Degree of acceptance
2. Process to reach a decision	(a) Intuition; charismatic leader; central decision-maker (b) Problem diagnosis (c) Theoretical knowledge as a guide; decision dictates preference (d) Once-and-for-all answer	(a) Interaction process (bargaining, mutual adjustment) (b) Problem-solving (c) Personal preference (volition) as a basis; preference dictates decision (d) Incrementalism (limited comparison at successive stages; partial answer)
3. Style of reasoning	(a) Clarity and consistency of goals and their rank order	(a) Lack of clarity and consistency of objectives; no well-established priority

Dimensions	Model I (Synoptic Model. Root Method. Rational Comprehensive Approach)	Model II (Strategic Model. Branch Method. Successively Limited Comparison)
	(b) Logical analysis of means and ends (i) well-isolated ends (ii) direct link of means to ends (c) Comprehensive analysis of all existing and theoretically possible factors and alternatives (d) Theoretically oriented	(b) Means-centred analysis (pragmatism) (i) Means and ends considered simultaneously (ii) No logical separation of means from ends (c) Non-comprehensive analysis (comparison of limited number of alternatives to the status quo) (d) Practically oriented
4. Perception of uncertainty	(a) Sufficient information on alternatives and their consequences (b) Full capacity for forecasting and planning (c) Unlimited capability to control consequences of each alternative (d) Attempts to absorb all uncertainty	(a) Inadequate information on alternatives and their consequences (b) Limited power in forecasting and planning (c) Limited ability in the mastery of the consequences of each alternative (d) Avoidance of uncertainty
5. Status of theory and procedure	(a) Prominent status of theory/knowledge (b) De-emphasis on procedure/rules of game/due process in decision-making (c) Correctness of substantive principles	(a) No need of theory/knowledge (b) Stress on procedure/due process/rules of game in decision-making process (c) Fairness of procedural rules

Dimensions	Model I (Synoptic Model. Root Method. Rational Comprehensive Approach)	Model II (Strategic Model. Branch Method. Successively Limited Comparison)
6. Organizational relationship	(a) Hierarchy, bureaucracy, and centralized system (b) Desirability of harmony, coherence, and integration	(a) Coalition, participation, and decentralized system (b) Value of conflict, diversity, and fragmentation
7. Views of society	(a) Unitary, bureaucratic, centralized State; autonomy of the State (b) Cohesive, organic, and class society (c) Command economy (d) Individual as a member of society; value of individual defined by his/her membership	(a) Federal, democratic, and decentralized State; State as an extension of society (b) Pluralistic society (c) Market economy (d) Individuals as basis of society; value of society defined in terms of preference of the individuals

Sources: Charles E. Lindblom, "The Science of "Muddling Through"', *Public Administration Review*, Vol. 19 (1959), pp. 79–99; Robert A. Dahl and Charles E. Lindblom, *Politics, Economics and Welfare* (New York, Harper & Row, 1953); Charles E. Lindblom, *The Intelligence of Democracy* (New York, The Free Press, 1965); Charles E. Lindblom, *Politics and Markets* (New York, Basic Books Inc., 1977).

APPENDIX 2 REMEDIAL RESPONSES WITHIN THE SYNOPTIC MODEL

Arenas	Administrative Approach		Preceptoral Approach	
	Functional Responses	Dysfunctional Responses	Functional Responses	Dysfunctional Responses
1. Ideological	(a) Seeking the truth from the facts	(a) Excessively high targets	(a) Mass-line	(a) Infallibility of the supreme leader and the Party
	(b) Observance of the law of economy	(b) Exaggerated sense of capacity and poor judgement of the situation	(b) Comradely criticism and self-criticism	(b) Politics in command (invincibility of class struggle)
	(c) Research and investigation	(c) 'Commandism', 'subjectivism', and 'bureaucratism'	(c) Constructive open-door rectification	(c) Political symbolism, retrospective justification, and dogmatism
2. Institutional	(a) Decentralization I and II	(a) Over-concentration of formal authority	(a) Effective bypassing mechanism from top to bottom	(a) Abuse and distortion of the directives of the supreme leader
	(b) 'Simple administration and crack troops'	(b) Overstaffing and procedural complexity; proliferation of meetings and paper work	(b) Dispatch of work-teams to the lower levels; downward transfer of cadres; the rotation of posts	(b) The 'Paris Commune' type of mass organization; 'link-up' among the masses; 'commando approach'

Arenas	Administrative Approach		Preceptoral Approach	
	Functional Responses	Dysfunctional Responses	Functional Responses	Dysfunctional Responses
3. Managerial	(a) Financial accountability and administrative discipline	(a) Excessive organizational slack, lack of accounting and efficiency	(a) Full mobilization of human resources; effectiveness but no lack of efficiency	(a) Relaxation and sometimes break-down of accounting and administrative rules; diversion of resources
	(b) Standardized wages and salaries balanced by collective welfare and political education	(b) One-sided emphasis on material incentives and individual's achievements	(b) A sense of mission, purpose, and commitment	(b) Overemphasis on moral appeal, and short-lived voluntarism and mass enthusiasm
	(c) Due respect to professional knowledge and technology	(c) Excessive privileges to 'experts'	(c) Appropriate role for experts but emphasis on consultation with the masses	(c) Attack on experts and professionals; too great importance of amateur-generalists (non-professionals and masses)
	(d) Adaptation of central policy to local situations and individual cases	(d) Arbitrary application of central politics	(d) Direct involvement of the masses in the implementation of policy	(d) Misrepresentation of demands of masses and deviation among low-echelon cadres

Arenas	Administrative Approach		Preceptoral Approach	
	Functional Responses	Dysfunctional Responses	Functional Responses	Dysfunctional Responses
	(e) The use of pilot programmes; summing up of experience; incrementalism guided by feedback	(e) Imposition and haste	(e) The use of pilot programmes; summing up of experience; incrementalism guided by feedback	(e) Symbolic use of model experience; and falsification of the experimental results
	(f) The use of policy precedents and past practices	(f) Bureaucratic rigidity and ritualistic adherence to established politics	(f) Policy guidance tailored to the concrete situation	(f) 'Destruction above construction'; innovative attempts without realistic appraisals
4. Political	(a) Polycentralism sanctioned by institutional framework	(a) Territoriality with excessive disparity between various sectors	(a) Charismatic leader answerable to crises	(a) The cult of personality
	(b) Balancing interests of central élite, local authorities, basic units, and individual producers	(b) Privileges, inequality, and alienation	(b) Comradeship, egalitarianism and meaningful participation	(b) Mob-ocracy
	(c) Everyone equal before the law	(c) Compartmentalism and mutual isolation	(c) A sense of community	(c) Anarchism and factionalism

Notes

NOTES TO CHAPTER 1

1. The State Statistical Bureau, the People's Republic of China (PRC), *Statistical Yearbook of China 1984* (Hong Kong, Economic Information and Agency, 1984), p. 419.

2. Franz Schurmann, *Ideology and Organisation in Communist China* (Berkeley, Calif., and London, University of California Press, 1968), pp. 226–35.

3. Stephen Andors, *China's Industrial Revolution* (New York, Pantheon Books, 1977), pp. 3–25.

4. Samuel P. Huntington and Joan M. Nelson, *No Easy Choice: Political Participation in Developing Countries* (Cambridge, Mass., Harvard University Press, 1976), pp. 42–78.

5. Yehezhel Dror, *Public Policy-making Re-examined* (Bedfordshire, England, Leonard Hill Books, 1973), pp. 163–96.

6. Charles E. Lindblom, *The Intelligence of Democracy* (New York, The Free Press, 1965), pp. 3–17.

7. A detailed analysis of various categories of documents at the Politburo level is given in Kenneth G. Lieberthal, *Central Documents and Politburo Politics in China* (Michigan Papers in Chinese Studies, No. 33, Ann Arbor, University of Michigan Press, 1978).

8. Dror (1973), pp. 163–96, note 5 above.

9. Charles O. Jones, *An Introduction to the Study of Public Policy* (Belmont, Calif., Wadsworth, second edition, 1977), pp. 8–9.

10. Michael D. Cohen, James G. March, and Johan P. Olson, 'A Garbage Can Model of Organizational Choice', *Administrative Science Quarterly*, No. 17 (March 1972), pp. 1–23; John W. Kingdon, *Agendas, Alternatives, and Public Policies* (Boston, Little, Brown and Company, 1984), pp. 88–94.

11. Dorothy J. Solinger, *Chinese Business under Socialism: The Politics of Domestic Commerce, 1949–1980* (Berkeley, Calif., and London, University of California Press, 1984).

12. Charles E. Lindblom, *Politics and Markets* (New York, Basic Books Inc., 1977), pp. 253–60.

13. Max Weber, *The Theory of Social and Economic Organization*, translated by A.M. Henderson and Talcott Parsons (New York, The Free Press, 1947), p. 88.

14. Herbert A. Simon, *Administrative Behavior* (New York, The Free Press, 1957).

15. Richard H. Hall, 'Closed-system, Open-system and Contingency-choice Perspectives' in Amitai Etzioni and Edward W. Lehman (eds.), *A Sociological Reader on Complex Organizations* (New York, Holt, Rinehart and Winston, third edition, 1980), pp. 32–43.

16. Richard M. Cyert and James G. March, *A Behavioral Theory of the Firm* (Englewood Cliffs, New Jersey, Prentice-Hall, Inc., 1963), pp. 26–43.

17. Amitai Etzioni, *The Active Society* (New York, The Free Press, 1968), pp. 282–4.

18. Anthony Downs, *Inside Bureaucracy* (Boston, Little, Brown and Company, 1967), pp. 32–40.

19. Andrew Shonfield, *Modern Capitalism: The Changing Balance of Public and Private Power* (New York and London, Oxford University Press, 1965).

20. Richard E. Flathman, *The Public Interest* (New York, John Wiley & Sons Inc., 1966).

21. Adam Smith, *The Wealth of Nations* (New York, Random House, Inc., 1937), p. 651.

22. Lindblom (1977), pp. 276–90, note 11 above.

23. For the strategic model upon which the economic approach rests, it is appropriate to employ the term 'intersubjectivity' to characterize the process of 'knowing', and therefore 'prescribing' (an essential element of policy-making). Many interacting policy-actors are involved and the issue is of concern to all participants in public policy-making. It is politically possible to prescribe and impose a consensus, such as the 'four fundamental principles' or, in the Chinese context, the 'law of economy'. Yet it is not tenable at the epistemological level to ascertain the existence of an absolute 'truth' on which such a policy is based. To do this one must assume the existence of an omniscient policy-maker, transcendental to human beings and their functions of feeling, observing, and reasoning. The term 'subjectivity' is untenable, not only for its pejorative meaning, but also for its assumption of private reasoning as applied to the public sphere. Epistemologically speaking, the implicit position derived from the concept of 'subjectivity' would initiate a series of debates on the possibility of private feeling, a private language, and a private ideology (or ethics). The author is of the opinion that ethical (or ideological) discourse, including both factual and evaluative components, is 'intersubjective' at three analytical levels. First, such a discourse has to be conducted according to the rule of 'universality', by applying an evaluative principle consistently to similar persons under similar circumstances. Second, a public language must be employed to identify and communicate ethical notions, and to make sense of 'private' or 'subjective' meanings. Third, the factual (or material) component concerns the public sphere, the definition of which can only evolve through 'symbolic interaction' or intersubjective interpretation. See Richard Flathman, *The Public Interest* (New York, John Wiley & Sons Inc., 1966); Kurt Baier, *The Moral Point of View: A Rational Basis of Ethics* (Ithaca, New York, Cornell University Press, 1958); Julius Kovesi, *Moral Notions* (London, Routledge and Kegan Paul, 1967); Philippa Foot, 'Moral Beliefs', in Philippa Foot (ed.), *The Theories of Ethics* (Oxford, Oxford University Press, 1967), pp. 83–100; A. J. Ayer, 'Can There Be a Private Language?', in George Pitcher (ed.), *Wittgenstein: The Philosophical Investigations: A Collection of Critical Essays* (Garden City, New York, Doubleday and Company, Inc., 1966), pp. 251–66; R. Rhees, 'Can There Be a Private Language?', in Pitcher (1966), pp. 267–85; John W. Cook, 'Wittgenstein on Privacy', in Pitcher (1966), pp. 286–323; Alan Donagan, 'Wittgenstein on Sensation', in Pitcher (1966), pp. 324–51.

NOTES TO CHAPTER 2

1. Shanghai shehui kexueyuan jingji yanjiusuo, *Shanghai zibenzhuyi gongshangye de shehuizhuyi gaizao* (*The Socialist Reform of the Capitalist Commerce and Industry in Shanghai*) (Shanghai, Shanghai renmin chubanshe, 1980).

2. Gao Gang, 'Zhanzai Dongbei jingji jianshe de zui qianmian' ('Stand on the Forefront of the Economic Construction in North-east China'), *Shenyang ribao* (*Shengyang Daily*), 6 June 1950, p. 2.

3. Dongbei fangzhi guanliju, 'Jingji hesuanzhi de zongjie' ('The Summary of the Experience in the Economic Accounting System'), *Xinhua yuebao* (*New China Monthly*), Vol. IV, No. 2, June 1951, pp. 353–6.

4. 'Zhengwuyuan guanyu yijiuwuyi nian guoying gongye shengchan jianshe de jueding' ('The Decision of the Government Administrative Council concerning the Production and Construction of the State-owned Industry in 1951'), *Xinhua yuebao*, Vol. IV, No. 1, May 1951, pp. 137–9.

5. Zhang Guanghua, 'Guoying qiye jingji jihua de bianzhi gongzuo' ('The Task in Formulating the Economic Plans of the State-owned Enterprise'), *Xinhua yuebao*, Vol. IV, No. 1, May 1951, pp. 129–32.

6. Zhang Dadian, 'Guoying gongye de cailiao gongying gongzuo' ('The Work of Material Supply in the State-owned Enterprises'), *Xinhua yuebao*, Vol. IV, No. 1, May 1951, pp.132–4.

7. 'Wancheng quannian jihua tigao shengchan gongzuo yingjie da guimao jianshe de xin shiqi' ('Fulfil the Annual Plans, Improve Production Work, Usher in a New Era of Large-scale Construction'), *Shenyang ribao*, 13 December 1952, p. 1; Che Zhenguo, 'Jinxing junheng you jiezou di shengchan bixu jiaqang keshi gongzuo' ('Strengthen the Work of Functional Departments, Maintain the Balance and Rhythm in Production'), *Shenyang ribao*, 25 June 1953, p. 2.

8. Gongye jihauchu jidianshi, 'Jixie si chang an zhishi tubiao zuzhi you jiezou shengchan de jingyan' ('The Experience of Organizing Rythmic Production on the Basic Indicative Table: The Case of the No. 4 Machinery Works'), *Shenyang ribao*, 13 May 1952, p. 2; 'Cong xinzhong wushu dao you jihua de shengchan' ('From No Calculation to Planned Production'), *Shenyang ribao*, 5 December 1952, p. 1.

9. 'Jixie sichang dui guojia jihua renshi bu zhengque' ('The No. 4 Machinery Works' Incorrect Understanding on the State Plan'), *Shenyang ribao*, 27 April 1953, p. 5.

10. 'Jia bao chengji pianqu xianjinchang chenghao' ('Falsification of Achievement to Obtain the Title of Advanced Factory'), *Shenyang ribao*, 10 June 1953, pp. 1 and 3.

11. 'Taolun guojia jihua de chengji he jingyan' ('The Achievement and Experience in the Discussion of the State Plan'), *Shenyang ribao*, 8 April 1953, p. 1.

12. Dongbei fangzhi guanliju, 'The Summary of the Experience...', *Xinhua yuebao*, Vol. IV, No. 2, June 1951, pp. 353–6, note 3 above.

13. Dongbei renmin zhengfu, 'Dongbeiqu guoying qiye guding zichan zhanxing guanli guicheng' ('Temporary Regulation of the Management of Fixed Assets in the State-owned Enterprises in the North-east Region'), *Xinhua yuebao*, Vol. III, No. 3, January 1951, p. 586.

14. 'Guanyu guoying qiye zai zengchan jieyue yundong zhong zhankai heding zijin gongzuo de zhishi' ('The Directive concerning the Task of Auditing the Working Capital in the Movement of Saving and Increase of Production'), *Xinhuo yuebao*, No. 1, January 1952, p. 146.

15. 'Lun dongbei gongying qiye guanli zhidu shang he jiandai zhidu shang de zhongda gaige' ('On the Major Reform of the Managerial System and Credit System of Public Enterprises in the North-east'), *Xinhua yuebao*, Vol. I, No. 4, February 1950, p. 937.

16. 'On the Major Reform of the Managerial System...', *Xinhua yuebao*, Vol. I, No. 4, February 1950, p. 937, note 15 above.

17. 'Zhonggongyebu zhishi ge qiye tuixing jingji hesuan zhi' ('The Directive of the Heavy Industry Ministry on the Implementation of the Enterprise Accounting System'), *Xinhua yuebao*, Vol. IV, No. 2, June 1951, p. 352.

18. 'The Summary of the Experience...', *Xinhua yuebao*, Vol. IV, No. 2, June 1951, pp. 353–6, note 3 above.

19. 'The Summary of the Experience...', *Xinhua yuebao*, Vol. IV, No. 2, June 1951, pp. 353–6, note 3 above.

20. William Brugger, *Democracy and Organization in the Chinese Enterprise, 1948–1953* (Cambridge, Cambridge University Press, 1976), pp. 124–38.

21. Gao Gang, 'Stand on the Forefront...', *Shenyang ribao*, 6 June 1950, p. 2, note 2 above.

22. Gao Gang, 'Stand on the Forefront...', *Shenyang ribao*, 6 June 1950, p. 2, note 2 above.

23. 'Buneng rongxu weifa jiaban jiadian' ('The Overtime Work is in Violation of Law and Should not Be Tolerated'), *Shenyang ribao*, 8 January 1951, p. 1.

24. Gao Gang, 'Stand on the Forefront...', *Shenyang ribao*, 6 June 1950, p. 3, note 2 above.

25. 'Dongbei fangzhi guanliju guanyu dinge guanli de zongjie' ('The Summing-up of Experience of the North-east Textile Managing Bureau on the Management of Norms'), *Xinhua yuebao*, Vol. 4, No. 2, June 1951, pp. 357–8; 'Zhonggong zhongyang dongbeiju jiaqiang chejian gong zuo jinyibu kaizhan zhengchan jieyue yundong de tongbao' ('The Circular of the North-east Bureau, CC, CCP, concerning Strengthening Work in Workshop and Launching the Increase of Production and Saving Movement'), *Shenyang ribao*, 7 December 1951, pp. 1–2; 'Gao Gang tongzhi zhishi jiaqiang gongchan chejian gongzuo' ('Comrade Gao Gang's Directive on Strengthening Work in the Workshop'), *Xinhua yuebao*, No. 27, January 1952, pp. 149–50.

26. Gao Gang, 'Stand on the Forefront...', *Shenyang ribao*, 6 June 1950, p. 2, note 2 above.

27. Gao Gang, 'Stand on the Forefront...', *Shenyang ribao*, 6 June 1950, p. 2, note 2 above.

28. 'Zhonggong zhongyang dongbeiju guanyu dang dui guoying qiye lingdao de jueyi' ('The Resolution of the North-east Bureau, CC, CCP, concerning the Leadership System of Public Enterprises'), *Shenyang ribao*, 7 September 1951, pp. 185–90.

29. 'The Resolution of the North-east Bureau...', *Shenyang ribao*, 7 September 1951, pp. 185–90, note 28 above.

30. James G. March and Herbert A. Simon, *Organizations* (New York, John Wiley & Sons Inc., 1958), pp. 12–33; Herbert A. Simon, *Administrative Behavior* (New York, The Free Press, 1957), pp. 140–1.

31. Brugger (1976), pp. 185–90, note 20 above.

32. 'The Resolution of the North-east Bureau...', *Shenyang ribao*, 7 September 1951, pp. 1–2, note 28 above.

33. 'The Resolution of the North-east Bureau...', *Shenyang ribao*, 7 September 1951, pp. 1–2, note 28 above.

34. 'The Resolution of the North-east Bureau...', *Shenyang ribao*, 7 September 1951, pp. 1–2, note 28 above.

35. Zhang Mingyuan, 'Gaijin women qiye de jingying guanli gongzuo' ('Improve our Tasks in the Enterprise Management'), *Xinhua yuebao*, Vol. II, No. 6, October 1950, p. 1375.

36. Brugger (1976), pp. 217–52, note 20 above.

37. Brugger (1976), pp. 202–4, note 20 above. Here Brugger gives some details of the chief engineer system. Franz Schurmann mentions the chief accountant system and the chief accountant's veto power over expenditures: see H.F. Schurmann, *Ideology and Organisation in Communist China* (Berkeley, Calif., University of California Press, 1968), pp. 249–50.

38. 'Kaishantun zaozhichang jiaqiang yusuan guanli' ('Strengthen Budgetary Management in Kaishantun Paper Factory'), *Zhongguo qinggongye (China's Light Industry)*, No. 14, 28 July 1956, pp. 23–4; 'Cong Dujiang fadianchang laikan tuixing chengben zuotanhui de zuoyong' ('To Assess the Effect of the Meeting on Cost in the Light of the Dujiang Power Plant'), *Renmin dianye (People's Electricity Industry)*, No. 21, 25 July 1956, pp. 16–18.

39. Zhang Mingyuan, 'Improve our Tasks...', *Xinhua yuebao*, Vol. II, No. 6, October 1950, p. 1375, note 35 above.

40. Zhang Mingyuan, 'Improve our Tasks...', *Xinhua yuebao*, Vol. II, No. 6, October 1950, p. 1375, note 35 above.

41. Harry Harding, *Organizing China* (Stanford, Stanford Unviersity Press, 1981), pp. 19–22.

42. Harding (1981), pp. 22–4, note 41 above.

43. 'Zhonggong zhongyang dongbeiju guanyu guoying chang kuang zhankai zengchan jieyue jingsai yundong yu wuliu yuefen zhongxin gongzuo de zhishi' ('The Directive of the North-east Bureau, CC, CCP, concerning the Launching of Competition-movement for Saving and Production in State-owned Mining and Industrial Enterprises Increase and Central Task in May and June'), *Shenyang ribao*, 9 May 1952, pp. 1–2.

44. Zhou Shaopeng, 'Zhongguo gongye jingji zerenzhi' ('The Economic Responsibility System of China's Industry'), *New Asia Academic Bulletin*, Vol. 5, 1983, p. 105.

45. Wang Mengkui, 'Qiye lingdao zhidu zhong de yige wenti' ('A Problem in the Enterprise Leadership System'), *Jingji yangjiu (Economic Research)*, No. 1, 1981, p. 39.

46. Mao Zedong, 'Zai zhongyang zhengzhiju kuoda huiyi shang de jianghua' ('The Talk at the Enlarged Conference of the Politburo of the CC, CCP, April 1956'), in *Mao Zedong sixiang wansui (Long Live Mao Zedong's Thought)* (n.p., n.p., 1969), pp. 35–6, hereafter cited as *Wansui*.

47. Mao Zedong, 'The Talk at the Enlarged Conference of the Politburo...', *Wansui*, pp. 35–6, note 46 above.

48. Li Xuefeng, 'Jiaqiang dang dui qiye de lingdao, guanche zhixing qunzhong luxian' ('Strengthen the Party's Leadership over Enterprises and thoroughly Carry out the Mass-line'), *Renmin ribao (People's Daily)*, 25 September 1956, p. 5.

49. Schurmann (1968), pp. 253–78, note 37 above; Brugger (1976), pp. 199–202, note 20 above; Stephen Andors, *China's Industrial Revolution* (New York, Pantheon Books, 1977), p. 53.

50. Mao Tse-tung, 'On Strengthening the Party Committee System', in *Selected Works of Mao Tse-tung* (Peking, Foreign Languages Press, 1967), Vol. IV, pp. 267–8.

51. 'Jiaqiang qiye dang zuzhi dui gongye shenchan de baozheng jiandu zuoyong' ('Strengthen the Role of the Enterprise Party Organization in Supervising and Guaranteeing Industrial Production'), *Shenyang ribao*, 17 March 1954, p. 1.

52. Wang Renzhong, 'Jiti lingdao de yuanze shibushi shiyong yu gongkuang qiye?' ('Is the Principle of the Collective Leadership Applicable to Mining and Industrial Enterprises?'), *Xinhua banyuekan (New China Bimonthly)*, No. 20, October 1956, pp. 54–6.

53. Wang Renzhong, 'Is the Principle of the Collective Leadership...', *Xinhua banyuekan*, No. 20, October 1956, pp. 54–6, note 52 above.

54. Li Xuefeng, 'Strengthen the Party's Leadership...', *Renmin ribao*, 25 September 1956, p. 5, note 48 above.

55. Anthony Downs, *Inside Bureaucracy* (Boston, Little, Brown and Company, 1967), pp. 158–66.

56. 'Zhongyang renmin zhengfu zhengwuyuan guanyu laodong jiuye wenti de jueding' ('The Decision of the Government Administrative Council of the Central People's Government concerning the Labour Employment Problem'), *Shenyang ribao*, 4 August 1952, p. 1.

57. 'Zhongyang renmin zhengfu zhengwuyuan guoying qiye neibu laodong guize gangyao' ('The Outline of the Labour Regulation within the State-owned Enterprises'), *Shenyang ribao*, 15 July 1954, p. 1.

58. Zhuang Qidong, *Laodong Gongzi Shouce* (The Manual of Labour and Wage) (Tianjin, Tianjin renmin chubanshe, 1984), pp. 1–14 and 22–8.

59. Brugger (1976), pp. 148–51, note 20 above.

60. 'Zhengque zhixing baji gongzizhi jiasu jingji huifu yu fazhan' ('Correctly Implement the Eight-grade Wage System, Accelerate the Economic Recovery and Growth'), *Shenyang ribao*, 22 June 1950, p. 1.

61. Gao Gang, 'Stand on the Forefront...', *Shenyang ribao*, 6 June 1950, p. 3, note 2 above.

62. 'Correctly Implement the Eight-grade Wage System...', *Shenyang ribao*, 22 June 1950, p. 1, note 60 above.

63. 'Correctly Implement the Eight-grade Wage System...', *Shenyang ribao*, 22 June 1950, p. 1, note 60 above.

64. 'Wei zhixing tiaozheng gongying qiye gongren jishu renyuan ji gai xing baji gongzizhi zhong ruogan wenti de zhishi' ('The Directive on Several Problems in Implementing the Adjustment of Salary of Technicians and Wage of Workers and Change to the Eight-grade Wage System in Public Enterprises'), *Shenyang ribao*, 9 July 1950, p. 1.

65. 'Zhixing baji gongzizhi zhong de jige wenti' ('Several Problems in Implementing the Eight-grade Wage System'), *Shenyang ribao*, 28 July 1950, p. 1.

66. Zhuang Qidong (1984), pp. 47–51, note 58 above.

67. Song Ping, 'Wei shime yao jinxing gongzi zhidu de gaige?' (Why Should We Proceed with the Reform of Wage System?'), *Xinhua banyuekan*, No. 10, 21 May 1956, pp. 73–5.

68. Ma Wenrui, 'Guanyu laodong gongzi gongzuo' ('On the Task in Workers' Wage'), *Xinhua banyuekan*, No. 15, 6 August 1956, pp. 115–18.

69. 'Dongbeiqu qiye jijian gongzizhi zhanxing guichen' ('The Provisional Regulation Piece-rate Wage System in Enterprises in the North-east Region'), *Xinhua banyuekan*, 19 April 1951, p. 2; 'Gengbao de tuixing jijian gongzizhi' ('Implement the Piece-rate Wage System in a Better Way'), *Xinhua banyuekan*, 19 April 1951, p. 2.

70. Zhuang Qidong (1984), pp. 66–71, note 58 above.

71. Zhuang Qidong (1984), pp. 59–66, note 58 above.

72. 'Qieshi zhixing laodong baoxian tiaoli' ('Thoroughly Implement the Labour Insurance Regulation'), *Shenyang ribao*, 1 March 1951, p. 3.

73. 'Zhonghu renmin gongheguo laodong baoxian tiaoli shishi xize caoan' ('The Draft of the Detailed Measures of the Labour Insurance Regulation of the People's Republic of China'), *Shenyang ribao*, 26 March 1951, p. 1.

74. Ma Wenrui, 'On the Task...', *Xinhua banyuekan*, No. 15, 6 August 1956, pp. 115–18, note 68 above.

75. 'Laodongbu Li Lishan buzhang guanyu Zhonghua renmin gongheguo laodong baoxian tiaoli caoan de jidian shuoming' ('Some Explanations by Minister Li Lishan of the Labour Ministry on the Draft Regulation of the Labour Insurance Regulation of the PRC'), *Shenyang ribao*, 1 March 1951, p. 3.

76. Joyce E. Kallgren, 'Social Welfare and China's Industrial Workers' in A. Doak Barnett (ed.), *Chinese Communist Politics in Action* (Seattle, University of Washington Press, 1969), p. 566.

77. 'Some Explanations by Minister Li Lishan...', *Shenyang ribao*, 1 March 1951, p. 3, note 75 above.

78. 'Mou chang gonghui gongzuo jidian jingyan zongjie' ('The Summary of Experience in the Work of a Labour Union in an Enterprise'), *Shenyang ribao*, 22 April 1951, p. 5.

79. Zhou Enlai, 'Zhangfu gongzuo baogao' ('The Report of Government Work'), in *Zhou Enlai xuanyji* (*The Selected Work of Zhou Enlai*) (Hong Kong, Yishan tushu gongsi, 1976), Vol. I, pp. 82–3.

80. Abraham Maslow, *Motivation and Personality* (New York, Harper & Brothers, 1954).

81. Deng Zihui, 'Zai zhongnan zonggonghui chou-wei kuoda huiyi shang de baogao'

('The Report to the Enlarged Conference of the Preparation Committee for the General Labour Union in the Central-South Region'), *Xinhua banyuekan*, Vol. II, No. 5, September 1950, p. 1034.

82. Lai Ruoyu, 'Wei wancheng guojia gongye jianshede renwu er fendou' ('Struggle for the Fulfilment of the Mission of the National Industrial Construction'), *Shenyang ribao*, 11 May 1953, p. 3.

83. Reinhard Bendix, *Work and Authority In Industry* (New York, Harper & Row, 1956), pp. 274–319.

84. Andrew G. Walder, 'Organized Dependency and Cultures of Authority in Chinese Industry', *Journal of Asian Studies*, Vol. XLIII, No. 1, November 1983, pp. 51–76.

85. 'Some Explanations by Minister Li Lishan...', *Shenyang ribao*, 1 March 1951, p. 3, note 75 above.

86. 'Miqie lianxi qunzhong gonggu yu kuoda gonghui zuzhi' ('Closely Ally with the Masses, Consolidate and Expand the Union Organization'), *Shenyang ribao*, 5 January 1951, p. 3; 'Zhengdun gonghui jiceng zuzhi de chubu zongjie' ('A Preliminary Summary of the Rectification of the Basic Echelon Labour Union'), *Shenyang ribao*, 15 May 1950, p. 1.

87. 'Zhonggong zhongyang dongbeiju guanyu jinyibu tuanjie gongying qiye zhong jishu renyuan yu zhiyuan de zhishi' ('The Directive of the North-east Bureau, CC, CCP, Concerning the Further Uniting with the Technicians and Staff Members in Public Enterprises'), *Shenyang ribao*, 20 April 1950, p. 1; 'Peiyang jishu liliang shi qiye lingdao de zhongyao renwu' ('The Important Mission for Enterprise Leadership is the Cultivation of Technical Manpower'), *Shenyang ribao*, 16 May 1954, p. 1.

88. 'Muqian gongying qiye zhong zhiyuan qingkuang yu dang de zhengce wenti' ('The Current Situation of the Staff Member in Public Enterprises and the Party's Policy Problems'), *Shenyang ribao*, 12 February 1950, pp. 1–2.

89. 'The Important Mission...', *Shenyang ribao*, 16 May 1954, p. 1, note 87 above.

90. 'Benshi guoying gongcheng dingli shi tu hetong qingkuang ji cunzai de wenti' ('The Situation and Existing Problems of Master-apprentice Contracts in the State-owned Enterprises in our City'), *Shenyang ribao*, 18 May 1950, p. 1; 'Shi tu jishu hetong shishi banfa' ('Implementing Measure of the Technical Contract of Apprenticeship'), *Shenyang ribao*, 23 August 1950, p. 1.

91. 'Jiaqiang laodong jilu quanmian chao'e wancheng guojia jihua' ('Strengthen Labour Discipline, Over-fulfil the State Plan'), *Shenyang ribao*, 9 July 1953, p. 1.

92. Mao Tse-tung, 'Report to the Second Plenary Session of the Seventh Central Committee of the Communist Party of China' in *Selected Works of Mao Tse-tung*, Vol. IV, p. 363, note 50 above.

93. Thomas R. Gottschang, 'Comparative Advantage and Government Policy in the Recent Economic Development of Liaoning Province' (a paper prepared for the Economic Bureaucracy Workshop, 20 July 1984, at the East-West Center, Honolulu, Hawaii), p. 4. Regarding the development of central planning under the Japanese administration from 1931 to 1945, see Kungtu C. Sun, *The Economic Development of Manchuria in the First Half of the Twentieth Century* (Cambridge, Mass., Harvard University Press, 1969), pp. 61–100.

94. Wong Foh-shen, 'China's Industrial Production, 1931–1946', in Ramon H. Myers (ed.), *Selected Essays in Chinese Economic Development* (New York and London, Garland Publishing Inc., 1980), pp. 1–6.

95. Gao Gang, 'Stand on the Forefront...', *Shenyang ribao*, 6 June 1950, p. 1, note 2 above.

96. There are disputes about the number of Japanese technicians retained after 1949. A number of authors, however, convincingly demonstrate that many Japanese technicians remained in factories in North-east China until 1953. See Thomas G.

Rawski, *China's Transition to Industrialism* (Ann Arbor, University of Michigan Press, 1980), p. 30; Chong-wook Chung, *Maoism and Development* (Seoul, Seoul University Press, 1980), pp. 29–31.

97. Rawski (1980), pp. 29–30, note 96 above; Chung (1980), pp. 31–4, note 96 above; Schurmann (1968), pp. 239–42, note 37 above.

98. Deng Xiaoping, 'Guanyu xiugai dang de zhangcheng de baogao' ('The Report concerning the Revision of the Party's Charter), *Xinhua banyuekan*, No. 20, 21 October 1956, pp. 27–9.

99. It is difficult to quantify the minimum conditions for the continuation and functioning of an organization. The shortages of technical and managerial staff mentioned by Chen Yun during his tour to North-east China in 1948 did not seem to be an obstacle or to defer the rise of the administrative approach — including rational industrial management. On the shortages of technical and managerial manpower, see Chen Yun, 'Zhengque chuli shin jieshou qiyezhong de zhiyuan wenti' ('Correctly Handling the Problems of Staff Members in Newly Taken-over Enterprises'), in Zhong gong zhongyang wenxian weiyuanhui (ed.), *Chen Yun wenxuan* (*Collected Essays of Chen Yun*) (Beijing, Renmin chubanshe, 1984), pp. 247–55; Huang Ou-dong, 'Muqian gongying qiye zhong zhiyuan qingkuang yu dang de zhengce wenti' ('The Current Situation of the Staff Members in Public Enterprises and the Party's Policy Problems'), *Shenyang ribao*, 12 February 1950, pp. 1–2; 'The Directive of the North-east Bureau, CC, CCP...', *Shenyang ribao*, 20 April 1951, p. 1, note 87 above.

100. Mao Zedong, 'Zai Chengdu huiyi shang de jianghua' ('Speech at the Chengdu Conference'), *Wansui*, p. 161, note 46 above.

101. 'Zhongguo gongchandang diqi jie zhongyang weiyuanhui juxing disi ci quanti huiyi de gongbao' ('The Communiqué of the Fourth Plenum of the Seventh Party Congress, CCP'), *Shenyang ribao*, 28 February 1954, p. 1.

102. Mao Zedong, 'The Talk at the Enlarged Meeting of the Politburo...'), *Wansui*, pp. 35–6, note 46 above.

103. Chou Fang, 'Explaining the Changes in the Organic Structure and Functions of People's Governments in Administrative Regions', *Summary of Mainland China Press* (hereafter referred to as *SMCP*), No. 494, 17–19 January 1953, pp. 36–8.

104. Deng Xiaoping, 'The Report Concerning the Revision...', *Xinhua banyuekan*, No. 20, 21 October 1956, pp. 27–9, note 98 above.

105. For example, in his report to the First Party Congress of the North-east Bureau of the Central Committee, CCP, in May 1950, Gao Gang put the following items on the agenda: improving planning procedures, establishing responsibility systems, one-man management, a congress of workers and staff, economic accounting, work norms, job classifications, and so on. These items were not put on the national agenda until three years later, in May 1953, when Jia Tuofu, Deputy Director of the Financial and Economic Commission made his report on the industrial situation. Standard eight-grade wage and piece-rate wage systems were introduced to North-east China in 1950, but they did not spread to the rest of the country between 1952 and 1956.

106. Chou Fang, 'Explaining the Changes in the Organic Structure...', *SMCP*, No. 494, 17–19 January 1953, pp. 36–8, note 103 above; 'Organic Law of Regional Government Councils' (passed by the Government Administration Council, 16 December 1949), *Current Background*, 8 April 1952, No. 170, p. 19; 'Sheng renmin zhengfu tongze' ('The General Regulations of the Provincial People's Government Organization'), *Xinhua yuebao*, Vol. I, No. 4, February 1950, pp. 866–7; 'Zhengwuyuan guanyu huafen zhongyang yu difang caizheng jingji gongzuo shang guanli zhiquan de jueding' ('The Decision of the Government Administrative Council concerning the Division of Management Jurisdiction between the Centre and Localities in Financial-economic Tasks'), *Xinhua yuebao*, Vol. V, No. 2, June 1951, p. 324.

107. Samuel P. Huntington and Joan M. Nelson, *No Easy Choice: Political Participation in Developing Countries* (Cambridge, Mass., Harvard University Press, 1976), pp. 29–35.

108. Schurmann (1968), pp. 225–35, note 37 above.

109. Chung (1980), pp. 34–6, note 96 above.

110. Here the post-Weberian perspective is given in a brief form, but it is formulated in various versions by a group of authors writing on organization theory. The first is the conception of 'bounded rationality', which stresses the mental and psychological limitations of organizational men relative to the complexity of evaluating and choosing alternatives as well as predicting and controlling their consequences. See Herbert A. Simon, *Administrative Behavior* (New York, The Free Press, 1957), pp. 61–109; see also Charles Perrow, *Complex Organization* (Glenview, Illinois, Scott, Foresman and Company, 1972), pp. 145–76. The second is the view of the cycle of purposive control, unanticipated consequences, and renewed control. See Nicos P. Mouzelis, *Organization and Bureaucracy* (Chicago, Aldine Publishing Company, 1967), pp. 59–62; still within the perspective of the control structure of a formal organization is Anthony Downs's observation of the cycle of degeneration and reorganization, see his *Inside Bureaucracy* (Boston, Little, Brown and Company, 1968), pp. 144–66. Michel Crozier treats this post-Weberian position in terms of the 'bureaucratic vicious circle', see his *The Bureaucratic Phenomenon* (Chicago, University of Chicago Press, 1964), pp. 175–208. The third version focuses on the irrationality arising from the uncertainty in the environment, see James D. Thompson, *Organizations in Action* (New York, McGraw Hill Book Co., 1967), pp. 3–13; see also Richard H. Hall, 'Closed System, Open System and Contingency Choice Perspectives', in Amitai Etzioni and Edward Lehman (eds.), *A Sociological Reader in Complex Organizations* (New York, Holt, Rinehart and Winston, third edition, 1980), pp. 32–43. The fourth version is the formulation of bureaucratic pathologies, emphasizing deviant behaviours within an organizational context, see Joseph Lapalombara, *Politics Within Nations* (Englewood Cliffs, Prentice-Hall, Inc., 1973), pp. 278–309.

111. Schurmann (1968), pp. 250–1, note 37 above; Andors (1977), pp. 56–8, note 49 above; and Brugger (1976), pp. 185–91, note 20 above.

NOTES TO CHAPTER 3

1. Chou Fang, 'Explaining the Changes in the Organic Structure and Functions of People's Government in Administrative Regions', *Summary of Mainland China Press* (hereafter cited as *SMCP*), No. 494, 17–19 January 1953, p. 37.

2. Franz Schurmann, *Ideology and Organisation in Communist China* (Berkeley, Calif., and London, University of California Press, 1968), pp. 293–6; Maurice Meisner, *Mao's China* (New York, The Free Press, 1977), pp. 384–9; Harry Harding, *Organizing China* (Stanford, Calif., Stanford University Press, 1981), pp. 1–31.

3. Zhou Enlai, 'Zhangfu gongzuo baogao' ('The Report of Government Work') in *Zhou Enlai xuanji* (*The Selected Works of Zhou Enlai*) (Hong Kong, Yishan tushu gongsi, 1976), Vol. I, pp. 73–5, hereafter referred to as *Zhou Enlai xuanji*.

4. Zhou Enlai, 'Guanyu fazhan guomin jingji dier ge wunian jihua de jianyi de baogao' ('The Report on the Proposal of the Second Five-year Plan of the Development of National Economy'), in *Zhongguo gongchandang diba ci quanguo daibiao dahui wenjian* (*The Documents of the Eighth Party Congress of the Chinese Communist*

Party) (Beijing, Renmin chubanshe, 1980), pp. 192–7, hereafter cited as *Wenjian* (1980).

5. Audrey Donnithorne, *China's Economic System* (London, George Allen and Unwin Ltd., 1967), p. 158.

6. Thomas G. Rawski, *China's Transition to Industrialism* (Ann Arbor, University of Michigan Press, 1980), pp. 112–45.

7. Deng Xiaoping, 'Guanyu xiugai dangzhang de baogao' ('The Report concerning the Revision of the Charter of the CCP'), in *Wenjian* (1980), pp. 133–4, note 4 above.

8. Liu Shaoqi, 'Zhongguo gongchandang zhongyang weiyuanhui xiang diba ci quanguo daibiao dahui de zhengzhi baogao' ('The Political Report of CC, CCP to the Eighth Party Congress'), in *Wenjian* (1980), pp. 53–4, note 4 above.

9. Zhou Enlai, 'The Report on the Proposal...', in *Wenjian* (1980), p. 219, note 4 above.

10. Anthony Downs, *Inside Bureaucracy* (Boston, Little o Brown and Company, 1967), pp. 56–8.

11. Downs (1967), pp. 56–8, note 10 above.

12. The concept is first used by Alexander Eckstein, *China's Economic Revolution* (Cambridge, Cambridge University Press, 1977), pp. 92–6; Schurmann refers to it as Decentralization II, that is, the delegation of power to the local level. See Schurmann (1968), pp. 175–8, note 2 above.

13. For the full text of the policy paper, see Mao Zedong, 'Lun shi da guanxi' ('On the Ten Great Relationships'), in Mao Zedong, *Mao Zedong xuanji* (*The Collected Works of Mao Zedong*) (Beijing, Renmin chubanshe, 1977), Vol. V, pp. 267–88.

14. Schurmann (1968), pp. 175–8, note 2 above.

15. Bo Yibo, 'Chongjing he huainian' ('My Deep Respect and Last Memory'), *Renmin ribao* (*People's Daily*), 3 July 1981, pp. 3–4.

16. Mao did mention that in December 1955, when these meetings were held, he summoned 34 ministers for a 'conversation'. Mao Zedong, 'Nanning huiyi shang de jianghua' ('Talk at the Nanning Conference'), in *Mao Zedong sixiang wansui* (*Long Live Mao Zedong's Thought*) (n.p., n.p., 1969), p. 151, hereafter cited as *Wansui* (1969).

17. Mao Zedong, 'On the Ten Great Relationships', in *Mao Zedong xuanji* (1977), Vol. V, p. 267, note 13 above.

18. 'Guanyu jinyibu gaijin guanli gongye he jianshe de zuzhigongzuo' ('Organizing Work for the Further Improvement of Industry Management and Construction'), *Dagong bao* (*Dagong Daily*), 11 April 1957, pp. 2–3; Sha Yihe, 'Dule guanyu jinyibu gaijin guanli gongye he jianshe de zuzhi gongzuo zhihou' ('After Reading "Organizing Work for the Further Improvement of Management of Industry and Construction"'), *Dagong bao*, 21 April 1957, pp. 1 and 3.

19. Mao Zedong, 'On the Ten Great Relationships', in *Mao Zedong xuanji* (1977), Vol. V, pp. 275–7, note 13 above.

20. Mao Zedong, 'On the Ten Great Relationships', in *Mao Zedong xuanji* (1977), Vol. V, pp. 273 and 277, note 13 above.

21. Mao Zedong, 'On the Ten Great Relationships', in *Mao Zedong xuanji* (1977), Vol. V, p. 276, note 13 above.

22. Zhou Enlai, 'The Report on the Proposal...', in *Wenjian* (1980), p. 218, note 4 above.

23. Zhou Enlai, 'The Report on the Proposal...', in *Wenjian* (1980), p. 218, note 4 above.

24. Zhou Enlai, 'The Report on the Proposal...', in *Wenjian* (1980), p. 219, note 4 above.

25. 'Diyi jijie gongyebu guanyu gaibian xianxing guanli zhidu de ruogan guiding'

('The Regulation of the First Ministry of Machine-building concerning the Change of the Current Managerial System'), in *Zhonghua renmin gongheguo fagui huibian* (*The Collected Laws of the PRC*), January–June 1957, pp. 195–200, hereafter cited as *Fagui huibian*.

26. Chen Yun, 'Guanyu gaijin gongye guanli tizhi de guiding' ('The Regulation concerning the Improvement of Managerial System in Industry'), in Chen Yun, *Chen Yun tongzhi wengao xuanji* (*The Collected Manuscripts of Comrade Chen Yun*) (Beijing, Renmin chubanshe, 1981), pp. 60–6, hereafter cited as *Chen Yun xuanji* (1981); Chen Yun, 'Guanyu gaijin shangye guanli tizhi de guiding' ('The Regulation concerning the Improvement of Managerial System in Commerce'), in *Chen Yun xuanji* (1981), pp. 67–9.

27. Chen Yun, 'Tizhi gaige yihou yinggai zhuyi de wenti' ('The Problems Deserving Attention after the Institutional Reforms'), in *Chen Yun xuanji* (1981), pp. 58–9, note 26 above.

28. 'Guowuyuan guanyu bufen fangzhi qiye xiafang difang guanli wenti de pifu' ('The Reply of the State Council to the Question of the Decentralization of Certain Textile Enterprises for Local Control'), in *Fagui huibian*, January–June 1958, p. 327; 'Zhongguo gongchandang zhongyang weiyuanhui guowuyuan guanyu gongye qiye xiafang de jixiang jueding' ('Several Decisions of the Central Committee, CCP and State Council concerning the Decentralization of Industrial Enterprises'), in *Fagui huibian*, January–June 1958, pp. 331–2; 'Guowuyuan guanyu zhongyang ge shangye bumen suoshu gongchang xiafang wenti de guiding' ('The Regulation of the State Council concerning the Decentralization of Factories under the Jurisdiction of Central Ministries in Commerce'), in *Fagui huibian*, January–June 1958, p. 322.

29. 'Guowuyuan guanyu gaijin gongye guanli tizhi de guiding' ('The Regulation of the State Council concerning the Improvement of Industrial Managerial System'), in *Fagui huibian*, July–December 1957, pp. 391–6.

30. 'The First Ministry of Machine-building...', in *Fagui huibian*, January–June 1957, pp. 145–200, note 25 above.

31. 'Zhongyang qiye 80% xiafang difang guanli' ('Eighty per cent of the Central Enterprises Have Been Transferred Downward to the Local Management'), *Xinhua banyuekan* (*New China Bimonthly*), No. 13, 1958, p. 63.

32. 'Zhongguo gongchandang zhongyang weiyuanhui guowuyuan guanyu gaijin jihua guanli tizhi de guiding' ('The Regulation of the Central Committee, CCP, and the State Council concerning the Improvement of the Managerial System of Planning'), in *Fagui huibian*, July–December 1958, pp. 96–9.

33. Mao Zedong, 'On the Ten Great Relationships', in *Mao Zedong xuanji* (1977), Vol. V, p. 273, note 13 above.

34. For Liu Shaoqi's tour to the Shijingshan Iron and Steel Works and Shijingshan Power-station, see 'Liu Shaoqi zai Shigang jinxing fangeming huodong de zuixing lu' ('The Criminal Record of Liu Shaoqi's Counter-revolutionary Activities in Shijingshan Steel and Iron Works'), *Beijing gongren* (*Beijing Workers*), No. 4, 17 May 1967; 'Jielu zhonguo heluxiaofu de yige fangeming xiuzhengzhuyi jingji gangling' ('Expose Counter-revolutionary Economic Platform of China's Khrushchev, 24 January 1968'), collection of the University of Chicago Library.

35. 'Expose Counter-revolutionary Economic Platform...', note 34 above.

36. Liu Shaoqi proposed a self-financed housing project after a briefing given by the Party committee members of Xiangjiang Machine-building Factory in March 1957. See Zhong gong Hunan sheng weiyuanhui, 'Hunan renmin shenqie huainian Liu Shaoqi tongzhi' ('The People of Hunan Commemorate Dear Comrade Liu Shaoqi'), in Hunan sheng renmin chubanshe (ed.), *Huainian Liu Shaoqi tongzhi* (*In Commemoration of Liu Shaoqi*), (Changsha, Renmin chubanshe, 1980), pp. 295–7.

37. Mao Zedong, 'Gongzuo fangfa liushi tiao' ('The Sixty Articles on Work Methods'), *Wansui* (April 1967), Article 23.

38. Mao Zedong, 'On the Ten Great Relationships', in *Mao Zedong xuanji* (1977), Vol. V, p. 272, note 13 above.

39. Zhuang Qidong, *Laodong gongzi shouce* (*The Manual of Labour and Wages*) (Tianjin, Tianjin renmin chubanshe, 1984) pp. 59–66.

40. Zhuang Qidong, *Laodong gongzi shouce* (1984), pp. 66–71, note 39 above.

41. The profit-sharing scheme began in 1953. Rulings were made in 1954 and 1956 and the State Council promulgated a document concerning the enterprise retained-profit system in 1958. 'Guowuyuan guanyu shixing qiye lirunliucheng zhidu de jixiang guiding' ('The Regulation of the State Council concerning the Implementing of the Enterprise Retained Profit System'), *Fagui huibian*, January–June 1958, pp. 239–42.

42. 'Guowuyuan zhuanfa caizhengbu Zongguo renmin yinghang guanyu guoying qiye liudong zijin gaiyou renmin yinhang tongyi guanli de buchong guiding de tongzhi' ('The Supplementary Regulation of the Ministry of Finance and the China People's Bank on the United Management of Working Capital of State-owned Enterprises by the People's Bank'), *Fagui huibian*, January–June 1959, pp. 122–4.

43. 'Guowuyuan dui chaizhengbu Zhongguo renmin yinhang guanyu gaijin guoying qiye liudong zijin gongying banfa de baogao de pifu' ('The Reply of the State Council to the Ministry of Finance and the People's Bank of China concerning the Improvement of the Supply of Liquid Capital of the State-owned Enterprises'), *Fagui huibian*, July 1960–December 1961, pp. 72–4.

44. 'The Criminal Record of Liu Shaoqi's Counter-revolutionary Activities...', *Beijing gongren*, No. 4, 17 May 1967, n.p., note 34 above; Mao Zedong, 'Sulian Zhengzhi jingjixue dushu biji' ('Reading Notes on the Soviet *Political Economy* 1961–1962'), *Wansui* (1969), p. 347, note 16 above.

45. 'Guowuyuan guanyu gaijin jiben jianshe caiwu guanli zhidu de jixiang guiding' ('The Regulation of the State Council concerning the Improvement of Financial Management in Basic Construction'), *Fagui huibian*, July–December 1958, pp. 123–4; 'Guowuyuan guanyu gaijin jiben jianshe caiwu guanli zhidu de jixiang buchong guiding' ('The Supplementary Regulation of the State Council concerning the Improvement of Financial Management in the Basic Construction'), in Caizhengbu (ed.), *Zhongyang caizheng fagui huibian* (*The Collected Laws of Finance of the Central Government*), January–June 1959, pp. 49–51; 'Guowuyuan guanyu jiben jianshe bokuan de jixiang guiding' ('The Regulation of the State Council on the Financial Appropriation in Basic Construction'), *Fagui huibian*, January 1962–December 1963, pp. 64–8.

46. Chung Chong-wook, *Maoism and Development: The Politics of Industrial Management in China* (Seoul, Seoul National University Press, 1980), pp. 118–19.

47. Parris H.C. Chang, *Power and Policy in China* (University Park and London, Pennsylvania State University Press, 1975), p. 58.

48. Mao Zedong, 'Zai zhongyang zhengzhiju kuoda huiyi shang de jianghua' ('Talk at an Enlarged Conference of the Politburo of the Central Committee'), *Wansui* (1969), pp. 35–8, note 16 above.

49. Deng Xiaoping, 'The Report concerning the Revision...', in *Wenjian* (1980), pp. 122–31, note 4 above.

50. Liu Shaoqi, 'The Political Report of CC, CCP...', in *Wenjian* (1980), pp. 122–31, note 4 above.

51. Mao Zedong, 'The Sixty Articles on Work Methods', in *Wansui* (April 1967), Article 23, pp. 33–4, note 37 above.

52. Mao Zedong, 'The Sixty Articles on Work Methods', *Wansui* (April 1967), Article 22, note 37 above.

53. Mao Zedong, 'Zai bajie erzhong quan hui shang de jianghua, disanci jianghua' ('The Talk at the Second Plenum of the Eighth Party Congress: the Third Talk'), *Wansui* (1969), pp. 210–11, note 16 above.

54. Mao Zedong, 'Zai bajie erzhong quan hui shang de jianghua, dierci jianghua'

('Talk at the Second Plenum of the Eighth Party Congress: the Second Talk'), *Wansui* (1969), p. 204, note 16 above.

55. 'Liu Shaoqi jiejian Suxiu waimao buzhang Bodeliqifu de tanhua zhaiyao' ('The Summary of Liu Shaoqi's Talk with the Minister of Foreign Trade of the Soviet Revisionists'), *Jingji pipan* (*The Economic Critique*), No. 5, 29 May 1967, unpaged.

56. Bo Yibo, 'Jishu geming de xin xingshi' ('The New Situation of Technical Revolution'), *Xinhua banyuekan*, No. 10, 1960, pp. 120-4.

57. Mao Zedong, 'Zai Nanning huiyi shang de jianghua' ('Talk at the Nanning Conference'), *Wansui* (1969), p. 153, note 16 above.

58. Mao Zedong, 'Zai bajie erzhong quan hui shang de jianghua' ('Talk at the Second Plenum of the Eighth Party Congress'), *Wansui* (1969), p. 192, note 16 above.

59. Mao Zedong, 'Zai zuigao guowu huiyi shang de jianghua jiyao' ('A Summary of the Speech at the Supreme Conference of State Affairs, 9 September 1958'), *Wansui* (1969), pp. 243-4, note 16 above; Mao Zedong, 'Zai Lushan huiyi jianghua' ('Talk at the Lushan Conference'), *Wansui* (1969), p. 302, note 16 above.

60. Michael C. Oksenberg, 'Policy Making under Mao, 1949-1968: An Overview', in John M.H. Lindbeck (ed.), *China: Management of a Revolutionary Society* (Seattle and London, University of Washington Press, 1971), pp. 104-5.

61. Mao Zedong, 'Zai bajie erzhong quan hui shang de jianghua' ('Talk at the Second Plenum of the Eighth Party Congress'), *Wansui* (1969), p. 192, note 16 above.

62. 'Diyi jixie gongyebu guanyu feichu he xiafang yi bufen guidzhang zhidu de tongzhi' ('The First Ministry of Machine-building's Circular concerning the Abolition and Downward-transfer of some Regulations and Systems'), *Fagui huibian*, January-June 1958, pp. 332-3.

63. 'Zhong gong Heilongjiang guoying Qinghua gongjuchang weiyuanhui guanyu ganbu canjia shengchan, gongren canjia guanli yewu gaige jingyan de chubu zongjie' ('The Preliminary Summary of Experience of Cadres' Participation in Production, Workers' Participation in Management, and the Managerial Reform by the Party Committee of the State-owned Qinghua Instrument Factory, CCP'), *Renmin ribao*, 25 April 1958, p. 3; 'Gaige qiye guanli gongzuo de zhongda chuangju' ('Great Innovation in the Work of Enterprise Management'), *Renmin ribao*, 7 May 1958, p. 1; Guo Huizhong, 'Baozheng dang dui qiye de juedui lingdao' ('Ensure the Party's Absolute Leadership over Enterprises'), *Renmin ribao*, 1 December 1958, p. 2; Wong Hefeng, 'Qiye guanli de zhongda gaige' ('Major Reform in Enterprise Management'), *Renmin ribao*, 26 April 1958, p. 3.

64. Wong Hefeng, Secretary of the Heilongjiang Party Committee, gave a detailed report on the origin of the formula, 'two participations, one reform and the three-in-one combination'. See Wong Hefeng, 'Gonggu fazhan liang can yi gai san jiehe quanmian tigao qiye de guanli shuiping' ('Consolidate and Develop the Two Participations, One Reform and Three-in-one Combination, Raise the Overall Standard of Enterprise Management'), *Hongqi* (*Red Flag*), No. 15, 1 August 1960, pp. 6-15.

65. Li Xuefeng, 'Guanyu qiye guanli fangfa shang de qunzhong luxian wenti' ('The Mass-line Problem concerning Enterprise Management'), *Hongqi*, No. 5, 1 August 1958, pp. 12-15.

66. Ke Qingshi, 'Guanyu gongye zhanxian shang de qunzhong luxian' ('On the Mass-line in the Industrial Front'), *Hongqi*, No. 21, 1 October 1959, pp. 1-9. Ke argued against the view that the mass movement should not be launched in the construction period, and emphasized the need to abolish unreasonable regulations and systems as well as to mobilize the masses fully.

67. 'Mao Zedong tongzhi zai jiuyuejian de zhongyao tanhua' ('Comrade Mao Zedong's Important Interview during September'), *Hongqi*, No. 16, 16 October 1958, pp. 1-2.

68. Chung (1980), pp. 135-40, note 46 above.

69. 'Fangeming xiuzhengzhuyi fenzi Bo Yibo shi da zuizhuang' ('The Great Crimes

of Counter-revolutionary Revisionist Bo Yibo'), *Jingangshan* (*Jingang Mountain*), Nos. 6 and 7, 1 January 1967, p. 6.

70. Bo Yibo, 'Yijiuwujiu nian gongye zhanxian de renwu' ('The Mission of the Industrial Front for 1959'), *Xinhua banyuekan*, No. 1, 1959, pp. 67–9.

71. 'Bo gongye zhanxian shang qunzhong luxian de huaiyipai' ('Repudiate the Sceptical Faction on the Mass-line of Industrial Front'), *Hongqi*, 16 November 1958, pp. 1–7.

72. Mao Zedong, 'He ge xiezuoqu zhuren de jianghua' ('A Talk to Directors of Various Regions of Economic Co-ordination'), *Wansui* (1969), pp. 251–2 and 258, note 16 above.

73. Mao Zedong, 'Zai sheng-shiwei shuji hui-shang de jianghua' ('Talk at the Conference of Provincial and Muncipal Party Secretaries'), *Wansui* (1969), p. 278, note 16 above.

74. Mao Zedong, 'Zai bajie liuzhong quanhui shang de jianghua' ('Talk at the Sixth Plenum of the Eighth Party Congress'), *Wansui* (1969), p. 266, note 16 above.

75. Ke Qingshi, 'Lun quankuo yibanqi' ('On the Whole Country as a Chessboard'), *Hongqi*, No. 4, 16 February 1959, p. 9.

76. Chen Yun, 'Dangqian jiben jianshe gongzuo zhong de jige zhongda wenti' ('Several Important Questions on the Current Tasks of Basic Construction'), *Hongqi*, No. 5, 1 March 1959, pp. 1–16.

77. Li Fuchun attended the conference and also delivered a speech. The purpose of the conference was to summarize the experience of the Great Leap Forward and discuss the 1959 annual plan.

78. 'Guojia jihua weiyuanhui caizhengbu guanyu jiaqiang chengben jihua guanli gongzuo de jixiang guiding' ('The Regulation of the State Planning Commission and the Ministry of Finance concerning the Strengthening of the Task of Cost, Planning and Management of the State Commission and Finance Ministry'), *Fagui huibian*, January–June 1959, pp. 112–15; see also 'Guowuyuan zhuanfa caizlengbu guanyu muqian qiye caiwu gongzuo zhong cunzai de jige wenti de baogao' ('The Report of the Finance Ministry concerning the Problems of the Current Financial Task in Enterprises'), *Fagui huibian*, January–June 1959, pp. 132–3; 'Caizhengbu guanyu guoying qiye kuaiji hesuan gongzuo de ruogan guiding' ('The Regulation of the Finance Ministry concerning Accounting Work in State-owned Enterprises'), *Fagui huibian*, July–December 1959, pp. 254–7; 'Guojia jihua weiyuanhui caizhengbu guanyu guoying gongye qiye shengchan feiyung yaosu chanpin chengben xiangmu he chengben hesuan de jixiang guiding' ('The Regulation of the State Planning Commission and Finance Ministry concerning Items of Production Expenses, Product Cost Categories and Cost Accounting in State-owned Industrial Enterprises'), *Fagui huibian*, July–December 1959, pp. 257–64.

79. 'Diyi jixiebu guanyu baozheng chanpin zhiliang de zhishi' ('The Directive of the First Ministry of Machine-building concerning Guaranteed Product Quality'), *Fagui huibian*, January–June 1959, pp. 200–2.

80. 'Diyi jixiebu gongyebu guanyu jiaqiang shebei weixiu gongzuo de zhishi' ('The Directive of the First Ministry of Machine-building concerning the Strengthening of Maintenance Work'), *Fagui huibian*, January–June 1959, pp. 205–7; 'Huaxue gongyebu guanyu jiben jianshe gongcheng jishu guanli de baxiang zhanxing guiding' ('The Eight Provisional Regulations on Technology Management of Basic Construction'), *Fagui huibian*, July–December 1959, pp. 163–9; 'Qinggongyebu jiben jianshe wenjian de shenpi banfa' ('The Measure concerning the Review and Approval of Documents in Light Industry'), *Fagui huibian*, July–December 1959, pp. 175–8.

81. Jin Ming, 'Jixu guzhu ganjing nuli jiangdi chengben' ('Continue to Exert the Utmost Effort and Endeavour to Reduce Costs'), *Caizheng* (*Finance*), No. 13, 9 July 1959, n.p.

82. 'Sichuan sheng jixie gongyeting zhaokai caiwu guanli zhidu zuotan hui' ('Forum on the System of Financial Meetings Held by the Engineering Office in Sichuan Province'), *Qiye kuaiji (Enterprise Accounting)*, No. 14, 22 July 1959, p. 15.

83. Bo Yibo, 'My Deep Respect...', *Renmin ribao*, 3 July 1980, pp. 3–4, note 15 above; 'Fupi zibenzhuyi de ji xianfeng, sanzi yibao de chuigushou' ('The Vanguard of Capitalist Restoration, Advocate of the Sanzi Yibo'), *Ba Yisan hongweibing (813 Red Guard)*, 28 April 1967, p. 7.

84. Li Rui, 'Shishi qiushi hexi wushamao' ('Seeking Truth from Facts, Officialdom Worthy of Nothing'), *Renmin ribao*, 31 December 1981, p. 5.

85. Mao Zedong, 'Talk at Lushan Conference...', *Wansui* (1969), p. 300, note 16 above.

86. Peng Dehuai has given some details of the episodes leading to his 'letter of opinions' of 14 July 1959. He stated that the letter was written after his talk to Mao's personal secretary Zhou Xiaozhou who had informed Peng that Mao shared some of Peng's views. As a result Peng wrote the letter which he intended to be an informal memo to Mao, but it was publicly circulated to the members of the conference without his consent. Only Peng himself and Zhou Xiaozhou knew of the letter beforehand; it was not, therefore, a result of concerted action against Mao. See Peng Dehuai zishu bianxie xiaozu (ed.), *Peng Dehuai zishu (Biography of Peng Dehuai)* (Beijing, Renmin chubanshe, 1981).

87. 'Qiye zhidu burong fugu' ('No Restoration of the Old Systems of Enterprise Management'), *Jiefang ribao (Liberation Daily)*, 3 November 1959, p. 4.

88. For Mao's comment, see *Hongqi*, No. 4, 1977, pp. 3–4 and *Beijing Review*, No. 14, 1 April 1977, pp. 3–4; for the report, see Zhonggong anshanshi weiyuanhui, 'Guanyu gongye zhanxian shang jishu gexin yu jishu geming yundong kaizhan qingkuang de baogao' ('The Report on the Situation in Developing the Movement of Technical Reform and Technical Revolution on the Industrial Front'), in *Dou-pi-gai (Struggle, Criticism, Transformation)*, No. 8, 1967, pp. 1–6.

89. Yang Shijie, 'Dang de lingdao he dagao qunzhong yundong zai Angang de zhongda shengli' ('Great Victory of the Party's Leadership and the Launching of the Mass Movement in a Big Way in the Anshan Iron and Steel Works'), *Renmin ribao*, 11 February 1960, p. 7.

90. 'Gangeming xiuzhengzhuyi fenzi Wu Lengxi gongci' ('Confession of the Counter-revolutionary Revisionist Element, Wu Lengxi'), *Gongren pinglun (The Workers Commentary)*, June 1968, n.p.

91. 'Mao Zhuxi guanyu Angang xianfa de pishi' ('Chairman Mao's Comment on the Anshan Constitution'), *Renmin ribao*, 22 March 1977, p. 1.

92. 'Zhongguo gongchandang dibaci quanguo daibiao dahui guanyu zhengzhi baogao de jueyi' ('The Resolution of the CCP on the Political Report to the Eighth Party Congress'), in *Wenjian* (1980), pp. 79–80, note 4 above.

93. Mao Zedong, 'Zai bajie san zhong quanhui shang de jianghua' ('Talk at the Third Plenum of the Eighth Party Congress'), *Wansui* (1969), pp. 122–3.

94. Deng Xiaoping, 'Guanyu diugai dangzhang de baogao' ('The Report concerning the Revision of the Charter of CCP'), in *Wenjian* (1980), pp. 135–40, note 4 above.

95. Liu Shaoqi, 'The Political Report of the CC, CCP...', in *Wenjian* (1980), p. 45, note 4 above.

96. Dwight H. Perkins, 'Industrial Planning and Management', in Alexander Eckstein, Walter Galenson, and Liu Ta-chung (eds.), *Economic Trends in Communist China* (Chicago, Aldine Publishing Company, 1968), pp. 616–32.

97. Mao Tse-tung, 'Turn the Army into a Working Force', in *Selected Works of Mao Tse-tung* (Peking, Foreign Language Press, 1967), Vol. IV, p. 337–8.

98. Mao Tse-tung, 'Report to the Second Plenary Session of the Seventh Central Committee of the Communist Party of China', in *Selected Works of Mao Tse-tung* (1967), Vol. IV, pp. 363–5, note 97 above.

99. Deng Xiaoping, 'Dui qica guanyu jianguo yilai dang de ruogan lishi wenti de jueyi de yijian' ('Opinion on the Resolution concerning Several Historical Questions of the Party since the Establishment of the Republic'), in *Deng Xiaoping wenxuan* (*Selected Essays of Deng Xiaoping*) (Beijing, Renmin chubanshe, 1983), p. 257.

100. Philip Bridgham, 'Factionalism in the Central Committee', in John Wilson Lewis (ed.), *Party Leadership and Revolutionary Power in China* (Cambridge, Cambridge University Press, 1970), p. 206.

101. Mao Zedong, 'Zai zhongyang zhengzhiju huibao huiyi shang de jianghua' ('Talk at the Conference of Briefing of the Politburo'), *Wansui* (1969), pp. 661–2, note 16 above; 'Zai zhongyang gongzuo huiyi shang de jianghua' ('Talk at the Work Conference of the Central Committee, CCP'), *Wansui* (1969), pp. 657–60, note 16 above.

102. Downs (1967), pp. 123–5, note 10 above.

103. Charles E. Lindblom, *The Intelligence of Democracy* (New York, The Free Press, 1965), pp. 83–4.

NOTES TO CHAPTER 4

1. A retrospective account is given by Xue Muqiao, 'Tiaozheng guomin jingji gaohao zhonghe pingheng' ('Readjust the National Economy, Maintain its Overall Balance'), *Xinhua yuebao* (*New China Monthly*), No. 2, 1981, p. 77.

2. Mao Zedong, 'Zai kuoda de zhongyang gongzuo huiyi shang de jianghua' ('Talk at the Enlarged Work Conference of the CC, CCP'), in Mao Zedong, *Mao Zedong sixiang wansui* (*Long Live Mao Zedong's Thought*) (n.p., n.p., 1969), pp. 414–16 (hereafter cited as *Wansui*); Ma Hong, Mei Xing, *et al.*, 'Jinian Li Fuchun tongzhi' ('In Commemoration of Comrade Li Fuchun'), *Xinhua yuebao*, No. 1, 1980, pp. 90–2.

3. Liu Shaoqi, 'Zai zhongguo gongchangdang di bajie quanguo daibiao dahui shang de zhengzhi baogao' ('The Political Report to the Eighth Party Congress of the Chinese Communist Party'), in Renmin chubanshe (ed.), *Liu Shaoqi xuanji* (*Collected Work of Liu Shaoqi*) (Beijing, Renmin chubanshe, 1985), Vol. II, p. 230.

4. Liu Shaoqi, 'Zai kuoda de zhongyang gongzuo huiyi shang de baogao' ('The Report to the Enlarged Work Conference of the Central Committee, CCP'), in *Liu Shaoqi xuanji* (1985), Vol. II, p. 359.

5. 'Zhong gong zhongyang guanyu dangqian gongye wenti de zhizhi' ('The Directive of the Central Committee, CCP concerning the Current Industrial Problems'), in Zhongguo Shehui Kexueyuan Gongye Jingji Yanjiusuo Ziliaoshi (ed.), *Zhongguo gongye guanli bufen tiaoli huibian* (*Selected Regulations of China's Industrial Management*) (Beijing, Beijing dizhi chubanshe, 1978), pp. 199–215 (hereafter cited as *Tiaoli huibian*).

6. 'The Directive of the Central Committee, CCP...', *Tiaoli huibian* (1978), pp. 200–5, note 5 above.

7. 'The Directive of the Central Committee, CCP...', *Tiaoli huibian* (1978), pp. 200–5, note 5 above.

8. Zhou Enlai, 'Guanyu fazhan guomin jingji di'erge wunian jihua de baogao' ('The Report on the Proposal of the Second Five-year Plan of the Development of the National Economy'), in Yishan Tushugongsi (ed.), *Zhou Enlai xuanji* (*Selected Works of Zhou Enlai*) (Hong Kong, Yishan Tushugongsi, 1976), Vol. II, pp. 309–10.

9. Xu Dihua, 'Liushiniandai chuqi gongye tiaozheng de jingyan zhide jiejian' ('The Experience of Industrial Readjustment during the Early 1960s Merited as a Reference'),

Gongye jingji guanli congkan (*Magazine of Industrial Economic Management*), No. 2, 1981, pp. 9–12.

10. Liu Shaoqi, 'The Report to the Enlarged Conference...', in *Liu Shaoqi xuanji* (1985), Vol. II, pp. 390–4, note 4 above.

11. 'Cong xilou huiyi kan caijing fangmian de fangeming xiuzhengzhuyi heixian' ('To Examine the Black Line of Counter-revolutionary Revisionism of Finance and Economy in the Light of the West Chamber Conference'), *Beijing gongshe* (*Beijing Commune*), No. 24, 26 May 1976, p. 2.

12. Xu Dihua, 'The Experience of Readjustment...', *Gongye jingji*, F3, 13, 1981, p. 43, note 9 above.

13. 'Guoying gongye giye gongzuo tiaoli' ('The Regulation of Tasks in State-owned Industrial Enterprises'), *Tiaoli huibian* (1978), p. 233.

14. 'The Regulation of Tasks in State-owned Industrial Enterprises', *Tiaoli huibian* (1978), p. 233, note 13 above.

15. Rong Wenzuo, 'Guanyu qinggongye shengchan zhuanyehua de ruogan wenti' ('Several Problems concerning the Specialization of Production in Light Industry'), *Jingji yanjiu* (*Economic Research*), No. 3, 1965, pp. 24–32, 46; Lu Lianping, 'Yong geming jingshen zuzhi jiagong gongye de zhuanyehua he xiezuo' ('Organize Specialization and Co-ordination in the Processing Industry with Revolutionary Spirit'), *Renmin ribao* (*People's Daily*), 12 April 1965, p. 5.

16. Li Biqing and Ren Yan, 'Lun gongye shengchan zhuanyehua jishu jinbu he jingji xiaoguo' ('On the Specialization in Industrial Production, Technological Progress and Economic Result'), *Jingji yanjiu*, No. 2, 1964, pp. 1–9; Qiao Rongzhang, 'Shilun woguo gongye shengchan xiezuo de xingzhi he zuoyong' ('On the Nature and Functions of Co-ordination in the Industrial Production of Our Country'), *Jingji yanjiu*, No. 5, 1965, pp. 20–5; Ji Chongwie, Li Lanqing, and Luo Jingfen, 'Zhuanyehua he xiezuo shi duo kuai hao sheng de fazhan gongye shengchanli de zhongyao tujing' ('Specialization and Co-ordination as an Important Approach to the Development of Industrial Production Force in Line of Quantity, Quality, Efficiency and Saving'), *Renmin ribao*, 20 February 1965, p. 5.

17. Yang Zhengmin, 'Zhai xiao er zhuan zhong er zhuan de jichu shang zuzhi jixie gongye shengchan' ('Organize the Machine Manufacturing on the Basis of "Small but Specialized" and "Medium but Specialized"'), *Renmin ribao*, 13 March 1965, p. 5; Fan Rongkang and Chen Chi, 'Shixing da zhong xiao jiehe zou zhuanyehua shengchan he xiezuo de daolu' ('Carry out the Integration of the Small, Medium and Big Factories, Take the Road of Specialized Production and Co-ordination'), *Renmin ribao*, 10 June 1965, p. 5.

18. 'Shanghai fazhan gongye de jiben zuofa' ('The Basic Approach to the Industrial Development in Shanghai'), *Qiye guanli* (*Enterprise Management*), No. 3, 1981, pp. 22–6; 'Guowuyuan tizhi gaige bangongshi, guowuyuan jingji yanjiu zhongxin, Changzhou fazhan jingji tiaozhen diaocha' ('The Survey of Economic Development in Changzhou'), *Hongqi* (*The Red Flag*), No. 13, 1982, pp. 21–6.

19. Yang Zhengmin, 'Organize the Machine Manufacturing...', *Renmin ribao*, 13 March 1965, p. 5, note 17 above; Fan Rongkang and Chen Chi, 'Carry out the Integration...', *Renmin ribao*, 10 June 1965, p. 5, note 17 above.

20. Xu Chanzhen, 'Gongye guanli tizhi gaige de lishixing changshi' ('A Historical Attempt in the Institutional Reforms of Industrial Management'), *Qiye guanli*, No. 3, 1981, pp. 15–18.

21. A Red Guard publication accused Liu Shaoqi, Deng Xiaoping, and Bo Yibo of illegally using the name of the Central Committee to endorse and issue this document. However, they were policy-makers and chief administrators on the 'first front' and they had the formal authority to decide upon the status of the document. See 'Liu Deng Bo zai gongjiao xitong daban tuolasi fupi zibenzhuyi zuize nantao' ('Inescapable Criminal Responsibility of Liu, Deng, Bo in Promoting Trusts in

Industrial and Transport System in a Big Way'), *Hongse gongjiao* (*Red Industry and Transport*), 14 April 1967, pp. 1, 3, and 4.

22. 'Chedi jielu he pipan Liu Shaoqi dagao tuolasi de zui'e yinmou' ('Thoroughly Expose and Criticize the Criminal Conspiracy of Liu Shaoqi in Promoting Trusts in a Big Way'), *Wei dong* (*Defence of Mao*), No. 16, 12 April 1967, p. 2.

23. 'Inescapable Criminal Responsibility...', *Hongse gongjiao*, 14 April 1967, pp. 1, 3 and 4, note 21 above.

24. 'Thoroughly Expose and Criticize the Criminal Conspiracy...', *Wei dong*, No. 16, 12 April 1967, p. 2, note 22 above.

25. 'Thoroughly Expose and Criticize the Criminal Conspiracy...', *Wei dong*, No. 16, 12 April 1967, p. 2, note 22 above.

26. 'Daban tuolasi shi Liu Shaoqi fupi zibenzhuyi de zui'e shouduan' ('To Promote Trusts is a Criminal Way of Liu Shaoqi in Restoring Capitalism'), *Beijing gongshe*, Nos. 21 and 22, 15 May 1967, p. 1.

27. Ye Ji, 'Woguo liushiniandai shiban luyegongsi de yixie qingkuang' ('Some Situation in Establishing Aluminium Corporation on a Trial Basis in the 1960s'), *Jingji yanjiu*, No. 1, 1979, pp. 75–6; 'Ji liushiniandai shiban zhongguo xiangjiao gongye gongsi de qingkuang' ('A Note of the Case of Chongqing Branch Corporation of China Rubber Industrial Corporation in the 1960s'), *Jingji yanjiu*, No. 1, 1979, pp. 5 and 77–8.

28. 'To Examine the Black Line of Counter-revolutionary Revisionism...', *Beijing gongshe*, No. 24, 26 May 1967, p. 2, note 11 above.

29. The two basic faults were discussed in Xu Chuanzhen, 'A Historical Attempt...', *Qiye guanli*, No. 3, 1981, pp. 15–18, note 20 above.

30. Liu Shaoqi, 'Shiban tuolasi' ('Trial-implementation of the Socialist Trust'), in *Liu Shaoqi xuanji* (1985), pp. 473–5.

31. For the case of the pharmaceutical industry in Shanghai, see 'Jiechuan yige fupi zibenzhuyi de dayinmou' ('Expose a Big Conspiracy in the Restoration of Capitalism') (n.p., n.p., 29 April 1967) (Far Eastern Library, The University of Chicago Library, 20 March 1968, AAS142); 'Guanyu Tianjin renmin zhiyaochang shiban tuolasi yilai de yixie qingkuang de diaocha baogao' ('Investigation Report on Some Situation of Organizing Trust in the Tianjin People's Pharmaceutical Factory'), *Jiu Liu zhanbao* (*The Combat Bulletin for Arresting Liu*), No. 4, 21 June 1967, pp. 2–4.

32. Liu Shaoqi, 'Trial-implementation of...', in *Liu Shaoqi xuanji* (1985), p. 474, note 30 above; 'Inescapable Criminal Responsibility...', *Hongse gongjiao*, 14 April 1967, pp. 1, 3, and 4, note 21 above.

33. Xu Chuanzhen, 'A Historical Attempt...', *Qiye guanli*, No. 3, 1981, pp. 15–18, note 20 above.

34. 'Investigation Report on Some Situation...', *Jiu Liu zhanbao*, No. 4, 21 June 1967, pp. 2–4, note 31 above.

35. 'Xiuzhengzhuyi de chuigushou' ('The Advocate of Revisionism'), *Beijing gongshe*, No. 24, 26 May 1967, p. 3.

36. 'Thoroughly Expose and Criticize the Criminal Conspiracy...', *Wei dong*, No. 16, 12 April 1967, p. 2, note 22 above.

37. Jin Qidong, 'Jiekai liu ji tuolasi de heimu' ('Raise the Black Curtain of Liu's Trusts'), *Hongse gongjiao*, No. 6, 15 May 1967, p. 1.

38. 'Thoroughly Expose and Criticize the Criminal Conspiracy...', *Wei dong*, No. 16, 12 April 1967, p. 2, note 22 above.

39. 'Thoroughly Expose and Criticize the Criminal Conspiracy...', *Wei dong*, No. 16, 12 April 1967, p. 2, note 22 above.

40. 'Thoroughly Expose and Criticize the Criminal Conspiracy...', *Wei dong*, No. 16, 12 April 1967, p. 2, note 22 above.

41. 'Thoroughly Expose and Criticize the Criminal Conspiracy...', *Wei dong*, No. 16, 12 April 1967, p. 2, note 22 above.

42. 'Thoroughly Expose and Criticize the Criminal Conspiracy...', *Wei dong*, No. 16, 12 April 1967, p. 2, note 22 above.

43. 'Thoroughly Expose and Criticize the Criminal Conspiracy...', *Wei dong*, No. 16, 12 April 1967, p. 2, note 22 above.

44. 'Thoroughly Expose and Criticize the Criminal Conspiracy...', *Wei dong*, No. 16, 12 April 1967, p. 2, note 22 above.

45. 'Expose A Big Conspiracy...', 29 April 1967, note 31 above; 'Investigation Report on Some Situation...', *Jiu Liu zhanbao*, No. 4, 21 June 1967, pp. 2–4, note 31 above.

46. 'Zhou Zongli de jianghua' ('Talk Given by Premier Zhou'), *Hong tiedao* (*Red Railway*), No. 3, February 1967, p. 3.

47. 'Inescapable Criminal Responsibility...', *Hongse gongjiao*, 14 April 1967, p. 1, note 21 above.

48. 'Thoroughly Expose and Criticize the Criminal Conspiracy...', *Wei dong*, No. 16, 12 April 1967, p. 2, note 22 above.

49. Liu Shaoqi, 'Zai kuoda de zhongyang gongzuo huiyi shang de jianghua' ('Talk at the Enlarged Work Conference of the CC, CCP'), in *Liu Shaoqi xuanji* (1985), pp. 436–7.

50. 'Inescapable Criminal Responsibility...', *Hongse gongjiao*, 14 April 1967, p. 1, note 21 above.

51. Mao Zedong, 'Zai zhengzhiju kuoda huiyi shang de jianghua' ('The Talk at the Enlarged Conference of the Politburo'), in Mao Zedong, *Wansui*, 1969, pp. 637–40, note 2 above.

52. Ma Hong, Mei Xing, *et al.*, 'In Commemoration of Comrade Li Fuchun', *Xinhua yuebao*, No. 1, 1980, pp. 90–2, note 2 above.

53. 'Chang Guanlou fangeming shijian de qianqian houhou' ('The Background of the Counter-revolutionary Incident of Chang Guanlou'), *Dongfang hong* (*East is Red*), 20 April 1967, p. 5.

54. Mao Zedong, 'Talk at the Enlarged Work Conference of the CC, CCP', in *Wansui*, 1969, p. 416, note 2 above.

55. Mao Zedong, 'Talk at the Enlarged Work Conference of the CC, CCP', in *Wansui*, 1969, p. 414, note 2 above.

56. Ma Hong, Mei Xing, *et al.*, 'In Commemoration of Comrade Li Fuchun', *Xinhua yuebao*, No. 1, 1980, pp. 90–2, note 2 above.

57. 'The Background of the Counter-revolutionary Incident...', *Dongfang hong*, 20 April 1967, p. 5, note 53 above.

58. Ma Hong, Mei Xing, *et al.*, 'In Commemoration of Comrade Li Fuchun', *Xinhua yuebao*, No. 1, 1980, pp. 90–2, note 2 above.

59. Ma Hong, Mei Xing, *et al.*, 'In Commemoration of Comrade Li Fuchun', *Xinhua yuebao*, No. 1, 1980, pp. 90–2, note 2 above; 'The Background of the Counter-revolutionary Incident...', *Dongfang hong*, 20 April 1967, p. 5, note 53 above.

60. 'Da ducao gongye qishitiao shi zenyang chulong de?' ('How Did the Big Poisonous Weed, "The Seventy Articles on Industry", Come out?'), *Dou-pi-gai* (*Struggle, Criticism, Transformation*), No. 8, 1967, pp. 28–37.

61. Ma Hong, Mei Xing, *et al.*, 'In Commemoration of Comrade Li Fuchun', *Xinhua yuebao*, No. 1, 1980, pp. 90–2, note 2 above.

62. 'Shenyang chengshi diaocha shi Liu Deng shexiang dangzhongyang Mao Zhuxi de yizhi dujian' ('Shenyang Urban Survey is a Poisonous Arrow Shooting at Party Centre and Chairman Mao'), *Wei dong*, No. 24, 15 May 1967, pp. 1–2.

63. Ma Hong, Mei Xing, *et al.*, 'In Commemoration of Comrade Li Fuchun', *Xinhua yuebao*, No. 1, 1980, pp. 90–2, note 2 above.

64. Liu Shaoqi, 'The Report to the Enlarged Work Conference...', *Liu Shaoqi xuanji* (1985), pp. 356–7, note 4 above.

65. All quotations from Liu's statements in this paragraph come from 'How Did the Big Poisonous Weed...?', *Dou-pi-gai*, No. 8, 1967, p. 28, note 60 above.
66. 'How Did the Big Poisonous Weed...?', *Dou-pi-gai*, No. 8, 1967, p. 29, note 60 above.
67. 'The Regulation of Tasks in State-owned Industrial Enterprises', *Tiaoli huibian* (1978), pp. 216–43, note 13 above.
68. 'The Regulation of Tasks in State-owned Industrial Enterprises', *Tiaoli huibian* (1978), pp. 216–41, note 13 above.
69. 'The Regulation of Tasks in State-owned Industrial Enterprises', *Tiaoli huibian* (1978), pp. 224, 238–40, and 242, note 13 above.
70. 'The Directive of the Central Committee, CCP...', *Tiaoli huibian* (1978), pp. 201–5, note 5 above.
71. Wang Haibo, Wu Jinglian, and Zhou Shulian, 'Bixu ba laodongzhe de yibufen shouru he qiye de jingying zhuangkuang jinmi di lianxi qilai' ('Link closely the Income of the Workers with the Performance of Enterprises'), *Jingji yanjiu*, No. 12, 1978, pp. 37–43.
72. Zhongguo gongye chubanshe (ed.), *Gongye qiye guanli wenxuan* (*Selected Articles on Industrial Enterprise Management*) (Beijing, Zhongguo gongye chubanshe, 1964), Vol. II (hereafter cited as *Guanli wenxuan*); 'Guojia jingji weiyuanhui guanyu gongkuang chanpin dinghuo hetung jiben tiaokuan de zhanxing guiding' ('The Provisional Regulation of the State Economic Commission concerning Basic Articles and Clauses of Ordering Agreements for Products in Mining and Industry'), *Fagui huibian*, January 1961–December 1962, pp. 182–94; 'Guowuyuan guanyu yange zhixing jiben jianshe chengxu yange zhixing jingji hetung de tongzhi' ('The Circular of the State Council concerning Vigorous Implementation of Basic Construction and Economic Agreements'), *Fagui huibian*, January 1961–December 1962, pp. 62–3; Deng Zhangming, 'Guanyu gongye qiye zhijian kaizhan jingji xiezuo de jige wenti' ('On Several Problems of the Development of Economic Co-ordination among Industrial Enterprises'), *Jingji yanjiu*, No. 3, 30 March 1965, pp. 16–19.
73. *Guanli wenxuan* (1964), Vol. I, note 72 above; Lee, Peter Nan-shong, 'China's Industrial Bureaucracy, 1949–73' (Unpublished Ph.D. dissertation, University of Chicago, 1975), pp. 76–80; 'How Did the Big Poisonous Weed...?', *Dou-pi-gai*, No. 8, 1967, p. 28, note 60 above.
74. 'Dadao Gongjiao zhanxian shang de heibawang sanfan fenzi Bo Yibo' ('Down with the Black Despot and Three Anti-elements on the Transport and Industry Front, Bo Yibo'), *Dongfang hong*, 15 February 1967, pp. 5–7.
75. Kuang Rian et al., 'Shilun guoying gongye qiye shixing yange jingji hesuan wenti' ('On the Vigorous Implementation of Economic Accounting in State-owned Industrial Enterprises'), *Jingji yanjiu*, No. 82, 27 August 1963; Xue Muqiao, 'Guanyu shehuizhuyi de jingji hesuan' ('On Socialist Economic Accounting'), *Hongqi*, No. 20, 1961, pp. 8–14; Li Chengrui and Zuo Chuntai, 'Guanyu shehuizhuyi qiye jingji hesuan de jige wenti' ('Several Problems of Economic Accounting in Socialist Enterprises'), *Hongqi*, No. 20, 1961, pp. 18–25.
76. Zhao Lukuang and Pan Jinyun, 'Lun jijian gongzi' ('On the Piece-rate Wage'), *Jingji yanjiu*, No. 2, 1979, pp. 49–50; Zhuang Qidong (ed.), *Laodong gongzi shoucie* (*The Manual of Labour and Wage*) (Jianjin, Tianjin renmin chubanshe, 1984), pp. 59–66.
77. Zhuang Qidong (1984), p. 26, note 76 above.
78. 'Chedi pipan Liu Shaoqi zai jingji lingyu de fangeming xiuzhengzhuyi zuixing' ('Thoroughly Criticize Liu Shaoqi's Counter-revolutionary Revisionist Crime in the Economic Sphere'), *Hongse gongjiao*, 26 May 1967, p. 2; Yang Shiyi, 'Jianli zongkuaijishi zhi de yixie zuofa' ('Some Practices in Establishing the Chief Accounting System'), in *Guanli wenxuan* (1964), Vol. VII, pp. 142–8, note 72 above; 'Jieshao

256 NOTES TO PAGES 89–93

angang chang kuang zongkuaijishi de zhize' ('Introduce the Duty and Responsibility of the Chief Accountant in Factories and Mines of the Anshan Iron and Steel Corporation'), in *Guanli wenxuan* (1964), Vol. III, pp. 137–41, note 72 above.

79. Liu Shaoqi, 'Shixing gudinggong he hetonggong bincun de zhidu' ('Implement the System Maintaining the Parallel Existence of the Fixed and Contractual Workers'), in *Liu Shaoqi xuanji*, Vol. II, pp. 470–2.

80. 'Down with the Black Despot...', *Dongfang hong*, 15 February 1967, pp. 5–7, note 74 above.

81. Wenhua Ziliao Gongyingshe (ed.), *Zhong-Su lunzhan wenxian* (*The Documents of the Sino-Soviet Polemics*) (Hong Kong, Ziliao gong yingshe, 1977).

82. 'How Did the Big Poisonous Weed...?', *Dou-pi-gai*, No. 8, 1967, p. 28, note 60 above.

83. 'Down with the Black Despot...', *Dongfang hong*, 15 February 1967, pp. 5–7, note 74 above.

84. 'Down with the Black Despot...', *Dongfang hong*, 15 February 1967, pp. 5–7, note 74 above.

85. 'The Regulation of the Tasks in ...', *Tiaoli huibian*, pp. 218–20, note 13 above. Cheng Qi *et al.*, 'Yansu duidai jihua baozheng wancheng jihua' ('Seriously Deal with Planning, Make Sure to Complete the Plans'), in *Guanli wenxuan* (1964), Vol. II, pp. 26–31, note 72 above.

86. Many articles and analyses published after 1961 indicate the methods, procedures, and problems of assessing and determining production capacity at the enterprise level. For a brief survey, see Hu Shiru and Li Douyuan, 'Gongye qiye shenchan nengli chading de jige wenti' ('Several Problems in the Assessment and Determination of the Production Capacity of Industrial Enterprises'), in *Guanli wenxuan* (1964), Vol. II, pp. 64–9, note 72 above; Zhu Chengkang, 'Guanyu queding huagong qiye chanping shengchan nengli de jige wenti' ('Several Problems regarding the Determination of Production Capacity of Products in Chemical Industries'), in *Guanli wenxuan* (1964), Vol. II, pp. 70–6, note 72 above; Diyi jijie gongyebu jihua caiwusi, 'Ruhe heding jijie gongye qiye de shengchan nengli' ('How to Assess the Production Capacity of Engineering Enterprises'), in *Guanli wenxuan* (1964), Vol. II, pp. 70–7, note 72 above; 'Renzhen jiaqiang qiye de ding'e guanli gongzuo' ('Assiduously Strengthen the Managerial Task of Norm-setting in Enterprises'), *Zhongguo qinggongye* (*China's Light Industry*), No. 3, 1963, pp. 85–9; Jiang Min, 'Jiaqiang ding'e guanli luoshi zengchan jieyue zhibiao' ('Strengthen Norm-setting Management and Implement the Indicators of Production and Savings'), *Zhongguo qinggongye*, No. 3, 1963, pp. 90–3.

87. 'The Background of the Counter-revolutionary Incident...', *Dongfang hong*, 20 April 1967, p. 6, note 53 above.

88. 'To Examine the Black Line of Counter-revolutionary Revisionism...', *Beijing gongshe*, No. 24, 26 May 1967, p. 2, note 11 above.

89. 'How Did the Big Poisonous Weed...?', *Dou-pi-gai*, No. 8, 1967, pp. 30–1, note 60 above.

90. 'How Did the Big Poisonous Weed...?', *Dou-pi-gai*, No. 8, 1967, pp. 30–1, note 60 above.

91. 'How Did the Big Poisonous Weed...?', *Dou-pi-gai*, No. 8, 1967, pp. 30–1, note 60 above.

92. 'How Did the Big Poisonous Weed...?', *Dou-pi-gai*, No. 8, 1967, pp. 30–1, note 60 above.

93. Charles E. Lindblom, *Politics and Markets* (New York, Basic Books, Inc., 1977), p. 65.

94. Mao Zedong, 'Guanyu gongzuo fangfa liushi tiao' ('On the Sixteen Articles on the Work Methods, May 1959'), in *Wansui*, 1967, p. 59, note 2 above.

95. Mao Zedong, 'Zai Chengdu huiyi shang de jianghua' ('Talk at Zhengtu Conference, March 1958'), in *Wansui*, 1969, p. 171, note 2 above.

NOTES TO CHAPTER 5

1. The main features of the Yenan type of military industry are described in Peter Schran, 'The Yen'an Origins of Current Economic Policies', in Dwight Perkins (ed.), *China's Modern Economy in Historical Perspective* (Stanford, Stanford University Press, 1975), pp. 279–337.

2. Dui Daqing jingyan de zhengzhi jingjixue kaocha xiezuozu (The Writing Group on the Investigation of the Political Economy of the Daqing Experience), *Dui Daqing jingyan de zhengzhi jingjixue de kaocha* (*Investigation of Political Economy of Daqing Experience*) (Beijing, Renmin chubanshe, 1979), pp. 266–7, hereafter cited as *Kaocha* (1979).

3. Xu Jinqiang, 'Gaoju Mao Zedong sixiang weida hongqi buduan jiashen qiye gemingua' ('Hoist High the Great Red Banner of Mao Zedong's Thought, continuously Deepen the Revolutionization of Enterprise'), *Jingji yanjiu* (*Economic Research*), No. 4, 1966, pp. 16–17.

4. Yu Qiuli, 'Quandang quanguo gongrenjieji dongyuan qilai wei puji Daqing shi qiye er fendou' ('Mobilize the Whole Party and the Working People of the Nation, Struggle for the Extension of Daqing Type of Enterprises'), in Sanlian shudian (ed.), *Quanguo gongye xue Daqing huiyi wenjian xuanbian* (*Selected Documents of National Conference of Learning from Daqing in Industry*) (Hong Kong, Sanlian shudian, 1977), p. 62, hereafter cited as *Wenjian xuanbian* (1977); Franz Schurmann, *Ideology and Organisation in Communist China* (Berkeley and Los Angeles, University of California Press, 1968), pp. 303–5; my interviews at the Beijing People's Machinery Factory in August 1979 indicated that in almost all large-scale enterprises, political departments were established as early as the Cultural Revolution.

5. 'Yu Qiuli cuowu yanxinglu' ('Quotations of the Erroneous Words and Deeds of Yu Qiuli'), *Ba yi ba zhanbao* (*August 18 and Combat Bulletin*), No. 18, 20 April 1967.

6. 'Yu Qiuli shige shemeren?' ('What Kind of Person is Yu Qiuli?'), *Changzheng* (*Long March*), No. 15, 19 April 1967, pp. 3–4; 'Shiyou tuolasi daodishi shenme house?' ('What Kind of Commodity is the Petroleum Trust really?'). *Changzheng*, No. 15, 19 April 1967, p. 4.

7. Song Zhenming, 'Gaoju Mao Zhuxi de weida qizhi zou woguo ziji gongye fazhan de daolu' ('Raise High the Great Banner of Chairman Mao, Take our Country's own Road of Industrial Development', *Wenjian xuanbian* (1977), pp. 18–21 and 102–3, note 4 above; Daqing gongye qiye guanli xiezuozu (The Writing Group on Industrial Enterprise Management in Daqing), *Daqing gongye qiye guanli* (*Industrial Enterprise Management in Daqing*) (Beijing, Renmin chubanshe, 1979), pp. 124–6, hereafter cited as *Qiye guanli*; *Qiye guanli* (1977), pp. 33–4; Xu Jinqiang, 'Hoist High the Great Red Banner...', *Jingji yanjiu*, No. 6, 1966, pp. 16–17, note 3 above; it is worthy of note that Xu Jinqiang failed to mention the work-post responsibility system in his 1966 article; this omission was probably because of the political climate at the beginning of the Cultural Revolution; 'Gangwei zerenzhi' ('Work-post Responsibility System'), *Renmin ribao* (*People's Daily*), 16 February 1977, p. 1; 'Du Mao Zhuxi de shu, ting Mao Zhuxi de hua, wei wuchanjieji shiye fendou yibeizi' ('Read Chairman Mao's Book, Listen to Chairman Mao's Words, Strive for the Proletarian Mission for a Whole Life'), *Renmin ribao*, 28 March 1977, pp. 1, 2, and 4.

8. Most successful State-owned enterprises provide workers and employees with a number of subsidies and services but Daqing oilfield is notable in affording housing, utilities, and fuel free of charge in the later stages of its development. See *Kaocha* (1979), pp. 124–7 and 266–319; 'Daqing jianshe cheng gongnong jiehe de xinxing kuangqu' ('To Build Daqing into a New Type of Mining Area with Worker-Peasant Integration'), *Jingji yanjiu*, No. 4, 1966, p. 27.

9. 'Zhanduan Liu Shaoqi shenxiang Daqing de mozhua' ('Chop Off the Demon's Claw of Liu Shaoqi Stretched to Daqing'), *Changzheng*, No. 15, 19 April 1967, pp. 1–2.

10. Yu Qiuli, 'Mobilize the Whole Party and the Working People...', *Wenjian xuanbian* (1977), pp. 62–3, note 4 above.

11. Song Zhenming, 'Raise High the Great Banner...', *Wenjian xuanbian* (1977), p. 100, note 7 above. Here Song expands upon the so-called 'three orientations' and five 'on-the-spots' policies to refer to the tasks of functional departments. However, it appears that the 'three orientations' and five 'on-the-spots' were originally mentioned in the context of materials and inventory management; see *Qiye guanli* (1979), pp. 166–70, note 7 above.

12. Zhang Dakai and Song Jinsheng, 'Qiye guanli shang de yiqe genben de gaige' ('A Fundamental Change in Enterprise Management'), *Renmin ribao*, 25 December 1964, p. 5.

13. Xu Jinqiang, 'Hoist High the Great Red Banner...', *Jingji yanjiu*, No. 6, 1966, p. 16, note 3 above.

14. Xu Jinqiang, 'Hoist High the Great Red Banner...', *Jingji yanjiu*, No. 6, 1966, pp. 17–19, note 3 above.

15. *Kaocha* (1979), pp. 37–8, note 2 above.

16. Yan Feng, 'What is the Essence of the "20 Articles"?', in *Selections from the People's Republic of China Magazines*, No. 884, 16 July 1976, p. 23, hereafter cited as *SPRCM*.

17. Yan Feng, 'What is the Essence of the "20 Articles"?', *SPRCM*, No. 884, 16 July 1976, p. 23, note 16 above.

18. See Stephen Andors, *China's Industrial Revolution* (New York, Pantheon Books, 1977), pp. 143–51.

19. 'Keshi yao zhudong we shengchan diyixian fuwu' ('The Functional Department Should Serve the First-Front Production'), *Gongren ribao (Workers' Daily)*, 14 April 1964, p. 1.

20. Hu Fengji, 'Jizhong dao changbu fuwu dao banzu shi qiye jingying guanli zhidu geminghua de yixiang biange' ('A Change Along the Line of Revolutionizing the Enterprise Management System, Centralization of Power to Factory Headquarters and Service to the Shifts and Teams'), *Guangming ribao (Guangming Daily)*, 21 June 1965, p. 4.

21. Zhang Dakai and Song Jinsheng, 'A Fundamental Change...', *Renmin ribao*, 25 December 1964, p. 5, note 12 above.

22. Zhang Dakai and Song Jinsheng, 'A Fundamental Change...', *Renmin ribao*, 25 December 1964, p. 5, note 12 above.

23. Zhang Dakai and Song Jinsheng, 'A Fundamental Change...', *Renmin ribao*, 25 December 1964, p. 5, note 12 above.

24. 'Danau qiye guanli geming shengchan mianmao huanran yi xi' ('Launch Enterprise Management Revolution, Put Production on an Entirely "New Footing"'), *Gongren ribao*, 23 February 1965, p. 2; 'Fuwu dao banzu' ('Services to the Shifts and Team'), *Gongren ribao*, 7 September 1965, p. 2.

25. Zhang Xingkui and Zhao Tingxin, 'Baituo shiwuzhuyi dao shengchan diyixian qu' ('Do away with Office Work and Go directly to the First Front of Production'), *Dagong bao (Dagong Daily)*, 14 May 1965, p. 2.

26. 'Lao zhang shi women de hao daitouren' ('Old Zhang is a Good Fellow who

Provides Leadership'), *Zhongguo xinwen* (*China News*), Press Release No. 5263, 4 September 1968, p. 1.

27. Alvin Gouldner, *Patterns of Industrial Bureaucracy* (New York, The Free Press of Glencoe Inc., 1954).

28. Zhang Dakai and Song Jinsheng, 'A Fundamental Change...', *Renmin ribao*, 25 December 1964, p. 5, note 12 above; Xu Jinqiang, 'Hoist high the Great Red Banner...', *Jingji yanjiu*, No. 4, 1966, p. 18, note 3 above.

29. *Qiye guanli* (1979), pp. 116–21 and 133–45, note 7 above; *Kaocha* (1979), pp. 223–4, note 2 above.

30. Andrew G. Walder, 'Industrial Organization and Socialist Development in China', *Modern China*, April 1979, p. 249.

31. Andrew G. Walder, 'Industrial Organization...', *Modern China*, April 1979, p. 249, note 30 above.

32. Thomas W. Robinson, 'Zhou Enlai and the Cultural Revolution in China', in Thomas W. Robinson (ed.), *The Cultural Revolution in China* (Berkeley, Calif., University of California Press, 1971), p. 165.

33. Zhou Enlai, 'Zai renmin dahuitang de jianghua' ('Talk at the Great People's Hall'), *Zhou Enlai xuanji*, Vol. III (Hong Kong, Yishan tushu gongsi, 1976), p. 622, hereafter cited as *Zhou Enlai xuanji*, Vol. III (1976).

34. 'Xiuzhengzhuyi de chuigoshou' ('The Advocate of Revisionism'), *Beijing gongshe* (*Beijing Commune*), No. 24, 26 May 1967, p. 3; Long Fei, 'Cong Yu Qiuli churen wei guojia jihua weiyuanhui zhuren kan Mao gong neibu douzheng' ('Examine the CCP's Internal Struggle in the Light of Yu Qiuli's Appointment to the Directorship of the State Planning Commission'), *Zhonggong yanjiu* (*The Research of the Chinese Communist Party*), Vol. 6, No. 12, December 1972, pp. 8–10.

35. Yu Qiuli was appointed Deputy Director of the State Planning Commission at the 159th meeting of the State Council. See 'Guowuyuan renmian mingdan' ('The Name List of Appointment and Dismissal of the State Council'), *Renmin ribao*, 29 November 1965, p. 2; 'Zhou Zongli de jianghua' ('Talk of Premier Zhou'), *Hong tiedao* (*Red Railway*), No. 3, 1 February 1967, p. 3.

36. 'Advocate of Revisionism', *Beijing gongshe*, No. 24, 26 May 1967, p. 3, note 34 above; Long Fei, 'Examine the CCP's Internal Struggle...', *Zhonggong yanjiu*, Vol. 6, No. 12, December 1972, pp. 8–10, note 34 above.

37. 'Gumu si bao Bo Yibo' ('Gu Mu Earnestly Protects Bo Yibo'), *Hongse gongjiao* (*Red Industry and Transport*), No. 7, 26 May 1967, p. 2.

38. See *Kaocha* (1979), p. 42, note 2 above.

39. 'Yu Qiuli de leilei zuixing bixu chedi qingsuan' ('Yu Qiuli's Numerous Crimes Must Be Settled Thoroughly'), *Jinjun bao* (*On March Bulletin*), No. 12, 26 March 1967, p. 2; 'Shede yishengua ganba Yu Qiuli laxia ma' ('Dismount Yu Qiuli from the Saddle even if it Means the Penalty of One Thousand Cuts'), *Jinggangshan* (*Jingang Mountain*), No. 20, 18 March 1967, p. 2.

40. According to Red Guard sources, Yu Qiuli viewed the Daqing Exhibition at least four times. See 'Dismount Yu Qiuli from the Saddle...', *Jinggangshan*, No. 20, 18 March 1967, p. 3, note 39 above.

41. 'Yu Qiuli duikang wuchanjieji silingbu zuixing nantao' ('Inescapable Crimes of Yu Qiuli in Opposing the Proletarian Headquarters'), *Jinjun bao*, No. 13, 1 April 1967, p. 4.

42. 'The Advocate of Revisionism', *Beijing gongshe*, No. 24, 26 May 1976, p. 3, note 34 above.

43. 'The Advocate of Revisionism', *Beijing gongshe*, No. 24, 26 May 1976, p. 3, note 34 above.

44. 'Yu Qiuli shi Liu Deng hei silingbu de ganjiang' ('Yu Qiuli is a Competent General in the Liu–Deng Black Headquarters'), *Jinggangshan*, No. 23, 26 March 1967, p. 4.

45. Zhou Enlai, 'Talk at the Great People's Hall', *Zhou Enlai xuanji*, Vol. III (1976), pp. 621–2, note 33 above.

46. Zhou Enlai, 'Dui pidou Yu Qiuli de zhishi' ('Instruction on the Criticism and Struggle against Yu Qiuli'), *Zhou Enlai xuanji*, Vol. III (1976), pp. 671–6.

47. Mao Zedong, 'Tingqu Gu Mu, Yu Qiuli huibao jihua gongzuo shi de zhishi' ('Instruction Given after the Briefing of Gu Mu and Yu Qiuli on the Task of Planning'), *Mao Zedong sixiang wansui* (*Long Live Mao Zedong's Thought*) (n.p., n.p., 1969), pp. 605–6, hereafter cited as *Wansui* (1969); Yu's role was confirmed by Zhou Enlai. See Zhou Enlai, 'Jiejian gong jiao kou geming zaofanpai de jianghua' ('Talk at the Reception of Revolutionary Rebel Factions on the Industrial and Transport Front'), *Zhou Enlai xuanji*, Vol. III (1976), pp. 629–30.

48. Zhou Enlai, 'Talk at the Great People's Hall', *Zhou Enlai xuanji*, Vol. III (1976), p. 622, note 33 above. Zhou suggested that he and Li Xiannian would be in charge of the Ministry of Railways because no other person could assume the responsibility.

49. Zhou Enlai, 'Instruction on the Criticism and Struggle...', *Zhou Enlai xuanji*, Vol. III (1976), pp. 629–30, note 46 above; Long Fei, 'Examine the CCP's Internal Struggle...', *Zhonggong yanjiu*, Vol. 6, No. 12, December 1972, p. 11, note 34 above.

50. 'Yi zhen huangliang zaixian' ('Another Dream of Grandeur') (n.p., n.p., 1967).

51. Donald W. Klein, 'The State Council and the Cultural Revolution', *China Quarterly*, No. 35, July–September 1968, pp. 80–2.

52. Long Fei, 'Dangqian Zhong gong wei guowuyuan zhuangkuang zhi yanxi' ('An Analysis of the Current Situation of the State Council'), *Zhonggong yanjiu*, Vol. 3, No. 7, July 1969, pp. 61–2.

53. Long Fei, 'An Analysis of the Current Situation...', *Zhonggong yanjiu*, Vol. 3, No. 7, July 1969, p. 64, note 52 above; Li Tianmin,. *Zhou Enlai pingzhuan* (*Biography of Zhou Enlai*) (Hong Kong, Union Research Institute, 1975), pp. 242–62.

54. Zhou Enlai, 'Instruction on the Criticism and Struggle...', *Zhou Enlai xuanji*, Vol. III (1976), pp. 671–6, note 46 above.

55. Long Fei, 'An Analysis of the Current Situation...', *Zhonggong yanjiu*, Vol. 3, No. 7, July 1969, p. 64, note 52 above.

56. Zhou Enlai, 'Tan shijie xingshi, dalianhe, sanjiehe, jiefang ganbu zhua geming, cushengchan he junguan wenti' ('Talk on the World Situation, Great Alliance, Triple Combination, Liberation of Cadres, Grasping of Revolution and Promoting Production and Military Control'), *Zhou Enlai xuanji*, Vol. III (1976), p. 659, note 33 above.

57. Zhou Enlai, 'Dui gedi tiedao gangkou jiaotong wenti de zhishi' ('Instruction on the Problems of Railway, Harbour and Transportation in Several Localities'), *Zhou Enlai xuanji*, Vol. III (1976), pp. 677–82, note 33 above.

58. Correspondence between Liu Shaoqi and Ma Wenrui, the Minister of Labour, was cited in an article, 'Dadao hetonggong zhidu de chuang daozhe gongzei Liu Shaoqi' ('Down with the Promoter of the Contract Workers System'), and the author(s) showed how the system was borrowed from the Soviet Union. See *Laogong zhanbao* (*The Combat Bulletin of Workers*), No. 2, 3 February 1978, p. 1.

59. Zhuang Qidong, *Laodong gongzi shouce* (*The Manual of Labour and Wage*) (Tianjin, Tianjin renmin chubanshe, 1984), pp. 25–6.

60. 'Guowuyuan guanyu guoying qiye shiyong linshigong de zhanxing guiding' ('The Provisional Regulations of the State Council Concerning the Employment of Temporary Workers in the State-owned Enterprises'), *Zhonghua renmin gongheguo fagui huibian* (*The Collected Laws of the PRC*), January 1962–December 1963, pp. 220–3, hereafter cited as *Fagui huibain*.

61. 'Zhongyang wenge xiaozu lingdao tongzhi jiejian quanguo hongse laodongzhe zaofan zongtuan daibiao tanhua jilu' ('Transcript of Conversation between Leading

Comrades of the Cultural Revolution Group and the Central Committee at the Reception of the Representatives of the All China Red Workers' Rebels Corps') (n.p., n.p., 26 December 1966). Chen Boda, Kang Sheng, Jiang Qing, Zhang Chunqiao, Qi Benyu, and Yao Wenyuan were among the participants.

62. Zhou Taihe *et al.* (eds.), *Dangdai Zhongguo de jingji tizhi gaige* (*The Economic Reform in Contemporary China*) (Beijing, Zhongguo shehui kexue chubanshe, 1984), pp. 131–2.

63. Shanghai People's Broadcasting Station, 29 February 1967, 9.00 pm. Zhou Enlai also made remarks on the issue on 1 February 1967 in Zhongnanhai and suggested that the issue of contract workers was not solely Liu Shaoqi's fault. See 'Zhou zongli de jianghua' ('Talk of Premier Zhou'), *Hong tiedao*, No. 3, 11 February 1967, p. 3.

64. Zhou Taihe *et al.* (eds.) (1984), p. 146, note 62 above.

65. 'Zhongguo gongchandang zhongyang weiyuanhui, guanyu wuchun jieji wenhua dageming de jueding' ('The Decision of CC, CCP Concerning the Great Proletarian Cultural Revolution, 8 August 1966'), *Hongqi* (*Red Flag*), No. 10, 10 August 1966, pp. 1–9.

66. 'Zhua geming cu shengchan' ('Grasp Revolution, Promote Production'), *Renmin ribao*, 7 September 1966, p. 1.

67. Hongfeng Combat Section, Honggi Combat Detachment, Peking Aeronautical Institute, 'Firmly Implement the Guideline of "Taking Firm Hold of the Revolution and Stimulating Production"', *Survey of Mainland China Press*, No. 3875, 6 February 1967, pp. 15–19, cited hereafter as *SMCP*.

68. 'Shanghai de yiyue geming jingyan' ('The Experience of the January Revolution in Shanghai'), *Guangyin hongqi* (*The Red Flag of Guangzhou Printing Factory*), No. 3, 23 November 1967, pp. 1, 3, and 4.

69. Chien Chunpang, 'Thoroughly Uncover the Big Conspiracy of Economism', *SMCP*, No. 3870, 30 January 1967, pp. 1–5.

70. 'Shanghai Revolutionary Rebels Hit at Economism, Score Great Victory', *SMCP*, No. 3869, 27 January 1967, pp. 16–21.

71. Raymond F. Wylie, 'Shanghai Dockers in the Cultural Revolution: the Interplay of Political and Economic Issues', in Christopher Howe (ed.), *Shanghai: Revolution and Development in an Asian Metropolis* (Cambridge, Cambridge University Press, 1981), pp. 110–24.

72. 'Quebao guojia yinhang jinrong shiye bushou pohuai' ('Make sure no Damage Done to the Banking and Monetary Apparatus of the State'), *Renmin ribao*, 14 January 1967, p. 2.

73. 'Creatively Study and Apply the "Three Old Articles" and Sweep away the Black Wind of Economism', *SMCP*, No. 3872, 1 February 1967, pp. 15–16.

74. 'Revolutionary Rebel United General Headquarters and Other Revolutionary Rebel Bodies in Chekiang Publish Urgent Notice on Striking down Counter-revolutionary Economism in the Countryside', *SMCP*, No. 3878, 13 February 1967, pp. 7–11; 'Four Revolutionary Organizations in Heilungkiang Province Make Urgent Appeal to Revolutionary Peasants of the Whole Province to Smash Economism thoroughly', *SMCP*, No. 3873, 2 February 1967, pp. 11–14; 'Revolutionary Rebel Organizations Issue Message to all Shanghai People' (NCNA — English broadcast, Shanghai, 21 January 1967), *SMCP*, No. 3867, 25 January 1967, pp. 24–7.

75. 'Cong Xilou huiyi kan caijing fanmian de fangeming xiuzheng zhuyi heixian' ('An Analysis of the Black Line of Counter-revolutionary Revisionism of Finance and Economy in the Light of the West Chamber Conference'), *Beijing gongshe*, 26 May 1967, p. 2.

76. 'Jingji tonggao' ('The Urgent Notice'), *Renmin ribao*, 12 January 1967.

77. 'Jingji tongdian' ('The Urgent Telegram'), *Renmin ribao*, 22 January 1967.

78. Hung Chanpien, 'Economism is the Corrosion of the Workers Movement', *SMCP*, No. 3867, 25 January 1967, pp. 19–20.

79. Chien Chunpang, 'Thoroughly Uncover the Big Conspiracy...', *SMCP*, No. 3870, 30 January 1967, p. 3, note 69 above.

80. 'Creatively Study and Apply the "Three Old Articles"...', *SMCP*, No. 3872, 1 February 1967, p. 15, note 73 above.

81. Harry Harding, Jr., 'Maoist Theories of Policy-making and Organization', in Robinson (ed.) (1971), pp. 113–42, note 32 above.

82. 'The Experience of the January Revolution...', *Guangyin hongqi*, No. 3, 23 November 1967, pp. 1, 3, and 4, note 68 above.

83. 'The Decision of CC, CCP Concerning the Great Proletarian...', *Hongqi*, No. 10, 10 August 1966, pp. 3–4, note 65 above.

84. 'The Experience of the January Revolution...', *Guangyin Hongqi*, No. 3, 23 November 1967, pp. 1, 3, and 4, note 68 above.

85. Mao Zedong, 'Dui Shanghai wenhua dageming de zhishi' ('Instruction on the Cultural Revolution in Shanghai'), *Wansui* (1969), pp. 667–72.

86. 'Shanghai boli chang jianli geming shengchan weiyuanhai' ('Shanghai Glassware Factory Establishes the Revolution Production Committee'), *Renmin ribao*, 14 January 1967, p. 1; 'Revolutionary Workers of Shanghai Factory Set Up "Revolution and Production Committee"', *SMCP*, No. 3869, 27 January 1967, pp. 1–3; 'Another New Product Nurtured by the Great Thought of Mao Tse-tung', *SMCP*, No. 3875, 6 February 1967, pp. 8–11.

87. Gong Xiaowen, 'Deng Xiaoping yu ershitiao' ('Deng Xiaoping and Twenty Articles'), *Xuexi yu pipan* (*Study and Critique*), No. 6, 14 June 1978, p. 18.

88. 'Heilongjiang sheng hongse zaofanzhe duoquan douzheng de jiben jingyan' ('The Basic Experience of the Struggle in Power Seizure by the Red Rebels in Heilongjiang Province'), *Hongqi*, No. 4, 1 March 1967, pp. 12–14.

89. 'Revolutionaries of Peking, Shanghai and Other Areas Acclaim New Experience Created by Heilongjiang Comrades-in-Arms in Embodying the Thought of Mao Tse-tung', *SMCP*, No. 3884, 21 February 1967, pp. 3–6.

90. 'Wei wuchanjieji geming shiye duodao quan zhanghao quan yonghao quan' ('Seize the Power, Employ the Power and Make Full Use of Power for the Proletarian Revolutionary Enterprise'), *Renmin ribao*, 1 March 1967, p. 1.

91. 'Dangqian Shanghai wenhua dageming de xingshi he renwu' ('The Current Situation and Mission in the Cultural Revolution in Shanghai'), *Hongqi*, No. 4, 1 March 1967, pp. 22–3.

92. 'Zhong gong zhongyang gei quanguo changkuang qiye geming zhigong geming ganbu de xin' ('The Circular of CC, CCP Concerning the Revolutionary Workers and Staff, and Revolutionary Cadres in Enterprises and Mines Throughout the Whole Nation'), *Hongqi*, No. 5, 30 March 1967, pp. 3–4.

93. 'Beijing geming zhigong daibiao huiyi jueyi' ('The Resolution of the Congress of the Revolutionary Workers and Staff in Beijing'), *Renmin ribao*, 24 March 1967, pp. 1 and 2.

94. 'Zai douzheng zhong shixian an hanye xitong de geming dalianhe, zhai dalianhe de jichu shang shixian geming de sanjiehe' ('Implement the Great Revolutionary Alliance according to the Branches of Industry, Carry out the Revolutionary Triple Alliance on the Basis of the Great Alliance'), *Renmin ribao*, 8 May 1967, p. 3.

95. 'An bumen dalianhe wei dou-pi-gai chuanzao youli tiaojian' ('Excellent Situation for Struggle, Criticism, and Transformation through Great Alliance on the Basis of Administrative Units'), *Renmin ribao*, 1 April 1967, p. 3.

96. 'Zunzhao Mao zhuxi zhishi, anzhao xitong shixing geming dalianhe' ('Follow Chairman Mao's Instruction, Form Great Revolutionary Alliance according to the System'), *Renmin ribao*, 19 October 1967, p. 1.

97. 'Naixin bangzhu ganbu dadan jiefang ganbu, fangshou shiyong ganbu' ('Patiently Help Cadres, boldly Liberate Cadres, and liberally Use Cadres'), *Renmin ribao*, 26 August 1967, p. 4; 'Daban xuexiban jiejue sanjiehe lingdao banzi wenti'

('Solve the Problems in the Triple Combination of Leadership Team through Study Group'), *Renmin ribao*, 27 February 1968, p. 2.

98. 'Yao reqiang dizhichi geming de xinganbu' ('Lend Enthusiastic Support to the Revolutionary New Cadres'), *Renmin ribao*, 16 November 1967, p. 1; 'Zhengque chuli laoganbu guanxi he gan-qun ganxi; geming weiyuanhui zai qunzhong zhong jianli geming guanwei' ('Correctly Handling the Relationship to Old Cadres, and that between the Cadres and Masses; Establishing the Revolutionary Authority of the Revolutionary Committees among the Masses'), *Renmin ribao*, 6 March 1968, p. 2.

99. Lin Biao, 'Zai Zhongguo gongchandang dijiuci quanguo daibiao dahui shang de baogao' ('The Report at the Ninth Party Congress, CCP'), *Hongqi*, No. 5, 1 May 1969, pp. 14–18.

100. 'Xunsu quanmian luoshi Mao zhuxi zuixin zhishi' ('Speedily and thoroughly Carry out Chairman Mao's Latest Instruction'), *Renmin ribao*, 13 January 1968, p. 1.

101. 'Jinyibu luoshi Mao zhuxi zuixin zhishi renzhen shixing lingdao banzi geminghua' ('Take a Further Step to Carry out Chairman Mao's Latest Instruction concerning the Revolutionization of Leadership Team'), *Renmin ribao*, 13 July 1968, p. 1. The editor's note reads: 'The Revolutionary Committees in all echelons determine to take Ling Bao county as a model, firmly grasping class struggle, thoroughly criticizing the counter-revolutionary revisionist line of China's Khrushchev in regime-building. Criticizing conservatism, smashing the resistance of the remnant force of the exploiting class, carrying out the rectification of the rank and file of the proletariat, practising crack troops and simple administration and allying closely with the masses in order to consolidate and score an even greater victory of the Great Proletarian Cultural Revolution.' (Translation supplied.)

102. Yao Wenyuan, 'Gongrenjieji bixu lingdao yiqie' ('The Working Class must Take Command over Everything'), *Hongqi*, No. 2, 25 August 1968, pp. 3–7.

103. 'Cong Shanghai jichuangchang kan peiyang gongcheng jishu renyuan de daolu' ('The Road for Cultivating Engineers and Technicians in the Light of Shanghai Lathe Works'), *Hongqi*, No. 2, 25 August 1968, pp. 26–31.

104. 'Dapo chongdie jigou, shixing jingbing-jianzheng jinmi lianxi qunzhong' ('Smash the Overlapping Apparatus, Practise the Crack Troop and Simple Administration, closely Ally with the Masses'), *Renmin ribao*, 16 July 1968, p. 2: 'Jinbing jianzheng shi yichang jianrui de jieji douzheng' ('Crack Troop and Simple Administration Is a Fierce Class Struggle'), *Renmin ribao*, 17 July 1968, p. 2; 'Mudanjiang fangzhichang dadan gaige buheli de guizhang zhidu' ('Boldly Reform Unreasonable Systems and Regulations in Mudanjiang Textile Factory'), *Renmin ribao*, 31 August 1968, p. 1.

105. 'Lirun guashuai wuzhi ciji de fangeming xiuzhengzhuyi miulun bixu chedi pipan' ('The Absurd Counter-revolutionary Revisionist Theory of Profit in Command and Material Incentive Must Be Criticized'), *Renmin ribao*, 9 July 1968, p. 4; 'Chongfen fahui gongrenjieji zai dou-pi-gai zhong de lingdao zuoyong, dali gaige buheli de guizhang zhidu xiagang keshi renyuan' ('Develop the Leadership Role of the Working Class in Struggle, Criticism, and Transformation; Reform Unreasonable Systems and Regulations, Transfer the Staff of Functional Departments Downward'), *Renmin ribao*, 22 September 1968, p. 1.

106. 'Develop the Leadership Role...', *Renmin ribao*, 22 September 1968, p. 1, note 105 above.

107. 'Fadong qunzhong gaige buheli guizhang zhidu quebao gongrenjieji zhangwo jishu lingdao daquan' ('Mobilize the Masses to Reform Unreasonable Systems and Regulations, Ensure the Working Class's Power over Technology'), *Renmin ribao*, 22 October 1968, pp. 1 and 2.

108. 'Zhuzhi gongren yeyu diaochazu kaijin keshi tuidong dou-pi-gai' ('Organize the Workers' Spare-time Investigation Group, Conduct Struggle, Criticism, and Transformation in Functional Departments'), *Renmin ribao*, 30 October 1968, p. 1.

109. 'Working Class must always Exercise Power of Leadership in Socialist Enterprises', *SMCP*, No. 4429, 9 June 1969, pp. 16–20; 'Advance in the Direction of Independence, Self-determination and Regeneration through Self Reliance', *SMCP*, No. 4433, 10 June 1969, pp. 6–13; 'Red Sun Illuminates Road forward for Tientsin Soda Plant', *SMCP*, No. 4500, 22 September 1969, pp. 13–16.

110. Lowell Dittmer, ' "Line-struggle" in Theory and Practice: the Origins of the Cultural Revolution Reconsidered', *China Quarterly*, No. 72, December 1977, pp. 675–712.

111. 'Kaizhan jiji sixiang douzheng shixian geweihui yiyuanhua lingdao' ('Launch Ideological Struggle, Carry out the Unified Leadership of the Revolutionary Committee'), *Nanfang ribao (Southern Daily)*, 15 January 1969, p. 2; 'Yong Mao Zedong sixiang zongjie dianxing jingyan zai zongjie jingyan zhong zijue gaizao shijieguang' ('Sum up Model Experience with Mao Zedong's Thought, Reform World View Conscientiously on the Basis of Summing-up Experience'), *Guangming ribao*, 28 March 1969, p. 2; 'Jingen Mao zhuxi jiushi shengli' ('Victory Comes When Chairman Mao is Closely Followed'), *Guangzhou Chinese News Service*, No. 5622, 29 August 1969, p. 1.

112. 'Gaige buheli de guizhang zhidu shi yichang geming' ('The Reform of Unreasonable Systems and Regulations Is a Revolution'), *Hongqi*, No. 6–7, 1 July 1969, pp. 73–8.

113. 'Ganbu jiefang chulai zenmeban' ('What to Do with the Liberated Cadres'), *Hongqi*, No. 8, 1969, pp. 59–64.

114. 'Zhuyi gongzuo fangfa' ('Pay Attention to the Work Method'), *Renmin ribao*, 5 November 1969, p. 1.

115. Mao Zedong, 'Zai waidi xunshi qijian tong yantu gedi fuze tongzhi de tanhua jiyao' ('Summary of Talks to Responsible Comrades during the Investigation Tour'), *Zhonggong yanjiu*, Vol. 6, No. 9, September 1972, pp. 91–2.

116. Zhou Taihe *et al.* (eds.) (1984), pp. 134–47, note 62 above.

117. Zhou Taihe *et al.* (eds.) (1984), p. 131, note 62 above.

118. Guojia jiwei xiezuo xiaozu (The Writing Group of the State Planning Commission), 'Let Us All Go into Action, Rely on Our Own Efforts', *Peking Review*, No. 37, 11 September 1970, pp. 17–20.

119. Guojia jiwei xiezuo xiaozu, 'Shenru kaizhan gongye zhanxian de zengchan jieyue yundong' ('Embark on the Movement of Savings and Increase of Production on the Industrial Front'), *Hongqi*, No. 2, 1971, pp. 39–47.

120. Long Fei, 'Examine the CCP's Internal Struggle...', *Zhonggong yanjiu*, Vol. 6, No. 12, December 1972, pp. 4–12, note 34 above.

121. Following an alleged *coup d'état* involving Lin, he and his family attempted to escape from China, but they were killed when the aeroplane in which they were travelling crashed.

122. Zhou Taihe *et al.* (1984), p. 148, note 62 above.

123. Zhou Taihe *et al.* (1984), p. 149, note 62 above.

124. Lin Biao, 'Zhongyang zhengzhiju kuoda huiyi shang de jianghua' ('Talk at the Enlarged Conference of the Politburo of the Central Committee'), in Zhonggong yanjiu zazhishe (ed.), *Yijiuqiling nian Zhonggong nianbao (The 1970 Yearbook of Chinese Communist Party)* (Taibei, Zhonggong yanjiu zazhishe, 1970), Section VII, pp. 50–6, hereafter cited as *Yijiuqiling* (1970).

125. Lin Biao, 'Zhongyang gongzuo huiyi shang de jianghua' ('Talk at the Work Conference of the Central Committee'), in *Yijiuqiling* (1970), Section III, pp. 56–62, note 124 above.

126. Mao Zedong, 'Gei Jian Qing de yifeng xin' ('A Letter to Jian Qing'), in Zhonggong yanjiu zazhishe (ed.), *Zhonggong nianbao (Yearbook of the Chinese Communist Party)* (Taibei, Zhonggong yanjiu zazhishe, 1973), Section VII, pp. 2–3, hereafter cited as *Zhonggong nianbao* (1973).

127. *Zhonggong nianbao* (1973), pp. 5–8, note 126 above.

128. Tang Tsou, 'Back from the Brink of Revolutionary-"Feudal" Totalitarianism', in Victor Nee and David Mozingo (eds.), *State and Society in Contemporary China* (Ithaca and London, Cornell University Press, 1983), pp. 53–88.

NOTES TO CHAPTER 6

1. 'Some Questions on Accelerating the Development of Industry', *Summary of People's Republic of China Magazines*, No. 926, 23 May 1977, pp. 8–28, hereafter cited as *SPRCM*.

2. Amitai Etzioni, *The Active Society* (New York, The Free Press, 1968), pp. 282–94.

3. Deng Xiaoping, 'Dangqian gangtie gongye bixu jijue de jige wenti' ('Several Problems to Be Solved regarding the Present Steel Industry'), in Zhongyang wenxian bianji weiyuanhui (ed.), *Deng Xiaoping wenxuan* (*Selected Essays of Deng Xiaoping*) (Beijing, Renmin chubanshe, 1983), pp. 8–11, hereafter cited as *Deng Xiaoping wenxuan*; Deng Xiaoping, 'Quandang jiang daju ba guomin jingji gaoshangqu' ('The Whole Party Should Emphasize the Overall Situation and Promote the National Economy'), *Deng Xiaoping wenxuan*, pp. 4–11.

4. 'Yichang cuandang duoquan de fangeming chouju' ('A Counter-revolutionary Farce in the Usurpation of the Party and Seizure of the State Power'), *Renmin ribao* (*People's Daily*), 16 July 1977, pp. 1–3.

5. Gong Xiaowen, 'Deng Xiaoping yu ershitiao' ('Deng Xiaoping and the Twenty Articles'), *Xuexi yu pipan* (*Study and Critique*), No. 6, 14 June 1976, p. 15.

6. Deng Xiaoping, 'The Whole Party Should Emphasize the Overall Situation...', *Deng Xiaoping wenxuan*, p. 5, note 3 above.

7. Deng Xiaoping, 'The Whole Party Should Emphasize the Overall Situation...', *Deng Xiaoping wenxuan*, pp. 4–11, note 3 above.

8. Gong Xiaowen, 'Deng Xiaoping and the Twenty Articles', *Xuexi yu pipan*, No. 6, 14 June 1976, pp. 14–15, note 5 above.

9. Deng Xiaoping 'The Whole Party Should Emphasize the Overall Situation...', *Deng Xiaoping wenxuan*, p. 4, note 3 above.

10. Gong Xiaowen, 'Deng Xiaoping and the Twenty Articles', *Xuexi yu pipan*, No. 6, 14 June 1976, pp. 14–15, note 5 above.

11. Deng Xiaoping, 'The Whole Party Should Emphasize the Overall Situation...', *Deng Xiaoping wenxuan*, pp. 4–7, note 3 above.

12. Deng Xiaoping, 'Several Problems to Be Solved...', *Deng Xiaoping wenxuan*, pp. 8–14, note 3 above.

13. Deng Xiaoping, 'Guanyu guofang gongye qiye de zhengdun' ('The Rectification concerning the Defence Industry'), *Deng Xiaoping wenxuan*, pp. 25–7, note 3 above.

14. Deng Xiaoping, 'Guanyu fazhan gongye de jidian yijian' ('Some Opinions concerning the Development of Industry'), *Deng Xiaoping wenxuan*, pp. 28–31, note 3 above.

15. 'A Counter-revolutionary Farce...', *Renmin ribao*, 16 July 1977, pp. 1–2, note 4 above.

16. Gong Xiaowen, 'Deng Xiaoping and the Twenty Articles', *Xuexi yu pipan*, No. 6, 14 June 1976, p. 15, note 5 above.

17. 'A Counter-revolutionary Farce...', *Renmin ribao*, 16 July 1977, pp. 1–3, note 4 above.

18. 'Some Questions on Accelerating the Development...', *SPRCM*, No. 926, 23 May 1977, pp. 8–28, note 1 above.

19. 'Some Questions on Accelerating the Development...', *SPRCM*, No. 926, 23 May 1977, pp. 8–28, note 1 above.

20. 'Some Questions on Accelerating the Development...', *SPRCM*, No. 926, 23 May 1977, pp. 8–28, note 1 above.

21. See 'Gongren jieji shi fanji youqing fanan feng de zhulijun' ('The Working Class is the Backbone Force in the Anti-rightist Tendency of Verdict-reversing Tide'), *Xuexi yu pipan*, No. 3, 14 March 1976, pp. 8–14.

22. 'Some Questions on Accelerating the Development...', *SPRCM*, No. 926, 23 May 1977, pp. 8–28, note 1 above.

23. 'Some Questions on Accelerating the Development...', *SPRCM*, No. 926, 23 May 1977, pp. 8–28, note 1 above.

24. 'Mao zhuxi guanyu Angang xianfa de pishi' ('Chairman Mao's Comments on the Anshan Constitution'), *Renmin ribao*, 22 March 1977, p. 1.

25. Yu Qiuli, 'Quandang quanguo gongren jieji dongyuan qilai wei puji Daqing shi qiye er fendou' ('Mobilize the Whole Party, the Working Class of the Whole Country in the Struggle for the Extension of the Daqing Type of Enterprises'), in Sanlian shudian (ed.), *Quanguo gongye xue Daqing huiyi* (*The National Conference of Learning from Daqing in Industry*) (Hong Kong, Sanlian shudian, 1977), pp. 57–61, hereafter cited as *Daqing huiyi*.

26. Sung Zhenming, 'Gaoju Mao zhuxi de weida qizhi zou soguo ziyi gongye fazhan de daolu' ('Hoist High the Great Banner of Chairman Mao, Travel along our own Road of Industrial Development'), *Daqing huiyi*, pp. 101–3, note 25 above.

27. Yu Qiuli, 'Mobilize the Whole Party, the Working Class...', *Daqing huiyi*, p. 64, note 25 above.

28. 'A Counter-revolutionary Farce...', *Renmin ribao*, 16 July 1977, pp. 1, 2, and 3, note 4 above.

29. Gong Xiaowen, 'Deng Xiaoping and the Twenty Articles', *Xuexi yu pipan*, No. 6, 14 June 1976, p. 16, note 5 above.

30. 'The Week: Wage Increases', *Peking Review*, Vol. 20, No. 49, 2 December 1977, pp. 3–4.

31. 'Guangyu anlao fenpei wenti de butong yijian' ('A Different View on "To Each according to Labour"'), *Guangming ribao* (*Guangming Daily*), 15 August 1977, p. 3.

32. Gong Shiqi, 'Guanyu anlao fenpei de jige wenti' ('Several Problems concerning Distribution according to Labour'), *Guangming ribao*, 15 August 1977, p. 3. 'Woguo jingji xuejie taolun anlao fenpei yu laodong baochou de juti xingshi wenti' ('Discussion within the Economic Circle of our Country on the Question of Distribution according to Labour and the Concrete Form of Payment for Work'), *Guangming ribao*, 21 November 1977, p. 3.

33. 'Discussion within the Economic Circle...', *Guangming ribao*, 21 November 1977, p. 3, note 32 above.

34. Hua Guofeng, 'Tuanjie qilai, wei jianshe shehuizhuyi xiandaihua qiangguo er fendou' ('Unite and Struggle for Building a Socialist, Modern, and Strong Country'), in Renmin chubanshe (ed.), *Zhonghua Renmin Gongheguo diwu jie quanguo renmin daibiao dahui diyi ci huiyi wenjian* (*The Documents of the First Session of the Fifth National People's Congress of the PRC*) (Beijing, Renmin chubanshe, 1978), p. 39, hereafter cited as *Huiyi wenjian*.

35. Deng Xiaoping, 'Jianchi anlao fenpei de yuanze' ('Insist on the Principle of Distribution according to Labour'), *Deng Xiaoping wenxuan*, pp. 98–9, note 3 above.

36. Deng Xiaoping, 'Jiefang sixiang shishi qiu shi tuanjie yizhi xianqiankan' ('Liberate Our Thought, Seek the Truth from Facts, and Look Forward'), *Deng Xiaoping wenxuan*, p. 136, note 3 above.

37. 'Huangpu gang zhuangxiegong shixing jijian gongzi de diaocha baogao' ('The Investigation Report of the Implementation of Piece-rate Wages among Dockers in

Huangpu'), *Guangming ribao*, 20 March 1978, p. 3; 'Guangzhou Huangpu gang zai douzheng zhong jianchi jijian gongzizhi' ('Insist on Piece-rate Wages in the Struggle of Huangpu Harbour of Guangzhou'), *Renmin ribao*, 14 April 1978, p. 1

38. 'Guanche zhixing anlao fenpei de shehuizhuyi yuanze' ('Thoroughly Implement the Socialist Principle of Distribution according to Labour'), *Renmin ribao*, 5 May 1978, pp. 1 and 3.

39. Jiang Yiwei, 'Shilun quanmian wuzi liyi de yuanji' ('On the Principle of Total Material Interest'), *Renmin ribao*, 14 July 1980, p. 5.

40. Caizhengbu Lilunzu, 'Wei jianshe qiangda de shehuizhuyi guojia jilei gengduo de zijin' ('Accumulate More Capital for the Establishment of a Powerful Socialist Country'), *Hongqi* (*Red Flag*), No. 8, 1977, pp. 70–3.

41. 'Deng Xiaoping fandong yanlun xuanpi' ('Selected Criticism of Deng Xiaoping's Reactionary Statements'), *Beijing daxue xuebao* (*The Journal of Beijing University*), No. 3, June 1976, p. 42.

42. Wu Jiajun, 'Shehuizhuyi jingji hesuan burong fuodong' ('Negation of the Socialist Economic Accounting Shall not Be Tolerated'), *Guangming ribao*, 18 July 1977, p. 3.

43. Wei Yue, 'Zhengque chuli guojia shengchan danwei he shengchanzhe geren guanxi' ('Correctly Handle the Relationship among the State, Production Unit, and Individual'), *Hongqi*, No. 5, 1977, pp. 57–63.

44. Ji Chongwei and Wang Zhenyuan, 'Guanyu zhengjia qiye yingli jiasu jijin jilei de wenti' ('Questions on the Increase of Enterprise Profits and the Acceleration of Capital Accumulation'), *Jingji yanjiu* (*Economic Research*), No. 4, 1978, pp. 8–16.

45. Sun Yefang, 'Yao Lizhi qizhuangdi zhua shehuizhuyi lirun' ('Approach the Socialist Profit in a Righteous Way'), *Jingji yanjiu*, No. 9, 1978, pp. 2–14.

46. Zhu Tiezeng, 'Quanmian tigao jingji xiaoguo shi fazhan woguo jingji de genben tujing' ('A General Rise of Economic Utility is the Fundamental Way in the Development of Our National Economy'), *Jingji yanjiu*, No. 5, 1981, pp. 35–8; 'Bixu jiangqiu jingji xiaoguo' ('We Must Heed Economic Utility'), *Renmin ribao*, 17 January 1980, p. 3; He Jianzhang, 'Zenyang tigao jingji xiaoguo' ('How to Improve Economic Utility'), *Guangming ribao*, 9 May 1980, pp. 1 and 3.

47. 'Yao nongqing shehuizhuyi shengchan de mudi' ('We Must Clarify the Objectives of the Socialist Production'), *Guangming ribao*, 23 October 1979, pp. 1 and 3.

48. 'Sung Zhenming jiu Bohai erhao zuanjinchuan fanchen shigu de jiantao' ('The Self-criticism by Sung Zhenming concerning the Incident of the Sinking of Bohai No. 2 Drilling Ship'), *Renmin ribao*, 26 August 1980, p. 1.

49. 'The Self-criticism by Sung Zhenming...', *Renmin ribao*, 26 August 1980, p. 1, note 48 above.

50. Meng Xianpeng, 'Ping Meiyou tiaojian chuangzao tiaojian yeyao shang' ('Criticize "We must Make it regardless of the Existing Conditions"'), *Renmin ribao*, 12 December 1980, p. 5.

51. Wu Jiang, 'Guanyu Lin Biao, sirenbang luxian de xingzhi he tedian' ('On the Nature and Characteristics of the Policy Line of Lin Biao and the Gang of Four'), *Renmin ribao*, 16 February 1979, p. 3.

52. Chen Shengchang, 'Jiben jianshe jizhong liliang da jianmiezhan fangzhen zhiyi' ('On Question the Principle of "Concentrating Superior Strength to Fight the Battle of Annihilation"'), *Jingji guanli* (*Economic Management*), No. 12, 1980, pp. 37–8; Li Mengbai and Lin Senlin, 'Zenyang renshi jiben jianshe jizhong liliang da jianmiezhan de fangzhen' ('How to Understand the Principle of Concentrating Superior Strength in the Battle of Annihilation'), *Jingji guanli*, No. 2, 1981, pp. 33–6.

53. Yan Fang, 'Suqing zuoqing sixiang yingxiang shi dangqian jingji gongzuo zhong de zhongyao renwu' ('To Eliminate the Leftist Ideological Influence Is the Important

Mission in the Current Economic Task'), *Jingji guanli*, No. 1, 1981, pp. 20–3 and 67.

54. 'The Draft Decision Concerning Some Problems in Speeding up the Development of Industry, Part I', *Issues and Studies*, Vol. XIV, No. 5, 1978, pp. 89–97.

55. 'Renzhen xuexi jianjue guanche gongye sanshitiao' ('Seriously Study and thoroughly Implement the Thirty Articles on Industry'), *Renmin ribao*, 4 July 1978, p. 1.

56. The date of issue of the 'Thirty Articles' by the Central Committee, CCP was first identified by Zhuang Qidong (ed.), in *Laodong gongzi shouce (The Manual of Labour and Wage)* (Tianjin, Tianjin renmin chubanshe, 1984), pp. 1–14; it was not formally announced in the *People's Daily* until 4 July 1978.

57. Deng Xiaoping, 'Gongren jieji yao wei shixian sige xiandaihua zuochu youyi gongxian' ('The Proletariat should Make Special Contribution to the Fulfilment of Four Modernizations'), in *Deng Xiaoping wenxuan*, pp. 124–9, note 3 above.

58. 'Xunsu tigao qiye guanli shuiping' ('Quickly Raise the Level of Enterprise Management'), *Renmin ribao*, 13 July 1978, p. 2; Gui Shiyong, 'Gongye shengchan zhong bixu jianli quanmian de zerenzhi' ('Establish a Comprehensive Responsibility System in Industrial Production'), *Jingji yanjiu*, No. 6, 1978, pp. 17–22.

59. 'Quickly Raise the Level of Enterprise Management', *Renmin ribao*, 13 July 1978, p. 2, note 58 above; 'Zhengdun he jianshe gongchang qiye lingdao banzi' ('Rectify and Bind up the Leadership Team of Industrial Enterprises'), *Renmin ribao*, 4 December 1979, p. 2.

60. 'Jianshe yige nengda shihua yingzhang de lingdao banzi' ('Build up a Leadership Team Capable of Waging Tough Battles of the Four Modernizations'), *Beijing ribao (Beijing Daily)*, 18 August 1979, p. 1.

61. Zhuang Qidong (ed.), *Laodong gongzi shouce*, pp. 56–8, note 56 above.

62. Zhuang Qidong (ed.), *Laodong gongzi shouce*, pp. 63–4, note 56 above.

63. 'Dui shixing jiangjin zhidu de jidian yijian' ('Some Opinions on the Implementation of the Bonus System'), *Gongren ribao (Workers' Daily)*, 8 December 1978, p. 1.

64. For a comprehensive summary of the major problems in the implementation of the bonus system and piece-rate wages, see 'Guanche zhixing anlao fenpei de shehuizhuyi yuanze' ('Thoroughly Implement the Socialist Principle of Distribution according to Work'), *Xinhua yuebao (New China Monthly)*, No. 5, 1978, pp. 58–70.

65. Zhuang Qidong, 'Dui muqian qiye zhong shixing de jiangjin zhidu de jidian kanfa' ('Several Views on the Trial-implementation of the Current Bonus System in the Enterprise'), *Gongren ribao*, 1 February 1979, p. 2; 'Zhengque di zhixing anlao fenpei de jiangji zhidu' ('Correctly Implement the Bonus System in Line with Distribution according to Labour'), *Renmin ribao*, 18 May 1979, p. 2; 'Jianjue zhizhi lanfa jiangjin de waifeng' ('Resolutely Stop the Deviant Tendency of Indiscriminate Payment of Bonus'), *Gongren ribao*, 13 December 1980, p. 3.

66. Deng Xiaoping, 'Muqian de xingshi he renwu' ('The Current Situation and Mission'), in *Deng Xiaoping wenxuan*, pp. 221–4, note 3 above.

67. 'Guanyu zhengque chuli shixing jiangli zhidu, jianjue zhizhi lanfa jiangji de jixiang guiding' ('The Regulation Concerning the Correct Implementation of the Bonus System and Resolute Prohibition of Indiscriminate Payment of Bonuses'), *Guowuyuan gongbao (The Communiqué of the State Council)*, No. 11, 1981, p. 342.

68. Peter N.S. Lee and Irene H.S. Chow, 'Incentive System in Chinese Factories: Continuity and Change in the post-Mao Era' (Paper presented to a conference on 'China's System Reforms' at the Centre of Asian Studies, University of Hong Kong, 17–20 March 1986) p. 22, hereafter referred to as Lee and Chow (1986).

69. Lee and Chow (1986), pp. 24–5 and 27–8, note 68 above; the State Statistical

Bureau, PRC, *Statistical Yearbook of China 1984* (Hong Kong, Economic Information and Agency, 1984) pp. 339 and 461.

70. Deng Xiaoping, 'Dang he guojia lingdao zhidu de gaige' ('The Reform of the Leadership Systems of the Party and the State'), in *Deng Xiaoping wenxuan*, p. 300.

71. Ma Hong, 'Guanyu gaige gongye qiye lingdao zhidu de tantao' (Discussion on the Reform of the Leadership System of Industrial Enterprises'), in Zhongguo jingji nianjian bianji weiyuan hui (The Editorial Board of the Almanac of China's Economy 1981) (ed.), *Zhongguo jingji nianjian 1981 (Almanac of China's Economy 1981)* (Hong Kong, Zhongguo jingji nianjian youxian gongse, 1981), pp. V. 218–23, hereafter cited as *Nianjian 1981*.

72. Wu Zhenkun, 'Lun guoying qiye lingdao zhidu de gaige fangxiang' ('On the Direction of the Reform of the Leadership System of the State-owned Enterprises'), *Renmin ribao*, 7 August 1981, p. 5.

73. Wang Mengqui, 'Qiye lingdao zhidu zhong de yige wenti — duiyu yizhangzhi de kaocha' ('One Problem in the System of Enterprise Leadership — Investigation concerning One-man Management'), *Jingji yanjiu*, No. 1, 1981, pp. 37–44.

74. Ji Zhong, 'Zongjie lishi jingyan, shixing changzhangzhi' ('Sum up the Historical Experience, Implement the Factory Director System'), *Jingji guanli*, No. 6, 1984, pp. 19–24.

75. Deng Xiaoping, 'Zai zhongyang zhengzhiju kuoda huiyi shang de jianghua' ('Speech at the Enlarged Meeting of the Political Bureau of the Central Committee'), *Zhong gong yanjiu (The Research of the Chinese Communist Party)*, Vol. 15, No. 7, 1981, pp. 135–8.

76. Deng Xiaoping, 'The Reform of the Leadership Systems...', in *Deng Xiaoping wenxuan*, pp. 280–2, note 3 above.

77. 'Guoying gongchang changzhang gongzuo zhanxing tiaoli' ('The Provisional Regulation of the Task of Factory Director of the State-owned Factory'), *Guanyuan gongbao*, No. 2, 1982, pp. 36–40.

78. Maurice Meisner, 'The Concept of the Dictatorship of the Proletariat in Chinese Marxist Thought', in Victor Nee and David Mozingo (eds.), *State and Society in Contemporary China* (Ithaca and London, Cornell University Press, 1983), pp. 116–17.

79. Mao Zedong, 'Sulian *Zhengzhi jingjixue* dushu biji' ('Reading Notes on the *Soviet Political Economy*'), in Mao Zedong, *Mao Zedong sixiang wansui (Long Live Mao Zedong's Thought)* (n.p., n.p., 1969), pp. 342–3, hereafter cited as *Wansui* (1969).

80. Ye Jianying, 'Guanyu xiugai xianfa de baogao' ('The Report concerning the Revision of the Constitution'), *Huiyi wenjian* (1978) pp. 114–16, note 34 above.

81. Lin Pei, 'Qiye minzhu guanli de wenti' ('The Problem of Democratic Management of the Enterprise'), *Renmin ribao*, 14 January 1980, p. 5; 'Fanzhan shehuizhuyi minzhu de zhongda cuoshi' ('An Important Measure in the Development of the Socialist Democracy'), *Gongren ribao*, 21 October 1980, pp. 1 and 3.

82. 'Guoying gongye qiye zhigong daibiao dahui zhanxing tiaoli' ('The Provisional Regulation of the Congress of the Staff and Workers in State-owned Industrial Enterprises'), *Guowuyuan gongbao*, No. 16, 1981, pp. 490–3.

83. Ma Hong, 'Discussion on the Reform...', *Nianjian 1981*, p. V. 221, note 71 above.

84. 'Guoying gongye qiye zhanxing tiaoli' ('The Provisional Regulation of the State-owned Industrial Enterprise'), *Guowuyuan gongbao*, No. 8, 1983, pp. 268–77.

85. Yuan Baohua, 'Gongye qiye zai zhengdun zhong qianjin' ('Industrial Enterprises Surge Forward in the Midst of Rectification'), *Nianjian 1981*, pp. VI. 43–4, note 71 above.

86. 'Guojia jingji weiyuanhui guanyu jiaqiang lingdao zhuahao qiye zhengdun

gongzuo de yijian' ('The Opinion of the State Economic Commission concerning the Strengthening of the Leadership and Carrying out the Task of Rectification of the Enterprise'), *Guowuyuan gongbao*, No. 24, 1981, pp. 752–3.

87. 'Qiye zhengdun yaoyi tuixing jingji zerenzhi wei tupo' ('Enterprise Rectification must Take the Implementation of the Economic Responsibility System as a Point of Breakthrough'), *Renmin ribao*, 5 August 1981, p. 1.

88. Zhao Ziyang, 'Dangqian jingji xingshi he jinhou jingji jianshe fangzhen' ('The Current Economic Situation and Guidelines for Economic Construction for the Future'), *Guowuyuan gongbao*, No. 26, 1981, pp. 831–3, note 88 above.

89. Zhao Ziyang, 'The Current Economic Situation...', *Guowuyuan gongbao*, No. 26, 1981, pp. 832–3, note 88 above.

90. 'Zhonggong zhongyang, guowuyuan guanyu guoying gongye qiye jinxing quanmian zhengdun de jueding' ('The Decision of the Central Committee, CCP, and the State Council to Carry out the Total Rectification of the State-owned Industrial Enterprises'), *Guowuyuan gongbao*, No. 15, 1982, pp. 647–54.

91. 'The Decision of the Central Committee, CCP...', *Guowuyuan gongbao*, No. 15, 1982, p. 653, note 90 above.

92. 'Guojia jingji weiyuanhui guanyu quanguo qiye zhengdun gongzuo zuotanhui qingkuang de baogao' ('The Reports of the State Economic Commission on the Situation of the National Conference on the Task of Enterprise Rectification'), *Guowuyuan gongbao*, No. 15, 1982, pp. 656–62.

93. 'Beijing shi lingdao qiye zhengdun gongzuo de sidian jingyan' ('Four Points of Experience of the Beijing Municipal Leadership in the Task of Enterprise Rectification'), *Jingji guanli*, No. 9, 1983, p. 38.

94. 'Four Points of Experience...', *Jingji guanli*, No. 9, 1983, pp. 23 and 39, note 93 above.

95. 'Yuan Baohua zai quanguo qiye zhengdun lingdao xiaozu huishang tichu yijiubasi nian qiye quanmian zhengdun gongzuo de renwu he yaoqiu' ('Yuan Baohua Proposes the Mission and Requirements for the Task of Total Rectification of Enterprises for 1984 at the Meeting of the Leadership Group for the National Rectification of Enterprises'), *Xinhua yuebao*, No. 12, December 1983, p. 133.

96. Anthony Downs, *Inside Bureaucracy* (Boston, Little, Brown and Company, 1967), pp. 147–55.

97. This analysis of the power relationships is based upon the author's 1977 paper, with modifications. See Peter Nan-shong Lee, 'The Gang of Four: Radical Politics and Modernization in China', in Steve S.K. Chin (ed.), *The Gang of Four: First Essays After the Fall* (Hong Kong, Centre of Asian Studies, University of Hong Kong, 1977), pp. 69–105.

98. The 'three directives' refer to (a) the study of proletarian politics, fighting, and preventing revisionism; (b) unity and stability; and (c) the development of the national economy. For background information on the politics of the three directives, consult the following: Yang Hua, 'Lun yijiuciliu nian de Deng Xiaoping shijian (II)' ('On the Deng Xiaoping Incident in 1976, Part 2'), *Zhonggong yanjiu*, Vol. 77, No. 11, 1977, p. 84; 'Yaohai shi fupi zibenzhuyi' ('The Crucial Point is the Restoration of Capitalism'), *Renmin ribao*, 17 February 1976, p. 1; 'Guanmian luoshi zhuagang zhiguo de zhanlue juece' ('Thoroughly Implement the Strategic Decision of Grasping Key Link and Restoring Order to the Country'), *Renmin ribao*, 11 April 1977, p. 1; Xiang Qun, 'Dazhe fanfupi de qihao gao fupi' ('Using the Anti-Restorationist Flag to Bring about Revolution'), in Renmin chubanshe (ed.), *Cuandang duoquan de yige dayinmou* (*The Big Conspiracy for Usurpation of the Party and Seizure of Power*) (Beijing, Renmin chubanshe, 1977), pp. 15–16.

99. The case is well documented in Hua Yang, 'Lun yijiuqiliu nian de Deng Xiaoping shijian (III)' ('On the Deng Xiaoping Incident in 1976, Part 3'), *Zhonggong yanjiu*, Vol. 12, No. 1, 1978, pp. 98–109; Kang Li and Yan Feng, 'Huibao tigang chulong

de qianqianhouhou' ('The Circumstances Surrounding the Appearance of the Outline of Summary Report'), *Xuexi yu pipan*, No. 4, 14 April 1976, pp. 20–7; private communication, 15 July 1983.

100. Xuan Mo, 'Sirenbang shijian yu Hua Guofeng dengtai' ('The Gang of Four Incident and the Rise of Hua Guofeng'), *Zhonggong yanjiu*, Vol. 10, No. 11, 1976, pp. 7–17; 'Da da yichang jiepi sirenbang de renmin zhangzheng' ('Wage a People's War in Exposing the Gang of Four'), in Sanlian shudian (ed.), *Jiefa pipan sirenbang wenxuan* (*Selected Articles for Exposing and Criticizing the Gang of Four*) (Hong Kong, Sanlian shudian, 1977), p. 11.

101. Deng Xiaoping, 'Zai quanjun zhengzhi gongzuo huiyi shang de jianghua' ('Talk at the Conference of the Political Work of the Whole Army'), in *Deng Xiaoping wenxuan*, pp. 108–23, note 3 above.

102. Hua Yang, 'On the Deng Xiaoping Incident... Part 3', *Zhonggong yanjiu*, Vol. 12, No. 1, 1978, pp. 98–109, note 99 above.

103. 'On the General Program for the Work of the Whole Party and the Whole Country', *SPRCM*, No. 921, 25 April 1977, pp. 18–37.

104. Deng Xiaoping, 'Duiqicao *Guanyu jianguo yilai dang de ruogan lishi wenti de jueyi* de yijian' ('Opinions Concerning *The Resolution on the History of the Party since the Establishment of the Republic*'), in *Deng Xiaoping wenxuan*, pp. 265–66.

105. Yuan Baohua, 'Industrial Enterprises Surge Forward...', *Nianjian 1981*, p. VI. 42, note 85 above.

106. 'Provisional Regulation of the State-owned Industrial Enterprise', *Guowuyuan gongbao*, No. 8, 1983, p. 268.

NOTES TO CHAPTER 7

1. Zhongguoqiye guanli baike quanshu bianji weiyuanhui (ed.), *Zhongguo qiye guanli baike quanshu* (*Encyclopedia of China's Enterprise Management*) (Beijing, Jiye guanli chubanshe, 1984), Vol. I, pp. 16–22.

2. The four forms of specialization and co-ordination are summarized from Article 10, 'Reorganizing Industry according to the Principle of Specialization and Co-ordination' of the 'Thirty Articles'. See 'Guanyu jiakuai gongye fazhan ruogan wenti de jueding' ('The Decision regarding the Acceleration of Industrial Development in "The Thirty Articles"') in *Zhonggong yanjiu* (*The Research of the Chinese Communist Party*), Vol. 12, No. 10, 1978, pp. 126–7.

3. Li Rui and Chen Shengchang, 'Shilun gongye qiye de guimo jiegou' ('On the Scale and Structure of Industrial Enterprises'), *Zhongguo shehui kexue* (*China's Social Sciences*), No. 1, 1981, pp. 65–76.

4. Zhou Jialin, 'Shilun yong dan wei zuhe fangshi guanli qiye' ('On the Managing of Enterprises with the Combination of "Units"'), *Tonggyue loncong* (*Collected Commentaries of Tonggyue*), No. 4, 1980, pp. 62–5; Yan Qiushi, 'Zai tiaozheng zhong tuijin jixie gongye de zhuanyehua gaizu' ('To Promote the Reorganization of the Machine-building Industry on the Basis of Specialization and in the Midst of Adjustment'), *Renmin ribao* (*People's Daily*), 12 May 1980, p. 5.

5. 'Gongye qiye kefou gaodian guan-ting-bing-zhuan' ('Whether Industrial Enterprises Should Engage in Closure, Stoppage, Merger and Transfer'), *Renmin ribao*, 13 March 1979, p. 2.

6. 'An zhuanyehua xiezuo yuanze gaohao gongye gaizu' ('Ensure the Success of Industrial Reorganization by Following the Principle of Specialization and Co-ordination'), *Renmin ribao*, 29 May 1979, p. 2.

272 NOTES TO PAGES 151–6

7. 'Ensure the Success of Industrial Reorganization...', *Renmin ribao*, 29 May 1979, p. 2, note 6 above.

8. Zhou Jialin, 'On the Managing of Enterprises...', *Tonggyue loncong*, No. 4, 1980, pp. 63–5, note 4 above.

9. Li Rui and Chen Shengchang, 'On the Scale and Structure...', *Zhongguo shehui kexue*, No. 1, 1981, pp. 65–76, note 3 above.

10. Xue Muqiao, 'Guanyu jingji tizhi gaige de yixie jijian' ('Some Views concerning the Reform of Economic System'), *Renmin ribao*, 10 June 1980, p. 5; Li Ling, 'Jianli zhuanyegongsi, lianhe gongsi de yuanze he fangfa de chutan' ('A Preliminary Investigation of the Principles and Methods in the Establishment of Specialized Corporations and Joint Corporations'), *Renmin ribao*, 1 July 1980, p. 5.

11. Li and Chen, 'On the Scale and Structure...', *Zhongguo shehui kexue*, No. 1, 1981, pp. 65–76, note 3 above.

12. 'Kefu xiao shengchan sixiang gaohao zhuanyehua xiezuo' ('Overcome the Mentality of Small Producers, Improve Specialized Co-ordination'), *Renmin ribao*, 14 October 1978, p. 1.

13. Audrey Donnithorne, 'China's Cellular Economy: Some Economic Trends Since the Cultural Revolution', *China Quarterly*, No. 52, October–December 1972, pp. 605–19.

14. Zheng Hai hang, 'Lun woguo gongye gongsi gaige wenti' ('On the Problems of Reform of Industrial Corporations in our Country'), *Jingji lilun yu jingji guanli* (*Economic Theory and Economic Management*), No. 2, 1981, pp. 59–61.

15. Liu Shuren, 'Lianhe shi shehuizhuyi shengchan fazhan de biran qushi' ('Combination is an Inevitable Trend in the Development of Socialist Production'), *Qiye guanli* (*Enterprise Management*), No. 4, 1980, pp. 15–17.

16. 'Guowuyuan guanyu tuidong jingji lianhe de zhan xing guiding' ('The Provisional Regulation of the State Council concerning the Promotion of Economic Combination'), in Zhongguo jingji nianjian bianji weiyuanhui (ed.), *Zhongguo jingji nianjian 1981* (*The Annual Economic Report of China, 1981*) (Beijing, Jingji guanli zhazhishe, 1981), Vol. II, p. 128, hereafter cited as *Nianjian* (1981).

17. 'The Provisional Regulation of the State Council...', in *Nianjian* (1981), Vol. II, p. 128, note 16 above.

18. 'Guowuyuan guanyu kaizhan he baohu shehuizhuyi jingzheng de zhanxing guiding' ('The Provisional Regulation of the State Council concerning the Development and Protection of Socialist Competition'), in *Nianjian* (1981), Vol. II, pp. 128–9, note 16 above.

19. 'Guojia jingji wenyuanhui guowuyuan tizhi gaige bangongshi, guangyu gongye guanli tizhi gaige zuotanhui huibao tigang' ('The Summary Report concerning the Forum on the Reform of Industrial Managerial Institutions'), *Guowuyuan gongbao* (*The Communiqué of the State Council*), No. 9, 1981, pp. 272–3.

20. Liao Jili, 'Cong heng xiang lianxi zongxiang lianxi tan tizhi gaige' ('Examine Institutional Reform from the Perspective of Horizontal and Vertical Linkage'), *Xinhua yuebao* (*New China Monthly*), No. 8, 1980, pp. 77–8.

21. Liao Jili, 'Examine Institutional Reform...', *Xinhua yuebao*, No. 8, 1980, pp. 78–81, note 20 above.

22. Bo Yibo, 'Chongqing shi de jingji tizhi zonghe gaige shidian he dui junmin jiehe daolu de tansuo' ('An Investigation of Pilot Programmes of the Comprehensive Economic Reform in Chongqing and the Road of "Military-civilian Integration"'), *Jingji guanli* (*Economic Management*), No. 8, 1983, pp. 2–5.

23. Zhou Taihe *et al.* (eds.), *Dangdai Zhongguo de jingji tizhi gaige* (*The Economic Reform of Contemporary China*) (Beijing, Zhongguo shehui kexue chubanshe, 1984), pp. 51–6, 77–8, 99–100, 137–8, and 160.

24. Zhou Taihe *et al.* (eds.) (1984), p. 308, note 23 above.

25. Zhou Taihe *et al.* (eds.) (1984), pp. 288–9 and 293–8, note 23 above.

26. Zhou Taihe *et al.* (eds.) (1984), pp. 300–1, note 23 above.

27. 'Jixie gongye an zhuanyehua xiezuo yuanze kaishi gaizu' ('The Machinery Industry Begins to Reorganize itself in Accordance with the Principle of Specialization and Co-ordination'), *Renmin ribao*, 28 August 1978, p. 2.

28. 'The Machinery Industry Begins to Reorganize...', *Renmin ribao*, 28 August 1978, p. 2, note 27 above.

29. Jing Qigai, 'Fazhan jixie gongye gongyi zhuanyehua' ('Development of Technical Specialization in the Machine-building Industry'), *Qiye guanli (Enterprise Management)*, No. 2, 1981, pp. 29–31.

30. Hua Huiyi, 'Nanjingshi rechuli gongyi zhuanyehua xiezuo yuegao yuehao' ('More and more Achievements in the Specialization and Co-ordination in Heat Treatment in Nanking Municipality'), *Jingji guanli*, No. 11, 1981, pp. 27–8.

31. Huang Juefei, 'Zhuanyehua cujin shehuihua' ('Specialization Promotes Socialization'), *Gongye jingji guanli congkan (Magazine of Industrial Economic Management)*, No. 1, 1981, pp. 58–61.

32. Wu Ming, 'Tantan woguo jixie gongye de gaizu he gaizao' ('On the Reorganization and Reforms of the Machine-building Industry in our Nation'), *Jingji guanli*, No. VI, 1981, pp. 7–11.

33. Zhou Taihe *et al.* (eds.) (1984), pp. 303–4, note 23 above.

34. Zhou Taihe *et al.* (eds.) (1984), pp. 306–7, note 23 above.

35. Li Huimin, 'Gaohao lianying, zou zhuanyehua fazhan xiliehua chanpin de daolu' ('Make Joint Production a Success, Take the Road of Specialization and Serialization of Products'), *Jingji guanli*, No. 8, 1984, pp. 43–6.

36. Zhou Taihe *et al.* (eds.) (1984), pp. 308–10, note 23 above.

37. 'Guojia jixie gongye weiyuanhui guanyu chengli zhongguo qiche gongye gongsi de baogao' ('The Report of the State Machinery Industrial Commission concerning the Establishment of China Automobile Corporation'), *Guowuyuan gongbao*, No. 1, 1982, pp. 25–7.

38. 'The Report of the State Machinery Industrial Commission...', *Guowuyuan gongbao*, No. 1, 1982, pp. 26–7, note 37 above.

39. Zhou Taihe *et al.* (eds.) (1984), p. 422, note 23 above.

40. Zhou Taihe *et al.* (eds.) (1984), p. 430, note 23 above.

41. Zhou Taihe *et al.* (eds.) (1984), p. 431–6, note 23 above.

42. 'Qinggongyebu guanyu shixing yancao zhuanying de baogao' ('The Report of the Ministry of Light Industry concerning the Implementation of the Tobacco Monopoly'), *Guowuyuan gongbao*, No. 10, 1981, pp. 316–17.

43. 'The Report of the Ministry of Light Industry...', *Guowuyuan gongbao*, No. 10, 1981, pp. 316–17, note 42 above.

44. 'Guojia wujiaju he zhongguo yancao zong gongsi guanyu jianjue zhizhi juanyan jiangjia qingxiao de bao gao' ('The Report of the State Price Bureau and China Tobacco General Corporation concerning the Prohibition of Price-cutting and Competition in the Sale of Cigarettes'), *Guowuyuan gongbao*, No. 17, 1983, pp. 782–5.

45. 'The Report of the State Price Bureau...', *Guowuyuan gongbao*, No. 17, 1983, pp. 782–5, note 44 above.

46. 'Yancao zhuanli tiaoli' ('Regulation of the Tobacco Monopoly'), *Guowuyuan gongbao*, No. 21, 1983, pp. 987–90.

47. 'Guojia jing wei guanyu zhongguo yancao zong gongsi dangqian jidai jiejue de jige zhuyao wenti de qingshi de tongzhi' ('The Circular of the State Economic Commission concerning the Petition by China Tobacco General Corporation regarding Several Major and Current Problems Meriting Urgent Solutions'), *Guowuyuan gongbao*, No. 21, 1984, pp. 728–30.

48. 'Guojia jingji weiyuanhui guanyu cujin lianhe kuoda mingpai zixingche shengchan shishi fangan de baogao' ('The Report of the State Economic Commission

274 NOTES TO PAGES 161-6

on the Implementation of the Proposal for Promoting Combination and Expansion of Production of Famous Brand Bicycles'), *Guowuguan gongbao*, No. 16, 1984, pp. 552-8.

49. Zhou Taihe *et al.* (eds.) (1984), pp. 541-5, note 23 above.

50. Han Zheyi, 'Shanghai fazhan gongye de jiben zuofa' ('The Basic Approach to Industrial Development in Shanghai'), *Qiye guanli*, No. 3, 1981, p. 22.

51. Han Zheyi, 'The Basic Approach to Industrial Development...', *Qiye guanli*, No. 3, 1981, pp. 22-3, note 50 above.

52. Tang Zhian and Huang Guochu, 'Shanghai huasheng dianshan chang zuzhi lianhe he xiezuo de diaocha' ('The Investigation of the Shanghai Hua-sheng Electrical Fan General Corporation in Organizing Combination and Co-ordination'), *Shehui kexue (Social Sciences)*, No. 3, 1981, p. 62.

53. 'Zuzhi lianhe fahui youshi' ('Form Combinations and Develop Superior Potential'), *Jingji guanli*, No. 12, 1983, pp. 16-19.

54. Zhou Muchang, 'Zujian Zhongguo Nanjing wuxiandian gongsi gaige guanli tizhi de yici changshi' ('An Attempt in the Reform of the Managerial System in the Establishment of the China-Nanjing Wireless Corporation'), *Gongye jingji guanli congkan*, No. 10, 1980, pp. 20-30; Zhou Muchang, 'Nanjing wuxiandian gongsi shixing dongshihui lingdao xia de jingli fuzezhi' ('The Manager's Responsibility System under the Leadership of the Board of Trustees in Nanjing Wireless Corporation's Trial Implementation'), *Jingji guanli*, No. 1, 1981, pp. 39-40; 'Zhongguo Nanjing wuxiandian gongsi zhangcheng' ('Charter of China-Nanjing Wireless Corporation'), *Gongye jingji (Industrial Economy)*, F3, 1981, pp. 52-7; 'Zou lianhe zhilu' ('Take the Path of Combination'), *Renmin ribao*, 20 July 1980, p. 1; Zhou Muchang, 'An Attempt in the Reform of the Managerial System...', *Gongye jingji guanli congkan*, No. 10, 1980, pp. 20-2.

55. Wang Daohan, 'Shanghai shi yu xiongshi diqu jian jingji jishu de xiezuo yu lianhe' ('The Co-ordination and Combination of Shanghai with the Brotherly Regions in the Economic and Technical Spheres'), *Gongye jingji guanli congkan*, No. 4, 1983, pp. 8-11.

56. 'Heilongjiang sheng qingfang gongye xitong xue Shanghai de jidian tihui' ('Some Observations on Learning from Shanghai in the Light and Textile Industries of Heilongjiang Province'), *Gongye jingji guanli congkan*, No. 8, 1981, pp. 31-6.

57. 'Benshi an zhuanyehua xiezuo yuanze gaizu gongye chujian chengxiao' ('The Initial Achievement of Industrial Reorganization according to the Principles of Specialization and Co-ordination in our City'), *Beijing ribao (Beijing Daily)*, 2 August 1979, p. 1.

58. Zhou Taihe *et al.* (eds.) (1984), p. 623, note 23 above.

59. Zhou Taihe *et al.* (eds.) (1984), pp. 631-2, note 23 above.

60. Zhou Taihe *et al.* (eds.) (1984), pp. 636-7, note 23 above.

61. Yu Xinmin, Guan Bai, and Sun Zhibo, 'Tianjin shiban qiyexing gongsi de youlai he fazhan' ('The Origin and Development of the Pilot Programmes of Enterprise-type Corporations in Tianjian'), *Jingji guanli*, No. VI, 1981, pp. 48-50 and 55.

62. Wu Jiapei and Li Wenrui, *Changzhou gongye fazhan de daolu (The Passage to Industrial Development in Changzhou)* (Beijing, Renmin chubanshe, 1979), pp. 53-9.

63. Zhou Taihe *et al.* (eds.) (1984), pp. 678-82, note 23 above.

64. Wu Jiapei and Li Wenrui (1979), p. 61, note 62 above.

65. Wu Jiapei and Li Wenrui (1979), p. 58, note 62 above.

66. Wu Jiapei and Li Wenrui (1979), pp. 62-4, note 62 above.

67. Zhou Taihe *et al.* (eds.) (1984), p. 681, note 23 above.

68. Gongye jingji yanjiusuo diaochazu, 'Zhengque chuli gongsi yu gongchan de guanxi' ('Correct Handling of the Relationship between the Corporation and Factory'), *Jingji guanli*, No. 2, 1981, pp. 37-41 and 48.

69. Zhou Taihe *et al.* (eds.) (1984), p. 682, note 23 above.
70. Zhou Taihe *et al.* (eds.) (1984), pp. 708–9, note 23 above.
71. Hu Xiang and Luo Qiang, 'Zhengque chuli gongsi neibu jiquan yu fenquan wenti' ('Correct Handling of the Problem of Centralization and Decentralization within the Corporation'), *Jingji guanli*, No. III, 1981, pp. 38–41.
72. Zhou Taihe *et al.* (eds.) (1984), pp. 712–13, note 23 above.
73. Yang Hui and Luo Qiang, 'Tiaozheng xuyao lianhe, lianhe cujin tiaozheng' ('Adjustment Must Depend upon Combination; Combination Promotes Adjustment'), *Hubei caijing xueyuan xuebao* (*The Journal of Hubei College of Finance and Economy*), No. 4, 1981, pp. 24–51.
74. Zhou Taihe *et al.* (eds.) (1984), p. 713, note 23 above.
75. Zhou Taihe *et al.* (1984), pp. 713–15, note 23 above; Luo Chuanyong, 'Zai lianhe tinei jiangu liangzhong suoyouzhi qiye liyi de yizhong hao banfa' ('One Good Way to Balance Enterprise Interests from Two Ownership Systems within the Conglomerates'), *Jingji guanli*, No. XI, 1981, pp. 33–6.
76. Zhou Taihe *et al.* (eds.) (1984), pp. 658–60, note 23 above.
77. Ding Jiatiao, 'Shixing kua sheng shi lianhe fahui zhongxin chengshi zuoyong' ('Implement Combinations across Provincial and Municipal Boundaries, and Develop the Function of Urban Centres'), *Jingji guanli*, No. 7, 1983, pp. 21–9; 'Zuo lianhe zhi lu da you kewei' ('Great Potential in Following the Road of Combination'), *Gongye jingji guanli congkan*, No. 3, 1980, pp. 40–3.
78. Chen Jiagui and Wang Lingling, 'Fahui jungong qiye youshi, wei minyong gongye jishu gaizao fuwu' ('Develop the Strength of Military Industrial Enterprises, Serve the Reconstruction of Civilian Technology'), *Jingji guanli*, No. 8, 1983, pp. 8–12; Qiu Jingji, 'Lianhe qilai shixing junmin jiehe' ('Combine together to Implement the Integration of Military and Civilian Sectors'), *Jingji guanli*, No. 8, 1983, pp. 12–15.

NOTES TO CHAPTER 8

1. Part of this chapter has been published with a different theoretical perspective: see Peter Nan-shong Lee, 'Enterprise Autonomy Policy in Post-Mao China: A Case Study of Policy-making, 1978–1983', *China Quarterly*, No. 105, March 1986, pp. 45–71.
2. Deng Xiaoping, 'Guanche tiaozheng fangzhen, baozheng anding tuanje' ('Implement the Readjustment Guideline, and Ensure Stability and Unity'), in *Deng Xiaoping wenxuan* (*The Collected Essays of Deng Xiaoping*) (Beijing, Renmin chubanshe, 1983), p. 313.
3. *Deng Xiaoping wenxuan* (1983), p. 313, note 2 above.
4. Zhou Taihe *et al.* (eds.), *Dangdai Zhongguo de jingji tizhi gaige* (*The Economic Reform of Contemporary China*) (Beijing, Zhongguo shehui kexue chubanshe, 1984), p. 171.
5. Hu's article was published on 6 October 1978. For an English translation, see Hu Qiaomu, 'Observe Economic Laws, Speed up the Four Modernizations', *Beijing Review*, Vol. 21, No. 45, 10 November 1978, pp. 7–15; Vol. 21, No. 46, 17 November 1978, pp. 15–23; Vol. 21, No. 47, 24 November 1978, pp. 13–21.
6. Xue Muqiao, 'Shehuizhuyi jingji de jihua guanli' ('The Planned Management of the Socialist Economy'), in Zhongguo shehui kexueyan jingji yanjiusuo *et al.*, *Shehuizhuyi jingji zhong jihua yu shichang de guanxi* (*Plan and Market in Socialist Economy*) (Beijing, Zhongguo shehui kexue chubanshe, 1980), Vol. I, pp. 15–23, hereafter cited as *Guanxi*.

7. Tang Zongkun, 'Jiazhi guilu shichang juzhi he shehuizhuyi jihua jingji' ('The Law of Value, Market Mechanism and Socialist Planned Economy'), in *Guanxi* (1980), Vol. I, pp. 158–60, note 6 above.

8. Liu Guoguang, 'Dui jingji tizhi gaige zhong jige zhongyao wenti de kanfa' ('Views concerning Important Problems of Reforms in the Economic System'), *Jingji guanli* (*Economic Management*), No. 2, 1979, pp. 12–13.

9. Liu Suinlian, 'Guanyu woguo jingji tizhi gaige fangxiang de tantao' ('Inquiry on the Direction of Reform of the Economic System in our Country'), *Jingji guanli*, No. 1, 1980, p. 4; 'Bixu kuoda qiye de quanli' ('The Power of Enterprises must Expand'), *Renmin ribao* (*People's Daily*), 19 February 1979, p. 1.

10. Luo Jingfen, 'Jingji guanli xitong tong zhengquan guanli xitong yingdang fenli'('The Economic Management System should be Separated from the Political Management System'), *Jingji guanli*, No. 10, 1979, pp. 15–19.

11. He Jianzhang and Zhang Zhuoyuan, 'Jiasu shehuizhuyi xiandaihua jianshe bixu zhongshi jiazhi guilu de zuoyong' ('To Accelerate the Socialist Modernization, Due Emphasis must be Placed on the Function of the Law of Value'), in *Guanxi* (1980), Vol. II, pp. 518–26, note 6 above; Chen Xiuchang and Tang Jinjun, 'Zijue liyong jiazhi guilu zaochao shangpin liutong' ('Conscientiously Apply the Law of Value, Facilitate the Circulation of Commodities'), in *Guanxi* (1980), Vol. II, pp. 735–46, note 6 above.

12. Luo Jingfen, 'The Economic Management System...', *Jingji guanli*, No. 10, 1979, pp. 15–19, note 10 above; Li Ruxun, 'Zijue yunyong jiazhi guilu he qiye xiangdui dulixing wenti' ('The Problem of Conscious Application of the Law of Value and the Relative Independence of Enterprises'), in Zhongguo shehui kexueyuan jingji yanjiusuo ziliaoshi *et al.* (eds.), *Shangpin shenchan jiazhi guilu he kuoda qiye quanxian* (*The Law of Value in Commodity Production and Expansion of Enterprise Autonomy*) (Beijing, Zhongguo shehui kexue chubanshe, 1980), Vol. I, pp. 317–28, hereafter cited as *Quanxian*; Shi Xiulin, 'Shengchan ziliao gongying yinggai shi jihua fenpei yu shichang xiaoshu xiang jiehe' ('The Supply of the Means of Production should be the Interaction between Planned Allocation and Market Sales'), in *Quanxian* (1980), Vol. I, pp. 295–308; Tang Zhongkun, 'Jiazhi guilu shichang jizhi he shehuizhuyi jihua jingji' ('The Law of Value, Market Mechanism and Socialist Planned Economy'), in *Guanxi* (1980), Vol. I, p. 139.

13. 'Chi daguofan shi shien mo shehuizhuyi?' ('What Kind of Socialism should it be Called if [the practice of] Eating out of a Big Rice Pot is Tolerated?'), *Beijing ribao* (*Beijing Daily*), 20 August 1979, p. 3.

14. 'Guanche zhixing an loa fenpei de shehuizhuyi yuanze' ('Thoroughly Implement the Socialist Principle of Distribution according to Work'), *Xinhua yuebao* (*New China Monthly*), No. 5, 1978, p. 58.

15. Hu Qiaomu, 'Observe the Economic Laws...', *Beijing Review*, Vol. 21, No. 45, 10 November 1978, pp. 7–15, note 5 above.

16. Liu Guoguang and Zhao Renwei, 'Lun shehuizhuyi jingji zhong jihua yu shichang de guanxi' ('On the Relationship between Planning and Market in the Socialist Economy'), in *Guanxi* (1980), Vol. I, pp. 69–70, note 6 above.

17. He Jianzhang, 'Woguo quanmin suoyouzhi jingji jihua guanli tizhi cunzai de wenti he gaige fangxiang' ('The Existing Problems and the Direction of Reforms in the Managerial System of the State Ownership and Planned Economy of our Country'), *Jingji yanjiu* (*Economic Reseach*), No. 5, 1979, p. 44.

18. Ma Hong, 'Guanyu jingji guanli tizhi gaige de jige wenti' ('Several Problems concerning the Reform of the Economic Managerial System'), *Jingji yanjiu*, No. 7, 1981, pp. 11–24.

19. Luo Gengmo, 'Guanyu jihua jingji shichang jingji he qita' ('On Planned Economy, Market Economy and Others'), in *Guanxi* (1980), Vol. I, pp. 44–5, note 6 above.

20. Xue Muqiao, 'Shehuizhuyi jingji de jihua guanli' ('Management by Planning in the Socialist Economy'), in *Guanxi* (1980), Vol. I, pp. 21–3, note 6 above.

21. Xue Muqiao, *Zhongguo shehuizhuyi jingji wenti de yanjiu* (*A Study of Problems of China's Socialist Economy*) (Peking, Renmin chubanshe, 1979), pp. 97–122; Feng Baoxing, Wan Xin, and Zhang Dajian, 'Shehuizhuyi jingji shi jihua jingji yu shangpin jingji de tongyi' ('The Socialist Economy is the Unity of Planned Economy and Commodity Economy'), in *Guanxi* (1980), Vol. I, p. 237, note 6 above.

22. He Jianzhang, 'The Existing Problems and the Direction of Reforms...', *Jingji yanjiu*, No. 5, 1979, p. 44, note 17 above.

23. Interview with Xue Boding, 1979.

24. Zhou Taihe *et al.* (eds.) (1984), pp. 164–5, note 4 above.

25. Dorothy J. Solinger, 'The Fifth National People's Congress and the Process of Policy Making: Reform, Readjustment and the Opposition', *Issues and Studies*, August 1982, pp. 63–106.

26. Deng Xiaoping, 'Jiefang sixiang shishiqiushi, tuanje yizhi xiangqian kan' ('Liberate our Thought, Seek Truth from Facts, and Unite and Look forward'), in *Deng Xiaoping wenxuan* (1983), pp. 135–6, note 2 above.

27. 'Zhongguo gong changdang dishiyi jie zhongyang weijuanhui disan ci quanti daibiao dahui gongbao' ('The Communiqué of the Third Plenum of the Eleventh Party Congress, CCP'), *Hongqi* (*Red Flag*), No. 1, 1979, p. 17.

28. Deng Xiaoping, 'Jianchi sixiang jiben yuanze' ('Insist on the Four Basic Principles'), in *Deng Xiaoping wenxuan* (1983), pp. 147–8, note 2 above.

29. The relevant commissions, ministries, and offices provided a long list of powers to be decentralized to enterprises, but each grant of power was limited and subject to the approval of the supervising authorities. This position remained the same from 1979 to 1984. See 'Guojia jingji weiyuanhui guanyu kuoda qiye zizhuquan shidian gongzuo qingkuang he jinhou yijian de baogaoshu' ('The Report and Opinions of the State Economic Commission concerning the [Current] Situation and the Future [Development] of the Task of Pilot Programmes of Expanding Enterprise Autonomy'), *Guowuyuan gongbao* (*The Communiqué of the State Council*), No. 14, 1980, pp. 419–27; 'Guojia jingji weiyuanhui guowuyuan tizhi gaige bangongshi guanyu gongye guanli tizhi gaige zuotanhui huibao tigang' ('The Outline Report of the State Economic Commission and the Institutional Reform Office of the State Council concerning the Conference on the Reform of the Industrial Management System'), *Guowuyuan gongbao*, No. 9, 1981, pp. 268–78; 'Guanche luoshi guowuyuan youguan kuoquan wenjian, gonggu tigao kuoquan gongzuo de juti shishi zhanxing banfa' ('The Provisional Measure on the Concrete Way to Consolidate and Improve the Work of Expansion of Autonomy and to Carry out thoroughly Related Documents of Autonomy of the State Council'), *Guowuyuan gongbao*, No. 14, 1981, pp. 439–51; 'Guowuyuan guanyu jinyibu kuoda guoying gongye qiye zizhuquan de zhanxing guiding' ('The Provisional Regulation of the State Council concerning the Further Expansion of the Autonomy of the State-owned Industrial Enterprises'), *Guowuyuan gongbao*, No. 10, 1984, pp. 323–5.

30. 'The Provisional Measure on the Concrete Way...', *Guowuyuan gongbao*, No. 14, 1981, p. 440, note 29 above.

31. A number of authors have argued that 'partial reform' is less likely to succeed in a Socialist country. However, total reform entails greater uncertainty, given the limited intellectual capacity of any one policy-maker, even a Socialist reformer. Of course, policy-makers who are able to take a broad and comprehensive perspective and to prepare thoroughly might be in a better position to introduce reform programmes in a command economy, in view of the interdependence of the components of the system in such an economy. See Susan L. Shirk, 'The Politics of Industrial Reform', in Elizabeth J. Perry and Christine Wong (eds.), *The Political Economy of Reform in Post-Mao China* (Cambridge, Mass. and London, Council

on East Asian Studies, Harvard University, 1985), pp. 199–204; Nina P. Halpern, 'China Industrial Reform', *Asian Survey,* Vol. XXV, No. 10, October 1985, pp. 998–1012.

32. 'The Outline Report of the State Economic Commission...', *Guowuyuan gongbao,* No. 9, 1981, p. 271, note 29 above.

33. Peter Nan-shong Lee, 'Enterprise Autonomy policy in Post-Mao China...', *China Quarterly,* No. 105, March 1986, pp. 45–71, note 1 above.

34. Zhonghua renmin gongheguo caizhengbu, 'Sanshiwu nian lai caizheng gongzuo de juda chengjiu' ('The Great Achievement of Financial Work for 35 Years'), *Caizheng (Finance),* No. 10, 1984, p. 3.

35. 'The Draft Decision concerning Some Problems in Speeding up the Development of Industry', *Issues and Studies,* Vol. XV, No. 1, January 1979, p. 74.

36. 'Guoying qiye shixing tiqu he shiyong qiye jijin' ('The Trial Implementation of Retention and the Use of Enterprise Funds in the State-owned Enterprises'), *Renmin ribao,* 20 December 1978, p. 1.

37. These five regulations are: (1) the Regulation of the Expansion of Managerial and Marketing Autonomy of State-owned Industrial Enterprises, (2) the Regulation of Implementation of Profit Retention in State-owned Enterprises, (3) the Provisional Regulation of the Increase of Depreciation Rates and Improvement of the Use of Depreciation Fees in State-owned Industrial Enterprises, (4) the Provisional Regulation of Levying Fixed Capital Tax in State-owned Industrial Enterprises, and (5) the Provisional Regulation of Bank Loans for the Full Quota of Working Capital in the State-owned Industrial Enterprise. The background of the five regulations was reported in the following: 'Guowuyuan banbu wuxiang gaige wenjian, jueding jiajin zhengdun guanli guoying qiye' ('The State Council Promulgates Five Policy Papers of Reform, Accelerates Rectification of the Management of the State-owned Enterprises'), *Dagong bao (Dagong Daily),* 30 July 1979, p. 1.

38. 'The Report and Opinions of the State Economic Commission...', *Guowuyuan gongbao,* No. 14, 1980, pp. 419–20, note 29 above.

39. 'The State Council Promulgates Five Policy Papers of Reform...', *Dagong bao,* 30 July 1979, p. 1, note 37 above.

40. Yuan Yu-sheng, 'Lun lirun liucheng de shishi he yuanze' ('On the Essence and Principle of Profit Retention'), *Kuaiji yanjiu (Accounting Research),* No. 3, 1980, pp. 56–7. Here Mr Yuan indicates that, out of 3,358 experimental enterprises, 1,982 units were directly approved by the State Council and 1,416 units were authorized by local governments.

41. The text of the July 1979 regulation of the profit-retention system is not available. But we can infer its key features from other sources. See 'Guoji jingji weiyuanhui caizhengbu guanyu guoying gongye qiye lirun liucheng shixing banfa' ('The Measure of the State Economic Commission and the Ministry of Finance on the Trial-implementation of Profit Retention in the State-owned Industrial Enterprises'), *Guowuyuan gongbao,* No. 1, 1980, p. 7.

42. 'The Measure of the State Economic Commission and the Ministry of Finance...', *Guowuyuan gongbao,* No. 1, 1980, pp. 7–11, note 41 above

43. 'The Report and Opinions of the State Economic Commission...', *Guowuyuan gongbao,* No. 14, 1980, p. 420, note 29 above.

44. 'The Report and Opinions of the State Economic Commission...', *Guowuyuan gongbao,* No. 14, 1980, pp. 420–1, note 29 above.

45. 'The Report and Opinions of the State Economic Commission...', *Guowuyuan gongbao,* No. 14, 1980, pp. 422–3, note 29 above.

46. 'The Report and Opinions of the State Economic Commission...', *Guowuyuan gongbao,* No. 14, 1980, p. 419, note 29 above.

47. 'The Provisional Measure on the Concrete Way...', *Guowuyuan gongbao,* No. 14, 1981, p. 440, note 29 above.

48. 'The Outline Report of the State Economic Commission ...', *Guowuyuan gongbao*, No. 9, 1981, p. 268, note 29 above.

49. 'The Outline Report of the State Economic Commission...', *Guowuyuan gongbao*, No. 9, 1981, p. 276, note 29 above.

50. 'Guojia jingji weiyuanhui guowuyuan tizhi gaige bangongshi guanyu shixing gongye shengchan jingji zerenzhi ruogan wenti de yijian' ('The Opinion of the State Economic Commission and the Institutional Reform Office of the State Council concerning Several Problems in the Trial Implementation of the Industrial Production Economic Responsibility System'), *Guowuyuan gongbao*, No. 24, 1981, pp. 758–9.

51. 'Guojia jingji tizhi gaige weiyuanhui guojia jingji weiyuanhui caizhengbu guanyu wanshan gongye jingji zerenzhi jige wenti' ('The Report of the State Economic Reform Commission, the State Economic Commission, the Ministry of Finance on Several Problems concerning Protection of the Industrial Economic Responsibility System'), *Guowuyuan gongbao*, No. 19, 1982, pp. 837–8.

52. 'The Opinion of the State Economic Commission and the Institutional Reform Office...', *Guowuyuan gongbao*, No. 24, 1981, pp. 758–9, note 50 above.

53. Yuan Yu-sheng, 'On the Essence and Principle...', *Kuaiji yanjiu*, No. 3, 1980, pp. 56–7, note 40 above.

54. Yehezhel Dror, *Public Policymaking Re-examined* (Bedfordshire, England, Leonard Hill Books, 1973), pp. 142–3.

55. On the early stages of the pilot programmes in Sichuan province in 1979–80, see Feng Ju and Zhou Zhenghua, 'Sichuan sheng wuge guoying gongye qiye zifu yingkui shidian de diaocha' ('The Investigation of the Pilot Programme of the Responsibility System for Profit and Loss in Five State-owned Industrial Enterprises in Sichuan Province'), *Zhongguo shehui kexue (China's Social Science)*, No. 3, 1981, pp. 83–96; Shen Caiyan, 'Cong kuoda qiye zizhuquan shidian de shijian kan qiye caiwu tizhi gaige de fangxiang' ('Analysis of the Direction of the Enterprise Financial System in Light of the Practice of the Pilot Programme of the Expansion of Enterprise Autonomy'), *Caizheng yanjiu (Research on Financial Policy)*, No. 5, 1980, pp. 27–36; Lin Ling, 'Kuoda qiye zizhuquan yu gaige qiye guanli' ('Expand the Enterprise Autonomy and Improve Enterprise Management'), *Xinhua yuebao*, No. 5, 1980, pp. 100–3; Lin Ling, 'Zhongguo jingji tizhi gaige zai Sichuan de shiyan' ('The Experiment of China's Economic Reform in Sichuan'), *Shehui kexue yanjiu (The Research of Social Science)*, No. 3, 1981, pp. 16–22; Lin Ling, 'Sichuan sheng liangnian lai jingji tizhi gaige de jingyan yu wenti' ('The Experience and Problems of Economic Reform in Sichuan Province for the Past Two Years'), *Jingji guanli*, No. 6, 1981, pp. 16–26; Qinggongyebu jingji tizhi diao yan zu, 'Sichuan sheng qinggongye qiye kuoda zizhuquan shidian qingkuang de diaocha baogao' ('The Investigation Report of the Pilot Programme of the Expansion of Enterprise Autonomy in the Light Industry in Sichuan Province'), *Jingji yanjiu*, No. 4, 1980, pp. 57–66; Fangzhi gongyebu diaochazu, 'Guanyu Sichuan fangzhi xitong kuoda qiye zizhuquan de qingkuang he jianyi' ('The Situation and Suggestions Concerning the Expansion of Enterprise Autonomy in the Textile Industrial System in Sichuan'), *Jingji guanli*, No. 3, 1981, pp. 30–3; Xue Shen, 'Chengshi he lidao' ('Ride on the Trend and Induce by Interest'), *Guangming ribao (Guangming Daily)*, 8 March 1980, p. 4, 15 March 1980, p. 2, 22 March 1980, p. 2, and 29 March 1980, p. 4; Yuan Yu-sheng, 'On the Essence and Principle...', *Kuaiji yanjiu*, No. 3, 1980, pp. 56–60, note 40 above; Tian Fang *et al.*, 'Chongqing shi kuoda qiye zizhuquan shidian de chubu diaocha' ('A Preliminary Investigation of the Pilot Programme of the Expansion of Enterprise Autonomy in Chongqing Municipality'), *Jingji yanjiu*, No. 3, 1981, pp. 28–35.

56. Lin Ling, 'The Experiment of China's Economic Reform...', *Shehui kexue yanjiu*, No. 3, 1981, p. 16, note 55 above.

57. Feng Ju and Zhou Zhenghua, 'The Investigation of the Pilot Programme...',

Zhongguo shehui kexue, No. 3, 1981, pp. 83–6, note 55 above; Shen Caiyan, 'Analysis of the Direction of the Enterprise Financial System...', *Caizheng yanjiu*, No. 5, 1980, pp. 26–7, note 55 above.

58. 'Wo sheng yibai qiye shixing kuoda qiye zizhuquan' ('The Trial Implementation of Expansion of Enterprise Autonomy in 100 Enterprises in our Province'), *Nanfang ribao (Southern Daily)*, 13 August 1979, p. 1; 'Wo sheng yibaige qiye kuoda zizhuquan chu jian chengxiao' ('The Initial Achievement of Expansion of Autonomy in 100 Enterprises in our Province'), *Nanfang ribao*, 27 October 1979, p. 1; 'Baohu xianjin qiye de jijixing' ('Protect the Activism of an Advanced Enterprise'), *Nanfang ribao*, 1 November 1979, p. 3; 'Renxin sigai' ('People Desire Change'), *Nanfang ribao*, 25 April 1980, p. 1.

59. 'Yichang guanyu kuoda qiye zizhuquan de bianlun' ('A Debate on the Expansion of Enterprise Autonomy'), *Nanfang ribao*, 16 August 1979, p. 1; 'Qingyuan jingyan jiangule guojia yu qiye geren de liyi' ('The Qingyuan Experience has Taken into Consideration the Interests of the State, Enterprise, and Individual'), *Nanfang ribao*, 21 August 1979, p. 1; 'Women dui Qingyuan shixing chao jihua lirun tichengjiang de kanfa' ('Our Observations of the Trial-implementation of Profit-sharing in the Case of Over-fulfilment of Plan in Qingyuan County'), *Nanfang ribao*, 19 August 1979, p. 1; 'Wo sheng jueding zai xian shu gongye qiye zhong tuiguang Qingyuan jingyan' ('Our Province Decided to Expand Qingyuan Experience to the Industrial Enterprises under the Jurisdiction of the County'), *Nanfang ribao*, 30 August 1979, p. 1; Ma Yipin, 'Yanjiu xinwenti zongjie xinjingyan' ('Investigate New Problems, Sum up New Experience'), *Nanfang ribao*, 17 September 1979, p. 2; 'Jiejue le popo duo, banshinan de wenti' ('The Problem of Many "Mother-in-laws" and Difficulties in Managing Business Have been Solved'), *Nanfang ribao*, 14 November 1979, p. 2; Zhong gong Qingyuan xian weiyuanhui, 'Guanyu Qingyuan xian guoying qiye shixing chao jihua lirun tichengjiang he gaige gongye guanli tizhi de qingkuang baogao' ('The Report of the Case of Trial Implementation of the Profit-sharing Prize in the Over-fulfilment of Annual Plans and of the Reform of the Industrial Managing System in State-owned Enterprises in Qingyuan County'), *Nanfang ribao*, 2 August 1980, pp. 2 and 4; 'Qingyuan jingyan de xinfazhan' ('The New Development of Qingyuan Experience'), *Nanfang ribao*, 23 August 1981, p. 2, and 26 August 1981, p. 2.

60. 'The Outline Report of the State Economic Commission...', *Guowuyuan gongbao*, No. 9, 1981, p. 276, note 29 above.

61. Zhu Yan and Cai Yifeng, 'Dui Shanghai shi kuoquan qiye lirun liucheng fenxi' ('The Analysis of Profit Retention in Enterprises with an Expansion of Power in Shanghai'), *Jingji yanjiu*, No. 9, 1981, pp. 6–12.

62. Chen Lingshu, 'Yi zhuguan ju wei danwei shixing lirun liucheng banfa de libi' ('The Advantages and Disadvantages in the Implementation of the Bureau-centred Profit-retention Measure'), *Jingji guanli*, No. 1, 1981, pp. 14–15 and 29.

63. An analysis of the case of the Textile Managing Bureau is given in: Bao Youde, 'Kending chengji buduan wanshan' ('Recognize the Achievement, and Make Improvement Continuously'), *Caizheng*, No. 10, 1981, pp. 12–13.

64. Chen Lingshu, 'The Advantages and Disadvantages...', *Jingji guanli*, No. 1, 1981, pp. 14–15 and 29, note 62 above.

65. Bao Youde, 'Recognize the Achievement...', *Caizheng*, No. 10, 1981, pp. 12–13, note 63 above.

66. Zhou Taihe *et al.* (eds.) (1984), pp. 552–3, note 4 above.

67. 'Guoying qiye yijiuwusi nian jihua lirun fencheng de shiyong banfa' ('Measures for Sharing and Use of Above-plan Profits of 1954 in the State-owned Enterprises'), *Zhonghua renmin gongheguo fagui huibian* (*The Collected Laws of the People's Republic of China*), June–December 1955, pp. 523–4, hereafter cited as *Wansui*.

68. Jin Jingqi, 'Beijing shi gongjiao qiye shixing lirun liucheng banfa de qingkuang' ('The Case of Trial Implementation of the Retained Profit Measure of the Enterprises

in Industry and Transport in Beijing Municipality'), *Jingji lilun yu jingji guanli* (*Economic Theory and Economic Management*), No. 3, 1981, pp. 58–63.

69. Wang Bingqian, 'Kaichuang caizheng gongzuo xin jumian' ('To Create the New Situation in the Financial Task'), *Caizheng jingji* (*The Economics of Finance and Trade*), No. 1, 1983, p. 3.

70. Liu Hongru, 'Liudong zijin guanli tizhi de gaige' ('The Reform of the Managerial System of Working Capital'), *Caizheng jingji*, No. 11, 1983, pp. 1–5.

71. 'Guojia jingji weiyuanhui, Guojia jihua weiyuanhui, Caizhengbu, Zhongguo renmin yinhang guanyu jiaqiang qiye liudong zijin guanli de baogao' ('The Report of the State Economic Commission, the People's Bank of China concerning the Strengthening of Management over Working Capital of the Enterprise'), *Guowuyuan gongbao*, No. 21, 1982, pp. 1029–30.

72. 'The Report of the State Economic Commission...', *Guowuyuan gongbao*, No. 21, 1982, pp. 1030–2, note 71 above.

73. 'Zhongguo renmin yinhang guanyu guoying qiye liudong zijing gaiyou renmin yinhang tongyi guanli de baogao' ('The Report of the People's Bank of China concerning the Change to Unified Management by the People's Bank over Working Capital of State-owned Enterprises'), *Guowuyuan gongbao*, No. 15, 1983, pp. 698–703.

74. 'The Report of the People's Bank of China...', *Guowuyuan gongbao*, No. 15, 1983, p. 698, note 73 above.

75. Xiao Jie, 'Qiye shengchan fazhan jijin yingdang yongzai wa ge gai shang' ('The Enterprise Development Fund should be Used for Tapping Potential, Technical Renovation, and Reconstruction'), *Jingji guanli*, No. 2, 1981, pp. 18 and 62.

76. Lin Qiushi, 'Tigao wa ge gai zijin xiaoguo de jige wenti' ('Several Problems in Improving the Utility of Funds for Tapping Potential and Technical Renovation and Reconstruction'), *Caizheng*, No. 4, 1981, pp. 11–16.

77. 'Guanyu jiaqiang xianyou gongye jiaotong qiye wa qian, gexin, gaizao gongzuo de zhanxing banfa' ('The Provisional Measure for Strengthening the Task of Tapping Potential, Technical Renovation and Reconstruction'), *Guowuyuan gongbao*, No. 7, 1980, pp. 207–11.

78. 'Guojia jihua weiyuanhui, guojia jiben jianshe weiyuanhui, caizhengbu, Zhongguo renmin jianshe yinhang guanyu shixing jiben jianshe bokuan gai daikuan de baogao' ('The Report of the State Planning Commission, the State Construction Commission, the Ministry of Finance and the People's Construction Bank of China concerning the Change from Financial Appropriation to Loans in Implementing Basic Construction'), *Guowuyuan gongbao*, No. 18, 1980, pp. 560–4.

79. 'Jiben jianshe xiangmu baogan jingji zerenzhi shixing banfa' ('The Provisional Measure of the Contracting-out Economic Responsibility System of the Basic Construction Projects'), *Guowuyuan gongbao*, No. 8, 1983, pp. 291–6.

80. 'The Provisional Measure of the Contracting-out Economic Responsibility System...', *Guowuyuan gongbao*, No. 8, 1983, pp. 295–6.

81. Nicos P. Mouzelis, *Organization and Bureaucracy* (Chicago, Aldine Publishing Company, 1967), pp. 59–62.

NOTES TO CHAPTER 9

1. Part of this chapter has been published with a different theoretical perspective. See Peter Nan-shong Lee, 'Enterprise Autonomy Policy in Post-Mao China: A Case Study of Policy-making, 1978–1983', *China Quarterly*, No. 105, March 1986, pp. 45–71.

2. State Statistical Bureau of the PRC, *The Statistical Yearbook of China 1984* (Hong Kong, Economic Information and Agency, 1984), p. 301.

3. The background is given by Xing Hua, 'Yijiubaling nian kaishi de caizheng tizhi zhongyao gaige' ('The Major Reforms of the Financial System Beginning in 1980, Parts I and II'), *Caizheng (Finance)*, No. 12, 1983, pp. 8–10 and No. 1, 1984, pp. 13–15.

4. 'Guanyu shixing huafen shouzhi, fenji baogan caizheng guanli tizhi de zhanxing guiding' ('The Provisional Regulation concerning the Financial System of the "Classification of Revenue and Expenditures", and "Contracting-out according to Hierarchy"'), *Guowuyuan gongbao (The Communiqué of the State Council)*, No. 1, 1980, pp. 3–6.

5. Xing Hua, 'The Major Reforms of the Financial System...', *Caizheng*, No. 12, 1983, pp. 8–9, note 3 above.

6. Zhou Taihe *et al.* (eds.), *Dangdai Zhongguo de jingji tizhi gaige (The Economic Reform in Contemporary China)* (Beijing, Zhongguo shehui kexue chubanshe, 1984), p. 460.

7. Liu Huanzhen, 'Lun caizheng guanli tizhi de gaige' ('On the Reform of the Financial Managerial System'), *Caizheng wenti (The Problems of Financial Administration)*, No. 2, 1983, pp. 68–73.

8. Zhao Ziyang, 'Yanjiu xinwenti, ba jingji gaige gaohao' ('Investigate New Problems, Set Economic Reform in the Right Direction'), *Renmin ribao (People's Daily)*, 21 April 1980, pp. 1 and 2.

9. Wang Bingqian, 'Xue xi guanche shier da jingshen kaichuang caizheng gongzuo xin jumian' ('Study and Implement the Spirit of the Twelfth Party Congress, and Create a New Situation of Financial Tasks'), *Caizheng yanjiu (The Research of Financial Administration)*, No. 1, 1983, p. 3.

10. Hsin Chang, 'The 1982–83 overinvestment crisis in China', *Asian Survey*, Vol. XXIV, No. 12, December 1984, pp. 1982–4.

11. Wang Shujiu, Zeng Kanglin, and Liu Bangshi, 'Luelun zhengqu woguo caizheng jingji zhuangkuang de genben haozhuan' ('A Brief Discussion on how to Make Fundamental Improvements in the Financial and Economic Situation of our Country'), *Caijing kexue (The Science of Finance and Economy)*, No. 1, 1983, pp. 26–32.

12. The State Statistical Bureau of the PRC (1984), p. 417, note 2 above.

13. The State Statistical Bureau of the PRC (1984), p. 419, note 2 above.

14. Liu Mingyuan, 'Guoying qiye ligaishui lilun yiju de tantao' ('A Discussion of the Theoretical Foundation of the Substitution of Taxation for Profit Remittance in State-owned Enterprises'), *Caizheng jingji wenti yanjiu (The Research of Economic Problems in Finance)*, No. 4, 1983, p. 39.

15. Rong Zihe, 'Dui dangqian caizheng gongzuo de jidian kanfa' ('Some Observations on Current Financial Tasks'), *Caizheng*, No. 8, 1983, p. 4.

16. Wang Shujiu, Zeng Kanglin, and Liu Bangshi, 'A Brief Discussion on the Fundamental Improvement...', *Caijing kexue*, No. 1, 1983, p. 27, note 11 above.

17. The State Statistical Bureau of the PRC (1984), p. 417, note 2 above.

18. The State Statistical Bureau of the PRC (1984), p. 419, note 2 above.

19. See Bo Yibo, 'Guanyu guomin jingji you jihua an bili fazhan de jige wenti' ('Several Problems of Planned and Proportional Development of the National Economy'), *Xinhua yuebao (New China Monthly)* No. 10, 1983, p. 118.

20. 'Caizhengbu guanyu yasuo guoying qiye guanlifei de zhanxing guiding' ('The Provisional Regulation of the Ministry of Finance concerning the Comprehension of Managerial Expenditure of the State-owned Enterprises'), *Guowuyuan gongbao*, No. 2, 1981, pp. 46–8.

21. 'Caizhengbu guanyu jiancha tou lou qian shui qingkuang he jia qiang shuishou gongzuo de baogao' ('The Report of the Ministry of Finance concerning the Situation

of Tax Fraud and Evasion and the Task of Strengthening Tax Collection'), *Guowuyuan gongbao*, No. 7, 1982, pp. 284–9.

22. 'Caizhengbu guanyu zhankai qiye caiwu jiancha qingkuang he jinhou yijian de baogao' ('The Report of the Ministry of Finance concerning the Beginning of Enterprise Financial Inspection and its Future Development'), *Guowuyuan gongbao*, No. 10, 1982, pp. 460–4.

23. 'Caizhengbu guanyu kaizhan caiwu da jiancha de qingkuang he jinyibu yansu caizheng jilu de baogao' ('The Report of the Ministry of Finance concerning the Situation of Implementing Major Financial Inspections and the Further Tightening up of Financial Discipline'), *Guowuyuan gongbao*, No. 11, 1984, pp. 325–9.

24. 'Guowuyuan guanyu jiejue qiye shehui fudan guozhong wenti de ruogan guiding' ('The Regulation of the State Council concerning the Settlement of the Problem of the Excessive Social Burdens of the Enterprise'), *Guowuyuan gongbao*, No. 18, 1982, pp. 774–7.

25. 'Guoying qiye chengben guanli tiaoli' ('The Regulation on Cost Management in the State-owned Enterprises'), *Guowuyuan gongbao*, No. 6, 1984, pp. 182–9.

26. State Statistical Bureau of the PRC (1984), p. 419, note 2 above.

27. 'Guowuyuan guanyu jiaqiang jiben jianshe jihua guanli, kongzhi jiben jianshe guimo de ruogan guiding' ('The Regulation of the State Council concerning the Strengthening of Planning Management and Control of the Scale of Basic Construction'), *Guowuyuan gongbao*, No. 4, 1981, pp. 107–11.

28. 'Zhonggong zhongyang guowuyuan guanyu zhengjia guojia nenyuan jiaotong zhongdian jianshe jijin de tongzhi' ('The Circular on the National Funds for the Key Constructions of Energy Sources and Transport'), *Guowuyuan gongbao*, No. 21, 1982, pp. 997–9.

29. 'Guowuyjan guanyu zhengque shixing jiangli zhidu, jianjue zhizhi lanfa jianjin de ji xiang guiding' ('The Regulations of the State Council concerning the Correct Implementation of the Bonus System and the Resolute Stop of the Indiscriminate Payment of Bonuses'), *Guowuyuan gongbao*, No. 11, 1981, pp. 339–42.

30. 'Guowuyuan guanyu guanche zhixing guowuyuan shi hao wenjian ruogan wenti de buchong guiding' ('Amendments of the State Council to Selected Problems in the Thorough Execution of the No. 10 Document of the State Council'), *Guowuyuan gongbao*, No. 11, 1981, pp. 343–6.

31. 'Guowuyuan guanyu yange zhizhi qiye lanfa jiaban jiadian gongzi de tongzhi' ('The Circular of the State Council concerning the Strict Prohibition of the Indiscriminate Payment of Overtime Wages by the Enterprises'), *Guowuyuan gongbao*, No. 8, 1982, pp. 336–8.

32. 'Laodong renshibu guanyu yijiubasan nian qiye tiaozheng gongzi he gaige gongzi zhidu wenti de baogao' ('The Report of the Ministry of Labour and Personnel concerning the Wage Adjustments and Wage Reforms of Enterprise for 1983'), *Guowuyuan gongbao*, No. 15, 1983, pp. 705–8.

33. 'Guojia jingji weiyuanhui, laodong renshibu, caizhengbu guanyu dangqian tuixing jinying zerenzhi gongzuo zhong youguan gongzi wenti de baogao' ('The Report of the State Economic Commission, the Ministry of Finance concerning Wage Problems in Current Tasks of Implementing the Marketing Responsibility System'), *Guowuyuan gongbao*, No. 10, 1983, pp. 439–41.

34. 'Guowuyuan guanyu guoying qiye fafang jiangjin youguan wenti de tongzhi' ('The Circular of the State Council concerning Related Problems in Bonus Payments'), *Guowuyuan gongbao*, No. 8, 1984, pp. 251–2; 'Laodong renshibu guanyu qiye heli shiyong jiangli jijin de ruogan yijian' ('Some Opinions of the Ministry of Labour and Personnel on the Reasonable Use of Bonus Funds'), *Guowuyuan gongbao*, No. 11, 1984, pp. 343–4.

35. Peter N.S. Lee and Irene H.S. Chow, 'Incentive System in Chinese Factories:

Continuity and Change in the Post-Mao Era' (Paper presented at a conference on China's System Reforms at the Centre of Asian Studies, University of Hong Kong, 17–20 March, 1986), pp. 12–16.

36. 'Guoying qiye jiangjinshui zhanxing guiding' ('The Provisional Regulation of the Bonus Tax of the State-owned Enterprises'), *Guowuyuan gongbao*, No. 6, 1984, pp. 550–2.

37. Lee and Chow (1986), pp. 12–16, note 35 above.

38. 'Sichuan wuge qiye shixing zifu yingkiu shidian de qingkuang' ('The Situation of the Pilot Programmes of the Responsibility System for Profits and Losses in Five Enterprises in Sichuan'), *Xinhua yuebao*, No. 9, 1980, pp. 115–20; Feng Ju and Zhou Zhenghua, 'Sichuan seng wuge guoying gongye qiye zifu yingkui shidian de tiaocha' ('The Investigation of the Pilot Programme of the Responsibility System for Profit and Loss in Five State-owned Industrial Enterprises in Sichuan Province'), *Zhongguo shehui kexue (China's Social Science)*, No. 3, 1981, pp. 83–6.

39. Shanghai shi qinggongye jixie gongsi (The Light Machinery Corporation of Shanghai Municipality), 'Gaohao yiligaishui cujin zengchan zengshou' ('Ensure the Success of the Substitution of Taxation for Profit Remittance, Promote the Increase of Production and Income'), *Jingji guanli (Economic Management)*, No. 6, 1981, pp. 44–7; Du Yanshuang and Zhao Kaitai, 'Guoying qiye gaizheng suodeshui wenti de tantao' ('The Discussion of the Problems of the State-owned Enterprises after the Change to the Collection of Enterprise Tax'), *Shehui kexue (Social Science)*, No. 6, 1980, pp. 17–20; Bao Shichuan, 'Duli hesuan guojia zhengshui zifu yingkui shidian yizhounian' ('One Year of the Pilot Programme of Independent Accounting, Taxation by the State, and the Responsibility for Profits and Losses'), *Shanghai guanli kexue (Shanghai Managerial Science)*, No. 1, 1981, pp. 7–12; Tao Youzhi and Huang Laiji, 'Shanghai caiyouji chang zifu yingkui shidian qingkuang' ('The Situation of the Pilot Programme of the Responsibility System for Profits and Losses in the Shanghai Combustion Machinery Factory'), *Jingji guanli*, No. 1, 1981, pp. 16–19.

40. 'Cong Liuzhou shuizhi gaige shidian kan guojia yu qiye lirun fenpei guanxi de jige wenti' ('An Analysis of Several Problems of the Distribution of Profits between the State and Enterprises in the Light of the Pilot Programme of Tax Reform in Liuzhou'), *Caizheng yanjiu*, No. 1, 1983, pp. 33–40.

41. 'Guojia jingji weiyuanhui guanyu kuoda qiye zizhuquan shidian gongzuo qingkuang he jinhou yijian de baogaoshu' ('The Report and Opinion of the State Economic Commission concerning the [current] Situation and the Future [Development] of the Task of Pilot Programmes of Expanding Enterprise Autonomy'), *Guowuyuan gongbao*, No. 14, 1980, p. 424.

42. 'Jingji guanli tizhi gaige lilun yu shijian wenti taolunhui jiyao' ('Summary of the Discussion on the Theoretical and Practical Problems of the Reform of Economic Management'), *Jingji guanli*, No. 7, 1981, p. 19.

43. Ma Hong, 'Guanyu jingji guanli tizhi gaige de jige wenti' ('Several Problems concerning the Reforms of the Economic Managerial System'), *Jingji yanjiu (Economic Research)*, No. 7, 1981, pp. 11–24.

44. Yang Ximin, 'Dui shuizhi gaige de jidian renshi' ('Some Observations of the Substitution of Taxation for Profit Remittance'), *Caijing kexue*, No. 2, 1983, p. 57.

45. Tian Jiyun, 'Guoying qiye shixing ligaishui shi jingji guanli tizhi de zhongda gaige' ('The Substitution of Taxation for Profit is a Major Reform in the Economic System'), *Xinhua yuebao*, No. 4, 1983, p. 121.

46. Zhao Ziyang, 'Guanyu diliu ge wunian jihua de baogao' ('The Report concerning the Sixth Five-year Plan'), in Quanguo renmin daibiao qahui changwu weiyuanhui bangongting (ed.), *Zhonghua renmin gongheguo diwu jie quanguo renmin daibiao dahui diwu ci huiji wenjian (The Documents of the Fifth Session of the Fifth NPC of the PRC)* (Beijing, Renmin chubanshe, 1983), pp. 112–16.

47. Wang Bingqian, 'Guanyu shixing ligaishui he qiye jishu de gaizao wenti' ('On

the Problem of Implementation of the Substitution of Taxation for Profit Remittance and Technical Renovation of the Enterprise'), *Cai mao jingji* (*Economics of Finance and Trade*), No. 6, 1983, p. 3.

48. 'Caizhengbu guanyu quanguo ligaishui gongzuo huiyi de baogao' ('The Report of the Ministry of Finance concerning the National Working Conference on the Substitution of Taxation for Profit Remittance'), *Guowuyuan gongbao*, No. 11, 1983, pp. 468–74.

49. 'Caizhengbu guanyu guoying qiye ligaishui shixing banfa' ('The Provisional Measure of the Ministry of Finance on the Substitution of Taxation for Profit Remittance in State-owned Enterprise'), *Guowuyuan gongbao*, No. 10, 1983, pp. 475–8.

50. Zhonggong shoudu gangtie gongye gongsi weiyuanhui, 'Gongye jingji zerenzhi de weili suozai' ('The Source of Strength of the Industrial Economic Responsibility System'), *Guangming ribao* (*Guangming Daily*), 21 January 1983, p. 3.

51. 'Caizhengbu guanyu quanguo ligaishui gongzuo huiyi de baogao' ('The Report of the Ministry of Finance concerning the National Work Conference on the Substitution of Taxation for Profit Remittance'), *Guowuyuan gongbao*, No. 11, 1983, p. 472.

52. Wang Peiling, 'Lun guoying qiye lirun fenpei zhidu gaige de fangxiang' ('On the Direction of the Distribution System of Profit in the State-owned Enterprise'), *Caijing wenti yanjiu* (*Research on Financial and Economic Problems*), No. 3, 1982, pp. 36–42; Xia Leshu, 'Zhengque chuli lirun fenpei zhongde maodun wenti' ('Correctly Handling Contradictory Problems in the Distribution of Projects'), *Caijing wenti yanjiu*, No. 2, 1983, pp. 57–62; Liu Mingyuan, 'Guoying qiye ligaishui lilun yiju de tantao' ('Discussion of the Theoretical Foundation of the Substitution of Taxation for Profit Remittance in the State-owned Enterprises'), *Caijing wenti yanjiu*, No. 4, 1983, pp. 37–41; Kang Zhennong, 'Guoying qiye shixing ligaishui shi guojia yu qiye zhijian fenpei guanxi de zhongda gaige' ('The Substitution of Taxation for Profit Remittance in the State-owned Enterprises is a Major Reform in the Relationship of Distribution between the State and Enterprise'), *Caizheng yanjiu*, No. 6, 1983, pp. 15–19; Wang Zhizheng, 'Dui guoying qiye ligaishui wenti de tantao' ('A Discussion concerning the Problems of Substitution of Taxation for Profit Remittance in the State-owned Enterprises'), *Caijing wenti yanjiu*, No. 5, 1983, pp. 59–62; Yuan Yu-sheng, 'Zhengque chuli guojia yu qiye zhijian de lirun fenpei guanxi' ('Correctly Handling the Relationship of Profit Distribution between the State and Enterprises'), *Caijing kexue*, No. 3, 1983, pp. 9–13.

53. Xia Leshu, 'Correctly Handling the Contradictory Problems...', *Caijing wenti yanjiu*, No. 2, 1983, pp. 59–60, note 52 above.

54. Cai Chuhan, 'Jianchi ligaishui de fangxiang' ('Insist on the Direction of the Substitution of Taxation for Profit Remittance'), *Caizheng*, No. 5, 1984, pp. 6–7.

55. 'The Report of the Ministry of Finance...', *Guowuyuan gongbao*, No. 11, 1983, pp. 468–74, note 48 above.

56. 'The Provisional Measure of the Ministry of Finance...', *Guowuyuan gongbao*, No. 10, 1983, pp. 475–8, note 49 above.

57. Wang Bingqian, 'Guanyu guoying qiye shixing ligaishui he gaige gongshang shuizhi de shuoming' ('An Explanation of the Implementation of the Substitution of Taxation for Profit Remittance and the Tax Reform of Industry and Commerce'), *Guowuyuan gongbao*, No. 23, 1984, p. 792.

58. 'Zhuajin shiji, jiji tuixing ligaishu dier bu gaige' ('Grasp the Opportunity, actively Carry out the Second Step of the Substitution of Taxation for Profit Remittance'), *Caizheng*, No. 8, 1984, pp. 2–5.

59. Wang Bingqian, 'An Explanation of the Implementation...', *Guowuyuan gongbao*, No. 23, 1984, p. 792, note 57 above.

60. 'Guoying qiye dier bu ligaishui shixing banfa' ('Provisional Measure for Trial

Implementation of the Second Step of the Substitution of Taxation for Profit Remittance in the State-owned Enterprises'), *Guowuyuan gongbao*, No. 23, 1984, pp. 798–803.

61. Bruce L. Reynolds, 'Reform in Chinese Industrial Management: An Empirical Report', in Joint Economic Committee, the Congress of the United States (ed.), *China under the Four Modernizations* (Washington, DC, United States Government Printing House, 1982), pp. 119–36; Althar Hussain, 'Economic Reforms in Eastern Europe and their Relevance to China', in Stephan Feuchtuang and Althar Hussain (eds.), *The Chinese Economic Reforms* (London, Croom Helm, 1983), pp. 91–120; Paul Hare, 'China's System of Industrial Planning', in Feuchtuang and Hussain (eds.) (1984), pp. 185–223; Cheng Chu-yuan, 'Economic Reform in Mainland China: In Comparison to Yugoslavia and Hungary', *Issues and Studies*, Vol. XIX, No. 9, September 1983, pp. 27–54; Gordon White, 'Socialist Planning and Industrial Management: Chinese Economic Reforms in the Post-Mao Era', *Development and Change*, Vol. 14, 1983, pp. 483–514.

62. Nina Halpern, 'China's Industrial Economic Reform', *Asian Survey*, Vol. XXV, No. 10, October 1985, pp. 998–1012; Christine Wong, 'The Second Phase of Economic Reform in China', *Current History*, October 1985, pp. 263–4; Susan Shirk, 'The Politics of Industrial Reform', in Elizabeth J. Perry and Christine Wong (eds.), *The Political Economy of Reform in Post-Mao China* (Cambridge, Mass., Council on East Asian Studies, Harvard University, 1985), pp. 199–364.

63. Richard M. Cyert and James G. March, *A Behavioral Theory of the Firm* (Englewood Cliffs, New Jersey, Prentice Hall, 1963), pp. 114–27.

64. 'Chengshi jingji tizhi gaige shidian gongzuo suotanhui jiya' ('The Summary of the Conference on the Task of Pilot Programmes in the Urban Economic Reform'), *Guowuyuan gongbao*, No. 11, 1984, pp. 346–52.

65. 'Zhonggong zhongyang guanyu jingji tizhi gaige de jueding' (The Resolution of the Central Committee, CCP, concerning the Reform of the Economic System'), *Dagong bao (Dagong Daily)*, 21 October 1984, pp. 2 and 6.

66. Zhao Ziyang, 'Dangqian de jingji xingshi he jingji tizhi gaige' ('The Current Economic Situation and the Reform of the Economic System'), *Renmin ribao (People's Daily)*, 12 April 1985, p. 1.

67. Zhao Ziyang, 'The Current Economic Situation...', *Renmin ribao*, 12 April 1985, p. 2, note 66 above.

68. Han Shaochu, 'Shilun qiye ligaishui' ('On the Substitution of Taxation for Profit Remittance'), *Caizheng yanjiu*, No. 4, 1984, pp. 32–7.

NOTES TO CHAPTER 10

1. Zhou Enlai, 'Zheng fu gongzuo baogao' ('The Report of Government Work'), in *Zhou Enlai xuanji (The Selected Works of Zhou Enlai)* (Hong Kong, Yishan tushu gongsi, 1976), Vol. I, pp. 73–5.

2. Zhou Enlai, 'Guanyu fazhan guoming jingji dierge wunian jihua de jianyi de baogao' ('The Report on the Proposal of the Second Five-year Plan of the Development of the National Economy'), in *Zhongguo gongchandang diba ci quanguo daibiao dahui wenjian (The Documents of the Eighth Party Congress of the Chinese Communist Party)* (Beijing, Renmin chubanshe, 1980), p. 80, hereafter referred to as *Wenjian* (1980).

3. Mao Zedong, 'Sulian Zhengzhi jingzhi xue dushu biji' ('Notes on the Soviet Textbook of Political Economy'), in *Mao Zedong sixiang wansui 1969 (Long Live*

Mao Zedong's Thought) (n.p., n.p., 1969), pp. 354–5, hereafter referred to as *Wansui* (1969).

4. *Wansui* (1969), pp. 354–5, note 3 above.

5. *Wansui* (1969), pp. 354–5, note 3 above.

6. Charles E. Lindblom, *Politics and Markets* (New York, Basic Books, Inc., 1977), p. 65.

7. David S. Lane, *The Socialist Industrial State* (London, George Allen and Unwin, 1978), pp. 28–43 and 143–74.

8. Alec Nove, *The Soviet Economic System* (London, George Allen and Unwin, 1977), pp. 288–322.

9. Jeremy R. Azrael, 'Varieties of de-Stalinization', in Chalmers Johnson (ed.), *Change in Communist Systems* (Stanford, Calif., Stanford University Press, 1970), pp. 135–52.

10. Maurice Meisner, *Mao's China* (New York, The Free Press, 1977).

11. Harry Harding, *Organizing China* (Stanford, Calif., Stanford University Press, 1981), pp. 1–31.

12. Martin King Whyte, 'Iron Law versus Mass Bureaucracy: Weber, Michels, and the Maoist Vision', in James Chieh Hsiung (ed.) *The Logic of Maoism: Critique and Explication* (New York, Praeger Publishers, 1974), p. 41; Francis Hearn, 'Rationality and Bureaucracy: Maoist Contributions to Marxist Theory of Bureaucracy', *Sociological Quarterly*, No. 19, Winter 1978, p. 39.

13. E.H. Carr, *The Bolshevik Revolution, 1917–1923* (London, Macmillan and Co. Ltd., 1963), Vol. II, pp. 361–2.

14. Carr (1963), p. 362, note 13 above.

15. Alec Nove, *Political Economy and Soviet Socialism* (London, George Allen and Unwin, 1979), p. 75.

16. Benjamin Higgins, *Economic Development* (London, Constable, 1968), p. 453.

17. Carr (1963), pp. 198–227, note 13 above.

18. Carr (1963), p. 189, note 13 above.

19. David A. Dyker, *The Soviet Economy* (London, Crosby Lockwood Staples, 1976), pp. 38–53; Barry M. Richman, *Soviet Management* (Englewood Cliffs, New Jersey, Prentice-Hall Inc., 1965), pp. 150–83; Alec Nove, *The Soviet Economic System* (London, George Allen and Unwin, 1977), pp. 85–119; Joseph S. Berliner, *Factory and Manager in the USSR* (Cambridge, Mass., Harvard University Press, 1957), pp. 182–206, 209–18, 261, and 316–27.

20. Jeremy R. Azrael, *Managerial Power and Soviet Politics* (Cambridge, Mass., Harvard University Press, 1966), p. 117; Gregory Bienstock, Solomon M. Schwarz, and Aaron Yugov, *Management in Russian Industry and Agriculture* (Ithaca and New York, Cornell University Press, 1948), pp. 17–31; Jerry F. Hough, *The Soviet Prefects: The Local Party Organs in Industrial Decision Making* (Cambridge, Mass., Harvard University Press, 1969), pp. 81–9 and 207–8.

21. Berliner (1957), pp. 231–43, note 19 above.

22. Beinstock *et al.* (1948), pp. 44–6, note 20 above; Berliner (1957), pp. 274–8, note 19 above.

23. David Granick, *The Red Executive: A Study of the Organization Man in Russian Industry* (Garden City, New York, Doubleday, 1960), p. 233.

24. Edward Crankshaw, *Khrushchev's Russia* (Baltimore, Penguin Books, 1959), p. 78; Merle Fainsod, 'The Party in the Post-Stalin Era', *Problems of Communism*, Vol. VII, No. 1, January–February 1958, p. 11; Nove (1977), pp. 70–5, note 8 above.

25. Crankshaw (1959), p. 93, note 24 above.

26. Crankshaw (1959), p. 93, note 24 above.

27. Crankshaw (1959), pp. 93–8, note 24 above.

28. Joel J. Schwartz and William R. Keech, 'Group Influence and the Policy Process in the Soviet Union', *American Political Science Review*, Vol. LXII, No. 3, September 1968, pp. 842–3.

29. Nove (1977), pp. 307–10, note 8 above.

30. Dyker (1976), p. 58, note 19 above.

31. Andrzej Korbonski, 'Political Aspects of Economic Reforms in Eastern Europe', in Zbigniew M. Fallenbuche (ed.), *Economic Development in the Soviet Union and Eastern Europe* (New York, Praeger Publishers, 1974), Vol. I, pp. 8–9.

32. Dennison Rusinow, *The Yugoslav Experiment 1948–1974* (London, C. Hurst and Company, 1977), pp. 32–80.

33. Fred Warner Neal, 'Worker Management of Industry in Yugoslavia — how it Operates and how it Is Controlled', in *American Universities Field Staff Reports, Southeast Europe Series*, Vol. 2, No. 3, 1954, p. 1.

34. Josip Broz Tito, 'Fifty Years of Revolutionary Struggle by the Communists of Yugoslavia', *Socialist Thought and Practice*, No. 33, January–March 1969, pp. 15–16.

35. Dusan Bilandzic, *Management of Yugoslav Economy, 1945–1966* (Belgrade, Yugoslav Trade Union, 1967), pp. 61–2.

36. Bilandzic (1967), pp. 63–4, note 35 above.

37. Ljubo Sirc, *The Yugoslav Economy Under Self-management* (London, Macmillan, 1979), pp. 6–9.

38. Fred Warner Neal, 'Decentralized Communism in Action', in *American Universities Field Staff Reports, Southeast Europe Series*, Vol. 4, November 1954, pp. 1–2.

39. Sirc (1979), p. 20, note 37 above.

40. Milovan Djilas, *The New Class: An Analysis of the Communist System* (New York, F.A. Praeger, 1957), pp. 37–44.

41. Dusan Popovic, 'Revolution of Intellectual Work', *Socialist Thought and Practice*, No. 27, July–September 1967, p. 45.

42. Adolf Dragicevic, 'Self-management by the Working Class', *Socialist Thought and Practice*, No. 23, July–September 1966, pp. 82–7.

43. Andrew J. Nathan, 'A Factionalism Model For CCP Politics', *China Quarterly*, No. 53, January–March 1973, pp. 34–66.

44. Michael Oksenberg, 'Occupational Groups in Chinese Society and the Cultural Revolution', in Chang Chun-shu, James Grump, and Rhoads Murphy (eds.), *The Cultural Revolution: 1967 in Review* (Ann Arbor, Center for Chinese Studies, University of Michigan, 1968), pp. 1–45.

45. Tsou Tang, 'The Cultural Revolution and the Chinese Political System', *China Quarterly*, No. 38, April–June 1969, pp. 63–91.

46. David M. Lampton, *The Politics of Medicine in China* (Boulder, Colorado, Westview Press, 1977).

47. H.F. Schurmann, *Ideology and Organisation in Communist China* (Berkeley and Los Angeles, University of California Press, 1968), pp. 17–53.

48. Stephen Andors, *China's Industrial Revolution* (New York, Pantheon Books, 1977).

49. Charles Bettelheim, *Cultural Revolution and Industrial Organization in China, Changes in Management and the Division of Labour* (New York and London, Monthly Review Press, 1974).

50. John Wilson Lewis, *Leadership in Communist China* (Ithaca, New York, Cornell University Press, 1963), pp. 101–44.

51. A. Doak Barnett, *Cadres, Bureaucracy, and Political Power in Communist China* (New York and London, Columbia University Press, 1967), pp. 427–46.

52. Michael Oksenberg, 'Methods of Communication within the Chinese Bureaucracy', *China Quarterly*, No. 57, January–March 1974, pp. 1–39.

53. Parris H. Chang, 'Research Notes in the Changing Loci of Decisions in the Chinese Communist Party', *China Quarterly*, No. 44, October–December 1970, pp. 169–94.

54. Kenneth G. Lieberthal, *Central Documents and Politburo Politics in China* (Michigan Papers in Chinese Studies, No. 33, Ann Arbor, University of Michigan Press, 1978).

55. Harry Harding, *Organizing China* (Stanford, Calif., Stanford University Press, 1981).

56. Audrey G. Donnithorne, *The Budget and Plan in China: Central-Local Economic Relations* (Canberra, Australian National University Press, 1972).

57. Nicholas R. Lardy, *Economic Growth and Distribution in China* (Cambridge, Cambridge University Press, 1978).

58. Thomas Rawski, *China's Transition to Industrialism* (Ann Arbor, University of Michigan Press, 1980).

59. William Brugger, *Democracy and Organization in the Chinese Industrial Enterprise, 1948–1953* (Cambridge, Cambridge University Press, 1976).

60. Graham T. Allison, *Essence of Decision: Explaining the Cuban Missile Crisis* (Boston, Little, Brown and Company, 1971) pp. 10–38; Amitai Etzioni, *The Active Society: A Theory of Societal and Political Processes* (New York, The Free Press, 1968), pp. 249–309.

61. This point has been demonstrated in another paper by this author. See Peter Nan-shong Lee, 'Enterprise Autonomy Policy in Post-Mao China: A Case Study of Policy-making, 1978–1983', *China Quarterly*, No. 105, March 1986, pp. 45–71.

62. Michael D. Cohen, James G. March, and Johan P. Olson, 'A Garbage Can Model of Organizational Choice', *Administrative Science Quarterly*, No. 17, March 1972, pp. 1–25; John W. Kingdom, *Agendas, Alternatives, and Public Policies* (Boston, Little, Brown and Company, 1984) pp. 88–94.

63. Charles E. Lindblom, *The Intelligence of Democracy* (New York, The Free Press, 1965), pp. 182–91.

64. Jurgen Domes, 'The "Gang of Four" and Hua Kuo-feng: Analysis of Political Events in 1975–1976', *China Quarterly*, No. 71, September 1977, pp. 473–97.

65. Nathan, 'A Factionalism Model...', *China Quarterly*, pp. 34–66, note 43 above; Tsou Tang, 'Prolegomenon to the Study of Informal Groups in CCP Politics', *China Quarterly*, No. 65, March 1976, pp. 98–114; 'Andrew J. Nathan replies', *China Quarterly*, No. 65, March 1976, pp. 114–17.

66. Tsou, 'Prolegomenon to the Study...', *China Quarterly*, p. 99, note 65 above.

67. Amitai Etzioni (1968), pp. 282–309, note 60 above.

68. Franklyn Griffiths, 'A Tendency Analysis of Soviet Policy-Making', in H. Gordon Skilling and Franklyn Griffiths (eds.), *Interest Groups in Soviet Politics* (Princeton, Princeton University Press, 1971), p. 358.

69. Andrew J. Nathan, 'Policy Oscillations in the People's Republic of China: A Critique', *China Quarterly*, No. 68, December 1976, pp. 720–33.

70. Lowell Dittmer, '"Line Struggle" in Theory and Practice: The Origins of the Cultural Revolution Reconsidered', *China Quarterly*, No. 72, December 1977, pp. 675–712; Harry Harding, 'Competing Models of the Chinese Communist Policy Process: Toward a Sorting and Evaluation', *Issues and Studies*, February 1984, pp. 19–23.

71. Dorothy J. Solinger, *Chinese Business under Socialism: The Politics of Domestic Commerce, 1949–1980* (Berkeley, Calif., and London, University of California Press, 1984), p. 62.

72. Solinger (1984), pp. 62–3, note 70 above.

Selected Bibliography*

Allison, Graham T., *Essence of Decision: Explaining the Cuban Missile Crisis* (Boston, Little, Brown and Company, 1971).

Andors, Stephen, *China's Industrial Revolution: Politics, Planning and Management, 1949 to the Present* (New York, Pantheon Books, 1977).

Armstrong, John A., *The Soviet Bureaucratic Elite* (New York, Frederick A. Praeger, 1959).

____'Sources of Administrative Behavior: Some Soviet and Western European Comparisons', *American Political Science Review*, Vol. LIX, No. 3, September 1965, pp. 643–55.

____'Party Bifurcation and Elites' Interests', *Soviet Studies*, Vol. XVIII, No. 4, April 1966, pp. 421–3.

Azrael, Jeremy R., *Managerial Power and Soviet Politics* (Cambridge, Mass., Harvard University Press, 1966).

____'Varieties of de-Stalinization', in Chalmers Johnson (ed.), *Communist Systems* (Stanford, Stanford University Press, 1970), pp. 135–52.

Barber, Michael P., *Public Administration* (London, Macdonald and Evans, second edition, 1978).

Barnett, A. Doak, *Cadres, Bureaucracy, and Political Power in Communist China* (New York and London, Columbia University Press, 1967).

____(ed.), *Chinese Communist Politics in Action* (Seattle, University of Washington Press, 1969).

Barry, Robert Farrell (ed.), *Political Leadership in Eastern Europe and the Soviet Union* (Chicago, Aldine, 1970).

Baum, Richard D., *Prelude to the Revolution, Mao, the Party and the Peasant Question, 1962–66* (New York and London, Columbia University Press, 1975).

Bell, Daniel, *The Coming of Post-Industrial Society, a Venture in Social Forecasting* (New York, Basic Books, Inc., 1976).

Bendix, Reinhard, *Work and Authority in Industry, Ideologies of Management in the Course of Industrialization* (New York, Harper & Row, 1956).

____*Max Weber: An Intellectual Portrait* (Garden City, New York, Doubleday & Company Inc., 1962).

Berliner, Joseph S., *Factory and Manager in the USSR* (Cambridge, Mass., Harvard University Press, 1957).

Bettelheim, Charles, *Cultural Revolution and Industrial Organization in*

---

* Works in the English language only.

China, Changes in Management and the Division of Labour (New York and London, Monthly Review Press, 1974).

Bienstock, Gregory, Schwarz, Solomon M., and Yugov, Aaron, *Management in Russian Industry and Agriculture* (Ithaca and New York, Cornell University Press, 1948).

Bilandzic, Dusan, *Management of Yugoslav Economy, 1945–1966* (Belgrade, Yugoslav Trade Union, 1967).

____'Workers' Management of Factories', *Socialist Thought and Practice*, No. 28, October–December 1967, pp. 30–47.

Blumer, Herbert, *Symbolic Interactionism, Perspective and Method* (Englewood Cliffs, New Jersey, Prentice Hall Inc., 1969).

Borison, O.B., and Koloskov, *Soviet – Chinese Relations, 1945–1970* (Bloomington and London, Indiana University Press, 1975).

Bornstein, Morris (ed.), *Economic Planning, East and West* (Cambridge, Mass., Ballinger Publishing Company, 1975).

Bridgham, Philip, 'Factionalism in the Central Committee', in John Wilson Lewis (ed.), *Party Leadership and Revolutionary Power in China* (Cambridge, Cambridge University Press, 1970), p. 206.

Brugger, William, *Democracy and Organization in the Chinese Industrial Enterprise, 1948–1953* (Cambridge, Cambridge University Press, 1976).

Brzezinski, Zbigniew K., and Huntington, Samuel P., *Political Power: USA/USSR* (New York, Viking Press, 1964).

Carr, E.H., *The Bolshevik Revolution, 1917–1923* (London, Macmillan and Co., 1963), Vol. II, pp. 361–2.

Chang, Hsin, 'The 1982–83 Overinvestment Crisis in China', *Asian Survey*, Vol. XXIV, No. 12, December 1984, pp. 1275–1301.

Chang, Parris H., *Power and Policy in China* (University Park and London, Pennsylvania State University Press, 1975).

____'Research Notes on the Changing Loci of Decisions in the Chinese Communist Party', *China Quarterly*, No. 44, October–December 1970, pp. 169–94.

Chao, Kang, *The Rate and Pattern of Industrial Growth in Communist China* (Ann Arbor, University of Michigan Press, 1965).

____*Capital Formation in Mainland China, 1952–1965* (Berkeley, Calif., and London, University of California Press, 1974).

Cheng, Chu-yuan, 'Economic Reform in Mainland China: In Comparison to Yugoslavia and Hungary', *Issues and Studies*, Vol. XIX, No. 9, September 1983, pp. 27–54.

Chung, Chong-wook, *Maoism and Development: The Politics of Industrial Management in China* (Seoul, Seoul National University Press, 1980).

Cohen, Michael D., March, James G., and Olson, Johan P., 'A Garbage Can Model of Organizational Choice', *Administrative Science Quarterly*, No. 17, March 1972, pp. 1–25.

Crankshaw, Edward, *Khrushchev's Russia* (Baltimore, Penguin Books, 1959).

Crozier, Michel, *The Bureaucratic Phenomenon* (Chicago, University of Chicago Press, 1965).

Cyert, Richard M., and March, James G., *A Behavioral Theory of the Firm* (Englewood Cliffs, New Jersey, Prentice-Hall Inc., 1963).

Dahrendorf, Ralf, *Class and Class Conflict in Industrial Society* (Stanford, Stanford University Press, 1966).

Dittmer, Lowell, ' "Line-Struggle" in Theory and Practice: The Origins of the Cultural Revolution Reconsidered', *China Quarterly,* No. 72, December 1977, pp. 675–712.

———'Bases of Power in Chinese Politics: A Theory and Analysis of the Fall of the "Gang of Four" ', *World Politics*, Vol. XXXI, No. 1, October 1978, pp. 27–60.

Djilas, Milovan, *The New Class: An Analysis of the Communist System* (New York, F.A. Praeger, 1957).

Domes, Jurgen, ' "The Gang of Four" and Hua Guo-feng: Analysis of Political Events in 1975–1976', *China Quarterly*, No. 71, September 1977, pp. 473–97.

Donnithorne, Audrey G., *China's Economic System* (London, George Allen and Unwin, 1967).

———*The Budget and Plan in China: Central-Local Economic Relations* (Canberra, Australian National University Press, 1972).

Downs, Anthony, *Inside Bureaucracy* (Boston, Little, Brown and Company, 1967).

Dragicevic, Adolf, 'Self-management by the Working Class', *Socialist Thought and Practice*, No. 23, July–September 1966, pp. 82–7.

Dror, Yehezhel, *Public Policy-making Re-examined* (Bedfordshire, England, Leonard Hill Books, 1973), pp. 163–96.

Dyker, David A., *The Soviet Economy* (London, Crosby Lockwood Staples, 1976), pp. 38–53.

Eckstein, Alexander, *China's Economic Development: The Interplay of Scarcity and Ideology* (Ann Arbor, University of Michigan Press, 1975).

———*China's Economic Revolution* (Cambridge, Cambridge University Press, 1977).

———, Galenson, Walter, and Liu, Ta-chung (eds.), *Economic Trends in Communist China* (Chicago, Aldine, 1968).

Eisenstadt, S. N., *Max Weber on Charisma and Institution Building* (Chicago and London, University of Chicago Press, 1968).

Etzioni, Amitai, *A Comparative Analysis of Complex Organization, On Power, Involvement and their Correlates* (New York, The Free Press, 1961).

———*The Active Society, A Theory of Societal and Political Processes* (New York, The Free Press, 1968).

Fainsod, Merle, 'The Party in the Post-Stalin Era', *Problems of Communism*, Vol. VII, No. 1, January–February 1958, p. 11.

Falkenheim, Victor C., 'Administrative Reform in Post-Mao China', *Pacific Affairs*, No. 53, Spring 1980, pp. 5–29.

Feuchtuang, Stephen, and Hussain, Athar (eds), *The Chinese Economic Reforms* (London, Croom Helm, 1983).

Flamengo, Ante, 'From Statism to Self-management', *Socialist Thought and Practice*, No. 26, January–March 1967, pp. 50–62.

Flathman, Richard E., *The Public Interest* (New York, John Wiley & Sons Inc., 1966).

Fleron, Frederick, jun. (ed.), *Technology and Communist Culture: the Sociocultural Impact of Technology under Socialism* (New York, Praeger Publishers, 1977), pp. 350–1.

Gehlen, Michael P., *The Communist Party of the Soviet Union: A Functional Analysis* (Bloomington, Indiana University Press, 1969).

Ginger, M.G., *Generalization in Ethics* (London, Eyre and Spottiswoode, 1963).

Gottschang, Thomas R., 'Comparative Advantage and Government Policy in the Recent Economic Development of Liaoning Province' (a paper prepared for the Economic Bureaucracy Workshop, 20 July 1984, at the East-West Center, Honolulu, Hawaii).

Gouldner, Alvin, *Patterns of Industrial Bureaucracy* (New York, The Free Press of Glencoe Inc., 1954).

Gramsci, Antonio, *Prison Notebooks*, edited and translated by Quintin Hoare and Geoffrey Nowell Smith (New York, International Publishers, 1975).

Granick, David, *The Red Executive: A Study of the Organization Man in Russian Industry* (Garden City, New York, Doubleday, 1960).

Green, Donald W., 'The Professional Engineer in Russian History', (Discussion paper No. 197, Annual Meeting of the American Association For the Advancement of Slavic Studies, Denver, March 1971).

Hall, Richard H., 'Closed-system, Open-system, and Contingency-choice Perspectives', in Amitai Etzioni and Edward W. Lehman (eds.), *A Sociological Reader on Complex Organizations* (New York, Holt, Rinehart, and Winston, third edition, 1980), pp. 32–43.

Harding, Harry, *Organizing China, the Problem of Bureaucracy 1949–1976* (Stanford, Calif., Stanford University Press, 1981).

——'Competing Models of the Chinese Communist Policy Process: Towards a Sorting and Evaluation', *Issues and Studies*, February 1984, pp. 13–33.

Hearn, Francis, 'Rationality and Bureaucracy: Maoist Contributions to Marxist Theory of Bureaucracy', *Sociological Quarterly,* No. 19, Winter 1978, pp. 37–54.

Hoffmann, Charles, *Work Incentive Practices and Policies in the People's Republic of China, 1953–1965* (New York, State University of New York Press, 1967).

Hough, Jerry F., *The Soviet Prefects: The Local Party Organs in Industrial Decision Making* (Cambridge, Mass., Harvard University Press, 1969).

Howe, Christopher, *Wage Patterns and Wage Policy in Modern China: Political Participation in Developing Countries* (Cambridge, Mass., Harvard University Press, 1976).

Huntington, Samuel P., and Nelson, Joan M., *No Easy Choice: Political Participation in Developing Countries* (Cambridge, Mass., Harvard University Press, 1976).

Johnson, Chalmers (ed.), *Change in Communist Systems* (Stanford, Calif., Stanford University Press, 1970).

Jones, Charles O., *An Introduction to the Study of Public Policy* (Belmont, Calif., Wadsworth, second edition, 1977).

Kardelj, Eduard, 'The Principal Dilemma: Self-management or Statism', *Socialist Thought and Practice*, No. 24, October–December 1966, pp. 3–29.

Kassof, Allen, 'The Administered Society: Totalitarianism without Terror', in F.J. Fleron, jun. (ed.), *Communist Studies and Social Sciences* (Chicago, Rand McNally, 1969), pp. 153–69.

Kerr, Clark, *et al.*, *Industrialism and Industrial Man, The Problem of Labour and Management in Economic Growth* (New York, Oxford University Press, 1964).

Kingdon, John W., *Agendas, Alternatives and Public Policies* (Boston, Little, Brown and Company, 1984).

Klein, Donald W., 'The State Council and the Cultural Revolution', *China Quarterly*, No. 35, July–September 1968, pp. 78–95.

Kolaja, Jiri, *Workers Council: The Yugoslav Experience* (New York, F.A. Praeger, 1966).

Krug, Barbara, 'The Economists in Chinese Politics', in David S.G. Goodman (ed.), *Groups and Politics in the People's Republic of China* (New York, M.E. Sharpe, 1984), pp. 40–67.

Kueh, Y.Y., 'Economic Reform in China at the *xian* Level', *China Quarterly*, No. 96, December 1983, pp. 665–88.

Lampton, David M., *The Politics of Medicine in China, the Policy Process, 1949–1977* (Boulder, Colorado, Westview Press, 1977).

Lane, David S., *The Socialist Industrial State, Towards a Political Sociology of State Socialism* (London, George Allen and Unwin, 1978).

Lardy, Nicholas R., *Economic Growth and Distribution in China* (Cambridge, Cambridge University Press, 1978).

Lee, Peter Nan-shong, 'A Comparative Study of Managerial Personnel: Soviet Russia (1981–   ), Communist China (1949–   ) and Yugoslavia (1945–   )' (Unpublished paper, 1974).

_____'China's Industrial Bureaucracy, 1949–1973' (Unpublished Ph.D. dissertation, University of Chicago, 1975).

_____'The Gang of Four: Radical Politics and Modernization in China', in Steve S.K. Chin (ed.), *The Gang of Four: First Essays after the Fall* (Hong Kong, Centre of Asian Studies, University of Hong Kong, 1977), pp. 69–106.

_____'Modernization and Managerial Power in China 1956–1966', in Steve S.K. Chin (ed.), *Modernization in China* (Hong Kong, Centre of Asian Studies, University of Hong Kong, 1979), pp. 71–89.

_____'Industrial Development and Mass-line Leadership in China, 1956–1966', in Ngok Lee and Chi-keung Leung (eds.), *China: Development and Challenge* (Hong Kong, Centre of Asian Studies, University of Hong Kong, 1979), pp. 101–26.

_____'The Modernization Programmes in the "Three Poisonous Weeds"', in Edward K.Y. Chen and Steve S.K. Chin (eds.), *Development and Change in China* (Hong Kong, Centre of Asian Studies, University of Hong Kong, 1981), pp. 31–53.

_____'Enterprise Autonomy Policy in Post-Mao China: A Case Study of Policy-making, 1978–1983', *China Quarterly,* No. 105, March 1986, pp. 45–71.

Lewis, John Wilson, *Leadership in Communist China* (Ithaca, New York, Cornell University Press, 1963).

_____'Leader, Commissar and Bureaucrat: The Chinese Political System in the Last Days of the Revolution', in Ping-ti Ho and Tsou Tang (eds.), *China in Crisis* (Chicago, University of Chicago Press, 1968), Vol. I, Book Two, pp. 449–500.

_____(ed.), *Party Leadership and Revolutionary Power in China* (Cambridge, Cambridge University Press, 1970).

Lieberthal, Kenneth G., *A Research Guide to Central Party and Government Meeting in China, 1949–1975* (White Plains, New York, International Arts and Science Press, 1976).

_____*Central Documents and Politburo Politics in China* (Michigan Papers in Chinese Studies, No. 33, Ann Arbor, University of Michigan Press, 1978).

Lin, Cyril Chihren, 'The Reinstatement of Economics in China Today', *China Quarterly*, No. 85, March 1981, pp. 1–48.

Lindbeck, John M. H. (ed.), *China: Management of a Revolutionary Society* (Seattle and London, University of Washington Press, 1971).

Lindblom, Charles E., *The Intelligence of Democracy, Decision-making through Mutual Adjustment* (New York, The Free Press, 1965).

_____*Politics and Markets, the World's Political Systems* (New York, Basic Books Inc., 1977).

_____'The Sociology of Planning: Thought and Social Interaction', in Morris Bornstein (ed.), *Economic Planning, East and West* (Cambridge, Mass., Ballinger Publishing Company, 1975), pp. 23–67.

Loucks, William N., 'Workers' Self-government in Yugoslav Industry', *World Politics*, Vol. XI, No. 1, October 1958, pp. 68–82.

Manion, Melanie, 'The Cadre Management System, Post-Mao: the Appointment , Promotion, Transfer and Removal of Party and State Leaders', *China Quarterly*, No. 102, June 1985, pp. 203–33.

Mao Zedong, *Collected Works of Mao Zedong* (Beijing, Foreign Languages Press, 1967).

March, James G., and Simon, Herbert A., *Organizations* (New York, John Wiley & Sons Inc., 1958).

Maslow, Abraham, *Motivation and Personality* (New York, Harper & Brothers, 1954).

Meisner, Maurice, *Mao's China, A History of the People's Republic of China* (New York, The Free Press, 1977).

Moody, Peter R., jun., *The Politics of the Eighth Party Congress of the Central Committee of the Communist Party of China* (Hamden, Connecticut, The Shoe String Press Inc., 1973).

Mouzelis, Nicos P., *Organization and Bureaucracy, an Analysis of Modern Theories* (Chicago, Aldine Publishing Company, 1967).

Nathan, Andrew J., 'A Factionalism Model For CCP Politics', *China Quarterly*, No. 53, January–March 1973, pp. 34–66.

____'Policy Oscillations in the People's Republic of China: A Critique', *China Quarterly*, No. 68, December 1976, pp. 720–33.

Neal, Fred Warner, 'Worker Management of Industry in Yugoslavia — how it Operates and how it Is Controlled', *American Universities Field Staff Reports, Southeast Europe Series,* Vol. 3, pp. 1–11.

____'Decentralized Communism in Action', *American Universities Field Staff Reports, Southeast Europe Series*, Vol. 4, November 1954, pp. 1–2.

____and Fisk, Winston M., 'Yugoslavia: Towards a Market Socialism', *Problems of Communism*, Vol. XV, No. 6, November–December 1966, pp. 28–37.

Nee, Victor, and Mozingo, David (eds.), *State and Society in Contemporary China* (Ithaca and London, Cornell University Press, 1983).

Nove, Alec, *Political Economy and Soviet Socialism* (London, George Allen and Unwin, 1979).

____*The Soviet Economic System* (London, George Allen and Unwin, 1977).

____'The Industrial Planning System: Reforms in Prospect', *Soviet Studies*, Vol. XIV, No. 1, July 1962, pp. 1–15.

Oksenberg, Michael, 'The Institutionalization of the Chinese Communist Revolution', *China Quarterly,* No. 36, October–December 1968, pp. 61–92.

____'Occupation Groups in Chinese Society and the Cultural Revolution', in Chang Chun-shu, James Grump, and Rhoads Murphy (eds.), *The Cultural Revolution: 1967 in Review* (Ann Arbor, Center for Chinese Studies, University of Michigan, 1968), pp. 1–45.

_____'Policy Making under Mao, 1949–1968: An Overview', in John M.H. Lindbeck, *China: Management of a Revolutionary Society* (Seattle and London, University of Washington Press, 1971).

_____'Methods of Communication within the Chinese Bureaucracy', *China Quarterly,* No. 57, January–March 1974, pp.1–39.

Perkins, Dwight H., 'Industrial Planning and Management', in Alexander Eckstein, Walter Galenson, and Ta-chung Liu (eds.), *Economic Trends in Communist China* (Chicago, Aldine Publishing Company, 1968), pp. 597–635.

_____*China's Modern Economy in Historical Perspective* (Stanford, Calif., (ed.) Stanford University Press, 1975).

Perrow, Charles, *Complex Organization: A Critical Essay* (Glenview, Illinois, Scott, Foresman and Company, 1972), pp. 145–76.

Perry, Elizabeth J., and Wong, Christine (eds.), *The Political Economy of Reform in Post-Mao China* (Cambridge, Mass., and London, Council on East Asian Studies, Harvard University, 1985).

Popovic, Dusan, 'Revolution of Intellectual Work', *Socialist Thought and Practice*, No. 27, July–September 1967, p. 45.

Pye, Lucian W., *The Spirit of Chinese Politics, a Psychological Study of the Authority in Political Development* (Cambridge, Mass., MIT Press, 1968).

Rawski, Thomas G., *China's Transition to Industrialism, Producer Goods and Economic Development of the Twentieth Century* (Ann Arbor, University of Michigan Press, 1980).

Reynolds, Bruce L., 'Reform in Chinese Industrial Management: An Empirical Report', in Joint Economic Committee, the Congress of the United States (ed.), *China under the Four Modernizations (Part I)* (Washington, DC, United States Government Printing House, 1982), pp. 119–37.

Richman, Barry M., *Soviet Management with Significant American Comparison* (Englewood Cliffs, New Jersey, Prentice-Hall Inc., 1965).

_____*Industrial Society in Communist China* (New York, Random House, 1969).

Rigby, T.H., 'Traditional, Market, and Organizational Societies and the USSR', *World Politics*, Vol. XVI, No. 4, July 1964, pp. 539–67.

Riskin, Carl, 'Maoism and Motivation: Work Incentive in China', *Bulletin of Concerned Asian Scholars*, Vol. 5, No. 1, July 1973, pp. 10–24.

Robinson, Thomas W. (ed.), *The Cultural Revolution in China* (Berkeley, Calif., and Los Angeles, University of California Press, 1971).

Rusinow, Dennison, *The Yugoslav Experiment 1948–1974* (London, C. Hurst and Company, 1977).

Ryavec, Karl W., 'Soviet Industrial Managers, their Superiors, and Economic Reform: A Study of an Attempt at Planned Behavioural Change', *Soviet Studies*, Vol. XXI, No. 2, October 1969, pp. 208–29.

Schram, Stuart R., *Authority, Participation and Cultural Change in China* (Cambridge, Cambridge University Press, 1973).

Schran, Peter, 'The Yen'an Origins of Current Economic Policies', in Dwight Perkins (ed.), *China's Modern Economy in Historical Perspective* (Stanford, Stanford University Press, 1975), pp. 279–337.

Schurmann, Franz, 'Politics and Economics in Russia and China', in Donald W. Treadgold, *Soviet and Chinese Communism* (London and Seattle, University of Washington Press, 1967), pp. 297–326.

____*Indeology and Organisation in Communist China* (Berkeley, Calif., and London, University of California Press, 1968).

Schurmann, H.F., 'Organizational Contrasts between Communist China and the Soviet Union', in Kurt London (ed.), *Unity and Contradiction: Major Aspects of Sino-Soviet Relations* (New York, Frederick A. Praeger Inc., 1962), pp.79–81.

Schwartz, Joel J., and Keech, William R., 'Group Influence and the Policy Process in the Soviet Union', *American Political Science Review*, Vol. LXII, No. 3, September 1968, pp. 841–51.

Seldon, Mark, *The Yenan Way in Revolutionary China* (Cambridge, Mass., Harvard University Press, 1971).

Shirk, Susan, 'The Politics of Industrial Reform', in Elizabeth J. Perry and Christine Wong (eds.), *The Political Economy of Reform in Post-Mao China* (Cambridge, Mass., Council on East Asian Studies, 1985), pp. 195–222.

____'Recent Chinese Labour Policies and the Transformation of Industrial Organization in China', *China Quarterly*, No. 85, December 1981, pp. 575–93.

Shonfield, Andrew, *Modern Capitalism: The Changing Balance of Public and Private Power* (New York and London, Oxford University Press, 1965).

Shoup, Paul, 'Comparing Communist Nations: Prospects for an Empirical Approach', *American Political Science Review*, Vol. LXII, No. 1, March 1968, pp. 185–204.

Simon, Herbert A., *Administrative Behavior, A Study of Decison-making Process in Administrative Organization* (New York, The Free Press, 1957).

____, Smithburg, Donald W., *et al.*, *Public Administration* (New York, Alfred A. Knopf, 1974).

Sirc, Ljubo, *The Yugoslav Economy under Self-management* (London, Macmillan, 1979).

Skilling, H. Gordon, 'Interest Groups and Communist Politics', *World Politics*, Vol. XVII, No. 3, April 1966, pp. 435–57.

____'Soviet and Communist Politics: A Comparative Approach', *Journal of Politics*, Vol. 22, No. 2, May 1966, pp. 300–13.

____and Griffiths, Franklyn (eds.), *Interest Groups in Soviet Politics* (Princeton, Princeton University Press, 1971).

Skinner, George William, and Winkler, Edwin, 'Compliance Succession in Rural Communist China, A Cyclical Theory', in Amitai Etzioni (ed.), *A Sociological Reader in Complex Organizations* (New York, Holt, Rinehart, and Winston, second edition, 1969).

Smith, Adam, *The Wealth of Nations* (New York, Random House Inc., 1937).

Solinger, Dorothy J., *Regional Government and Political Integration in Southeast China, 1949–1954: a Case Study* (Berkeley, Calif., and London, University of California Press, 1977).

——'Economic Reform via Reformulation in China: Where Do the Rightist Ideas Come From?', *Asian Survey*, Vol. XXI, No. 9, 1981, pp. 947–61.

——'The Fifth National People's Congress and the Process of Policymaking: Reform, Readjustment, and the Opposition', *Issues and Studies*, August 1982, pp. 63–106.

——*Chinese Business under Socialism: The Politics of Domestic Commerce, 1949–1980* (Berkeley, Calif., and London, University of California Press, 1984).

Solomon, Richard H., *Mao's Revolution and the Chinese Political Culture* (Berkeley, Calif., and London, University of California Press, 1971).

Starr, John Bryan, 'From the 10th Party Congress to the Premiership of Hua Guo-feng: the Significance of the Colour of the Cat', *China Quarterly*, No. 67, September 1976, pp. 457–88.

Stepan, Alfred, *State and Society: Peru in Comparative Perspective* (Princeton, New Jersey, Princeton University Press, 1978).

Strauss, Anselm (ed.), *George Herbert Mead on Social Psychology* (Chicago, University of Chicago Press, 1965).

Sun, Kungtu C., *The Economic Development of Manchuria in the First Half of the Twentieth Century* (Cambridge, Mass., Harvard University Press, 1969).

Thompson, James D., *Organizations in Action* (New York, McGraw Hill Book Co., 1967).

Tito, Josip Broz, 'Fifty Years of Revolutionary Struggle by the Communists of Yugoslavia', *Socialist Thought and Practice*, No. 33, January–March 1969, pp. 15–16.

——'Power Must Remain in the Hands of the Working Class', *Socialist Thought and Practice*, No. 26, April–June 1967, pp. 3–29.

Tonkovic, Stipe, 'The Humanistic and Ethical Aspect of Worker Management', *Socialist Thought and Practice*, No. 18, April–June 1965, pp. 65–89.

Townsend, James R., *Politics in China* (Boston and Toronto, Little, Brown and Company, 1980).

Tucker, Robert C., 'On the Comparative Study of Communism', *World Politics*, Vol. XIX, No. 2, January 1967, pp. 242–57.

Tsou Tang, 'The Cultural Revolution and the Chinese Political System', *China Quarterly*, No. 38, April–June 1969, pp. 63–91.

——'The Values of the Chinese Revolution', in Michael Oksenberg, *China's Developmental Experience, Proceedings of the Academy of Political Science,* No. 31, March 1973 (New York, Praeger, 1973).

——'Mao Tse-tung Thought, the Last Struggle for Succession, and the post-Mao Era', *China Quarterly*, No. 71, September 1977, pp. 498–527.

——'Revolution, Reintegration, and Crisis in Communist China: Framework for Analysis', in Ping-ti Ho and Tsou Tang (eds.), *China in Crisis* (Chicago, University of Chicago Press, 1968), Vol. I, pp. 277–347.

Vogel, Ezra F., 'From Friendship to Comradeship: The Change in Personal Relations in Communist China', *China Quarterly*, No. 21, January–March 1965, pp. 46–60.

——*Canton under Communism: Programs and Politics in a Provincial Capital, 1949–1968* (Cambridge, Mass., Harvard University Press, 1969).

Walder, Andrew G., 'Industrial Organization and Socialist Development in China', *Modern China*, April 1979, pp. 233–72.

——'Organized Dependency and Cultures of Authority in Chinese Industry', *Journal of Asian Studies*, Vol. XLIII, No. 1, November 1983, pp. 51–76.

Ward, Benjamin, 'Workers' Management in Yugoslavia', *The Journal of Political Economy*, Vol. LXV, October 1957, pp. 373–86.

Weber, Max, *The Theory of Social and Economic Organization*, translated by A.M. Henderson and Talcott Parsons (New York, The Free Press, 1947).

White, Gordon, 'Socialist Planning and Industrial Management: Chinese Economic Reforms in the Post-Mao Era', *Development and Change*, Vol. 14, 1983, pp. 483–514.

Whiteley, C.H., 'Rationality in Morals', *Proceedings of the Aristotelian Society*, New Series, Vol. L, 1949–50.

Whyte, Martin King, 'Bureaucracy and Modernization in China: The Maoist Critique', *American Sociological Review*, Vol. 38, No. 2, April 1973, pp. 149–63.

——'Iron Law versus Mass Democracy: Weber, Michels and the Maoist Vision', in James Chieh Hsiung (ed.), *The Logic of 'Maoism': Critique and Explication* (New York, Praeger Publishers, 1974), pp. 37–61.

——*Small Groups and Political Rituals in China* (Berkeley, Calif., University of California Press, 1974).

Womack, Brantly, 'Politics and Epistemology in China since Mao', *China Quarterly*, No. 88, December 1979, pp.768–9.

Wong, Christine, 'The Second Phase of Economic Reform in China', *Current History*, October 1985, pp. 263–4.

Wong Foh-shen, 'China's Industrial Production, 1931–1946', in Ramon H.

Myers (ed.), *Selected Essays in Chinese Economic Development* (New York and London, Garland Publishing Inc., 1980).

Wortzel, Larry M., 'Incentive Mechanisms and Remuneration in China: Policies of the Eleventh Central Committee', *Asian Survey*, Vol. 21, No. 9, September 1981, pp. 961–76.

Wylie, Raymond F., 'Shanghai Dockers in the Cultural Revolution: The Interplay of Political and Economic Issues', in Christopher Howe (ed.), *Shanghai: Revolution and Development in an Asian Metropolis* (Cambridge, Cambridge University Press, 1981), pp. 110–24.

Chronology

1948

3–4 August   Chen Yun, Chairman-elect of the All-China Federation of Labour, delivered a speech on 'The General Mission of the Labour Movement in Contemporary China' at the Sixth National Labour Congress.

7 August   The North-east Bureau of the Central Committee (CC) of the Chinese Communist Party (CCP) made 'The Decision concerning Staff Problems in Public Enterprises' (drafted by Chen Yun).

August   Chen Yun, Director of the Financial and Economic Commission of the North-east People's Government, filed the Report entitled 'The Financial and Economic Task on the Agenda' to the Central Committee of the Chinese Communist Party.

1949

16 December   The Government Administration Council (GAC) passed 'The Organic Law of the Regional Government Councils'.

1950

February   The Government Administration Council (GAC) promulgated 'The General Regulations of the Provincial People's Governments in the Administrative Regions'.

13 February   The GAC held the National Financial and Economic Conference, discussing the centralization of power over revenue and expenditure, personnel establishment, trades, and banking.

28 February   The Financial and Economic Commission (FEC), GAC, promulgated 'The Directive regarding the Establishment of the Factory Management Committee in State and Public Enterprises', requesting the establishment of the Factory Management Committee

and the Congress of Representatives of Workers and Staff to practise managerial democracy.

21 March   The Fuel Industry Ministry issued 'The Circular concerning the Abolition of the Gang-boss System in Coal-mines throughout the Country'.

20 April   The North-east Bureau, the Central Committee, CCP, issued 'The Directive concerning Uniting with Technician and Staff Members in Public Enterprises'.

6 June   Gao Gang, Chairman of the North-east People's Government, Director of the North-east Military Administrative Committee, and Secretary of the North-east Bureau, Central Committee, CCP, delivered a speech entitled 'Stand on the Forefront of the Economic Construction in North-east China', giving a briefing on the economic situation in North-east China, and also instructions and recommendations on industrial management.

6–9 June   The Third Plenum of the Seventh Party Congress, CCP, was convened; Mao Zedong delivered the speech 'Struggle for Basic Improvement of the National Financial Conditions'; Chen Yun made a 'Report on Financial and Economic Task'.

16 June   The GAC announced 'The Directive concerning the Relief of the Unemployed Workers'.

17 June   The Ministry of Labour, GAC, issued 'The Provisional Measures of the Unemployed Workers'.

29 June   The GAC promulgated 'The Labour Union Law of the People's Republic of China'.

9 July   The North-east People's Government issued 'The Directive concerning Several Problems in Wage Readjustments of Workers and Technicians for the Implementation of the Eight-grade Wage System'.

24 July   The Financial and Economic Commission, GAC, made 'The Decision on the Work Relationship between the Labour Bureaux and Local State Enterprises of Provincial and Municipal Governments'.

25 December   The Textiles Industry Ministry, GAC, made 'The Decision on the Establishment and Strengthening of the Production Responsibility System', including provisions pertaining to the administrative responsibility system of managers and staff members (or one-man management).

29 December   The GAC passed 'The Provisional Regulation of Private Enterprises'.

1951

12 January   The GAC issued 'The Supplementary Directive concerning the Unemployed Intellectual'.

26 January   The Ministry of Labour, GAC, made 'Amendments to the Implementation Measures of the Labour Insurance Regulation of the People's Republic of China'.

January   The North-east People's Government issued 'The Directive concerning the Task of Auditing Working Capital in the Saving and Production-increase Movement'.

January   The North-east People's Government promulgated 'The Provisional Regulation of the Management of Fixed Assets in State Enterprises in the North-east Region'.

12 February   The Financial and Economic Commission, GAC, sponsored the 'National Conference of Industry', in order to implement reforms of enterprise management and introduce planning management, the economic accounting system, the factory director responsibility system, as well as the eight-grade wage system and the piece-rate wage system.

25 February   The GAC promulgated 'The Labour Insurance Regulations of the People's Republic of China'.

27 February   The Ministry of Labour announced 'The Regulation concerning the Registration Procedures of Labour Insurance'.

1 March   Li Lishan, Minister of the Labour Ministry, provided 'An Explanation concerning the Draft Regulation of the Labour Insurance Regulation of the PRC'.

7 March   The Financial and Economic Commission, GAC, promulgated 'The Regulation of the Composition of the Total Wage Bill'.

29 March   The GAC announced its policy of classification of revenue and expenditure on the basis of a three-tier managerial system (the centre, the administrative region, and the province) and a three-tier taxation system.

20 April   The Ministry of Labour announced 'The Accounting System of the Labour Insurance Fund' (amended 21 February 1953).

4 May   A meeting of the GAC passed 'The Decision on Dividing Managerial Powers over Financial and Economic Tasks between the Centre and Localities', to authorize the delegation of power over State enterprises and financial and economic management to the localities.

9 May   The Ministry of Labour, GAC, provided 'An Explanation of Several Problems concerning the Regulation of the Composition of the Total Wage Bill'.

15 May   The Ministry of Labour, GAC, announced 'The Provisional Regulations on the Recruitment of Workers and Staff in Various Places'.

May   The GAC made 'The Decision concerning the Division of Managerial Jurisdiction over Financial and Economic Tasks between the Centre and Localities'.

May   The GAC made 'The Decision concerning the Production and Construction of State Industry in 1951'.

June   The Textiles Industry Bureau, North-east People's Government, released the document 'The Summary of Experience in the Economic Accounting System'.

June   The Heavy Industry Ministry issued 'The Directive on the Implementation of the Enterprise Accounting System'.

25 July   The GAC issued 'The Directive concerning the Relief of Unemployed Teachers and School Students'.

7 September   The North-east Bureau of the Central Committee, CCP, passed 'The Resolution concerning the Leadership System of Public Enterprises'.

November   The Financial and Economic Commission, GAC, sponsored the 'National Conference of Planning', and decided to carry out planned production in 29 major categories of industrial products.

1952

13 January   The Financial and Economic Commission (FEC), GAC, issued 'The Provisional Measure concerning the Task of Basic Construction', centring on the establishment of centralized planning management in basic construction.

15 January   The FEC, GAC, issued 'The Provisional Measure of the Retention of the Enterprise Bonus Fund in State Enterprises'.

January   The FEC, GAC, issued 'The Provisional Measure of Drafting the National Economic Plan', prescribing the planning procedure on the basis of the central ministries and the administrative regions, assigning to the FEC responsibility for the National

Economic Plan, and defining factories and enterprises as basic units of planning.

6 August   The GAC announced 'The Decision concerning Labour and Employment', proposing the establishment of labour and employment committees in various localities and unified operations for the registration, training, and remoulding of the unemployed, and planned arrangement of unemployment.

1953

1 January   The beginning of the First Five-year Plan.

19 April   The Central Committee, CCP, endorsed and transmitted the FEC's 'Report concerning Managerial Problems in State Industrial and Mining Enterprises', proposing to formulate production plans in enterprises, to carry out managerial reform, and to introduce an economic accounting system.

25 April   The Central Committee, CCP, and GAC promulgated the 'Outline of the 1953 National Economic Plan', requiring the strengthening of the planning and statistical apparatus and the establishment of responsibility systems in industrial safety, quality control, construction projects, and so on.

28 May   The Heavy Industry Ministry issued 'The Directive concerning the Establishment of the Responsibility System in Mining and Manufacturing Industry'.

1954

4 March   The Central Committee, CCP, endorsed and circulated the FEC's 'Report concerning the Planning Conference for the Expansion of Public and Private Industries'.

5 September   The GAC promulgated 'The Provisional Regulation of Public–Private Joint Industrial Enterprises'.

20 September   The First National People's Congress was convened in Beijing; the Constitution of the PRC was passed and promulgated; the GAC was converted into the State Council; and the administrative regions were abolished as a major tier in the hierarchy of the State apparatus.

1955

12 April   The Central Committee, CCP, endorsed and circulated the papers of 'The Second National Planning Conference', demanding the strengthening of planning tasks and an interconnection and balance among economic sectors, localities, and types of ownership.

31 August   The State Council promulgated 'The Decree of a Change to a Wage System and Monetary Payment for all Personnel in State Organs'.

29 October   Mao Zedong, Zhou Enlai, and Chen Yun spoke on the Socialist reform of private industry and commerce in a forum of the All-China Federation of Industry and Commerce, signalling the complete transformation of private enterprises into State enterprises.

1956

10 January   Completion of public–private joint enterprises in approximately 50 cities.

14 April   The National Wage Conference was convened.

25 April   Mao Zedong delivered the speech 'On the Ten Great Relationships' at the Enlarged Conference of the Political Bureau (Politburo), Central Committee, CCP.

May–August   The State Council sponsored the National Conference on Economic Institutions; it also passed three resolutions for the improvement of institutions in industry, commerce, and finance.

25 September   Li Xuefeng, Head of the Department of Industry and Transport, CC, CCP, delivered a speech to the Eighth Party Congress, CCP, entitled 'Strengthen the Party's Leadership over Enterprises and thoroughly Carry out the Mass-line'.

15–27 September   The Eighth Party Congress of the CCP was held. 'The Proposal concerning the Second Five-year Plan of the Development of the National Economy' was passed; Zhou Enlai spoke on the improvement of economic institutions and Chen Yun discussed the problems to be faced after the completion of the Socialist transformation.

16 October   The State Council passed 'The Regulation concerning

Several Problems of Wage Reform in New Public–Private Joint Enterprises'.

1957

20 September–9 October   The Third Plenum of the Eighth Party Congress was convened and two reports were presented: Zhou Enlai's report on labour and wages, labour insurance, and welfare; and Chen Yun's 'Report on the Problems concerning the Improvement of the Administrative and Managerial Institutions of the State', including the increase of agricultural production. The Plenum passed the following policy papers: 'The Outline for the Development of National Agriculture, 1956–67 (Draft)' and drafts on the improvement of economic institutions in industry, commerce, and finance.

15 October   Having secured the approval of the Standing Committee of the National People's Congress, the State Council promulgated the following policy papers: 'The Regulation concerning the Improvement of Industrial Managerial Institutions (Draft)', 'The Regulation concerning the Improvement of Financial Management (Draft)', and the 'Regulation concerning the Improvement of Commercial Managerial Institutions (Draft)'.

1958

Early March–26 March   The Central Committee, CCP, convened the Chengdu Conference, at which there were extensive discussions on the reform of managerial systems in the fields of planning, industry, basic construction, material supply, finance, pricing, commerce, and education, and the delegation of power to the local level was stressed.

5 April   The Central Committee made several rulings concerning co-ordination between enterprise units and the need for balance in the planning process, adopted the 'double-track' system of planning, and lessened central control in the planning process.

11 April   The State Council, after extensive discussion, passed the following policy papers: 'Several Rulings concerning the Decentralization of Industrial Enterprises', the 'Circular concerning the Change of Local Financial Discretion over Revenue and

Expenditure, the Income and Disbursement Categories, and the Proportion of Revenue-sharing according to a Fixed Five-year-term System'.

26 April   Wong Hefeng delivered a speech on 'Major Reform in Enterprise Management', summarizing the experience of mass-oriented management in Heilongjiang province.

22 May   The State Council promulgated 'The Regulation concerning the Implementation of the Enterprise Profit-retention System'.

2 June   The Central Committee, CCP, issued the 'Regulation concerning the Decentralization of Enterprise Units, Business Units, and Technical Manpower'. It required the downward transfer of all enterprises in the fields of industry, transport, commerce, and agriculture before 15 June.

9 June   The State Council promulgated 'The Regulation concerning the Improvement of the Taxation System', delegating the administration of six types of taxation to local government and a portion of industrial and commercial tax to the local level.

5 July   The State Council promulgated 'Several Rulings concerning the Improvement of the Financial System of Basic Construction', introducing the 'contracting-out' responsibility system of capital investment.

24 September   The State Council passed the 'Regulation concerning the Improvement of Planning Management', 'Several Rulings on the Improvement of the Material Supply System', and 'Several Rulings concerning Further Improvement of Financial Management and the Banking Systems of Loans and Credits (Draft)'.

1959

January   The Ministry of Finance and the People's Bank of China announced the policy paper entitled 'The Supplementary Regulation concerning the Improvement of the Supply of Working Capital in State-owned Enterprises'.

29 June   Comrade Mao Zedong had an exchange of views on economic tasks with several leaders in Lushan, admitting that four powers (personnel, finance, commerce, and industry) had been decentralized excessively and at a rash pace, and this had resulted in some chaos; accordingly he stressed the need for unified command, centralized leadership, and recentralization of power.

2 June–16 August   The Enlarged Conference of the Politburo and the Eighth Plenum of the Eighth Party Congress were held, starting with a 'summing-up' of experience and ending with a critique of the rightist opportunistic tendency.

15 October   The Central Committee and the State Council decided to implement the dual command system over mining enterprises, with ministries playing the key role, as from 1 January 1960.

1960

22 March   Mao Zedong endorsed 'The Report concerning Technical Reform and the Technical Revolutionary Movement on the Industrial Front', filed by the Secretary of the Anshan Municipal Party Committee.

1961

14–18 January   The Ninth Plenum of the Eighth Party Congress was convened; it proposed the guideline of 'readjustment, consolidation, enrichment, and upgrading', and, in the meantime, it decided to establish six bureaux of the Central Committee, CCP, in North China, North-east China, East China, Central-south China, South-west China, and North-east China.

15 January   The Central Committee, CCP, and the State Council approved and circulated 'The Opinion of the Ministry of Finance concerning the Improvement of Financial Systems', which recommended the centralization of financial power to the centre, the administrative regions, provinces, municipalities, and special districts; the adoption of annual revenue-sharing on the basis of the total volume of revenue as well as a reduction in profit retention by enterprises; the change from the contracting-out financial responsibility system to appropriation and supervision by the banks.

20 January   The Central Committee, CCP, formulated 'Several Rulings concerning the Readjustment of Managerial Institutions', which recommended the recentralization of enterprises, the unified management of the defence industry and the railway system, as well as the implementation of the principle of the 'whole country as a

chessboard' (that is, overall arrangement) in production and basic construction.

20 January   The Central Committee, CCP, endorsed the recommendation by the Ministry of Finance to reduce the retained profit of State-owned enterprises from 13.2 per cent to 6.9 per cent of total realized profit.

15 September   The Central Committee, CCP, issued the 'Directive concerning the Current Industrial Problems', requiring the centralization of managerial power over industry to the central level (including the regional bureau level) and making a unified arrangement and allocation of manpower, finance, and material supply throughout the country.

15 September   The Central Committee, CCP, issued the 'Regulation of Tasks in State-owned Industrial Enterprises (Draft)' (or the 'Seventy Articles').

1962

11 January–7 February   The Central Committee, CCP, convened the Enlarged Work Conference (or the 'Seven Thousand People Conference') at which Mao Zedong and Zhou Enlai, among others, made important speeches; Liu Shaoqi delivered a written report on behalf of the Central Committee with regard to the failings of the Great Leap Forward and remedies.

10 March   The Central Committee, CCP, made the 'Decision concerning the Rigorous Adoption of Centralization and Unified Management of the Task in Banking, and of Tight Control over Monetary Volume' (or the 'Six Articles on Banking').

21 April   The Central Committee, CCP, issued the 'Decision concerning Rigorous Control in Financial Management' (or the 'Six Articles on Finance').

1 May   The Central Committee, CCP, endorsed and circulated the State Economic Commission Party Group's 'Opinions concerning the Adoption of Centralized, Unified, and Total Management of Tasks in Material Supply'.

31 May   The Central Committee, CCP, endorsed and circulated a report by the State Planning Commission concerning the strengthening of the management of basic construction and reaffirming the procedures of review and approval over medium and large-scale construction projects.

27 September   The Central Committee, CCP, made the 'Decision concerning the Problems of Work in Commerce'.

1963

16 March   The Central Committee, CCP, decided to establish the China Tobacco General Corporation, which was given a monopoly over the procurement, production, and distribution of tobacco.

1964

17 August   The Central Committee, CCP, decided to carry out a trial implementation of socialist trusts in 12 branches of industry on the basis of the report filed by the State Economic Commission.

21 September–19 October   The National Planning Conference recommended a gradual decentralization of managerial power in 19 categories of non-industrial basic construction to the local level, in addition to the 'five small industries'.

1965

14 April   The Central Committee, CCP, endorsed, in principle, 'The Outline of Tasks in Industry and Transport for 1965', recommending the streamlining and simplification of factory headquarters and functional departments, the abolition of staff organizations within workshops, and the emphasis on a service orientation in functional departments, in direct relationship to the shifts and teams in large industrial and mining enterprises; it also proposed the abolition of workshops, a two-tier rather than a three-tier system of management, and the abolition of functional departments (but not staff functions) in small and medium factories and mines; it proposed a reform of the material supply system.

1966

8 August   The Central Committee, CCP, passed the 'Sixteen-point

Resolution', setting out rules on how to conduct the Cultural Revolution.

1967

9 January   Thirty-four 'rebel organizations' in Shanghai issued an urgent notice to urge industrial workers to stay at their work posts, to strive to over-fulfil the annual plan, and to postpone the settlement of wage adjustments, back-pay, and welfare issues until the end of the Cultural Revolution.

18 January   The Finance and Trade System issued another urgent telegram with regard to accounting, taxation, revenues, wages, bonuses, welfare, public property and funds, and banking procedures during the Cultural Revolution.

10 February   Heilongjiang's experience of the 'triple combination' for seizing power was publicized and the form of the revolutionary committee spread to the enterprise level.

5 June   The *Liberation Daily* began to criticize the 'Seventy Articles'.

1968

August   Yao Wenyuan wrote an article entitled 'The Working Class must Take Full Command', signalling the start of the 'struggle, criticism, and transformation' campaign.

1969

16 February–24 March   The National Planning Conference was convened; the socialist trusts and 'short-circuited' balancing in the planning procedure were criticized; horizontal command (local control) in industrial management was recommended.

1970

15 February–21 March   The National Planning Conference was

convened and the outline of the Fourth Five-year Plan (Draft) was formulated. The outline proposed the following: (a) the establishment of economic regions; (b) the majority of enterprise units were to be decentralized to the local level, with a minority adopting 'dual command' by ministries and local governments; (c) the contracting-out responsibility system was introduced to basic construction on a trial basis; (d) the contracting-out responsibility system was introduced to material supply; (e) the contracting-out responsibility system was introduced to the financial management of revenue and expenditure; and (f) the method of 'from the bottom to the top' and the combination of vertical and horizontal commands (emphasizing horizontal command) were recommended in the planning process.

May   The Central Committee, CCP, decided to decentralize 2,600 enterprises from the central to the local level.

20 June   The Light Industry Ministry decided to transfer 72 enterprise units to the local level, in order to fulfil the aim of commodity self-sufficiency within each province or special district.

25 June–20 August   The Ministry of Finance convened the 'National Conference of Finance and Banking', recommending measures to implement the contracting-out responsibility systems in finance, capital investment, and agricultural loans.

26 September   The Ministry of Foreign Trade recommended the decentralization of its enterprise units to the local level, where they would be managed by a dual command system stressing the role of local command.

18 December   Mao Zedong, in his talk with Edgar Snow, reaffirmed the principle of two initiatives (central and local) and recommended the giving of more discretion to the local level, minimizing central intervention.

December   The State Council drafted 'The Summary of the 1972 National Planning Conference', emphasizing the need for a unified State plan, enterprise rectification, and the establishment of systems and regulations.

1971

1 March   The Ministry of Finance issued the 'Circular concerning the Implementation of the Contracting-out Responsibility System of Revenue and Expenditure', and decided to carry out a system of

'fixed revenue and expenditure, contracting-out responsibility, guaranteed financial remittance (or subsidy for differentials), retention of surplus, and annual adjustment'.

30 October   The State Council decided to promote the following workers: those who were in the third grade before 1957; those who were in the second grade before 1960; and those who were in the first grade before 1966. In total 28 per cent of industrial workers were involved.

1972

6 September   The Ministry of Finance changed the contracting-out financial responsibility system to a new system, featuring 'a fixed percentage of retained revenue, the sharing of incremental revenue, and expenditure according to contracted-out targets'.

October   The State Planning Commission drafted 'The Regulation concerning the Insistence on Unified Planning, and the Strengthening of Economic Management', emphasizing the rectification theme.

1975

13–17 January   The First Session of the Fourth National People's Congress was convened in Beijing; the Constitution of the PRC was passed; Zhou Enlai delivered a report of government work, reaffirming the objectives of the four modernizations.

25 February and 8 March   The Central Committee, CCP, held the National Conference of Party Secretaries in Industry, issued the 'Directive on Strengthening Railway Work', and decided to authorize the Ministry of Railways to carry out unified management, centralized command, a ministry-wide allocation of manpower, and to establish the necessary regulations and systems.

5–26 April   'The National Conference of Basic Construction' decided to implement the contracting-out responsibility system in capital investment.

8–10 May   The Central Committee, CCP, convened the 'Forum on the Steel Industry', calling for rectification of the steel industry. It also recommended the establishment of a powerful leadership team from the ministerial to the enterprise level, of regulations and systems, and an effective production command structure.

18June–11 August The State Council convened the work conference on planning, which reviewed the planning procedures and apparatus, recommended central control over large-scale enterprises and large-scale construction projects, redrew the jurisdictions over material allocation, and centralized a portion of the depreciation fund.

26 October–23 January 1976 The National Planning Conference was convened; it recommended a new scheme for allocating the depreciation fund: 40 per cent to enterprises, 30 per cent to the local and ministerial levels, and 30 per cent to the State Treasury.

1976

January-August The Anti-Deng Xiaoping Campaign took place.

6 October The Gang of Four were arrested.

11 November The State Council authorized Jiangsu province to carry out the trial implementation of the contracting-out revenue responsibility system; it allowed the provincial level to retain 42 per cent of the revenue collected and to remit 58 per cent to the State Treasury. The State Council also adopted a new system of material supply, encouraging regional co-operation.

1977

13 November The State Council endorsed and circulated the Ministry of Finance's 'Regulation concerning the Management of Tax Collection', stressing central control and regulation over all matters concerning taxation.

1978

26 February–5 March The Fifth National People's Congress was convened in Beijing and the Constitution of the PRC was passed.

20 April The Central Committee authorized the trial

implementation of the 'Decision concerning Problems of the Speeding-up of Industrial Development (Draft)' (or the 'Thirty Articles').

22 April The State Planning Commission, the State Basic Construction Commission, and the Ministry of Finance promulgated the following: 'Several Rulings concerning the Strengthening of the Management of Basic Construction', 'The Decision to Strengthen the Management of Basic Construction in Self-financed Projects', 'Several Rulings concerning Basic Construction Procedures', 'The Regulation concerning the Classification of Large-scale and Medium Basic Construction Projects', and 'The Regulation of the Classification of the Funding of Basic Construction and other Items'.

7 May The State Council issued 'The Circular concerning the Implementation of the Bonus and Piece-rate Wage System'.

25 May The Second Session of the Standing Committee of the Fifth NPC approved in principle 'The Provisional Measure of the State Council concerning the Retirement and Resignation of Workers'.

2 June–9 September The State Council convened conferences on economic reform, proposing to move away from the old framework of the administrative approach, to make full use of economic leverage and organizations, to change the 'feudalistic-bureaucratic style' of management entirely, to introduce a specialization policy and a contractual system, to expand enterprise autonomy and legal rights, and to implement the principle of 'to each according to his labour' in wages policy.

6 October Hu Qiaomu published his article 'Observe the Law of Economy, Speed up the Four Modernizations'.

11 November The Ministry of Labour, the State General Labour Bureau, and the State General Material Supply Bureau issued 'The Circular concerning the Special Awards Measure in the Trial Implementation of Energy Conservation and the Saving of Raw Materials'.

25 November The State Council authorized the trial implementation of the enterprise fund system in State-owned enterprises and the restoration of the bonus system.

18–23 December The Third Plenum of the Eleventh Party Congress was convened, reaffirming the transformation from the 'class struggle' to the four modernizations, and the necessity for institutional reforms.

1979

5-28 February   The People's Bank of China convened a conference of branch managers and adopted differentiated interest rates as well as the principle of selectivity in its loan policy.

30 March   Deng Xiaoping delivered the speech 'Insist on Four Basic Principles' at a Party conference on theory.

5-28 April   The Central Work Conference was convened, and it promulgated the guideline, 'Readjustment, reform, rectification, and improvement' in the development of the national economy.

June   The Financial and Economic Commission established its 'Research Group on Economic Reforms', headed by Zhang Jinfu.

13 July   The State Council promulgated five policy papers and authorized pilot schemes of the enterprise autonomy policy. The five policy papers were: (a) 'Several Rulings concerning the Expansion of Managerial and Marketing Autonomy in State-owned Industrial Enterprises'; (b) 'The Regulation of Profit Retention in State-owned Enterprises'; (c) 'The Provisional Regulation of a Fixed-asset Tax in State-owned Enterprises'; (d) 'The Regulation of an Increase in the Depreciation Rate and an Improvement in the Use of Depreciation Fees in State-owned Enterprises'; and (e) 'The Provisional Regulation concerning the Use of Bank Loans for the Total Amount of Working Capital in State-owned Enterprises'.

28 August   The State Council endorsed and issued 'The Measure concerning the Trial Implementation of Bank Loans for Basic Construction' and the 'Regulation concerning the Trial Implementation of Bank Loans for Basic Construction', and decided to carry out a trial implementation of the change from financial appropriations to bank loans.

1980

20 January   The State Council promulgated 'The Provisional Measure of Profit Retention in State-owned Industrial Enterprises'. It applied to the enterprises involved in the pilot schemes of the enterprise autonomy policy, and it effected a change from the 'total-sum method' of profit retention to one based upon retention of the basic profit plus the incremental profits.

1 February   The State Council promulgated 'The Provisional

Regulation concerning the Financial Management System of the Classification of Expenditure and Income and Contracting-out Responsibility according to Hierarchy'. It was applicable to 15 provinces, but did not include Beijing, Tianjin, Shanghai, Fujian, Guangdong, Jiangsu, and the eight autonomous regions.

12 February   The Thirteenth Session of the Fifth NPC decided to establish the Machine-building Commission of the State Council to afford unified leadership over the machine-building sector.

1 April   The State Planning Commission, the State Economic Commission, and the General Bureau of Labour announced the 'Provisional Measure of the Piece-rate Wage in State-owned Enterprises' and authorized its trial implementation.

8 May   The State Council decided to establish the 'Office of Institutional Reform', headed by Tu Hsing-heng.

2 September   The State Council endorsed the 'Report concerning the Work Situation and the Views for the Future of the Pilot Schemes of the Expansion of Autonomy in Enterprises'. It allowed enterprises to adopt a variety of profit-retention schemes and recommended decentralization in all aspects of enterprise management.

29 October   The State Council promulgated the 'Provisional Regulation concerning the Development and Protection of Socialist Competition', encouraging competition between sectors of the economy and between enterprises.

21 November   The State Economic Commission, the Ministry of Finance, and the China People's Construction Bank issued a joint circular authorizing a change from financial appropriations to bank loans for funding renovation projects and technical improvements.

25 November   The State Council decided to change from financial appropriations to bank loans for funding basic construction in enterprises which enjoyed an independent accounting status and were capable of repaying their debt.

16–25 December   The Central Work Conference was convened in Beijing and reaffirmed the economic readjustment policy.

1981

16 January   The State Council issued the document 'Several Rulings concerning the Correct Implementation of the Bonus System and the Stoppage of Indiscriminate Payment of Bonuses'.

26 January   The State Council issued 'The Directive concerning the Financial Balance of Expenditure and Disbursement and the Strengthening of Financial Management'.

3 March   The State Council issued 'Several Decisions concerning the Strengthening of the Planning Management of Basic Construction and Control over the Scale of Basic Construction'.

4 March   The State Council endorsed the 'Summary of the Briefing concerning Several Problems of Readjustment in the Machine-building Industry'.

6 March   The State Economic Commission promulgated the 'Provisional Regulation concerning the Contracts of Industrial and Mining Products'.

1 April   The State Council endorsed the 'Summary of Briefing of the Forum on Institutional Reform in Industrial Management', recommending a curtailment of the further expansion of enterprise autonomy experiments, but a continuation of industrial reorganization on the basis of 'specialization and co-ordination'.

15 May   The State Council authorized the establishment of China's General Tobacco Corporation, in line with the report concerning the tobacco monopoly filed by the Light Industry Ministry.

20 May   The State Economic Commission, the Office of Institutional Reform, and other units promulgated the 'Provisional Measure concerning the Thorough Implementation of Papers of Expansion of Enterprise Autonomy, and Consolidation and Improvement of the Task in Expansion of Enterprise Autonomy'.

20 May–6 June   The National Conference of Chiefs of Material Supply Bureaux was convened, and recommended a double-track system of planned allocation of raw materials (that is, administrative and market).

31 May   The State Council issued a supplementary ruling concerning the bonus problem, and the establishment of ceilings for wage control.

13 July   The Central Committee, CCP, circulated the 'Provisional Regulation of the Congress of Workers and Staff Members in State-owned Industrial Enterprises'.

29 October   The State Council endorsed a policy paper by the State Economic Commission and the Office of Institutional Reform: 'The Opinion on Several Problems of the Industrial-production Economic-responsibility System'.

7 November   The State Council issued 'The Provisional Measure

concerning the Rigorous Application of the Policy on the Retirement and Resignation of Workers'.

30 November–1 December   Premier Zhao Ziyang outlined 10 policy guidelines on economic reform in his report on government work to the Fourth Session of the Fifth NPC.

31 December   The State Council authorized the establishment of China's Automobile Industrial Corporation.

1982

2 January   The Central Committee, CCP, promulgated 'The Provisional Regulation of the Task of Factory Directors in State-owned Factories', defining the principles of enterprise management, the collective leadership of the Party Committee, the democratic management of staff and workers, and administrative command by the factory director.

25 January   Chen Yun reaffirmed, in his talk to the State Planning Commission, that the central plan should be given a principal place and that the market should play a supplementary role in the national economy.

4 March   Zhao Ziyang pointed out, in the Work Conference on Transport and Industry, that economic reform should follow the principle of overall planning combined with limited freedom, overall concentration combined with small-scale decentralization, and the full play of local initiative under the framework of the principle of the 'whole country as a chessboard'.

8 March   Zhao Ziyang proposed the reorganization of the State Economic Commission, to incorporate the State Agricultural Commission, the State Machine-building Commission, the State Energy Commission, and the Finance and Trade Small Group.

16 March   The State Council promulgated 'The Provisional Regulation concerning the Managerial Systems of Nation-wide Specialized Corporations', allowing nation-wide specialized corporations to become economic entities outside the framework of the administrative apparatus of the State Council.

March   The State Council approved pilot schemes of the comprehensive economic reform in Changzhou municipality.

10 April   The State Council promulgated 'The Regulation of Awards and Punishments for Staff and Workers in Enterprises'.

4 May   The State Council recommended the establishment of the

State Institutional Reform Commission, headed by Premier Zhao Ziyang.

12 May   The State Council endorsed the establishment of the China Shipping Industrial Corporation.

1 September   The Twelfth Party Congress was convened.

8 November   The State Council promulgated 'Several Problems concerning the Improvement of the Current Industrial Economic-responsibility System'.

30 November   Premier Zhao Ziyang, in his report to the Fourth Session of the Fifth NPC, presented the highlights of the economic reforms which had taken place in the last three years of the Sixth Five-year Plan: the gradual introduction of the tax-for-profit schemes, the restructuring of the relationship between the State and enterprises, the full development of the role of the central cities, the alleviation of the strain between horizontal and vertical command, the improvement of commercial channels and commodity exchange, and so on.

7 December   The Central Committee, CCP, issued 'The Circular concerning Several Problems in the Improvement of the Organizational Apparatus of Local Government and the Party'.

24 December   The State Council issued 'The Supplementary Regulation concerning Tight Control over the Scale of Investment in Fixed Assets', proposing a 30 per cent tax for any self-financed investment project which exceeded the State plan.

1983

22 January   The State Planning Commission put forward 'The Opinion concerning the Improvement and Strengthening of Planning Management'.

8 February   The Central Committee and the State Council authorized pilot schemes of the comprehensive economic reform in Chongqing.

19 February   The Central Committee, CCP, and the State Council approved the establishment of the China Petroleum Chemical General Corporation.

22 February   The Ministry of Labour issued 'The Circular concerning the Rigorous Trial Implementation of Labour Contracts'.

25 February   The Ministry of Labour announced its 'Provisional

Regulation concerning the Recruitment and Evaluation of Workers and Appointments by Merit'.

3 March   The State Planning Commission, the State Economic Commission, the Ministry of Labour, and China People's Construction Bank jointly promulgated the 'Provisional Measure of the Contracting-out Responsibility System in Basic Construction Projects'.

25 March   The State Council approved reform proposals concerning the Yangtze River navigation system.

1 April   The State Council promulgated 'The Provisional Regulations of State-owned Industrial Enterprises'.

12 April   The Ministry of Finance issued 'The Provisional Measure concerning the Substitution of Taxation for Profit Remittance'.

25 April   The Ministry of Labour announced the 'Provisional Regulation of the Technical Assessment of Workers'.

29 April   The Ministry of Finance issued 'The Provisional Regulation concerning the Income Tax of State-owned Enterprises', stipulating that State-owned enterprises should pay an income tax of 55 per cent of realized profit.

6 June   Premier Zhao Ziyang, in his report on government work to the First Session of the Sixth NPC, stressed that to prepare for the Seventh Five-year Plan, three major items should be on the agenda: (a) the reform of the planning apparatus to strengthen the management of the national economy, (b) the development of Socialist markets and the organization of production and distribution according to the requirements of large-scale socialized production, and (c) the reform of the financial system, the labour and wage system, and the relationships among the centre, localities, enterprises, and workers.

3 September   The State Council issued 'The Circular concerning the Rigorous Rectification of the Work of Recruiting the Children of Retired and Resigned Workers'.

1984

5 March   The State Council issued 'The Regulation on Cost Management in State-owned Enterprises'.

June   The Ministry of Finance issued 'The Provisional Measure concerning the Trial Implementation of the Second Step of the Substitution of Taxation for Profit Remittance in State-owned Enterprises'.

21 October The Central Committee, CCP, passed 'The Resolution concerning Economic Reform'.

INDEX